# Tradition, Revolution, and Market Economy
# in a North Vietnamese Village,
# 1925–2006

# Tradition, Revolution, and Market Economy in a North Vietnamese Village, 1925–2006

Hy V. Luong

University of Hawai'i Press
Honolulu

Revised and expanded edition of *Revolution in the Village:
Tradition and Transformation in North Vietnam, 1925–1988* (1992)

16  15  14  13  12  11  10   6  5  4  3  2  1

**Library of Congress Cataloging-in-Publication Data**
Luong, Hy V.
   Tradition, revolution, and market economy in a North Vietnamese village,
1925–2006. — Rev. and expanded ed.
      p.   cm.
   Rev. and expanded ed. of: Revolution in the village: tradition and
transformation in North Vietnam, 1925–1988.
   Includes bibliographical references and index.
   ISBN 978-0-8248-3370-1 (hardcover : alk. paper) —
   ISBN 978-0-8248-3423-4 (pbk. : alk. paper)
  1.  Son Duong (Vietnam)—History.   2. Vietnam—History—20th century.
3.  Vietnam—Economic conditions—20th century.   4. Vietnam—Social
conditions—20th century.   I. Luong, Hy V. Revolution in the village.   II. Title.
   DS559.93.S66L86 2010
   959.7'1—dc22
                                        2009038155

University of Hawai'i Press books are printed on acid-free
paper and meet the guidelines for permanence and
durability of the Council on Library Resources.

Designed by the University of Hawai'i Press Production Staff

Printed by Edwards Brothers, Inc.

# Contents

# Preface

In 1992 I published *Revolution in the Village: Tradition and Transformation in North Vietnam, 1925–1988.* This book examines the political, economic, and sociocultural changes over six decades in the small village of Sơn-Dương in northern Vietnam, spanning the French colonial era, through the violent conflicts with French and American powers and the socialist construction, and the reforms within the command economy framework.

When I revisited the village of Sơn-Dương in 1998, it was in the middle of local political turmoil during which the majority of villagers were refusing to pay irrigation and numerous other local fees. I was struck by the extent to which villagers' relations with authorities were undergoing a profound transformation. Although the political turmoil in Sơn-Dương in 1998 made it impossible for me as a researcher from North America to conduct a full restudy of the village without the closest surveillance by Vietnamese security agents, I was intrigued by the transformation dynamics in Sơn-Dương and elsewhere in rural Vietnam in the context of Vietnam's reintegration into the global economy. I also learned soon after my visit that the Vietnamese National Archives contained a number of files on Sơn-Dương from the French colonial era, archives that had not been available a decade earlier to scholars based outside Vietnam. Archival research in Hanoi in 2003 and field visits to Sơn-Dương in 2004 and 2006 provided me with data of great historical depth and with extensive contemporary materials on Sơn-Dương. This research lays the groundwork for the present book. The first five chapters covering the colonial period and the rise of Marxism have been revised from my original study with additional archival materials. Chapters 6, 7, and 8 are new and extend the study to 2006, thus showing the transformation from a command economy to a market economy and the accompanying cultural, social, and political changes in the village. The book now takes readers through eight decades of major upheaval—anticolonial uprisings, wars, the rise and transformation of a Marxism-inspired revolution, and the re-emergence of a market economy tempered by socialist-revolutionary legacies. The book examines a microcosm of events and the restructuring of the political economy and the local sociocultural framework in Sơn-Dương in relation to the larger trends in the northern Vietnamese countryside and in other rural areas of Vietnam, as well as in relation to the theoretical literature on agrarian revolution.

# Acknowledgments

I first learned of Sơn-Dương village in 1984, when my colleague Sidney Mintz introduced me to Nguyễn Đắc Bằng. Mr. Bằng, an octogenarian exile living in Toronto then, had received two death sentences from the French regime in Vietnam for having participated in an anticolonial uprising in 1930 organized by the Vietnamese Nationalist Party. Both sentences were commuted, and he was subsequently sent to French Guiana, together with other Vietnamese inmates, to open up the interior of this sparsely populated French colony in South America. Mr. Bằng eventually escaped to Georgetown, Guyana, where he became heavily involved in the mobilization of local support for Hồ Chí Minh's government in the period from 1946 to 1975. His political activities in South America led to an official visit to Cuba in 1962. Sidney Mintz had met Bằng in 1966 at an academic conference in Georgetown, Guyana.

In interviews in Toronto in 1985–1986, Bằng discussed his life history with me in depth. Despite his advanced age, he was able to provide valuable information on the structure of his village before 1930 and on his prison experiences in Vietnam. Bằng also introduced me to his relatives in Vietnam to facilitate my field research in Sơn-Dương village in the summer of 1987. Although I conducted all of the research and analysis in this book myself, without Nguyễn Đắc Bằng, this book on the village of Sơn-Dương would not have been written.

Despite the relative depth of oral history and archival materials in Canada and France, this book was considerably enriched by my field and library research in Vietnam in the summers of 1987, 1988, 1998, 2003, 2004, and in December 2006. I am grateful to many individuals for assistance during those trips. Professor Ngô Vĩnh Long encouraged me to submit a research visa application to the Vietnamese government and actively supported my application. During my research in Vietnam in summer 1987, the late professor Phạm Huy Thông of the Social Science Committee of Vietnam asked Professor Lê văn Lan of the Institute of History and Mr. Nguyễn văn Kự of its Department of International Cooperation to assist me. Mr. Kự helped to untangle the bureaucratic red tape in Hanoi, and Professor Lê văn Lan coordinated my fieldwork in Sơn-Dương magnificently. Dr. Ngô Quang Nam, director of the Office of Cultural Services in the province of Vĩnh-Phú, and Mr. Nguyễn Đức Qũy, a Sơn-Dương native and a nephew of Nguyễn Đắc Bằng, introduced me to the village leadership and the rest of the village population. Professor Diệp Đình Hoa coordinated my revisits to Sơn-Dương in 1988 and 1991, and Mr. Lê Hướng took Photos 1–2 and 5–6 for this book in 1991. I revisited Sơn-Dương under the sponsorship of the National University of Vietnam in Hanoi in 1998, of the Vietnam Institute of Ethnology in 2004, and of the Vietnam Institute of Culture and Information in 2006. Drs. Trần Hà and Đặng Thanh Phương and Mssr. Lê Minh Anh and Tạ Hữu Dực of the Vietnam Institute of Ethnology and Dr. Phan văn Dốp of the Southern Institute of Sustainable Development provided valuable assistance in the survey of 321 Sơn-Dương households in 2004. Professor Lương Hồng Quang accompanied me on my quick revisit to Sơn-Dương in December 2006. I would also like to thank Professor Phan Huy Lê of the National University of Vietnam-Hanoi, and Professor Nguyễn Văn Huy and Mr. Phạm Văn Dương of the Vietnam Museum of Ethnology for their support for my revisit to Sơn-Dương in 1998. Most importantly, had it not been for the tolerance of Sơn-Dương villagers and the village leadership for an anthropologist's intrusion into their lives, this study could not have been completed. To all these individuals I am truly indebted.

Sidney Mintz has been supportive of my project from its inception, and he offered valuable advice on the first draft of the manuscript. Professors Christine White, David Marr, David Hunt, Dr. Vũ Huy Phúc (Vietnam Institute of History), and three remaining anonymous readers for the University of Hawaiʻi Press made many useful and detailed comments on the book. It was a challenge to respond adequately to the advice these scholars offered from different disciplinary and theoretical perspectives. Claudia Vicencio, Pamela Kelley, Susan Stone, and Margaret Black made useful editorial suggestions on different editions of this book. Mr. Huỳnh Ngọc Thu of the Department of Anthropology at the National University of Vietnam in Hồ Chí Minh City drew Maps 1–5 for this new edition of the book. Ms. Trần Thu Lan, a doctoral advisee of mine in Toronto, entered tax and demographic data from the French colonial period that I had collected in the Vietnamese archives. I also benefited from the comments of several students in my course on Vietnam at Johns Hopkins University. I am solely responsible for any remaining errors.

During my archival and library research in France and Vietnam, the staff at the Bibliothèque nationale (Paris), the Archives nationales, Section d'outre-mer (Aix-en-Provence), the Centre des études de l'Asie du sud-est et du monde insulindien (Valbonne), the Vietnamese National Library (Hanoi), and the Vietnamese National Archives (Hanoi) kindly provided a large amount of material on short notice. I also benefited from Mr. Lê Vĩnh Phúc's preliminary translation of Nguyễn Đắc Bằng's Vietnamese-language account of the major political events in his life. My sisters Thérèse Kim-Trang Luong and Isabelle Kim-Cúc Luong provided valuable assistance in transcribing the tapes of my interviews with Mr. Bằng. The discussion of Vietnamese kinship in this book is based on my previously published article "Vietnamese Kinship: Structural Principles and the Socialist Transformation in Northern Vietnam," which appeared in the *Journal of Asian Studies* in 1989 (vol. 48, pp. 741–756). Parts of Chapters 8 and 9 are drawn from my chapter "The State, Local Associations, and Alternate Civilities in Rural Northern Vietnam" in the book *Civil Society, Globalization, and Political Change in Asia,* edited by Robert Weller and published by Routledge.

The research on which this book is based was assisted by grants from the University of Toronto, as well as from the Joint Committee on Southeast Asia of the American Council of Learned Societies and the Social Science Research Council with funds provided by the National Endowment for the Humanities and the Ford Foundation.

Finally, and most important of all, this book would not have been completed without the sacrifice by my family members. I greatly appreciate their understanding.

# Abbreviations and Units of Measure

## Abbreviations

| | |
|---|---|
| AOM-P-NF | Archives nationales, Section d'outre-mer, Paris, Indochine-Nouveaux fonds |
| AOM-AP-I | Archives nationales, Section d'outre-mer, Aix-en-Provence, Indochine |
| AOM-AP-RST | Archives nationales, Section d'outre-mer, Aix-en-Provence, Résidence supérieure du Tonkin |
| DRV | Democratic Republic of Vietnam |
| GGI-DAP | Gouvernement général de l'Indochine, Direction des affaires politiques et de la Sûreté générale, Contribution à l'histoire des mouvements politiques de l'Indochine française |
| ICP | Indochinese Communist Party |
| TTLTQG1-PT | Trung tâm lưu trữ Quốc gia 1 (National Archive Center 1 of Vietnam), Phú-Thọ Files |
| VND | Vietnamese currency *(đồng)* |
| VNP | Vietnamese Nationalist Party |

## Vietnamese Units of Measure

| | |
|---|---|
| *đấu* | 1 liter, or 0.91 quart (dry) |
| *mẫu* | 3600 square meters, or 0.9 acre |
| *sào* | 360 square meters, or 0.09 acre |

# Introduction

Like virtually all other rural communities in the Red River delta of North Vietnam, the village of Sơn-Dương, lying behind a bamboo hedge, is well hidden from the paved provincial highway. In order to get to the village, one has to turn off the provincial highway onto a pothole-ridden dirt road. A one-mile ride along this road into the village leaves a vehicle completely covered either with dirt or red mud from the potholes, depending on whether the road has been baked in the hot sun or watered by a tropical summer downpour. The dirt road continues well beyond Sơn-Dương, plowing through the rice fields of this small fertile plain and turning back toward Việt-Trì, the provincial capital of Vĩnh-Phú and one of the three major industrial centers of the north. Familiar eyes can recognize the village of Sơn-Dương from afar among other bamboo clusters dotting the rural landscape by tracing the road against a background of mountain peaks rising in the west on the other side of the Red River. Arriving in Sơn-Dương, one leaves behind the main delta of North Vietnam to enter the midland district of Lâm-Thao in the heartland of the first Vietnamese kingdom, the kingdom of the Hùng dynasty (which lasted up to the third century B.C.E.).[1] In the courtyards of many houses in the village are huge haystacks for oxen and buffalo, the draft animals used in the rice paddies. Towering over the cultivators' dwellings are the areca palm trees. These provide the highly valued nut, chewed with betel leaves in a long-exiting practice that is widespread in the southeastern part of Asia. The physical landscape may seem at first glance to have been frozen since time immemorial.

Such an impression is misleading. Events behind the bamboo hedge have been partly shaped by the Chinese and Western capitalist world systems in the course of their economic, political, and ideological expansion.

1

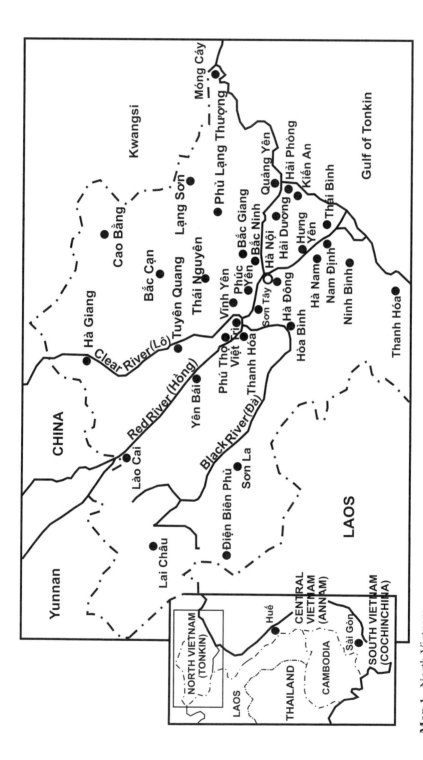

**Map 1.** North Vietnam

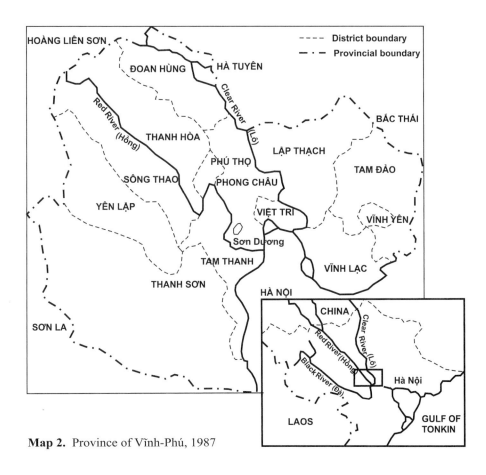

**Map 2.** Province of Vĩnh-Phú, 1987

Sơn-Dương has withstood repeated foreign ravages throughout the past century, first by the Chinese, then by the French, and finally by the Americans. At the same time it has undergone fundamental ecological, demographic, socioeconomic, and political changes in one the most important revolutions of our time.

As early as June 1965, three months into the sustained U.S. air war against North Vietnam, many young Sơn-Dương villagers experienced for the first time the bitter taste of modern technological destruction:

The sky was vividly blue above the village of Sơn-Dương, Lâm-Thao district, in the afternoon of June 24, 1965. Members of the [agricultural] cooperative all prepared to leave for the field, when two American "pirate" planes zoomed into sight. Incomprehensibly,

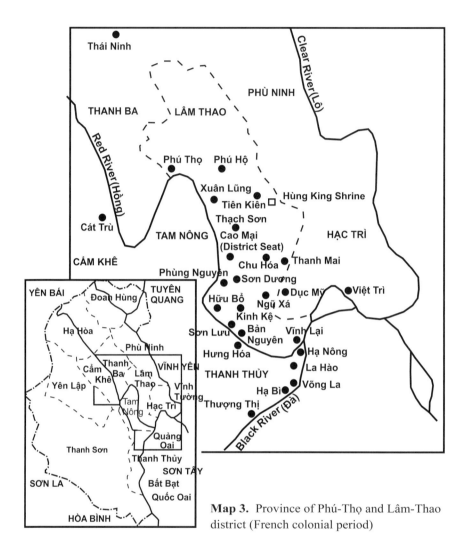

**Map 3.** Province of Phú-Thọ and Lâm-Thao district (French colonial period)

bombs exploded in the village. Fires instantly erupted. Smoke billowed into the blue sky. The burning smell of bomb powder filled the air. The earth shook....

[As soon as the bombing was over] the ground surrounding [the] bomb craters became the informal meeting place for almost 200 people denouncing [the] crime of [the] American "pirate." The mourning cries of little Hồ's father [over his bombing-victim son] and sister Ái's five small children, now rendered motherless...registered deeply in the hearts and minds of every villager. (Phú-Thọ, July 9, 1965)

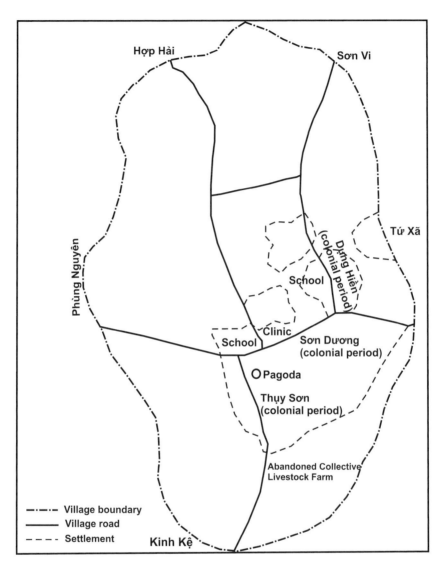

**Map 4.** Sơn-Dương village, 1987

This article in the provincial Communist Party newspaper, *Phú-Thọ,* was a harbinger of tough days ahead for Sơn-Dương villagers, even though they had heard of the U.S. bombing along the North Vietnamese coast in the summer of 1964. On July 24, 1965, the intensified second Indochina War struck home to the people in Sơn-Dương personally (estimated 1965 population 2,700). Bombs heavily damaged the village's

**Map 5.** Province of Phú-Thọ, 2006

junior high school and a few nearby houses. They also left deep craters in the surrounding rice fields. In the eleven years of the intensified armed conflict that followed (1964–1975), the village sent to the front, in both the north and the south, 360 of its own sons, of whom 41 died in the war in this period. Their names are engraved on tombstones in the village's war memorial cemetery, which honors the 73 village sons who died between 1930–1983 for the Vietnamese revolution and defense of the country. The bitter memory of war lives on in the minds of many villagers. During my research in the village in the summer of 1987, for example, a ranking village cadre referred obliquely to the unforgettably devastating impact of B-52 bombing on his battalion in the south during the war. He remained openly suspicious and hostile to my research throughout my visit. To this day, villagers still wonder why Sơn-Dương became a U.S. bombing target on July 24, 1965.

Sơn-Dương had endured many foreign ravages during the seven decades of French colonialism in North Vietnam (1883–1954), and many other ravages well before that. Firmly supporting Hồ Chí Minh's Vietminh forces during the first Indochina War (1946–1954) against the French, the village was bombed four times in 1951 by the French colonial air force. The bombing reportedly killed over thirty villagers and destroyed seventy-eight houses. In early 1930, in what was then Phú-Thọ province, the village had been a hotbed of anti-French activity. In retribution following an abortive anticolonial uprising in the provinces of Phú-Thọ and Yên-Báy, colonial troops burned the majority of the houses in Sơn-Dương. They also guillotined a native son in the town of Phú-Thọ, then the provincial capital, and the colonial government sent nineteen others to penitentiaries, some as far away as French Guiana in South America. Earlier, in the first wave of resistance to French colonialism (1884–1895), Sơn-Dương had also been active. In the turmoil of the first anti-French resistance movement, Chinese troops who initially participated against the French at the request of the Vietnamese court reportedly massacred about 120 villagers due to personal animosity between the anti-French guerrilla leader in Sơn-Dương and certain other anticolonial leaders (TTLTQG1-PT 534, cf. Sơn-Dương 1987).

Sơn-Dương has not only suffered from war. Caught in a precarious balance between a rapidly expanding population and millennium-old rice fields, its socioeconomic structure has also undergone a fundamental transformation. Despite the impression of a physical landscape frozen in time, the irrigation canals along the provincial highway and the road leading into the village were only constructed in the 1950s. Prior to this major water-control project, large portions of the low-lying village fields were inundated in the tropical summer and fall monsoons, and the high-lying sections were too dry for winter and spring cultivation. Before the completion of the canals in 1957, most village fields yielded only one staple crop annually, and some even lay fallow for the entire year. By 1987 the same land was yielding at least two, if not three, crops. These ecological changes came not a moment too soon. From 1954 to 1987 the cultivated area shrank from 1,009 *mẫu* (363 hectares, or 908 acres) to 820 *mẫu* (295 hectares, or 737 acres). In the same period the village population increased from 2,144 to 3,828, not counting the increasing number of villagers temporarily residing elsewhere for advanced schooling, armed service, or other government service.[2]

The most significant changes remain the land-reform campaign and the cooperative program that Hồ Chí Minh's government launched after its consolidation of power in the north in 1954. The land reform of 1954 redistributed approximately 300 *mẫu* (108 hectares, or 270 acres) of rice fields from landlord and rich peasant households to other members of the village of Sơn-Dương.[3] The formation of agricultural cooperatives five years later was the first step toward the communal ownership of virtually all the cultivable land in Sơn-Dương. Despite a significant policy shift in 1981—a radical decentralization of the production process, which raised the rice crop yield by more than 100 percent in the 1982–1988 period— this collective ownership of land remains the fundamental principle in the socioeconomic structure of the village.

As an administrative unit, under Hồ Chi Minh's government, Sơn-Dương is a commune *(xã)* that was formed through the merger of the three villages of Sơn-Dương, Dụng-Hiền, and Thuỵ Sơn. The trend to merge many villages into communes began accelerating in northern Vietnam in the late 1940s and 1950s. In most localities in northern Vietnam this is simply an administrative merger, and rural dwellers still strongly identify nowadays with their villages (*làng* in vernacular Vietnamese, or *thôn* [hamlet] in administrative terms). However, over time, for historical reasons (discussed below), in Sơn-Dương, the boundaries separating the three villages of Sơn-Dương, Dụng-Hiền, and Thuỵ-Sơn have lost their significance to villagers. The terms "village" *(làng)* and "commune" *(xã)* are now interchangeable for the people of Sơn-Dương and are used interchangeably in the following analysis of the socioeconomic structure and historical events in Sơn-Dương.

The following study examines the revolutionary processes in the village of Sơn-Dương over the past eight decades as discovered through the voices of elderly villagers, the findings from archival and field research in France and North Vietnam, and a survey of village households. As a study of the interplay of structure and history in a Vietnamese community from the colonial to the socialist era, including the current period of re-integration into the global capitalist system, this book differs from the few Western-language village studies of Vietnam in some important respects.[4] Studies before 1992 examined a Vietnamese community either in ethnographic or sociological-statistical terms without including an in-depth historical dimension (Hickey 1964; Houtart and Lemercinier 1981) or from a historical perspective without a detailed microscopic investigation of structure in the colonial or socialist era (Phạm-Cường and Nguyễn-văn-Bá 1976; Trullinger 1980).[5] The following study also differs from important anthropological and historical research on rural Vietnam in the past decade and a half because it closely examines how local structure in a village on the one hand, and anticolonial historical events and market development on the other, have mutually shaped each other (cf. Kleinen 1999, Gammeltoft 1999, Nguyễn Tùng 1999, Malarney 2002, Papin and Tessier 2002, Taylor 2007; see also Luong 2006).

I was not aware that anticolonial resistance had simmered in Sơn-Dương for a large part of the past century when I selected the village for study. I chose the community through a chance encounter with an exiled octogenarian revolutionary from there, Nguyễn Đắc Bằng. Originally a member of the Vietnamese Nationalist Party (VNP), Bằng had participated in the VNP-organized uprising in North Vietnam in 1930. Having obtained a copy of Mr. Bằng's memoir on the major events of his political career, I found fascinating his life trajectory, which spanned different corners of the French and British empires and bridged the colonial and socialist eras of twentieth-century Vietnam. With Bằng's collaboration and with his memoir as my starting point, I decided in 1985 to undertake a study of how historical events in Bằng's life in particular and in Sơn-Dương in general interplayed with both the microstructure of Sơn-Dương village and the French colonial system. With the encouragement of Vietnamese diplomatic authorities, I planned a research visit to Bằng's native village in order to complement archival research in France and interviews in Canada in the summer of 1985. I hoped to combine the life-history method and archival research in order to illuminate the interplay of local tradition and history—an interplay seen both in the continuity and discontinuity of a community and in the lives of community members.

My field research in Sơn-Dương was conducted in the summer of 1987 under difficult circumstances. Although the U.S. war in Vietnam had ended twelve years earlier, tension and hostility lingered on both sides. The United States continued to maintain a trade embargo on Vietnam, had refused to normalize relations, and had exerted pressure on its allies and international organizations for widespread economic sanctions. As a researcher from the United States, I was viewed with suspicion by certain cadres within the community as well as by Vietnamese officials in Hanoi responsible for national domestic security. Vietnamese academic authorities were also cautious, although more understanding. Through the arrangements of Vietnamese social science authorities a member of the provincial Party leadership personally introduced me to Sơn-Dương Party leaders and informed them that my study had provincial authorization. Although I had visited the village earlier in the summer as a fictive

kinsman of Nguyễn Đắc Bằng, a relation structured by the use of kin
terms common among unrelated Vietnamese, with this formal introduction I was able to gain access to a wider network of villagers, including
the Party leaders. I selected most of my interlocutors through informal
consultations with acquaintances and through my past research on the village. The interview sample included males and females of different class
backgrounds, whose lives involved different degrees of political activism.
Despite the hostility of one ranking Party member, the village leadership
consented to all my interview requests. One Party leader was assigned to
coordinate my research and to introduce me to the requested villagers in
their homes. After an initial meeting or a formal interview, I visited many
of my interviewees again informally, at times unexpectedly, for follow-
up inquiries. The duration of my field research in 1987 was limited by
national security officials as well as by the common practice among Vietnamese ethnologists and sociologists of spending no more than six weeks
in any particular community at one time. I extended my research briefly
to include a two-day research revisit to the village in the summer of 1988.
In my three visits to Sơn-Dương in the late 1980s, relying primarily on the
life-history approach, I interviewed in some depth sixteen mostly elderly
villagers.

In the summer of 1998, I revisited Sơn-Dương in order to donate the
royalties from the publication of my book *Revolution in the Village* to a
worthy local cause and to learn what changes had taken place in the village
over a decade of market-oriented reforms in Vietnam.

In 1997 the province of Vĩnh-Phú in which Sơn-Dương had been
located was divided into Vĩnh-Phúc and Phú-Thọ, and Sơn-Dương now
belonged to the latter.[6] In the village I was startled by the profound crisis
that had arisen between the local population and the commune administration. As a reflection of the magnitude of the crisis, between 1993 and
1998, under strong local social pressures, three Communist Party secretaries and three presidents of the People's Committee had quickly succeeded
one another. Relations between the local population and the government
of Sơn-Dương reached a boiling point during my visit: local families were
reportedly refusing to pay not only their irrigation fees but also commune
taxes. These arrears had totaled US $18,000 for half a year. As a result,
Sơn-Dương's cumulative debt to the state irrigation authorities had spi-
raled to approximately US $15,000. Peasants reported that the flow of
irrigation water to the commune had slowed significantly, causing them
considerable hardship during the rice cultivation season. Nor, for half a
year, had commune cadres received their salaries because of this politi-

cally rooted financial crisis. At a major meeting during which the Party secretary reviewed commune activities in the first half of 1998, one villager was reported to have asked publicly who had elected this political leader to a position of authority. About half of the local Communist Party members sided with the protesters in their prolonged confrontation with commune authorities. From the time I first visited Sơn-Dương in 1987, relations between the local population and the state seem to have undergone a fundamental transformation, one that paralleled the proliferation of village- and kinship-based local associations. Because Sơn-Dương was considered a political "hot spot" in 1998, my visit there was closely monitored by provincial authorities. I proceeded with formal and highly informative interviews on the village's economy and society, while in informal conversations with a number of villagers being told in rich detail about local tensions. However, within a few days I became aware of the very close surveillance of my research in the village by provincial security agents. I was not allowed to take any picture in the village, not even of the village pagoda, despite the intervention of a major figure in Vietnamese academia in Hanoi. The local atmosphere in the summer of 1998 was clearly not conducive to an in-depth restudy of Sơn-Dương. I decided to end my research after one week, for continuing my research would have caused complications for my academic sponsor in Hanoi and led to unnecessary questions from the Vietnamese security authorities about my academic work.

In the summer of 2003 I discovered a number of French colonial archival documents about Sơn-Dương and its two neighboring villages of Dụng-Hiền and Thuy-Sơn in the Vietnamese national archives. Then in 2004, when relative calm had returned to Sơn-Dương, I returned for a restudy. By then, the district of Phong-Châu had been divided into the districts of Lâm-Thao and Phù-Ninh, and Sơn-Dương was made part of Lâm-Thao again.

Besides conducting in-depth interviews with numerous villagers from all walks of life, I also commissioned a survey of 321 households (29 percent) selected on the basis of a random probability sampling of 1,093 village households. All members of 38 of the selected households had already migrated elsewhere but still maintained their houses, land, and registration status as village residents. From their closest relatives in the village, we obtained the most basic information on the members of these households, such as name, age, relationship to the household head, dates of most recent departures from Sơn-Dương, and current place of residence. A full survey was conducted on the remaining 283 households. Quantitative survey data provided a rich complement to the interview and archival materials, especially on village life under market-oriented reforms. The vivid narratives of elderly villagers bridged the different historical eras of twentieth-century Vietnam, spanning the transition from French colonialism to nationalistic socialism and global market participation. The significant people with whom they interacted ranged from the French colonial masters and the last generation of Vietnamese Confucian literati to the Marxist cadres of socialist formation and to capitalist entrepreneurs. I have used their narratives at some length to provide a detailed ethnographic portrait of village structure as it bears upon the major historical events of the past eight decades, especially since no nonfictive in-depth accounts were available on the structure of any Vietnamese community in the French colonial period.

Although shaped by the historically constituted context of the narration and inextricably linked to the narrator's reconstruction of his self, the narrative of the major interlocutor (Nguyễn Đắc Bằng) is substantiated by available archival and newspaper accounts, except for a small number of details that will be noted (see also Luong 1991; cf. Knudsen 1990). Other Sơn-Dương villagers related the events of their lives within this tightly knit community where their life histories are part of public knowledge. However, due to a sharp conceptual distinction between village members and outsiders, a few influential members of the Sơn-Dương community were concerned that villagers might relate politically sensitive developments to a researcher whom they considered a part of the alien outside world. In order to protect those narrators, I have not presented their stories in full. For the same reason, many interlocutors of the postcolonial period cannot be identified except in terms of their socioeconomic backgrounds.

The following study has two basic goals. First, in examining the socioeconomic structure and historical events in a north Vietnamese village through eight decades of Western encounter, the study seeks to highlight the dynamics of a major revolution of our time. Given the research objective and the fieldwork constraints, the book does not attempt to provide a full ethnographic description of Sơn-Dương village. It is less concerned with the structure and events of a microtemporal order presented in standard ethnographies than with the interplay of tradition and events in historical time. In the metaphor of the well-known French historian Fernand Braudel, the book situates historical events—the surface ocean waves—in the major undercurrents of socioeconomic formations, more specifically, in terms of the encounter between Western colonialism and capitalism, on the one hand, and a Chinese-influenced indigenous system, on the other.

Second, since ethnohistorical and fieldwork data bear upon the debates on the dynamics of the Vietnamese revolution and market-oriented reforms, the study also seeks to refine theoretical models of modern revolutionary processes in agrarian societies—theoretical models that are firmly embedded in the major traditions of contemporary Western social theory represented by John S. Mill, Karl Marx, Emile Durkheim, and Ferdinand de Saussure. The following survey of these major theoretical traditions provides the background for my analysis of tradition and historical events in the 1925–2006 period in the village of Sơn-Dương in particular and in Vietnam in general—an analysis that is most critical of the Millean tradition of inquiry.

## Revolutionary Processes in Agrarian Societies: Theoretical Models of Structure and History

In the Millean tradition of inquiry, structure is assumed to be derived from the goal-directed acts of self-interested individuals. The significance of structure is thus rendered peripheral in the analysis of historically embedded revolutionary processes and of human action in general. In the literature on revolution and agrarian unrest, the political scientist Samuel Popkin's rational-choice model offers a good example of this theoretical framework (1979). The human act and historical events are examined not in systematic relation to the structure of the capitalist world system and the native sociocultural framework but primarily in terms of the logic of individual self-interest. In his study of the Vietnamese revolution, Popkin examines the behavior of the peasantry and the elite in their search for individual material gains. He emphatically rejects the view that modern agrarian movements involve defensive reactions to the violation of precapitalist normative structures by the colonial and capitalist order. In Popkin's argument the incorporation of indigenous agriculture into the capitalistic world market, the establishment of the colonial regime, and the expansion of state power are not necessarily deleterious to peasants' welfare. The single-stranded relations of the market actually free peasants from dependence on monopolistic local lords. According to Popkin, colonialism brings vital stability and an improved communication system that keeps prices from fluctuating widely and thus keeps peasants alive in times of local famine.

Along the same line of analysis, Popkin argues that modern revolutionary movements such as the Vietminh do not succeed because of the decay of an old normative order. Rather, these movements succeed because, as political entrepreneurs, their leaders can offer peasants concrete welfare improvements and effective organization against marauding lords and notables. Popkin's analysis of revolutionary movements develops as a direct corollary to Mancur Olson's neoclassical thesis that "class-oriented action will not occur if the individuals that make up a class act rationally" (1965:105).

According to Olson, since the provision of collective good as by land reform benefits all the members of a group (this is, the peasant class), rational individuals will not incur the heavy cost of that collective good in order to further group interests unless there also exist selective incentives available only to active contributors to the collective cause. Popkin's rational peasant actors are primarily projected as Hobbesian men who act in an environmental and sociocultural vacuum and who, beyond family circles, engage in a war of all against all for maximum personal gain. Underlying Popkin's model of revolutionary processes and his analysis of the Vietnamese revolution is the tradition of Western thought that has dominated economics and shaped major theoretical endeavors in sociology (for example, Homans), political science (for example, Riker, Frohlich), and anthropology (for example, Malinowski, Barth).

In contrast, the Marxist tradition seeks to situate revolutionary movements and historical events in general within the structure of conflict-ridden class relations.[7] The Marxist analyses of class relations and revolutionary dynamics in the past century were strengthened by the development of Immanuel Wallerstein's world-system theory, which seeks to situate them within a broader international context—the context of unequal exchange between the core and the periphery of the world capitalist system. A new phase of core-periphery relations emerged in the nineteenth century, when the different states within the capitalist core began to compete with one another on a global scale as they sought territorial expansion. The competition did not necessarily arise because of the immediate profitability of colonial conquests: it arose at least in part out of the concern of many states that they would be denied access to potential markets and resource bases in Asia and Africa (Murray 1980:10–15).

Instead of defining capitalism in terms of one particular method of labor control (wage labor), Wallerstein views capitalism as essentially involving "the maximization of surplus creation" (Wallerstein 1979: 285). Since wage labor is more costly in the capitalist core than in the periphery, and given the unequal exchange relations between the core and the periphery, the capitalist world system utilizes a variety of labor methods in the periphery, including coercive labor, in order to maximize surplus appropriation.[8] In the capitalist world system, the proletariat is either largely located in the periphery or composed of "ethnicities" originating in the periphery; the bourgeoisie is heavily concentrated in, although by no means restricted to, the core. Within the world-system framework, class conflict takes on an international dimension, and revolution is seen as originating in the periphery, where proletarian class interests emerge most clearly. As Wallerstein puts it, "The primary contradiction is between the interests organized and located in the core countries and their local allies on the one hand, and the majority of the population on the other. In point of fact then, an 'anti-imperialist' nationalist struggle is in fact a mode of expression of class interest" (Wallerstein 1979:200). In other words, ethnonationalism can serve the interests of the oppressed classes within the capitalist world system despite its frequent manipulation by an indigenous elite. On the relationship between class interest and ethnonationalism outside the capitalist core, Wallerstein suggests:

> It is no accident that the great social revolutions of the twentieth century (the Russian, Chinese, Vietnamese, Cuban) have been at one and the same time "social" and "national." To be "social," they had to be "national," whereas those "revolutions" which claimed to be "national" without being "social" (for example, that of the [Chinese] Kuomintang) could not in fact defend "national" interests. . . . The fundamental political reality of that [capitalist] world economy is a class struggle which however takes constantly changing forms: overt class consciousness versus ethno-national consciousness, classes within nations versus classes across nations. (Ibid.:230; see also Ngô-Vĩnh-Long 1978b)

Within the same Marxist framework, although he does not explicitly adopt Wallerstein's key concepts of core and periphery, the sociologist Jeffery Paige examines in depth the greater historical probability of revolution outside the capitalist core, especially in areas of the underdeveloped world that export agricultural products:

> The expansion of the [agricultural] export sectors led to vast population movements, including the international slave trade, massive appropriations of traditional landowners, the creation of armies of agricultural laborers, and the replacement of traditional communal social ties with commercial market relations. The new forms of export

agricultural organization created new social classes and destroyed old ones and introduced new patterns of class conflict. Conflict developed between the foreign owners of the new agricultural organizations and their wage laborers, between the new agrarian upper class and the old pre-industrial landlords it replaced, and between landlords converted into commercial entrepreneurs and their former tenants now bound by ties of wages and rent. The strength of colonial and imperial political controls long prevented the political expression of these conflicts, but with the decline of colonial power in the postwar era, the commercial export sectors of the underdeveloped world have become centers of revolutionary social movements. (Paige 1975:3)

Assuming inherent conflicts between agricultural producers and the dominant class, Paige attempts to construct an overall model of the forms that class conflict takes (Paige 1975; 1983). Paige deduces behavior patterns and the form of agrarian unrest from the income sources of the involved actors. More specifically, he proposes, on the one hand, that the economic base of the landed dominant class is narrower, more static, and less efficient than that of its commercial and industrial counterparts. The former's economic weakness gives rise to zero-sum class conflict as well as to its tyrannical political control of the means of production (both land and labor). On the other hand, the broader, more dynamic and efficient capital base of the commercial or industrial upper class can expand nonproducers' resources. This factor facilitates the adoption of more compromising solutions by the dominant class. In this context class conflict involves the economic distribution of goods and products rather than the political control of labor and land. Adopting Marx's theoretical arguments in his analysis of the French peasantry (Marx 1963; cf. Mitrany 1951), Paige further hypothesizes that cultivators' dependence on land as their main source of income gives rise to a conservative, competitive, and structurally dependent peasantry. In contrast, their dependence on wages would result in a more radical, solidary, and structurally interdependent cultivator class.

Based on the premise of inherent class conflict and with its focus on the structure of class relations at the expense of both individual choices and the native sociocultural universe, Paige's model predicts that agrarian unrest will take the form of rebellion only when both cultivators and noncultivators derive their incomes from land, as is the case in north and central Vietnam. Furthermore, a combination of non-cultivators dependent on income from land and cultivators dependent on income from wages leads to revolution. Such a combination of income sources is typical of sharecropping and migratory labor estate systems.... In sharecropping systems [as in South Vietnam] the dominant ideology is likely to be Communist, while in migratory labor systems [for example, Kenya] the dominant ideology is likely to be nationalist. Revolutionary socialist movements are most likely in decentralized sharecropping systems, and revolutionary nationalist movements are most likely in colonial settler estate systems. (Paige 1975:71; also Paige 1983:706)

In contrast, although they have been influenced to varying degrees by the Marxist approach, anthropological analyses of agrarian revolutions and of historical events in general have paid closer attention to the dynamic interplay between capitalism and indigenous noncapitalist social formations as sociocultural systems (E. Wolf 1969; Smith 1984; see also James C. Scott 1976). For example, Carol Smith suggests that political unrest involves not necessarily and not only class conflict within the local system but a clash between Western capitalism as a sociocultural system and native organizational frameworks. In her examination of the ongoing Guatemalan revolution, Smith argues,

It cannot be accidental that wherever closed corporate peasant communities have formed, the social formations holding them have been plagued by the 'agrarian problem'—peasantries that refuse to be easily proletarianized —as well as by countless peasant rebellions, control of state apparatus by powerful landed oligarchies, and persistent ethnic divisions that shape the way in which regional and national political processes operate." (Smith 1984:195; cf. Luong 1985)

In James C. Scott's moral-economy model, agrarian unrest is examined in terms of the reactive response of the peasantry in a precapitalist social formation to capitalism and colonialism. In the context of the world market and the colonial state, the subsistence ethic of the precapitalist order by which lords and the state are supposed to respect peasants' right to subsistence in exchange for legitimacy is often violated. Given the peasants' concern with subsistence and the precarious relations between nature and the production process, they are hypothesized to prefer a variable to a fixed tax and rent policy. Scott's framework defines exploitation not merely in terms of the amount of resources extracted, but in fact, more importantly, also in terms of the nature and timing of this extraction from the peasantry. The expansion of Western capitalism and the establishment of European colonies eventually lead to the violation of the subsistence ethic through the erosion of patron-client ties and the existing welfare mechanisms in the relation between cultivators and noncultivators. As a corollary, Scott suggests that peasant rebellions essentially involve a conception of social justice. Peasant movements are seen as quintessentially defensive reactions of a moral nature —defensive reactions against the violation of the subsistence ethic and the increasingly serious threat to their survival during subsistence crises. Under this threat and violation, any significant natural or human-induced disaster can spark agrarian unrest. The prominent role of third-world peasants in twentieth-century political movements, Scott argues, involves a dynamic interplay between a precapitalist sociocultural order, on the one hand, and colonialism and capitalism, on the other. Unrest is thus defined, within the Durkheimian tradition of social thought, in terms of a breakdown of the normative framework during a period of transition (cf. Gran 1975).

From a different analytical angle, while still situating modern anticolonial movements in the context of the structure and processes of Western colonial expansion, the political scientist Rupert Emerson deemphasizes the significance of class conflict:

> Save in the sense that Western-inspired changes in the economic structure underlay much of the disruption of the older societies, it is doubtful that the economic aspects were as significant as the political and social in turning the new colonial elites to nationalism.... [The ample grounds for hostility to colonial economic systems, such as the favoring of metropolitan interests over indigenous enterprises] were not generally the original source from which the more basic hostility sprang.... The more fundamental elements were the sense of inferiority inherent in colonialism, the indignation aroused by determination of status on racial grounds, and the gnawing consciousness of being a second-class citizen in one's own country. (Emerson 1960:54–55)

Emerson suggests two major conditions for the rise of nationalism in the colonial context: the disruption of the precolonial order and the emergence of a Westernized bourgeois elite—an elite who are particularly sensitive to the incongruity between Western egalitarian and democratic ideals and the colonial structure of racial and ethnic inequality.

In the first place, the greater the disruption of the old society under the impact of the intruding Western forces—assuming that the disruption takes the form of a development of modern enterprise and administration and not merely the suppression of the native population—the speedier and more complete the assertion of nationalism is likely to be....The elements of...[the] population which have been most drastically divorced from the close-knit pattern of their traditional society are the most susceptible to the appeal of nationalism. (Ibid.: 44)

Emerson suggests that it is nationalism that serves as the major basis for both the emergence of anticolonial movements and the integration of the modern nation-state. If the colonial encounter initially provokes a xenophobic reaction on the part of the indigenous system, the anticolonial movements of a later stage tend to involve both a nationalist ideology and a progressive orientation (ibid.: 11). Emerson proposes that the nationalism emerging from colonial contexts has stronger democratic roots than the nationalism in comparable noncolonial societies for two reasons. First, the modern anticolonial and nationalist leadership comes not so much from the traditional elite but from the ranks of the Western-educated intelligentsia, whose world view is shaped, at least to a certain extent, by Western democratic ideals. Second, democratic emphases enable the anticolonial leadership to gain greater legitimacy and mass support (ibid.: 213–237).[9] According to Emerson, Marxism owes its appeal among the anticolonial leaders in the (former) colonies of European empires not to the inherent class conflict between workers and the owners of the means of production, but to the nationalist ideology onto which it is grafted. To the extent that Emerson's thesis centers on the notion of an integrated normative order— an order that colonialism disrupts and nationalism serves to achieve—it is also under a Durkheimian influence.

On a general theoretical level both the Marxist and Durkheimian approaches stand in sharp contrast to J. S. Mill's utilitarian framework in that they examine historical events and revolutionary dynamics in structural terms, either in terms of the structure of class relations or the disjuncture between an expanding Western capitalism and local indigenous systems. In this respect all the models in which the notion of structure constitutes a fundamental analytical concept are generally congruent with Fernand Braudel's situation of historical events within deeper socioeconomic undercurrents. The critical difference among these models of the relationship of structure to historical events lies in the extent to which they pay attention to the structure of native categories. Paige's model, for example, focuses almost exclusively on the structure of class relations at the expense of the ideological dimensions of capitalism and indigenous noncapitalist formations. In contrast, within the Saussurean-Durkheimian tradition, Marshall Sahlins, for example, situates historical events in the conjuncture of different systems of meanings. In the case of the early period of contact between Westerners and the Hawaiian kingdom, he analyzes how the arrival of Captain Cook was metaphorized within the supposedly integrated Hawaiian scheme of conceptual categories (Captain Cook as the Hawaiian god Lono) and how the historically specific conjuncture of Western and Hawaiian systems shapes the latter through the mediation of events and practice (for example, the murder of Captain Cook in accordance with Hawaiian categories; see Sahlins 1981 and 1985).[10] The theoretical issues emerging in the three major theoretical approaches to historical events constitute the background for the following analysis of tradition and history in the village of Sơn-Dương in the 1925–2006 period.

Part I of the present study examines in microscopic detail the interplay of anticolonial events in the 1884–1930 period and the colonial social structure in the village of Sơn-Dương and the district of Lâm-Thao. The second part of the book analyzes the rise of Marxist power and the socialist revolution in the village in the past eight decades. The third part of the book examines the dynamics of local economic, sociocultural, and political changes as Vietnam shifts from a command economy to an era of market-oriented reforms and global economic integration since the late 1980s. I argue that the events in Vietnam during the most violent phases of the Western colonial and capitalist encounter (1930–1975) cannot be fully understood by applying a narrow cost-benefit analysis to historical agents, as emphasized in Popkin's model and the Millean tradition of inquiry. As emphasized respectively in Wallerstein's work and the aforementioned anthropological analyses of agrarian unrest, those events should instead be situated both in the structure of Western capitalist imperialism and in the indigenous sociocultural framework—a framework in which the kinship-centered model of hierarchical relations exists in a dialectical tension with the collectivistic ideology. More specifically, the Vietnamese revolution is rooted in two sets of conditions of the native system. First are the fundamental inequality and contradictions in the relationship between the European metropolis and the capitalist core on the one hand and the colonies and the periphery of world capitalism on the other. It is a relation in which the racial diarchy of the colony stands in sharp contrast to the discourse of "liberty, equality, and fraternity" of the European metropolis. It is a system in which, at least in the perception of anticolonial leaders, the policy of the colonial state is geared more often than not toward the process of capital accumulation by and for the capitalist core. Second, and equally significant, is the degree of divergence of local tradition from the practice of capitalist imperialism as well as the strength of this tradition in providing the ideological support and organizational resources for revolutionary movements. Against Paige's analysis of the Vietnam case (Paige 1975 and 1983), I argue that, throughout the past century, the greater divergence of local tradition in northern and central Vietnam from the imperialist capitalist framework accounts both for the generally greater intensity of armed unrest against French and American intervention and for the greater receptivity to a mild form of collectivism there than in southern Vietnam. In other words, the greater degree of armed unrest and receptivity to collectivism relate to the greater strength of both the collectivistic ideology and the kinship-centered model of hierarchical relations in the local tradition of the center and the north. I suggest that these forces also underlie the trajectory of Sơn-Dương villagers' participation in the market economy and their responses to many events in the village in the two decades under market-oriented reforms in Vietnam. In sum, I suggest that the structures of both the capitalist system and the indigenous social formation have powerfully shaped historical events in Vietnam in the past century. And these structures are in turn themselves shaped by historical events.

PART I

# Historical Events and Village Structure in Colonial Northern Vietnam

# CHAPTER 1

# Vietnamese Anticolonialism, 1884–1930

## A Microscopic Perspective on Historical Events

On February 10, 1930, the Ministry of Colonies in Paris received a "most urgent" cable reporting that two Vietnamese companies in the colonial infantry had revolted in Yên-Báy, a town located 153 kilometers northeast of Hanoi (AOM-P-NF, 322–2614). Other "urgent" cables reported armed violence in the northern provinces of Phú-Thọ, Thái-Bình, and Hải-Dương, as well as bombing incidents at colonial government buildings in Hanoi. The initial report of three casualties among the ranking French officers in Yên-Báy was subsequently revised upward to ten. The revolt received heavy coverage in the press of both the French metropolis and the Far Eastern colony. Most accounts initially blamed the uprising on communist agitation.[1] However, it was not until three months later that the Indochinese Communist Party (ICP) launched its own movement—a fifteen-month insurrection in which half a million Vietnamese in twenty-five provinces actively participated.[2] The short-lived Yên-Báy precursor of the ICP-led soviet movement was actually organized by the Vietnamese Nationalist Party (VNP, Việt Nam Quốc Dân Đảng). It marked the beginning of a period of unrest in which members of the French-educated intelligentsia played, for the first time, an active role in Vietnamese anticolonialist movements.

The unfolding of the Yên-Báy drama had a profound significance for the members of the village of Sơn-Dương, at that time in the province of Phú-Thọ. It was in this village that a large number of the bombs for the Yên-Báy uprising were manufactured. It was also at Sơn-Dương that the VNP vice-president, the Confucian scholar Xứ Nhu, established his command post for the armed movement in the provinces of Phú-Thọ and Yên-Báy.[3]

According to French reports, on February 9, 1930, many male and female villagers from Sơn-Dương and some other villages in the district of Lâm-Thao pretended to make a pilgrimage to a well-known pagoda in the town of Yên-Báy.[4] They carried bombs, scimitars, flags, bandoliers, and badges in suitcases and baskets. The baskets were covered with fruit, flowers, votive paper, and incense. The "pilgrims" got off the train at three different stations near the town in order to avoid attracting the attention of the local police. From these stations they were led to temporary hide-outs by soldiers in the colonial forces stationed in Yên-Báy (Report 78 c.s. of the *résident supérieur* of Tonkin to the governor general of Indo-china, pp. 28–29, AOM-P-NF, 323–2626; also AOM-P-NF, 322–2614). Over 100 bombs as well as revolutionary leaflets had been produced at the Sơn-Dương house of a French-trained schoolteacher, Nguyễn Đắc Bằng. Bằng and his wife's cousin, the local Confucian teacher Toại (Đồ Toại), had actively organized Sơn-Dương villagers in preparation for the armed movement in Yên-Báy and Phú-Thọ.

Not only did the village of Sơn-Dương become a bomb factory, a major point of political mobilization, and the command post for the Yên-Báy insurrection, a large number of its members also actively participated in the armed attacks on the local colonial headquarters in Phú-Thọ. On the evening of February 9, 1930, according to a French Sûreté report,

> Around eight or nine o'clock...the rebels gathered in three locations in Sơn-Dương, some at Toại's house, some at Bằng's residence, and others in the fields of Sơn-Dương where they would soon be joined by the other two groups. Around eleven or midnight, Xứ Nhu divided the contingent into two groups, one [heading for the district seat of] Lâm-Thao, the other led by Xứ Nhu himself to [the native guard barrack in] Hưng-Hoá, with Toại as second in command. Each rebel received two bombs and a scimitar, with the exception of Xứ Nhu, who armed himself with a pistol. Some wore khaki uniforms and sashes. The two groups departed around one o'clock in the morning.
>
> Of the Xứ Nhu-led contingent heading for Hưng-Hoá...one group crossed the river on the public ferry, the other on sampans....They gathered on the sand bank of Bản-Nguyên, where it seems that other participants had arrived in sampan from the Hạ-Bì and Võng-La areas of Thanh-Thuỷ district....[With additional participants from nearby villages, the rebel ranks swelled to thirty-three to forty men, and] Xứ Nhu ordered an arms redistribution, gave final and detailed instructions to his men, [and waited for the attack signal from the Lâm-Thao district seat]....
>
> As a glimmer of light was finally detected from Lâm-Thao, Xứ Nhu gave the order to march to the native guard post of Hưng-Hoá by skirt-

ing the administrative building and passing the town post office. It was around three in the morning then. Arriving at the foot of the complex, the revolutionaries exhorted the sentry guards to open the doors and join them. They had expected the defection of the guards and an easy achievement of their objective. But they were greeted with rifle shots. The rebels soon threw bombs into the yard of the post, the barracks, and the residence of the commanding officer. They burned gasoline near a side door and forced open the gates. Some entered the yard and attempted an entry into the residence of the commanding officer. Together with his wife, he managed to [flee to] the blockhouse.... The attack lasted about forty-five minutes. As the attackers encountered heavy fire, they quickly retreated and fled toward the river, carrying with them the unused arms. Some dispersed into the surrounding areas. Three arrests were subsequently made and seventeen unexploded bombs were found in the yard of the post.

The same night, a group of approximately twenty individuals showed up at the house of the instructor Nguyễn Quang Kính of Kinh-Kệ village [next to Sơn-Dương]. He lived with his two wives, the two sisters Mã thị Chế and Mã thị Báu, in a house at the [village] school located at some distance from the village [center]. The rebels forced him to follow them. Chế was also led away when she attempted to catch up with the group and to give her husband some clothes to take along. The following morning Chế was found dead on the dike near Sơn-Lưu, her chest pierced by a pistol bullet. Kính was seriously wounded with scimitar strikes at the wrist, on the shoulder, and on the face. He could not name the attackers. In striking him, they only said: "We have just assassinated the district chief. Now it is your turn."... Kính had been affiliated with the VNP. It is probable that the Hưng-Hoá group wanted him to join them for the attack, but they killed him when he refused. (French Sûreté report of March 1, 1930, AOM-P-NF, 323–2626)

Having earlier done propaganda work among the native guards of the Hưng-Hoá post, the VNP attack contingent had expected the guards' cooperation. Unknown to the attack force, however, the French had sent a fifty-troop reinforcement to the post the day before on the basis of an anonymous tip from a local source about a possible attack. As a major VNP leader in Sơn-Dương village and a participant in the Hưng-Hoá attack, the schoolteacher Bằng recounted the unfolding of events differently from the official French report:

[After we forced our entry into the yard in our assault on the Hưng-Hoá post] from the second floor of the blockhouse, the enemy counterattacked. A rain of bullets began falling all around us. Donning a beige khaki uniform, a cap, a pair of sandals, and a banner across my shoulder saying "Revolutionary Armed Forces: Every Sacrifice for the Liberation of the Fatherland and the Vietnamese People," I rushed to the house of the commanding French officer with my scimitar. Breaking in the door, I saw only a frightened French woman in her pajamas. She cried and begged for her life. "Don't be afraid," I told her. "We are revolutionary soldiers. We are looking for your husband, the commanding officer; we respect the lives of women and children." The three of us, myself and two comrades, frantically and thoroughly searched the entire house for the officer. When we rushed across the yard to the two-story blockhouse to continue our search, we heard an order in French from the second floor to open more fire. There was the French second lieutenant, the post commander!

Bullets heavily rained down in the darkness around us, and we found no comrades at all in the area. I sensed immediately that something had gone wrong. We rushed toward the back and escaped through the gate at the corner of the vegetable garden. I knew by heart the nooks and crannies of the town of Hưng-Hoá, having attended school there a number of years earlier. We rushed through the deserted streets in the darkness of the night and ran back to the river. It was indeed a miracle that none of us got hurt! Perhaps the Vietnamese soldiers, among whom we had done a lot of propaganda work, simply fired into the air as a warning to us.

Arriving at the river bank well past three o'clock, we found Xứ Nhu and other comrades anxiously waiting there for the sampans to take them back across the river.

Reaching the other side of the river, we were informed of our next battle plan: we were all to move to the Lâm-Thao district seat to reinforce our troops there and then all together on to the Phú-Thọ provincial capital, where we would wait for our fighters to arrive on the afternoon train from Yên-Báy before launching the attack on the Phú-Thọ military barracks. After the takeover of the Phú-Thọ post, we would advance toward Sơn-Tây and the rest of the provinces in the Red River delta.... In the darkness of the night, as we passed through the village of Kinh-Kệ on a shortcut route to Lâm-Thao, Xứ Nhu asked us: "Does the French hunting dog teacher Kính live in this village?" Upon my nod, he gave the French-trained Syria vet-

eran in our ranks the pistol and the execution order.... We left behind
Kính's body and the wailing cries of his wife and children, and it was
almost dawn when we reached the fields of Sơn-Dương village. I
was ordered to remain behind to mobilize the inhabitants to join the
uprising.

Bằng's narrative and the French reports may not fully reflect reality.
The former VNP member, Kính, may have simply been left for dead by the
anticolonial forces. And the French woman whom Bằng reported to have
encountered may not have been the wife of the commanding officer of the
Hưng-Hoá post. But it is significant that Bằng's narrative highlights his
humanitarian voice in this encounter during the attack on the Hưng-Hoá
barrack, while ignoring the assassination of the former VNP member's
wife reported in the French Sûreté account. Bằng's selective discursive
emphasis, like that in the French report, constitutes a part of the larger
ideological struggle couched in the idiom of humanitarianism. However,
the assassination of the former VNP member's wife is shadowed by the
larger chain of events as Bằng narrated them:

A few hours later [after the return to Sơn-Dương from Hưng-Hoá],
on the morning of the tenth, I received the first news of our victory at
Lâm-Thao. The revolutionary fighters had taken the district seat and
captured the weapons of administrative guards, despite the escape of
the district chief. I was told that thanks to the propaganda efforts of
my young brother Tăng and his friends, peasant women had happily
brought to our fighters rice, meat, cakes, and soup; and the inhabitants of the surrounding villages had been coming to the district seat
in large number to volunteer to join our ranks, shouting en route
the slogan "long live the success of the Vietnamese revolution!" On
learning the news, although exhausted by the lack of any sleep for
several consecutive nights, I felt an intense euphoria. I rushed to all
the corners of the village, calling for my fellow villagers to join our
forces at Lâm-Thao.

However, the good news did not last long. Within half an hour I
was stunned when a young pupil rushed back to inform us that a company of Vietnamese and French soldiers led by the deputy *résident*
and a French captain had counterattacked and that our fighters, after
a valiant defense for over an hour with small arms, had had to retreat
and disperse because they were outnumbered and outgunned. I was
also told that the veteran of Syria in our ranks had been wounded in

the leg and that our soldiers were then trying to regroup to move on to the provincial capital.

The news that Bằng had received of the development in the Lâm-Thao district seat was essentially correct. The attack troops had not only captured arms from the administrative guards, but they had also set fire to the residence of the hated and corrupt district chief and raised their own flag on the main gate of the district administration building. It was Bằng's adolescent brother who had read the revolutionary army's proclamation of victory in the district seat. However, the victory was short-lived. Under the daylight counterattack by a detachment of twenty native guards led by the Phú-Thọ deputy *résident* (the de facto deputy province chief), the VNP forces had to make a full retreat. Xứ Nhu was seriously wounded and reportedly attempted suicide several times, succeeding only on his third attempt (Cố-Nhi-Tân 1969:103–104; Hoàng-Phạm-Trân 1949:96–97).

The major uprising in Yên-Báy had not unfolded smoothly either, despite the active cooperation of many Vietnamese soldiers in the colonial infantry battalion. The anticolonial forces did succeed initially in seizing the arms warehouse, and they caused the French numerous casualties among their twenty-nine officers and warrant officers. That night they proclaimed victory. The yellow-and-red pennants of their revolutionary army waved over the barracks, while white-and-red revolutionary flags were raised at the district seat. The leaders of the insurrection also sent a patrol into the town to invite the populace to join them in the uprising, claiming that all the French officers and warrant officers had been killed. The colonial armed forces in Yên-Báy were, however, far from united in their support for the insurrection. In contrast to the colonial infantry, the native guards did not join the uprising. The native guards even gathered to defend French civilians and the main administrative building in the provincial capital. Having failed to gain the support of native guards, the revolutionary fighters did not proceed to seize the train station and other major provincial buildings as previously planned (AOM-P-NP, 323–2626). Toward daybreak a small number of colonial infantry soldiers managed to report to their French commanders in the still French-controlled upper barracks, claiming earlier coercion by the revolutionary forces. As the revolutionary forces had forgotten to cut the telegraph line, a reconnaissance plane was sent in from Hanoi in response to reports from Yên-Báy, and the French counterattack began at daybreak. Once firing began from a French airplane, according to one revolutionary participant from Phú-Thọ (Nguyễn-Hải-Hàm 1970), the revolutionary forces quickly retreated. The French reports also mention that the fighters fled after only two shots from the counterattacking forces (Wintrebert report, AOM-P-NF, 323–2626; cf. Sûreté report 2967/s, AOM-AP-I, 7F–57). The most important attack in the VNP insurrection scheme quickly turned into a rout. Although the uprising had been prepared with some care, the Vietnamese Nationalist Party leadership had apparently not planned for unexpected developments.

It is not surprising that the VNP armed movement in the rest of the Red River delta fizzled out in the face of subsequent tight French security measures throughout Tonkin (north Vietnam), particularly in the provinces along the route to Hanoi from the Chinese province of Yunnan. A curfew was imposed in Hanoi for twelve days. The isolated bombing incidents in Hanoi on February 10, 1930, did not succeed in preventing the colonial authorities from sending French troop reinforcements to Phú-Thọ and the neighboring provinces of Yên-Báy, Sơn-Tây, and Tuyên-Quang. French and legionnaire troops were also sent to the previously all-Vietnamese garrisons at Sept-Pagodes, Phủ-Lạng-Thương, as well as to the potentially troublesome provinces of Hải-Dương, Nam-Định, and Kiến-An (Robin report 1930, 14-16, AOM-P-NF, 323–2626). Many VNP suspects, both within and outside the colonial armed forces, were arrested in the provinces of Hải-Dương and Bắc-Ninh.

These moves by the colonial government notwithstanding, six days after the Yên-Báy and Phú-Thọ incidents, the VNP leadership mounted a last-ditch challenge to the French in two districts on the boundaries of Hải-Dương and Thái-Bình provinces. In Thái-Bình a hundred-strong VNP force led by a village schoolteacher and a deputy canton chief attacked the district seat of Phủ-Dực. Many fighters disguised themselves in the uniforms of the colonial infantry. The local administrative guards were taken in by the ruse, and the revolutionary forces subsequently destroyed the Phủ-Dực post, wounded three guards and one of the district chief's daughters, and captured the district guards' rifles. A similar attack took place in the neighboring district of Vĩnh-Bảo (Hải-Dương province) on the same night. After killing the district chief, the VNP forces occupied Vĩnh-Bảo for one day before being dislodged to Cổ-Am, a village well known for its strong tradition of Confucian scholarship and civil service. The village was subsequently bombed at the order of the French *résident supérieur* for Tonkin (Robin report 1930, 20, and police report, AOM-P-NF, 323–2626). As a warning to the rest of the Vietnamese population, the French *résident supérieur* ordered the French provincial chiefs to give maximum publicity to the Cổ-Am bombing (ibid., 20). A 200-man native-guard column was sent in for a mopping-up operation, which moved gradually from the

Phủ-Dực-Vĩnh-Bảo region to the provinces of Kiến-An, Bắc-Ninh, Sơn-Tây, and Yên-Báy (Robin 1930, 21-22, AOM-P-NF, 323–2626). By February 21 all the VNP front commanders had been arrested, including party president Nguyễn Thái Học himself.

The village of Sơn-Dương was not spared the French punitive measures in the aftermath of the VNP insurrection. Damages were reported in the village president's letter to the newspaper *Le petit parisien.* The letter was fully couched in colonialist rhetorical discourse to invoke the sympathy of readers among the colonial masters:

Dear Sir:

I hope that for the sake of all of us and of our unfortunate families, you will represent France and respond to my request as the president of the village of Sơn-Dương, Lâm-Thao district, province of Phú-Thọ (Tonkin), in order to conduct an investigation [into the French burning of Sơn-Dương houses]. Of the sixty-nine homeowners [in Sơn-Dương] whose properties were burnt down in a punitive measure [by the colonial government], only five deserved the punishment for having participated in the revolt.... Đậu, Toại, Tín, Sỹ, Tín. The rest were innocent victims who [unfortunately] lost their homes.... Please imagine our misfortune when, instead of finding our houses, we found only embers and ashes.... The fire destroyed everything we had: not only our houses, but also all our belongings, cereals, objects, clothes, and even our sacred ancestral altars. We could not save anything because, before the disaster bell tolled, we had to line up two by two, men and women, the young and the elderly, at the end of the village under the command of armed soldiers. We had to face two machine guns that forced us to remain silent.... But that was not the end. Despite our misery and our pain, and besides the 200-piaster penalty, we were required to carry our bamboo to the district seat and to reconstruct the buildings destroyed by the revolutionaries as well as to deliver bamboo to the provincial capital at a distance of sixteen kilometers. The magnitude of our misfortune could hardly be greater, because our poor village lost considerably with this cruel punishment, more than Xuân-Lũng, Cao-Mại, Kinh-Kệ, Phùng-Nguyên, La-Hào, Võng-La.

Not knowing how to make the mother country understand all our misfortunes at [such a great] distance, we trust and beg you, Sir, to kindly help the weak like ourselves see the light of French justice....

May these lines prove to the Mother Country our loyalty, of which the living proof is our more than twenty foreign-war veterans [Viet-

namese fighting for France in Europe during World War I] who nonetheless lost their houses for no understandable reasons.

May our grievances lead to your assistance and to redress for the
unjustly big losses imposed upon us without any pity, losses similar to those that the Chinese pirates caused to our ancestors in a still
memorable past era. May our poor peasants with their pitiful earnings benefit from the kindness of the noble maternal France, which
undoubtedly did not order the imposition of those terrible punishments
[upon us]....

President of the village of Sơn-Dương

I could not ascertain from oral historical or archival sources whether
Sơn-Dương had as many as twenty foreign-war veterans, if any at all,
returning from World War I in Europe. However, the village president
clearly hoped that the adoption of the dominant discursive practice of a
"noble maternal France" would signify the acceptance of the colonial masters' ideological hegemony and invoke their sympathy for the submissive
colonized subjects. The letter was enclosed with a receipt from the French
*résident* in Phú-Thọ for 200 piasters as a "contribution to the expenses
incurred by the rebellion in which certain members of the village have
participated" (Viollis 1935:204–206).

It was not entirely unpredictable that the Yên-Báy insurrection would
fail, although the magnitude of the revolt did catch the French by surprise.
In contrast to the first wave of Vietnamese anticolonial resistance against
the French at the end of the nineteenth century and the Communist-led
armed movements in both 1930–1931 and 1946–1975 (to be discussed
below in depth), the VNP leadership relied on a quick-strike strategy for
seizing urban centers. Although it faced an enemy with overwhelmingly
superior arms, the VNP leadership neither prepared for protracted guerrilla
warfare in the countryside nor systematically cultivated strong rural support among the indigenous masses as a precondition for such a strategy.

Moreover, the colonial government had received signals of a coordinated armed uprising in Tonkin. These ranged from the reports from a
high-ranking VNP informer in late 1929 to numerous and large discover-
ies of tracts, bombs, and other weapons in different Tonkinese locations
between October 1929 and January 1930. The invaluable informer was in
fact the head of military affairs on the VNP Central Committee.[5] Questions
had been raised about the loyalty of native troops in the colonial forces in
Hanoi and Nam-Định and the possibility of breaking up Vietnamese units
or transferring them to more remote regions of north Vietnam had been

discussed (Robin report 1930, 46–55, 66–67, AOM-P-NF, 323–2626). A number of Vietnamese warrant officers in the Tonkinese colonial forces had been arrested or transferred in 1929, and such moves within the colonial infantry had weakened the party structure in the armed forces. Arrests of other VNP members in 1929 had also shattered the VNP infrastructure in many Tonkin provinces.[6] With the active participation of the same high-ranking informer on the VNP Central Committee, the colonial authorities had come close to arresting the entire top VNP leadership at a December 25, 1929, meeting in the Phú-Thọ village of Võng-La, not too far from Sơn-Dương. Although the informer's collaboration with the French had been exposed by this arrest attempt, the colonial authorities still received sufficient information in two northern provinces about an insurrection planned around the Vietnamese New Year (early February 1930). They ordered provincial chiefs and military commanders to be on the alert throughout the New Year period and emphasized the need for close collaboration between military and civilian authorities in order to suppress revolutionary propaganda among the troops.[7] In the province of Phú-Thọ, tipped off by a written warning of an impending attack on the town of Hưng-Hoá, colonial authorities responded with troop reinforcements in the town. Unknown to the local VNP command, fifty additional native guards had been ordered to the Hưng-Hoá post on the eve of the uprising (Sûreté report of March 1, 1930, AOM-P-NF, 323–2626).

The French crackdown and the precautionary measures on the eve of the Yên-Báy uprising disrupted the VNP leadership's insurrection plan. The party president's order to postpone the uprising by five days arrived in the village of Sơn-Dương only after the departure of many villagers for Yên-Báy. In the end the colonial government regained control of Yên-Báy in less than half a day.

From a historical perspective, however, the significance of the Yên-Báy insurrection transcends the events in February 1930. The uprising and the local popular support for it in the fertile agricultural district of Lâm-Thao and in Phú-Thọ in general were far from isolated developments. For most of the period following the official establishment of French colonial power in Tonkin and Annam in 1883, anticolonial resistance had simmered in this long-settled area of northern Vietnam. The *pax colonia* and the history of Western capitalist expansion in this part of the country were punctuated by eruptions of armed unrest, the first wave coming in 1884–1893, the second, a relatively minor one during World War I, the third under VNP leadership in 1930, and finally, the most serious one, from 1941 until the violent end of French colonialism in 1954.

The first anticolonial movement in the Phú-Thọ area followed the fall of the Sơn-Tây citadel in December 1883, an encounter with the West that seems to have left the populace with a bitter aftertaste and to have consequently strengthened their resolve to resist. The French attack on Sơn-Tây took place in the aftermath of the Harmand convention of August 1883, which ceded Tonkin to the French as a protectorate and effectively gave the colonial regime access to the vast Chinese market from the south (see Trương-Bửu-Lâm 1968:16–23). This treaty notwithstanding, Tonkin was far from secure, and French control was limited to a number of areas in the Red River delta.

The province of Sơn-Tây, which at this time included the district of Lâm-Thao and the village of Sơn-Dương, had long served as a base for Black Flag troops to harass and attack French forces near Hanoi (Marr 1971:41–43). Black Flag soldiers came from the ranks of the troops in the Taiping movement who had sought refuge in north Vietnam following the defeat of the movement in China in 1865. They maintained de facto control of the region along the Sino-Vietnamese border. Enlisting their services, the Huế court appointed the Black Flag leader to be ranking military commander of the provinces of Sơn-Tây, Hưng-Hoá, and Tuyên-Quang in 1880. In addition to the Black Flag troops, since late 1881 regular Chinese government troops had been crossing into Vietnam in response to the Western threat to a country under Chinese suzerainty.

In December 1883, in order to reduce the military threat to French forces in the Hanoi area, the French mobilized 5,500 troops for the assault on the Vaunbanesque Sơn-Tây citadel. Although Black Flag forces mounted a valiant defense, suffering an estimated 1,000 casualties and inflicting 403 casualties on the French-commanded troops, the citadel fell on the third day to the technologically superior invading troops (McAleavy 1968:26–27; Trần-Trọng-Kim 1964:537; James G. Scott 1885:86). The French victory terrorized the Vietnamese population, as a British journalist in Tonkin at the time reported:

That was a terrible night in Sontay. The Turcos [Turks in the French Foreign Legion] had entered, with comparatively little opposition, by the eastern gate, and they admittedly killed men, women, and children—every living thing they came across. The French troops were not so bad, but the butchery of Chinamen and cropped-headed Annamese [under the Vietnamese governor general's command]...was sickening....

Even so late as May 1884...most of the houses remained gutted and empty....Liu Jung-fu [or Lưu-Vĩnh-Phúc, the Black Flag troop commander] carried off all the inhabitants, so say the French, but the Chinese say the French killed them all. Women are very scarce in Son-tay still, and that can be said of no other post where the French are in Tongking. The sacking of the place was a terrible affliction, which the Tongkinese will not forget readily. (J. G. Scott 1885:85–86)

With the fall of the Sơn-Tây citadel, Black Flag troops temporarily withdrew to the citadel of Hưng-Hoá, across the river from the village of Sơn-Dương. In direct violation of orders from the conciliatory and resigned Huế court, a ranking Sơn-Tây official, Treasury Director Nguyễn văn Giáp, like quite a few other Vietnamese mandarins, retreated to the district of Lâm-Thao, where he set up two major anticolonial guerrilla bases in Thanh-Mai and Thạch-Sơn (see Map 3). Both villages neighbor on the Lâm-Thao district seat and are situated at a distance of five kilometers from the village of Sơn-Dương (Lê-Tượng and Vũ-Kim-Biên 1981:113–114). Another anti-French mandarin appealed to the populace:

The provincial citadel [of Sơn-Tây] has been lost, and it becomes increasingly painful for us to receive the orders,

The garrisons have been withdrawn and the imperial edicts reach us in bitterness.

The French plots are indeed fearful. They are like silkworms gnawing at the mulberry leaves.

Lương văn Dật [a petty officer] was a God-cursed traitor who acted like a worm in one's bones. He delivered the citadel to the enemy.

Because of that, the situation now is almost desperate and the country disintegrates.

Because the court's officials were cowards and excessively anxious to save their lives, they hurriedly surrendered to the enemy.

Given that advantage, the enemy now moves freely and kills our people with impunity,

But people like us must try to preserve the country in which we live. Shall we just stare at our decay? . . .

Since we are determined not to live with the enemy, we shall not be deterred by their overwhelmingly superior forces,

Since we believe that success rests upon the people's will, we shall not fret over our futile efforts. (translated in Trương-Bửu-Lâm 1967:113–115)

Despite the small odds for success, anticolonial support among the population seems to have been partly sustained by the native sociocul-

tural logic that places greater emphasis on effort than on short-term consequences, as can be seen in the last phrase of the appeal. The achievements
of native actors were measured in terms of the moral nobility of their acts
as much as on the basis of concrete results.

After seizing the Bắc-Ninh citadel in March 1884, the French turned
their attention to Hưng-Hoá and began a campaign to consolidate control
of mountainous regions close to the Sino-Vietnamese border. On April 5,
1884, 8,000 troops advanced toward Hưng-Hoá. Although they encountered some resistance at the conjuncture of the Red and Black rivers, the
French troops moved steadily upstream with few casualties. The Vietnamese governor of Hưng-Hoá (Nguyễn Quang Bích) and Black Flag commanders seem to have ordered the harassment of French troops only in
order to buy time for the organization of their retreat: the citadel was burnt
and abandoned on April 12 with practically no resistance (James G. Scott
1885:176–185; McAleavy 1968: 231–232; cf. Lê-Tượng and Vũ-Kim-
Biên 1981:114). The surrounding countryside, including the other side of
the river where Sơn-Dương is located, was virtually depopulated, possibly
because the retreating troops drafted able-bodied men to carry weapons
from the citadel but most probably because the widely reported Sơn-Tây
massacre had frightened the peasant population in this part of the country
(McAleavy 1968; cf. James G. Scott 1885:185). Part of the Black Flag
force withdrew toward Lâm-Thao. Bích moved to the hilly area on the
other side of the Red River, near the boundaries of Cẩm-Khê, Hạ-Hoà,
and Yên-Lập districts, to lead the guerrilla resistance in coordination with
Giáp in Lâm-Thao.

The village of Sơn-Dương was located precisely on the route of attack
and counterattack between the French-controlled town of Hưng-Hoá and
the major guerrilla base of Thanh-Mai in Lâm-Thao (see Kiều-Hữu-Hỷ et
al.1961:9; Đặng-Huy-Vận 1967:48–49). As the French attempted to seize
control of the rest of Tonkin, and Chinese troops and Vietnamese guerrillas
counterattacked the invading forces, this area of northern Vietnam up to
the Vietnam-China border became a major battle zone. In November 1884,
for example, Chinese government and Black Flag troops began moving
from northern Phú-Thọ and Yên-Báy to encircle the French-controlled
Tuyên-Quang citadel, where they carried out a three-and-a-half-month
siege. The more mountainous districts of Hưng-Hoá (Trấn-Yên, Văn-
Chấn, Yên-Lập) and Sơn-Tây (Hạ-Hoà and Thanh-Ba) fell back under the
control of anti-French forces (Đặng-Huy-Vận 1967:48). In March 1885,
as Chinese troops from Kwangsi defeated a French force of 35,000 in
Lạng-Sơn, Black Flag troops and Vietnamese guerrillas also intensified

their attacks in the Lâm-Thao area and four other agriculturally fertile districts of Sơn-Tây province (ibid.:48–49).[8]

It was at this juncture in early April 1885 (the twenty-eighth day of the second lunar month) that, according to an official village report in 1897, a hundred villagers were massacred, and the majority of village houses were burnt down (TTLTQG1-PT–534). This report provided the names of seventy-three adult men massacred in 1885 and mentioned specifically that the list did not include massacred women and children (ibid.); village legends recorded a century later put the number massacred at 300 (Sơn-Dương 1987:12). Given a listing of 198 households in another 1897 report, the number of village households in 1885 was unlikely to have significantly exceeded 200, and the death of 100 adult villagers was a major disaster to Sơn-Dương. This disaster became a part of the village's collective memory, and a ceremony to commemorate these deaths was added to the village's annual ritual calendar (ibid.:12). The exact circumstances of these killings, however, remain shrouded in mystery. Village oral history speaks of an attack by Chinese Black Flag troops whom a major anti-French leader in Lâm-Thao district, Lãnh Mai, had successfully enlisted to eliminate the Sơn-Dương guerrilla leader, Đội Bốn, supposedly a follower of yet another anti-French leader, Đề Kiều. Đội Bốn was reportedly killed in this 1885 Chinese attack (ibid.:12). However, a different historical source lists Đội Bốn as a local guerrilla leader during the second period of anti-French activity, which extended into the early 1890s (Lê-Tượng and Vũ-Kim-Biên 1981:119–120). In any case, Sơn-Dương was clearly under the control of the anticolonial resistance when the entire district of Lâm-Thao fell into Vietnamese and Chinese (Black Flag) hands in May 1885. From this base and from the other side of the Red River, guerrilla forces intensified their attacks on other districts, seizing the strategically located town of Việt-Trì and the districts of Bất-Bạt and Quảng-Oai, and destroying the French military post in Hưng-Hoá in May and June of the same year (Đặng-Huy-Vận 1967:49).

The anticolonial resistance in the Lâm-Thao area in particular and in northern Vietnam in general took a major turn in the summer of 1885. In July 1885 King Hàm-Nghi fled the capital at Huế and issued an anti-colonial "Aid-the-King" edict to his subjects.[9] As the historian Trương-Bửu-Lâm has remarked, "The edict…was warmly received by the population and immediately set in motion the strongest resistance the French had encountered since they first set foot on Vietnamese soil" (1968:25). In terms of the relationship between the court and the populace, the royal edict lent legitimacy to the resistance movement: "Royal sanction was thus squarely behind popular resistance—too late for any temporal success, but still of great importance in sustaining resistance through its most barren years. With the flight of the monarch, indignation could no longer turn against him and therefore focused increasingly on the French" (Marr 1971:51). One month earlier Chinese government troops had begun withdrawing from Vietnam following the Franco-Chinese Tientsin agreement, according to which China recognized Vietnam as a French colony and protectorate in exchange for an end to French attacks on Taiwan and other points along the Chinese coast. The Vietnamese anticolonial movement thus became strongly rooted in the indigenous soil, relying primarily on the local population for support. Its leadership was provided primarily by Confucian literati: of the thirty-four prominent leaders whose biographical data were available, twenty-two were former mandarins, and eight others were Confucian degree holders (Trần-Huy-Liệu, Văn-Tạo, and Nguyễn-Khắc-Đạm 1957:70–82).

At this point in 1885 the Hưng-Hoá area became the liaison center for the anticolonial movement in the north, as the fugitive monarch bestowed on the Hưng-Hoá regional guerrilla commander, former governor Nguyễn Quang Bích, the titles of minister of rites (including foreign affairs), marquis, and deputy troop commander of Tonkin.[10] The countryside in which the village of Sơn-Dương is located thus constituted a major northern base in the first wave of Vietnamese anticolonialism (1883–1896), with links to the Aid-the-King headquarters in Thanh-Hoá province through the hilly Mường country of Hoà-Bình.[11]

It is not surprising, then, that the area around Sơn-Dương also became a point of concentration for French military power. In October 1885 the French mobilized 6,000 troops armed with cannons to attack the guerrilla base at nearby Thanh-Mai (Lê-Tượng and Vũ-Kim-Biên 1981:116). Overwhelmed in number and firearms, the guerrillas had to retreat to the other side of the Red River and farther upland. The French set up military posts in many locations. But taking advantage of the difficult but familiar terrain and the strong support of the local population, the guerrilla forces selectively attacked administrative seats and military posts throughout the province, and temporarily dispersed into the surrounding hills whenever they encountered overwhelming enemy forces. The anticolonial resistance made maximal use of a guerrilla strategy in which they relied on their own mobility in the midland hills as well as the peasants' food supply and intelligence for tactical advantages. At the same time guerrilla forces arrested and even executed certain mandarins and local officials who collaborated with the French (ibid.:117–119). Some district chiefs sought refuge in the military posts. It was a classic guerrilla war that prefigured the strategy of the Communist-led armed movement against the French and American forces from 1930 to 1975.

At the end of 1888 a newly emerging commander from the ranks of Giáp's staff, Đốc Ngữ (General Ngữ), and other guerrilla commanders began a successful strategy of bolder attacks on French forces in the Hưng-Hoá area. The Lâm-Thao district seat was sacked on December 30 and 31, 1888. Sơn-Dương was reported to be one of three main anticolonial bases in the district, the other two being the neighboring village of Ngũ-Xã and the traditional base of Thanh-Mai (ibid.:120). Approximately one year later, in late 1889, all of the administrative and military staff members in the Lâm-Thao district seat joined the anticolonial movement and took their arms to a guerilla base in Thanh-Ba district (ibid.:119). According to a French Catholic priest, in 1889 "the rebels became stronger and more numerous [in Hưng-Hoá and Sơn-Tây]. In the districts of Quảng-Oai, Lâm-Thao, Bất-Bạt, Tam-Nông, An-Lạc, Cẩm-Khê, Sơn-Vi, Hạ-Hoà, and Thanh-Ba, rebel groups roamed freely at night and occasionally even during the day.... I would say that in these districts, the rebels have more control than the protectorate government forces do. The authority of the protectorate government is more formal than real" (Puginier, quoted in Đặng-Huy-Vận 1967:49–50). Another observer remarked that "in all the villages there exist two mayors, one with real power and collecting taxes for the rebels; the other a puppet mayor, an official working for the French government and lying to the latter from dawn to dusk" (Girod, quoted in ibid.:50). A French native guard commander in the Hưng-Hoá area remarked: "Everywhere that we have passed, and no matter how much good will our own chiefs have, we have actually left regrettable traces of our passage. A house destroyed? A buffalo disappearing? As soon as we have left, Đề Kiều [the major guerrilla commander mentioned earlier] has sent the peasant a buffalo or money equivalent to the price of the house" (Pouvourville 1892:10). Đề Kiều reportedly also maintained strict discipline among his troops and meted out harsh punishments, including execution, to troops pillaging the property of nonhostile populations (ibid.:14).

By mid-1890 conditions had deteriorated for the French in Lâm-Thao district. French military posts were set up only along the rivers, and there existed no civil guard posts in the central part of the district (April 30, 1890, report of the French *résident* in Hưng-Hoá, AOM-AP-RST, 27–656). Many villages were reportedly abandoned, with land having lain fallow for up to three years, although the exact reasons for this abandonment were not clear (May 5, and July 31, 1890, reports of the

French *résident* AOM-AP-RST, 27–656). Guerrilla troops in the district were estimated at three to four hundred. The French chief administrator for Sơn-Tây province commented specifically on Lâm-Thao district in a report to Hanoi: "I am convinced that many canton chiefs and village mayors are accomplices to the pirates [guerrillas]. I suspect [the complicity of] even certain higher-ranked Vietnamese authorities. I have ordered the surveillance of many" (April 1890 report, AOM-AP-RST, 27–656). After a temporary calm in July 1890, guerrilla activities intensified again in the fall. The same administrator described guerrilla troops as numerous, well organized, well disciplined, and roaming the area with impunity (Oct. 14, 1890, report, AOM-AP-RST, 27–656). At one point numbering as many as 1,200 in the Hưng-Hoá and Lâm-Thao area, the guerrilla force was armed with modern weapons and hundreds of thousands of bullets, either purchased in China or seized from French forces (Pouvourville 1892:72–73; Pouvourville 1923:317). It was in this context of intensified guerrilla activities that in 1890, according to a 1897 report from Sơn-Dương village to colonial authorities, over twenty villagers, including thirteen specific men, were killed by the anti-French guerrilla force (TTLTQG1-PT–534).[12] Sơn-Dương village was clearly in a fighting zone between anticolonial guerrillas and French troops.

In October 1890 the guerrilla force successfully attacked the major Sơn-Tây citadel and released a large number of their imprisoned comrades (Đặng-Huy-Vận 1967:53; Lê-Tượng and Vũ-Kim-Biên 1981:121). Three months later they attacked the provincial capital of Hoà-Bình and seized a large amount of ammunition (Lê-Tượng and Vũ-Kim-Biên 1981:121). Defeats of French forces along the Red and Black rivers in this period from 1889 to 1893 were numerous and substantial (Đặng-Huy-Vận 1967:51–55; Lê-Tượng and Vũ-Kim-Biên 1981:119–124). The resistance movement reportedly gained the collaboration of certain high-ranking Vietnamese mandarins, such as the district chief of Cẩm-Khê and the second-ranked official in Sơn-Tây province (Đặng-Huy-Vận 1967:50). To "pacify" the country the colonial regime had to station a regiment of native guards in the town of Việt-Trì in 1890 and one company of the elite marine forces in nearby Đoan-Hùng district from 1891 onward (Lê-Tượng and Vũ-Kim-Biên 1981:124).

In order to force guerrilla leaders to surrender and to pressure their villages into delivering them to the colonial authorities, the French ordered the arrest of their families, the seizure of their property, the removal of the sacred bones of their ancestors from ancestral graves, and the arrest of key notables (Oct. 28, 1890, report, AOM-AP-RST, 27–656). They also attempted to divide anticolonial forces along ethnic lines, pitting ethnic Mường against Vietnamese, and to gain the alliance of local officials. However, it was not until the 1893 assassination of Đốc Ngữ and the surrender that same year of Đề Kiều, the guerrilla leader and a major landlord in Cẩm-Khê district on the other side of the Red River, that the French regained control of the area of the future province of Phú-Thọ (Lê-Tượng 1967:54).

The end of the guerrilla movement in Phú-Thọ in 1893 marked the virtual completion of the French pacification campaign in Tonkin. It brought to a close the nineteenth-century spontaneous resistance to the French invasion in north Vietnam—a resistance that grew out of patriotism, monarchical loyalty, and attachment to tradition. The remaining incidents of resistance involved the Đề Thám movement, which until 1913 militarily harassed the French all the way from the hilly Yên-Thế area to the neighboring provinces of Phúc-Yên and Vĩnh-Yên (later merged with Phú-Thọ into Vĩnh-Phú). This movement combined elements of patriotism and defense of tradition with a Robin Hood-type redress of social grievances (Trương-Bửu-Lâm 1967:27–28; Marr 1971:73–75; Lê-Tượng and Vũ-Kim-Biên 1981:141–144). However, it was not of such a magnitude as to prevent the colonial regime from turning its attention to the consolidation of political control and the development of capitalism in the land.

The French Indochinese Union was formed in 1887, including Tonkin (north Vietnam), Annam (central Vietnam), Cochinchina (south Vietnam), and Cambodia, to which Laos was added in 1899. Cochinchina was a direct French colony headed by a French governor. In the four other parts of the union, nominally French protectorates, the French appointed *résidents supérieurs*. For easier military and political control of the largely mountainous and strongly resistant Hưng-Hoá province, the colonial regime divided the territory west of the Red River into smaller provinces: Hoà-Bình (an ethnic Mường province, 1886), Sơn-La (1895 [1886]), Yên-Báy (1900), Lào-Cay (1907 [1886]), and Lai-Châu (1909) (Vũ-văn-Tính 1970b: 60-63; Vũ-văn-Tính 1970a: 44).[13] The new province of Hưng-Hoá was formed from the remaining provincial territory, together with Lâm-Thao district of Sơn-Tây province (merged in September 1891) and most of Đoan-Hùng district of Tuyên-Quang (merged in 1895). Its capital was moved in 1903 to the town of Phú-Thọ, situated over sixty miles from Hanoi on the strategic Hanoi-Yunnan railway, which the French had constructed to facilitate the movement of goods into the southern Chinese market and the movement of troops into the northwestern frontiers of north Vietnam. The province itself was also renamed Phú-Thọ in 1904. Like other northern provinces, it was headed by a French *résident* and supported by a French provincial staff, French commanders of the native guards, and Vietnamese mandarins, including a nominal governor, a provincial native court judge, and district chiefs. The nominal authority of the Vietnamese governor was reflected in the fact that district chiefs reported directly to the French *résident* and requested directly from him authorization even for a few days of home visits or sick leaves for themselves and their staff (TTLTQG1-PT 485). Sustained partly by alternating the myth of the French civilizing mission and that of French-Vietnamese coexistence (*huyền thoại khai hóa* and *huyền thoại Pháp Việt đề huề;* see Nguyễn-văn-Trung 1963), the colonial system was also maintained by the use of a combination of naked coercive power and rewards to the collaborators who constituted the majority of the native intelligentsia.

Parallel to the consolidation of political control was the development of a colonial economic policy that created conditions favorable to the capitalist exploitation of land, labor, and other natural resources and that compounded the problems faced by peasants in maintaining their livelihoods. Specific colonial measures in Indochina included the introduction of direct and indirect taxation and the conversion of tax payments from kind to cash in order to facilitate capitalist growth, the concession of indigenous land to colonial settlers for the development of major cash crops, the appropriation of labor through a corvée system, and the introduction of repressive labor laws to hold down labor costs for capitalist agromineral ventures.

In the province of Phú-Thọ the capitalist sector of the economy consisted primarily of French tea and wax-tree plantations in the hilly parts of the province, a tea-processing plant in Phú-Hộ, and a small pulp mill in Việt-Trì. The plantations were set up on land conceded to French settlers and Vietnamese collaborators—concessions amounting to 10,969 hectares, or approximately 22 percent of the province's cultivable land in the 1930s (Phạm-Xuân-Độ 1939:62–63; Henry 1932:23).[14] In the late 1930s, Phú-Thọ annually exported 1,100 tonnes of wax-tree resin to China and Japan (Phạm-Xuân-Độ 1939:69). The province also exported 900 tonnes of dried tea a year to France, North Africa, and the New World (ibid.). By 1931 the concessions of indigenous land in Vietnam to European settlers alone amounted to 890,000 hectares—approximately 19 percent of cultivable acreage at the time (see Table 1).

The land concessions for capitalist agricultural development involved a labor-intensive capital accumulation with a most limited capital reinvest-

**Table 1.** European land concessions in colonial Vietnam (in thousands of hectares)

|  | Cultivable land | Land occupied by concession | Part of concession land actually cultivated |
|---|---|---|---|
| Tonkin | 1,200 | 120 (10%) | 30 |
| Annam | 1,000 | 170 (17%) | 25 |
| Cochinchina | 2,400 | 600 (25%) | 300 |
| Total | 4,600 | 890 (19%) | 355 |

*Source:* J. Chesneaux, reprinted in Murray 1980: 66.

ment in the local economy. In Phú-Thọ, for example, despite the importance of tea as an export commodity, tea pressing and drying machines were not introduced until 1938 (Lê-Tượng and Vũ-Kim-Biên 1981:131). Although land in the village of Sơn-Dương, unlike many other villages in the province and in the midland region of north Vietnam as a whole, was not appropriated for colonial exploitation, the colonial system did adversely affect the lives of many villagers through the close monitoring by the French of poll tax lists and the requirement that taxes be paid in cash, as well as through a significant increase in both direct and indirect taxes.

In the 1890s local officials in Sơn-Dương and neighboring villages wrote to higher officials on quite a few occasions to dispute the latter's figures about the number of people required to pay poll taxes. In November 1897 Sơn-Dương notables argued that the number of male adult poll-tax payers residing in the village had actually declined to 150 due to a large number of deaths in the previous decade: 100 deaths (including 73 adult men) in an 1885 massacre by Chinese troops; over 20 deaths (including 13 adult men) in 1890 in anticolonial warfare; 30 men, plus many women and children, dead of cholera in 1895; and 8 more dead of cholera in 1896. Sơn-Dương village notables provided specific names of the adult male villagers who had died in 1885, 1890, and 1895 and complained that the higher officials had reduced the number of poll-tax payers by only 15 (TTLTQG1-PT–534). In June 1898, February 1899, and August 1899, officials of neighboring Dụng-Hiền village also complained that the poll-tax imposition had increased from 34 in 1897 to 49 in 1898, while the village had only 42 men between the ages of seventeen and sixty (TTLTQG1-PT–527). In 1907 Sơn-Dương complained again about having to pay poll taxes for 27 people who were eligible for official exemption, including 6 soldiers, 10 reserve soldiers, 8 students and scholars having passed qualifying tests for regional examinations, 1 canton chief, 1 village mayor, and 1 deputy mayor (TTLTQG1-PT–534). While Sơn-Dương village officials and notables complained repeatedly of overtaxation, the higher authorities accused them of tax evasion: in 1902, the district chief of Lâm-Thao reported to the French *résident* that Sơn-Dương village officials had collected poll taxes from 230 adult male villagers but reported only 209 to the higher officials (TTLTQG1-PT–534). Correspondence between Sơn-Dương village officials and the district and provincial authorities reveal a recurrent tension between villages and higher-level bureaucrats. Village notables wanted a financial cushion, whether sanctioned by the state or not, while the state wanted to fill state coffers, both through close monitoring of the tax rolls and through an increase of both direct and indirect taxes.

As an example of a tax increase, within the three decades from the end of the nineteenth century to the mid-1920s, the colonial government increased poll taxes by 500 percent, to 2.5 piasters for both property owners (de jure) and landless male laborers (de facto). However, the price of first-class rice increased only 200 to 300 percent in this same period (August 1898 and August 1900 reports of Hưng-Hoá *résident,* AOM-AP-RST, 27–664; *Bulletin économique de l'Indochine*). More significantly, the precolonial tax exemptions and reductions in cases of natural calamity were no longer granted. Moreover, additional charges were imposed to finance cantonal schools and public works. Even in the province of Phú-Thọ, where skilled agricultural laborers commanded wages four times higher than in overpopulated Thái-Bình province of the lower delta, the poll tax inflicted serious hardships on many poor families in periods of crop losses or low rice prices. Its adverse impact on the lives of the village poor is probably best highlighted by the case of a Sơn-Dương villager, the elderly Thành, whose labor her father had to mortgage for 5 piasters in order to pay his poll tax in 1918:

> My family conditions were very difficult in those days [in my youth], especially during the tax season. The poll tax for a man, starting at the age of eighteen, amounted to 3 piasters, equivalent to the purchase price of a thatch hut—an amount we could not count on our relatives for much help with. It was because of the need for money to pay my father's poll tax that my parents had to mortgage my labor for 5 piasters to a wealthy relative, the owner of 11 *mẫu* of rice fields. I ended up working for this relative for twelve years.

Although many major direct tax increases had been introduced by 1910, between 1911 and 1930 the colonial state's direct tax revenues in Tonkin were even further increased, by 109 percent, in comparison with 115 percent and 130 percent respectively for Annam and Cochinchina.

The colonial government also introduced indirect taxes through its opium, alcohol, and salt monopolies. Monthly and quarterly reports from the French *résident* in Phú-Thọ in the first decade of the century meticulously delineated the quantities of opium and alcohol sold through the government monopolies. The fines imposed on villages for any moonshine activity on their territories were at one point so stiff that, short of cash, villagers had to deliver oxen and buffalo to the provincial offices (November 1899 report from the *résident* of Hưng-Hoá, AOM-AP-RST, 27–664). In the early days of the colonial establishment, the overwhelming majority of local court cases involved moonshining and opium-smuggling: eighty-four of the ninety-eight court verdicts in 1905, for example, involved infringements of government monopolies (1905 report from the *résident* of Hưng-Hoá, AOM-AP-RST, 27–664). In 1907, after a 25 percent decline over the previous year in the sale of monopolized alcohol, the provincial administration actually considered instituting a forced consumption measure based on the number of adult male villagers. The French *résident* in Phú-Thọ discussed in great detail, in October 1910, his efforts to promote the sale of monopoly alcohol:

In my meetings with district and canton chiefs and with village authorities, I have attempted to make the populace understand its own advantages from the new sale regime that is to be rigorously put into effect next January. I have repeated numerous times [to the native population] that they have an interest in not stopping through smuggling the flow of this indispensable revenue source to the protectorate [government]— the [very] revenue that has allowed the government to undertake large hydraulic projects to enrich the country. However, one cannot hide the reality that smugglers will continue to be active so long as the moonshine is sold to consumers at a price lower than that offered by the monopoly and so long as consumers seem to prefer the taste of the moonshine to that of the alcohol on sale by the administration.... I reproduce in their entirety the instructions that I gave to the provincial authorities on March 25, 1909, soon after I assumed this office:

The Compagnie générale [government monopoly] has informed me that the alcohol sale figure in Phú-Thọ leaves much to be desired. Smuggling is quite active. The instructions that I have recently received from the *résident supérieur* [of Tonkin] on this subject are precise. Smuggling is an act that disturbs public order, for which, with the support of all the indigenous authorities, I am responsible. I would therefore like to ask...you, all the district chiefs, to exert maximum effort in order to discover clandestine distilleries. Despite accusations, I do not believe that the mandarin chiefs of the six districts willingly close their eyes to the clandestine production houses known to them. The support that I expect and demand from the district chiefs does not consist only of the occasional arrest of a coolie or a destitute woman carrying a bottle of moonshine. Such a repressive method is ineffective and disturbing to the populace because the penalties are out of proportion to the reported misdemeanor. I would like the district chiefs, upon receiving these instructions, to secretly find through their informers the moonshine producing houses....I would like to inform you, the chiefs of districts, that I will pay the closest attention to the manner in which these instructions are followed and that I will take seriously into account your achievements in this respect when I make promotion recommendations. (AOM-AP-RST, 27–665)

By the first quarter of 1911, as a result of district officials' sales pressure and a new retailing system in which well-off villagers were recruited to manage the sale of government alcohol within their communal boundaries, sales by the government monopoly had increased by 50 percent from 1906 (Reports of the *résident* of Phú-Thọ in the fourth quarter of 1910 and on March 31, 1911, AOM-AP-RST, 27–665). Due to a price reduction in 1913, sales doubled over the previous level.

The colonial government also used its monopoly of salt to set the price of salt five to ten times higher than the price that producers obtained. The general colonial budget, approximately 70 percent of which was derived from indirect taxation through the government monopolies on alcohol, salt, and opium, increased from twenty million piasters in 1899 to sixty-five million in 1924 (Murray 1980:68–81).

The revenue increase financed the expansion of the administrative apparatus, the provision of new medical and educational services, and the construction of a modern communication system. The annual mortality rate in Phú-Thọ declined from 4 percent in 1900 to 2.2 percent in 1929, although as late as 1943 there still existed only three hospitals in the province and one doctor for 77,000 natives (Lê-Tượng and Vũ-Kim-Biên 1981:129). Access to modern education beyond third grade was limited mainly to the children of the upper indigenous social stratum because of the considerable direct and indirect expenses of an education beyond this level. By 1933 in the entire province of Phú-Thọ (est. pop. 270,000) there were only four primary schools (through the sixth grade), including one in Lâm-Thao district. In addition to the cost, most families that sent their children to primary school were deprived of the children's labor. The monthly tuition, room, and board for a boarding student in Hanoi might cost up to 10 piasters. But even in the midland region of Phú-Thọ, where the income of an annually hired agricultural worker was on average four times higher than in the lower Red River delta of north Vietnam, it amounted to only 36 to 40 piasters a year.

By the mid-1930s the modern communication system included 73 kilometers of rail line, 140 kilometers of paved roads, and 396 kilometers of unpaved roads in the province of Phú-Thọ (Phạm-Xuân-Độ 1939:72–73) and 2,000 kilometers of rail line and 28,000 kilometers of paved and generally passable unpaved roads in all of Indochina (Murray 1980:172, 177). Constructed mainly by means of compulsory labor (thirty to forty-eight days a year) in the first few decades of the colonial order, this transportation infrastructure primarily served the government's military purposes and the interests of capitalist agromineral ventures. In the province of Phú-Thọ it was no coincidence that by 1940, aside from the national and interprovincial highways with their clear strategic and commercial value, one of the three other year-round passable provincial roads ran through the major tea plantation area (called the Tea Road, or đường Chè)—an area with an export-oriented economy (Phạm-Xuân-Độ 1939:76). On the colonial landscape were thus juxtaposed a new export-oriented system of roads and barefoot peasants too poor to afford modern transportation walking up to eighty kilometers a day to gain their livelihood. Plans for a water-control project for the Lâm-Thao-Hạc-Trì plain of Phú-Thọ were never realized in the colonial period. As suggested by the French scholar Paul Mus (1949:269), the livelihood of peasants was sustained within a subsistence-oriented framework, but their taxes were calculated in terms of a capitalist world economy.

Despite the ideologies of *mission civilisatrice* and Franco-Vietnamese association, as well as the material and status rewards to collaborators among the native intelligentsia, in the twilight of the Confucian era a minority of the Confucian-educated elite could never come to terms with French colonialism. Realizing the futility of blind, uncoordinated resistance to the technologically superior French forces, in the first quarter of the twentieth century some advocated popular social reforms as the means to progress, turned a critical eye on tradition, and mounted a thinly veiled

## Hierarchy and Collectivism in Village Structure

On the eve of the February 1930 uprising, the community of Sơn-Dương included three different villages: Sơn-Dương itself (known as Mương in the vernacular language), Dụng-Hiền, and Thuy-Sơn. According to official colonial tax records, the three villages possessed a total of 1,279 *mẫu* (460.44 hectares) of rice fields: Sơn-Dương had approximately 825 *mẫu* (297 hectares) for a population of 1,464; Dụng-Hiền had 298 *mẫu* (107.28 hectares) for 240; and Thuy-Sơn, a single-lineage village, had 153 *mẫu* (55.08 hectares) for 70 people (land data for 1921 from TTLTQG1-PT–1368; 1927 demographic data from Ngô-vi-Liên 1928:134, 323, 351).[1] The cultivated surface per inhabitant averaged 2,595 square meters for the three villages as a whole and 2,028 square meters in the original village of Sơn-Dương. The figure for Sơn-Dương is about 38 percent higher than the average both for the province of Phú-Thọ (1,460 square meters) and for north Vietnam in general (1,470 square meters) (Henry 1932:23).

   Throughout the colonial period Sơn-Dương relied on agriculture for its livelihood and on women's marketing activities as a secondary source of income. In the fields of Sơn-Dương, only one rice crop could grow each year. Rice seedlings were transplanted into the low-lying fields in either the twelfth or the first lunar month for a harvest four months later *(lúa chiêm)*. Inundated in the summer, these fields served as the village fishing ground during this period. In the high-lying fields, transplanting was done in the fifth or sixth lunar month, and this rice *(lúa mùa)* was harvested in the tenth or the eleventh month (see Tạ-Long 1976:83). These fields were then plowed for the growing of melons and vegetables (onions, leeks, peas, gourds, and pumpkins). Of the agricultural tasks, plowing was normally assigned to men, transplanting to women, and weeding and harvesting to both; in Phú-Thọ women at times took charge of plowing and most other tasks (Phạm-Xuân-Độ 1939:38). Female villagers, regardless of class background, often engaged in marketing activities, moving from one rural market to another, in order to supplement their family incomes. Most markets were held periodically, usually for six days a month. For example, the Sơn-Dương market met on the third and the eighth day of each ten-day cycle; the neighboring Ngũ-Xã market, on the second and seventh days; the Cao-Mại market in the district seat, on the fourth and ninth days; and the Phú-Thọ provincial market, on the fifth and tenth days (ibid.:70). Some women even traveled as far as the neighboring provincial capital of Yên-Báy, a distance of 80 kilometers, on foot. Sơn-Dương did not produce any handicrafts. The weaving of textiles, such as was done in neighboring Ngũ-Xã village, did not spread to Sơn-Dương until the very end of the colonial period, in the 1940s.

Throughout the French colonial period, despite occasional disputes, Sơn-Dương, Dụng-Hiền, and Thuy-Sơn were linked together administratively, ritually, historically, economically, and sociopolitically. In terms of administration, the original Sơn-Dương was the head village in a canton of the same name; besides Dụng-Hiền and Thuy-Sơn, it included four other villages (pops. 871, 719, 504, 74) and was administered by a canton chief and a deputy chief. From 1921 onward each village was ruled by a village executive council, called the Lineage Representative Council (Hội Đồng Tộc Biểu). Headed by a president and a vice-president (respectively, *chánh hương hội* and *phó hương hội*), the council included a directly elected mayor and deputy mayor as well as council-appointed officials (such as secretary, treasurer, and village guard chief, among others; see Trần-Từ 1984:60–81).[2] Ritually, Sơn-Dương, Dụng-Hiền, and Thuy-Sơn worshiped the same tutelary deity, albeit at three different communal houses. At a major area festival on the third day of the third lunar month, the members of the three villages, male and female, young and old, allied in a ritual fight against the residents of Ngũ-Xã in the neighboring canton of Vĩnh-Lại. Members of the three villages also shared one Buddhist pagoda located in the village of Sơn-Dương (TTLTQG1-PT–532). Historically, according to a local Communist Party historian, it was not until the early nineteenth century that the Kiều lineage seceded from Sơn-Dương to form the tiny village of Thuy-Sơn and that Dụng-Hiền followed suit.[3] Economically, the three villages shared the same periodic rural market, which was located by the gate of Sơn-Dương village, in front of its pagoda. The market met six times each lunar month, on the third, eighth, thirteenth, eighteenth, twenty-third, and twenty-eighth days. Sociopolitically, the elites of at least Sơn-Dương and Dụng-Hiền, if not of all three villages, were closely linked. As the head village, Sơn-Dương had the only elementary school (up to the third grade) in the canton, and at the time of the 1930 uprising, students from throughout the canton attended school there. The elite of Sơn-Dương village were thus linked with the area's young intelligentsia through school ties. These bonds were reinforced by marital alliances that overrode the local preference for village endogamy.

The three villages of Sơn-Dương, Dụng-Hiền, and Thuy-Sơn also had disputes, mainly over land and taxes, and these occasionally drew the attention of district and provincial officials. Being the largest and the original village of the three, Sơn-Dương had a small number of inhabitants who owned cultivable land in Dụng-Hiền and Thuy-Sơn. In 1901 Sơn-

Dương notables claimed that 9.9 *mẫu* of Dụng-Hiền rice fields that were owned by Sơn-Dương villagers belonged to Sơn-Dương. District officials rejected this claim (TTLTQG1-PT–534). In 1906 Sơn-Dương and Thuy-Sơn had a land dispute over 16.9 *mẫu* of rice fields. As arbitrator, the district chief awarded 8 *mẫu* to Sơn-Dương and the rest to Thuy-Sơn (ibid.). In 1917 Sơn-Dương and Thuy-Sơn officials got into a dispute again, this time over tax collection on Thuy-Sơn land owned by Sơn-Dương villagers. While the owners of 12 *mẫu* paid their land taxes directly to Thuy-Sơn, the land taxes on over 30 *mẫu* were collected by Nguyễn Đắc Bằng's father, who had been the mayor of Sơn-Dương since 1910 (TTLTQG1-PT–473). The mayor *(lý trưởng)* of Thuy-Sơn and Bằng's father did not agree on the tax rate or on the total amount of taxes on the land owned by Sơn-Dương villagers. The mayor of Thuy Sơn had three head of cattle seized from Sơn-Dương village. The district chief ordered Thuy-Sơn to accept the amount of taxes handed over by Bằng's father and fined the Thuy-Sơn mayor for seizing cattle instead of reporting the problem to the district chief (TTLTQG1-PT–537).

Occasional disputes notwithstanding, Sơn-Dương, Dụng-Hiền, and Thuy-Sơn were closely linked. Beneath the structure of all three villages also lay a shared ideological tension between collectivism, on the one hand, and a class-structured, kinship-centered, male-oriented hierarchy, on the other.

### Collectivism and the Village Network

Inside the bamboo hedge surrounding a rural community like Sơn-Dương, members related to one another within the framework of a corporate peasant village. Villagers were considerably differentiated in wealth and status yet linked together by extensive social ties. Although Sơn-Dương's sense of communal unity and collectivism may have seemed attenuated, given its weaker communal land tradition than that in a number of northern villages, villagers still shared the annual cycle of communal deity worship, a sharp distinction between insiders *(nội tịch)* and outsiders *(ngoại tịch),* and the corporate fiscal and nonfiscal responsibilities (corvée and draft quota) to both the precolonial and the colonial state. (Village insider status was granted only after one's family had settled in the village for a few generations.) It was in the village rituals and the communal land institutions that the collectivist ideology was clearly manifested.

Sơn-Dương villagers worshiped as their tutelary deity General Quý Minh of the Hùng dynasty (to the third century B.C.E.) at the communal house, and General Lân Hồ of the Trần dynasty (thirteenth century) at a village shrine *(đền)*. In light of the considerable anticolonial activities in Sơn-Dương over the past century, it is significant that General Quý Minh was believed to have played a major role in defending the Hùng dynasty against external forces (Lê-Tượng and Nguyễn-Khắc-Xương 1987:69–70, Vũ-Kim-Biên 1999:526–528).[4] Similarly, General Lân Hồ, who died from a serious battle wound in 1287 in Ngũ-Xã village, was a major hero in the struggle against the Mongols (Lê-Tượng and Vũ-Kim-Biên 1981:89–90, Vũ-Kim-Biên 2002:132).[5] Thuy-Sơn and Dụng-Hiền villagers reportedly shared the worship of General Lân Hồ at the Sơn-Dương shrine, where they gathered on the tenth day of the eighth lunar month. They also wor- shipped General Quý Minh, but at their own communal houses. Besides tutelary deity worship, villagers participated in many other annual rituals, some of which marked temporal transitions in the annual village calendar and enhanced the solidarity of old-timer insider families vis-à-vis the more recently arrived outsider families, whereas others functioned to alleviate the anxiety of securing a daily livelihood. For example, during the New Year celebration, work, loud speech, and demands for the repayment of debts, among other things, were tabooed. These taboos remained in effect until village literati and officials had made an offering to the tutelary deity at the communal house. On the fifteenth day of the first month, villagers planted reeds in paddy baskets, which they offered to the deities, symbol- izing the growth of paddy even from reeds (Tạ-Long 1976:79). On the first day of the sixth month, they participated in the ritual of (paddy) field descent *(lễ hạ điền)* on a communal field to mark the beginning of the rice cultivation season and to pray for good crop growth. And on the third day of the third lunar month, they joined together in a ritual fight against the villagers of Ngũ-Xã.

The annual rituals and certain other institutions in the three villages were partly sustained by communal land, which amounted to 56.56 *mẫu* (20.36 hectares) in 1942, according to village regulations at the time. It thus amounted to 4.4 percent of their cultivated area, as compared with the average of 9.1 percent in the province of Phú-Thọ and 21 percent in Tonkin (Henry 1932:23, 109). In 1942 the amount of communal land was reported at 1.69 *mẫu* for Thuy-Sơn and 1.57 *mẫu* for Dụng-Hiền, and in both cases the income from this land was used for collective ritual expenses (Thuy- Sơn 1942 and Dụng-Hiền 1942). Of the 53.3 *mẫu* of communal land in Sơn-Dương, 39.3 *mẫu*, once reserved as a source of supplementary income for soldiers *(binh điền)* and to cover the expenses of a village school *(học điền)*, were rented out.[6] The land rental income was put into a general public fund, some of which was used to defray the expenses of a village school. Fourteen *mẫu* were allocated to support ritual activities: 1.6 *mẫu* for activities at the communal house, 5.3 *mẫu* for the Buddhist pagoda, 4.5 *mẫu* for the Literati Association, and 2.6 *mẫu* rotated annually among neighborhood groups (*khu* and *giáp*), which used the proceeds from the land to pay for village feasts and ceremonies (Sơn-Dương 1942, article 72). These rites of solidarity, which excluded the more recently arrived village outsiders, reinforced the strong conceptual distinction between village insiders *(nội tịch)* and outsiders *(ngoại tịch)*. In 1916, of the 299 male adults in the eighteen-to-sixty age range required to pay poll taxes in Sơn-Dương, 204 were classified as insiders, and 95 as outsiders. The number of insiders and outsiders among poll tax payers was respectively 32 and 11 in Dụng-Hiền, and 7 and 4 in Thuy-Sơn (TTLTQG1-PT–1274). The conceptual categories of insiders and outsiders involved a rigid distinction of community membership that was both reflected in and reinforced by an extraordinarily high level of village endogamy. Although precise figures for colonial Sơn-Dương are not available, in the pre-1945 northern rural communities for which data were available, endogamy reached at least 80 percent (see Luong 1984:298). The distinction between village insiders and outsiders constituted part of a general and persistent conceptual distinction between members and nonmembers of a social unit—whether kinship, communal, or ethnic—that underlay the northern tradition of great formality in interaction with outsiders.

Beyond communal linkages, villagers in Sơn-Dương related to one another extensively through territorial and voluntary association ties as well as through genealogical and fictive kinship. The village of Sơn-Dương was divided into five hamlets *(khu),* each of which was further divided into patrilineage-dominated neighborhood groups (*giáp* or *phe*), for a total of thirteen groups. Each hamlet or neighborhood group comprised households of different patrilineages, although due to territorial clustering of relatives within a smaller unit, each neighborhood group was normally dominated by one patrilineal group. At birth, each boy was registered with a *giáp,* a patrilineage *(họ),* and a *khu* to prepare for fuller participation in public activities within the kinship and communal frameworks later on. In a household with two sons, the first son belonged to the same *giáp* as his father, with whom he normally resided. Although also residing with his father, the second son shared *giáp* membership with his mother's father, who usually resided in another hamlet because most marriages involved villagers from different hamlets and because women moved into

the households of their husbands' parents upon marriage (patrilocal residence). As a result, although the nucleus of a *giáp* membership resided
within the same territorial unit, the *giáp* always had many male members from other hamlets in the village. In general, *giáp* membership was
considerably more significant than *khu* membership because a portion of
the communal land was rotated among the *giáp* for cultivation. In return,
the *giáp* in charge of ritual communal land was obligated to contribute to
public expenses as well as to provide food (for example, glutinous rice,
pork, and chicken) for the worship of communal tutelary deities and for
communal house feasts on festival and New Year occasions (*ngày cầu;* cf.
Trần-Từ 1984:46–60). On the third day of the first lunar month, the entire
*giáp* also participated in a pig husbandry competition at the communal
house. In order to meet its communal obligations, a *giáp* contracted with
its own members who had achieved a certain seniority to receive the land
for the year and to prepare for the feasts from the yield of the earth. The
fact that two brothers who resided in the same household and shared the
same patrilineage membership belonged to different *giáp* in different hamlets increased the cross-cutting ties within the community.

Villagers of the same socioeconomic standing also formed voluntary
associations to meet their various needs. Most notable were two village-
wide associations, the exclusively male Literati Association (Hội Tư Văn
or Hội Văn Thân) and the elderly women's Buddhist Association (Hội Chư
Bà). The former included both Confucian teachers and, as a reflection of
the colonial transformation, those who held the Franco-Vietnamese Certificat d'Études Élementaires (for the successful completion of the third-
grade examination). It organized the annual worship of Confucius at the
literary shrine *(văn chỉ).*[7] In the colonial period the Literati Association
was still assigned the honored task of delivering formal speeches at communal deity worship rituals at the communal house *(đình).* The elderly
women's Buddhist Association, in contrast, met at the village pagoda,
constructed around 1810, for the worship of Buddha on the first and the
fifteenth day of each lunar month. Other voluntary associations included
the female-controlled rotating credit associations *(họ)* and the household-
centered ceremony assistance associations. Members of these associations
came mainly from within a hamlet. The five to twenty members of a typical *họ* took turns obtaining the periodic contributions necessary to meet
their own financial needs. The elderly Thanh, whose labor was mortgaged
at the age of seven for her father's tax payment, discussed how her family
was able to purchase 1.2 *mẫu* of rice fields in the 1930s, thereby becoming
a middle-peasant household:

People wondered how I obtained the money to purchase the rice field. But I bought the field without any help from relatives. I did it by saving pennies and by joining a small credit association in the village. I repaid the loan obtained for the purchase of the rice field over two and a half years, 100 kilograms of rice from each crop and twice a year.

The ceremony assistance associations assisted members on the occasions of weddings, examination success, rituals honoring the elderly, and funerals. The associations were called *họ tiền, họ gạo,* or *họ cỗ,* depending on whether the assistance took the form of cash, rice, or labor at the time of a ceremony. Most village households participated in at least one mutual assistance association. Bằng's narrative regarding the funerals of his father and his father's senior mother (that is, his grandfather's first wife) illustrates the role of these mutual assistance associations in village life:

My father died in 1928 of a gastrointestinal disease. My grandfather's first wife died in early 1929 in her old age. These two funerals were the two major ones in my life. At the funeral for my father, visitors came from all over Lâm-Thao district since he had had many pupils and because he had been president of the village council. Buddhist nuns also came in large numbers for prayer sessions. Relatives and acquaintances from elsewhere came to pay their respects. Visitors squeezed into the courtyard, bringing with them cash, rice, meat, and boiled chicken as funeral offerings and contributions. They kowtowed and, as the sons of the deceased, we had to reciprocate. We wore special mourning dresses made of coarse white fabric and donned banana-leaf hats and belts. We had to walk stooped over with canes both in the house and during the funeral procession. My knees became bruised from all the kowtowing during the three days of funeral ceremony. My brothers and I were joined by [our cousin] Mai [a son of Bằng's father's junior half-brother, raised by Bằng's father] in kowtowing to visitors in reciprocation for their kowtows to my deceased father. He wore the filial funeral dress for the occasion [that is, he ritually assumed the role of a son]. We had to welcome and provide a feast for a lot of people. As a result, many pigs were sacrificed during the funeral.

The entire village had to contribute to my father's and grandmother's burials because my parents had been members of feast associations. Association membership ranged from nine to eighteen individuals, who came mostly from the same neighborhood. A member of a rice association usually contributed a basket of rice [twenty liters]. A member of a cash association might contribute 6 or 7 piasters to the ceremony. The members of feast-preparing associations contributed their labor to prepare the feast to feed visitors from within and from outside the village. When my father died, the members of the associations with which he had been affiliated had to pay their dues.

Beyond territorial and voluntary association ties, as in other northern villages the intracommunal social network in Sơn-Dương was rendered more intricate by extensive kinship ties, both fictive and nonfictive. In an agricultural environment with high infant mortality, many well-off families without sons or with few (surviving) offspring adopted children, either actually or nominally, both within the local community and beyond. In addition to contributing to the household labor force, adoption was prevalent because it involved native beliefs about the necessity of patriline continuity, which could occur only through sons, and in the role that adoption could play in warding off the decimation of one's own offspring by evil supernatural forces. Bằng's narrative highlights the frequent adoption process in his household:

It was partly out of a belief in supernatural causes of deaths that many adoptions, real or nominal, took place in my youth. My paternal grandfather adopted a daughter, who in turn had two daughters. I had to address these two women as *chị* (elder sister). Because my grandfather's adopted daughter did not have any sons, her husband and she in turn had to adopt a nephew as the heir to their wealth—someone who could continue their line and worship them after death....

My senior mother also adopted a daughter after failing to raise any of her first seven children. This eldest sister of mine was adopted during a big flood in the region of Nam-Định and Phủ-Lý in the lower delta, when her real mother had taken her along to the midland region and begged for food at the Cao-Mại market [in the Lâm-Thao district seat]. That was how my sister had the nickname Mòn [picking the leftovers]. After this adoption and after my birth, my senior mother succeeded in raising two sons. My parents also gave me up for nominal adoption by the employer of my first love, Lư. The practice of nominal adoption was prevalent in the old days, especially among those whose children were few or whose many children died young.

I myself also adopted three sons altogether. One of the three, Dần, came from my village. Dần was actually a distant relative of mine, although not in my patrilineage. Because he seemed a bright kid, I asked his father why he was not sent to school. His father mentioned the poverty of the family. I told the father that I would be willing to adopt Dần and take care of his schooling, given his apparent intelligence. His father agreed. My wife and I raised Dần together with our first son even when my father was still alive [before 1928]. After my father's death, I adopted two other sons among my pupils, one from Hữu-Bổ village and the other a son of a Chinese medicine practitioner in my native Lâm-Thao district. Both came from poor families. As the former's father had also died, his widowed mother could not support his schooling after a while. My senior mother was kind to them, raising them like her grandsons and encouraging their schooling. My wife and I had two sons. But my first son died quite early because we did not have a maternity clinic in those days. We had to rely on old village women using unhygienic instruments during delivery. That was why my son's health was poor. If he had survived, he would be over fifty years old now.

The kinship network within the village was formally organized into a number of patrilineages *(họ)* whose membership was passed from father to son. In Sơn-Dương, as well as in other northern rural communities, the different patrilineages in a village were linked by affinal ties—an extensive network that resulted from the strong preference for village endogamy. The affinal ties were by no means insignificant because a married-out woman continued to maintain ritual obligations toward the members of her natal patriline or local patrilineage. She was expected to bring her children to her parents' home to attend the important death anniversaries in her family of birth. At the wedding of any of her children, ancestral offerings were made not only to her husband's ancestors (including offerings at the houses of her husband's patrilineage chief and lineage branch chief), but also to the ancestors of her own father and mother. The extensive social ties reduced the possibility of permanent cleavages within the corporate community, a community also bounded by tutelary deity worship and other annual rituals, corporate responsibilities (corvée, taxes, and military draft) to the state, and the institution of communal land.

**Class, Gender, and Hierarchy**

Despite a degree of communal solidarity among villagers, the structure of Sơn-Dương and other northern villages in the colonial period was clearly dominated by a considerable class cleavage and a class-structured, kinship-centered, and male-oriented hierarchy. This class- and gender-based hierarchical framework dominated village institutions from the household to the communal level. The hierarchy was male-oriented despite the significant labor contribution of women, regardless of their class background.

Village households were considerably differentiated in wealth and status, with numerous cases of class mobility even within a single generation. Even by the time of the Marxist-organized 1954 land reform, when large landholders with a sense of the political wind had already partially dispersed their holdings, the twelve Sơn-Dương households classified as landlords and rich peasants (2.6 percent of the households and 4.5 percent of the population) still owned 23 percent of the rice fields in the village (230 *mẫu*). The wealthiest villager still retained 110 *mẫu* or 11 percent of the cultivable land. At the other end of the spectrum were landless and poor peasant households, which, at the time of the 1954 land reform, made up 70 percent of the village households. The process of socioeconomic differentiation seems to have proceeded slightly further in Sơn-Dương and in the district of Lâm-Thao than in the rest of the province of Phú-Thọ because the percentage of landless and poor peasant households in Phú-Thọ in 1954–1955 was only 54.16 percent (White 1981:423). The data on land distribution in the native population also suggest a slightly greater socioeconomic differentiation in Lâm-Thao district in the late 1920s (see Table 2).

As a result of the greater socioeconomic differentiation and an unfavorable people-to-land ratio in Sơn-Dương, many poor villagers found work in other villages in the area. Although probably incorporating to some extent the discourse of the Marxist-led class struggle of the 1950s, the narrative of Bằng's cousin Tế remains quite informative on the working conditions of a hired laborer in the 1930s—conditions that seem to have remained essentially the same throughout the colonial period:

I was born into a well-to-do family. My paternal grandparents had bequeathed my father and his two brothers more than thirty *mẫu* of rice fields. My senior uncle occupied the position of a deputy canton chief in the area. However, my father had treated my mother very poorly in favor of his second wife. My mother and I left the household

**Table 2.** Distribution of cultivable rice fields under native ownership in Lâm-Thao and Phú-Thọ (percent)

|  | Lâm-Thao District | Province of Phú-Thọ |
|---|---|---|
| 0–1 *mẫu* | 62.5 | 59.1 |
| 1–5 *mẫu* | 29.6 | 34.6 |
| 5–10 *mẫu* | 6.1 | 5.2 |
| 10–50 *mẫu* | 1.7 | 1.0 |
| 50–100 *mẫu* | 0.03 | 0.02 |
| Over 100 *mẫu* |  | 0.002 (1 landowner) |

*Source:* Henry 1932:92–93.

to work for other people when I was only five. When my father fell seriously ill around 1930, he called me back. But my father's second wife beat me heavily and fed me little. I left again to join my mother.

Late in 1931 my father died in poverty, since a large part of the ancestral land had been sold in the aftermath of the VNP uprising to secure the release of my senior uncle. As a result of their frustration and depression after this abortive uprising, whatever remained was lost through their gambling and opium smoking. Even the family pond and half of the 3 *sào* of ancestral residential land were sold. Few people came to our house in my father's final hours, partly because of our poverty and partly because of the rumor that he had contracted the contagious disease of tuberculosis. I still remember vividly his final moments: a chicken was tied to the foot of the bed, a piece of paper was placed over his mouth to check his breath, and I silently sat in a corner of the house on the floor. He was buried on the same day by eight pall bearers.

When my father's junior wife left to remarry, my mother and I returned to the pitiful house, a two-room hut with a termite-bored bunk bed. Yet at the approach of the lunar new year we had to hide away from the house to avoid our creditors. We returned only on New Year's Day, since it was a taboo to demand debt payments on the first few days of the new year. We cooked our rice cake in an earthen pot. We had no copper one.

Feeling bad about the family's poverty and my mother's hardships, I began working again at the age of twelve, this time as a babysitter. I worked for an aunt and then for another household. I was paid 4 piasters a year plus sufficient food for myself. In the colonial period children could pursue education beyond the second or third grade only if their families were wealthy.

At the suggestion of my acquaintances, I soon gave up babysitting in order to apprentice as a plowman for Mayor Hữu in the village of Vĩnh-Lại. I remember that on the first day he beat me left and right with a bamboo rod in the field as I tried the plow. The following morning, weeping and holding the plow but determined to master the technique, I succeeded at the task. I became an accomplished plowman at the age of fourteen or fifteen. The work schedule was heavy. At the first cock crow of the day, I would get up to gather three to four baskets of water lentils and to pound them in the mortar so that the wife of my employer could just pick them up for sale in the morning in the market. The food was seldom sufficient to fill my stomach. I usually had just about three hundred grams of leftover rice for breakfast, two bowls for lunch, and the same for dinner. At lunch and dinner time I had some banana broth to add a taste to the rice. I had to go into the field rain or shine. When it rained, I had to check the condition of the banks of my employer's field in order to ensure their strength to contain rain water. When the sun was scorching, I had to catch field crabs and tend the buffalo. The work was demanding, as the employer tried to make the most of the salary that I received from him. I did whatever he ordered: plowing, transplanting, weeding. He simply supervised. I always went to work hungry. Even at their family celebrations, I ate the leftovers when I returned from the field. My annual salary was 30 piasters, two pairs of brown coarse cotton pajamas, a belt, and, in those days, a turban. If we bargained well, we might obtain a brown coarse-cloth formal dress instead of two pairs of pajamas. I was allowed to go home for major death anniversaries and for the New Year celebration only upon my mother's request to the employer. It was a heavily exploitative system.

I worked for six years as a live-in plowman and jack-of-all-trades in Vĩnh-Lại, where many of my fellow Sơn-Dương villagers also found work. We did not work in Sơn-Dương because our village was more densely populated and because we were not fed as well as in Vĩnh-Lại. For all those years, my mother remained a hired laborer in Sơn-Dương.

Fortunately, I did not run into any difficulty with local officials regarding the payment of taxes. Any failure to pay in time would lead to the arrest and minor torture of one's brother or adult family member in the communal house courtyard. No matter whether one could afford it or not, under the circumstances, one had no choice but to contribute a few dimes toward a close relative's tax obligations. I paid only 2.5 to 3 piasters a year for poll tax and less than a dime on the piece of residential land. I managed all right.

Opportunities for upward mobility through educational achievements and other means were not as limited as Tế suggests. Bằng's favorite student and later the president of the Sơn-Dương Communist Party branch, Mr. Lê văn Tiềm, obtained a Certificat d'Études Primaires and became a village teacher despite the economic hardships of his family:

> I owed a lot to Mr. Bằng, who, finding me quite intelligent among his thirty to forty students, cared a great deal about my educational success. My family was so poor at the time that I had only rice soup, as occasionally we did not even have enough rice to cook steamed rice. We did not own any land because my father was addicted to opium. It was my mother who supported the family as a seasonal seedling transplanter. Despite our poverty, my parents made the sacrifice for my education, and our relatives lent us some money and rice whenever necessary, because Mr. Bằng and everybody else had said that I was quite intelligent. We were so poor that [unable to pay for room and board] I had to ask for a free sampan ride across the river daily to attend the provincial school in Hưng-Hoá. Working quite hard, I passed the examination for the Certificat d'Études Primaires quite early, on my first try. It took other students four or five tries before they succeeded. In 1931, at the age of eighteen, I became a private tutor in the house of a landlord in the neighboring village of Phùng-Nguyên. My salary amounted to a few piasters a month.

The elderly Thành (born 1912) recounted at length her experiences as a poor villager and her family's upward mobility in the 1920s and 1930s:

> I worked very hard [as a laborer] after marriage [at the age of nineteen] because my husband and I were so poor that we had to live initially on the land of his uncle. Even when tending buffalo for somebody else, I managed to dig and collect two baskets of tubers such as potatoes and manioc in fields that the owners seemed to have harvested cleanly. I sold them in the market. We purchased rice for our meals on a day-to-day basis. Still, we managed to pay our taxes in order not to get into trouble with the government. Five years

later we purchased a small thatch hut for 3 piasters. We purchased
the land for the hut the following year and 1.2 *mẫu* of rice fields
(0.432 hectares) the year after for 27 piasters. I also began raising this
younger brother of mine [pointing to a younger brother], since my
parents had died.

   In those days, without a draft animal to plow the land, I had to
loosen the earth with a hoe in preparation for planting. I hoed 1.5 *sào*
of land [0.12 acre] a day. [I did all the farmwork because] at the time
my husband and his two brothers jointly owned a sewing machine and
worked on the other side of the river, around the town of Hưng-Hoá.
During the slack season my adolescent brother helped to cook for
them. For the rest of the year he assisted me with minor agricultural
tasks. After each harvest he and I also picked the fallen grains and
leftover potatoes. Furthermore, even while transplanting for the spring
crop in the middle of the winter, I always managed to catch at least a
basket of fish before going home. The water was so cold at that time
that the fish became sluggish and were unable to swim. Every few
days I would go to the district seat market in Cao-Mại [approximately
6 kilometers away] to sell my fish. At night, my sleep was less than
sound as I worried about getting up by two o'clock in the morning in
order to have an early start at the working day. When not working the
land, I walked 80 kilometers a day to a market near the capital of the
neighboring province, Yên-Báy. I left the house at six o'clock in the
morning and reached there after nightfall. I sold onions and bought
dried fish, which I exchanged for manioc and rice. Later, we managed
to obtain the co-ownership of an ox. I worked so hard that I could not
bear any children myself.

Despite such examples of upward mobility, downward mobility was
not insignificant, as illustrated in the case of Tế's family, and the poor in
Sơn-Dương labored under difficult conditions. Poor villagers who chose
sharecropping did not fare much better than laborers: landlords reportedly
took one-half to two-thirds of the harvest, depending on whether the landlord paid for the seeds and the land taxes.
   In contrast, most sons of elite families in Sơn-Dương engaged in a long
and arduous educational process in preparation for rather leisurely lives,
at times in positions as teachers and village officials. Bằng, the French-
educated teacher, described in detail the division of labor in his family,
which, with 20 to 30 *mẫu* of rice fields, ranked among the wealthiest 2
percent of village households:

I was born into a family that had been well-off for generations, although it did not own a large amount of land. We had 20 to 30 *mẫu* of rice fields, a few buffaloes, at least two live-in workers-cum-plow-men, and sharecroppers. My family ranked fifth or sixth in the village in terms of wealth. During the transplanting and harvesting seasons we hired, in addition, several seasonal laborers to work on the land that we cultivated directly. We also received half of the crop from the sharecropped land. My family also had a brick factory when I was a small kid. As a result, our pigsty, buffalo stable, and entire courtyard were constructed with bricks. It was one of approximately one dozen brick houses in the village. All the rest were made of bamboo, wood, and thatch.

My father had studied Sino-Vietnamese and Confucian classics. Qualified to take the regional Confucian examination, he passed the first two tests to get into the third of the four rounds. He did it a few times but was not able to advance into the final round. Frustrated, he stopped taking the examinations. After a short stint as a teacher of Sino-Vietnamese in the village, he became the mayor of Sơn-Dương and then moved up to the position of president *(chánh hương hội)* of the Lineage Representative Council [village executive council]. While a village chief, he also ran for the position of canton chief. However, he lost to a poorer candidate because he offended people with an arrogant statement.[8] Nevertheless, he achieved more than my paternal grandfather, who reached only the position of mayor and did not master Confucian classics to become a candidate at the regional examinations. My father was called Chánh Ty after his highest title and after my original name Ty, Nguyễn Doãn Ty. He was called after me because I was his first son, although I have two older sisters and although my mother was only his third-ranked wife.

[My mother died of a supernaturally induced illness when I was only five.] I was raised by my senior mother, who was very kind to me. At the age of six, I entered a village school where modern Vietnamese, Chinese characters, and Confucian morality were taught. . . . Three years later I began attending a Vietnamese public school in the village. Finding me intelligent, the village schoolteacher suggested to my father that he allow me to continue with primary education at a provincial school. . . . With the concurrence of my senior mother, my father followed [my teacher's] suggestion. He was progressive, because older women in the village had discouraged people from learning the modern Vietnamese script. They cited the strange-looking and unsacred nature of modern writing. In those days villagers even used the paper from modern Vietnamese books as paper towels or toilet tissue. Nobody dared to trash Sino-Vietnamese books.

I was already in my teenage years—it was around 1916—when I took the entrance exam for the provincial Franco-Vietnamese school in Việt-Trì. Because there was an age limit, we had to make a new birth certificate in order to lower my official age by four years. My name was also consequently changed from Nguyễn Doãn Ty to Nguyễn Đắc Bằng. . . . I stayed in Việt-Trì for over a month. Then I moved to the provincial capital of Phú-Thọ where I entered the second grade and lived for over a year. As my future good friend Lập of neighboring Kinh-Kệ village and a few of my cousins went to the Hưng-Hoá school, I was sent along with them to Hưng-Hoá. Later, my brothers Tăng and Gia followed me there. I was in the third grade when I moved to Hưng-Hoá. I also got married at this point. I still remember that after the wedding, my wife carried thirty *đấu* of rice every month to Hưng-Hoá in order to pay for my room and board. I usually returned home on Saturday and left early on Monday for school.

Although I was the best student in my class in Hưng-Hoá and received the honors prize, I twice failed the examination for the Certificat d'Études Primaires. Candidates had to pass all five written tests (two math, one drawing, one essay, and one dictation test) before they could be admitted to the last round of oral examinations. I had problems primarily with the dictation test because my French teachers were all Vietnamese and the dictation examiner was French. I eventually obtained the Certificat d'Études Primaires on the third try. It was thanks to my father's progressive attitude, my senior mother's kindness, and my intelligence inherited from my mother's father, a mandarin and a doctorate degree holder *(phó bảng)*.[9]

After obtaining the Certificat d'Études Primaires, I studied for two years at the private teacher-training school Trí-Tri in Hanoi. It cost a little less than 10 piasters a month in those days. My parents paid 5 or 6 piasters for room and board at a boarding house on the outskirts of Hanoi. After graduating with the Brevet Élementaire, *mention péda-gogique*, I returned to my native village in early 1927, started private elementary classes, and began my career as a schoolteacher. Such an education was the privilege of the sons of relatively well-off families. Scholarships were not available then as they are now.

[Throughout all those years of schooling] my brothers and I were not allowed to get involved much in manual labor. During my earlier years of Sino-Vietnamese education in the village, I usually tended buffalo in the afternoon after my return from school—not because I had to but because I liked to get a chance to play games with other buffalo tenders from different villages. The buffalo were simply permitted to roam in the fields near the wood. It was so much fun that I had to compete with household members to be allowed to take the buffalo to the fields. I occasionally also watered the trees and plants in the yard. After I started learning French, my father prohibited me from getting involved in those tasks and required me to study after school. My brothers Tăng and Gia never got involved in those tasks, even when they were young.

Bằng's father's prohibition of menial labor represented the rigid distinction between mental and menial labor and the Confucian emphasis on the role of educated men in providing moral leadership for society at large. Because of this Confucian ideal, the sons of elite families went through a long educational process, while their mothers, sisters, wives, and daughters made a significant contribution to the household and village economy. The labor contribution of women from elite families is elaborated in Bằng's continuing narrative:

*Given the amount of land owned by your family, did the members of your family work on the land at all? Do I assume correctly that laborers were hired to work all the land?*
My family members did contribute their labor. My elder sister, my older female cousin, my wife, and the wives of my two brothers Tăng and Gia all worked and worked very hard. Waking up before dawn, they divided the various tasks among themselves, including pounding and dehusking the rice paddy, boiling water, cooking rice, and feeding the pigs and chickens. During the peak agricultural seasons, not only did they cook for a lot of day laborers, but they also had to help with transplanting and harvesting. In the evening they had the same tasks to perform: pounding paddy, cooking rice, and feeding the pigs and chickens. They could not go to bed until midnight. Meals had to be cooked five times a day in my family during these seasons. In my youth, for example, in the early morning while my brothers, my father, and I were still sleeping, my elder sisters and female cousin had to cook for my paternal grandmother, my father's wives,

and the workers leaving early for the field. We men did not wake up until about halfway through the morning, that means, around eight o'clock. My father then had a porridge of rice, peas, and eggs. Each of us boys got one bowl and then we left for school. My brothers and I came back around eleven o'clock for lunch. The workers were also fed around that time. In the afternoon, after the workers had left, we had dinner around five o'clock. We had two main meals a day besides breakfast; those working in the field had three main meals a day. It was the same when I became a teacher in my village. During other seasons the young female members of my family grew vegetables and melons. It was always one crop or the other on my family's land. My wife, cousin, and sisters-in-law had to retail the secondary crops in periodic rural markets. They occasionally had to walk 16 kilometers each way to the Phú-Thọ provincial market. The market in Sơn-Dương was held only six times a month. So was the only other market in the neighboring villages, located in Ngũ-Xã, held on alternate days. Produce peddlers had to move from one market to another to sell their produce. During my school days in the provincial capital of Phú-Thọ, the women from my native village would already have arrived there on foot when I was responding to nature's call in the yard early in the morning.

Bằng's narrative on the division of labor in his household not only reveals in sharp detail the significant labor contribution of women in elite families, but also confirms his cousin Tế's account of the conditions of the poor:

Our live-in workers took charge of heavier work, such as plowing. Usually coming from poor families outside my patrilineage, they were paid 36 to 40 piasters a year and two pairs of pajamas. They were given three days of vacation as well as rice, meat, wine, and cash gifts at New Year's. The work in the fields was supervised by my cousin Mai, the grandson of my paternal grandfather by his mistress. Mai lived in the same house with us and woke up at around four o'clock in the morning like my wife and sisters-in-law.

The conditions of our live-in workers might not be great, but workers who could not till the land received little more than food for themselves, the poll tax payment, and two pairs of pajamas for a year of work. Many women also worked as migrant laborers, moving from one village to another as part-time seedling transplanters. Working from dawn till dusk, each normally received two working meals of a mixture of rice and other cereals, and one *đấu* of rice to take home. In my youth a lot of villagers were poor, working for a few landholding families in Sơn-Dương and elsewhere. The landless people were in particularly dire circumstances in those days in our country. In a very poor family the migrant-laborer mother could only take care of her children in the evening, usually breastfeeding a baby and then cooking for others the rice that she had been paid at the end of the day. Although the village had over a dozen *mẫu* of communal land, it was not sufficient to distribute among the poor.... The poor did not benefit much from communal land in Sơn-Dương.... Life was not easy for either the seasonal and live-in workers or the young female members of the landowning families, especially during the transplanting and harvesting seasons.

The gender-based division of labor derived from the exclusive reserve of public power and societal leadership roles for men. In the Confucian view widely accepted by the indigenous population at the time, educated men in particular played a vital role in the moral leadership and ideological formation of society. In order to fulfill this mission, the educated had to transcend their financial self-interest and maintain exemplary behavior. For example, Bằng's salary payment as a private schoolteacher had to be handled by a committee of his pupils' parents and not directly by Bằng himself. When Bằng became heavily involved in gambling for entertainment, his senior mother successfully intervened to end his gambling activities with the argument that as a teacher, he had to set a moral example for his students and other villagers.

In the communal life of Sơn-Dương, both the role of educated men and socioeconomic differences were ritualized through communal house feasts from which women and male outsiders *(ngoại tịch)* were excluded and at which any violation of the codified seating order and food distribution arrangements could lead to litigation. According to the 1942 village regulations in Sơn-Dương, first-place mats were reserved for those with examination successes; second-place mats were for male villagers at least sixty years old and with mandarinal ranks or titles; third-place mats were for elderly men (aged fifty or above) without titles and village officials; fourth-place ones were for honorary village officials who had purchased their titles; and fifth-place mats were for ordinary villagers (Sơn-Dương 1942, article 77). Similarly, in Thuy-Sơn, first-place mats were for male villagers with major examination successes and officials; second-place mats were for those with junior secondary school completion certificates, government office clerks, current and former canton officials, members of provincial consultative councils, honorary mandarins, and those above the age of seventy; third-place mats were for Confucian scholars who had passed the qualifying tests for regional Confucian examinations and villagers with modern primary school certificates, lowest-level honorary bureaucrats (second level of the ninth [lowest] bureaucratic grade or *tùng cửu phẩm*), current and former mayors, deputy mayors, and chairs/vice-chairs of the Lineage Representative Council, and other villagers aged sixty or above; fourth-place mats were for other village officials, honorary mayors, honorary deputy mayors, and honorary village titleholders; fifth-place mats were for ordinary male villagers. The seating order in the communal house of Dụng-Hiền was quite similar to that in Thuy-Sơn, except that the fifth-place mats were reserved for villagers purchasing honorary Literati Association memberships and that ordinary male villagers were excluded altogether (Dụng-Hiền 1942, article 10). The seating arrangements in communal houses reflected an interplay not only of wealth, bureaucratic power, and age, but also of the well-entrenched Confucian emphasis on scholarship.

The male-oriented, class-centered model of social hierarchy played an equally prominent role in structuring relations within the household and the patrilineage. It was a hierarchical model in which descent was traced through men, residence was patrilocal, and authority, both domestic and public, rested primarily with wealthy and educated men not engaged directly in manual labor, the prominent role of women in household production processes notwithstanding.

In early 1928 Bằng's household was a classic polygynous, patrilineally extended family that, both in terms of household formation and gender relations, was firmly rooted in the Vietnamese male-oriented model of kinship. The household formation approached the Confucian ideal of *ngũ đại đồng đường* (a family with members of five consecutive generations together under the same roof). Bằng's household had sixteen members belonging to four consecutive generations, including all the surviving male descendants of the three wives of the household founder (that is, Bằng's paternal grandfather). As seen in Figure 1, the household comprised Bằng's paternal grandfather's (A1) first wife and her granddaughter (C1, temporarily separated from husband); the three-member nuclear family of Bằng's grandfather's grandson (C7) by the grandfather's third wife; Bằng's father (B2, born of Bằng's grandfather's second wife) and the father's two surviving wives; Bằng (ego, C6), his wife, a son, and

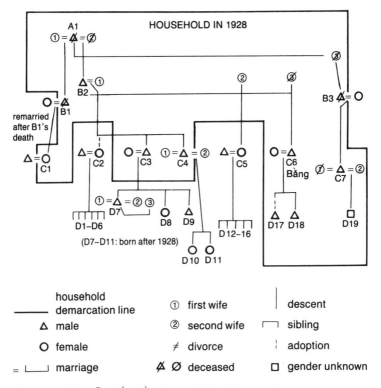

**Figure 1.** Nguyễn Đắc Bằng's partial family genealogy

an adopted son; as well as Bằng's two senior brothers Tăng and Gia (C3 and C4) and their two respective wives. The formation did not merely highlight the patrilineal linkage to the household founder (ego's paternal grandfather) at the expense of matrilateral ones (the founder's three wives), it also strictly followed the rule of patrilocal residence. Bằng's married half-sister (C5) and his father's adopted daughter (C2) had moved to their husbands' households. By the same principle, Bằng's wife and his half-brothers' wives, all of whom had married their husbands when their husbands were only thirteen or fourteen years old, resided with their husbands' large extended family.

Bằng's early 1928 household exemplifies the male- and elite-oriented model in Vietnamese kinship—a model clearly dominant among the precolonial and colonial elite. Centering on a male-female hierarchy and its isomorphic relation to other conceptual dichotomies such as center versus periphery and spatially bound versus spatially unbound, the male-oriented model emphasized the rule of patrilocal residence (male/female :: center/

periphery :: spatially bound/spatially unbound), a formal separation of the sexes, the domestic-centered role of women in patrilineally extended families, and the public-domain orientation of male household members. In this model, even when the wife actively participated in the labor market, as she did in Sơn-Dương in the precapitalist and colonial eras, ideally it did not replace her domestic-centered role but merely increased the financial resources of the unit for which she was responsible. A woman's financial contribution was made without any necessary increase in her authority. Formal education as an avenue to public status was not available to women in Sơn-Dương until Bằng started teaching in 1927. In terms of domestic authority, despite the presence of Bằng's grandfather's first wife in the household at the time, it was Bằng's father (B2, born ca. 1865–1870) who officially headed the household. The main room of the house was a male domain where important guests were received and where the ancestral altar was located. Not only were junior female members of the household such as Bằng's wife unable to enter this main room in the presence of guests, but they reportedly had to cover their faces with conical hats when passing in front of it in the presence of male guests. Male and female household members were separated to the extent that married male members continued to sleep in the main room of the house apart from their spouses. When questioned about the consummation of his marriage at the age of fourteen, Bằng responded:

> It took quite a while for the marriage to be consummated. After the wedding, I still slept with my brothers and my cousin Mai in the living room, where the ancestral altar was located. My wife slept with my senior female cousin. For intimate moments with my wife, I had to wait until everybody fell asleep. We had to spend time together discreetly in a corner of the house.

The male-oriented model emphasized the male-centered continuity of the kinship unit, which, in the internal logic of this model, was ensured by polygyny. In addition, polygyny also delivered an important labor source, given the significant role of wives in the domestic economy. Bằng's grandfather and father each had three wives. The wealthiest Sơn-Dương villager, whose second wife was a sister of Bằng's father's second wife, had seven wives altogether. The second wealthiest man, who also occupied the position of village mayor *(lý trưởng),* had at least four wives, albeit with no children. The rank of children in polygynous families depended primarily on their mothers' seniority: a younger son born of the first wife was senior to and addressed as *anh* (elder brother) by his older half-siblings.

In Sơn-Dương the sons of the elite got married through parental arrangements at an early age, usually before the age of fifteen. Because of the need for female labor, the daughters-in-law were slightly older women who could contribute their labor to the household production processes. However, through an arrangement between the bride's and the groom's families, a bride might be able to stay with her natal family in order to help her parents for up to three years after the wedding. In this context of parental arrangements, the young couple did not always fully understand the significance of the marital bond. Bằng related his naive reaction to his marriage at the age of fourteen:

> Despite the big wedding, I was still too young then to understand that
> my wife, Mrs. Lan, had moved into my family after the ceremony.
> I asked her after three days why she still remained in my house, not
> yet returning to her home. My elder sisters had to tell me: "She is
> your wife." ... You see, when my half-sister got married, thanks to her
> mother's wealth and power, she could remain at home for almost one
> year before moving to her husband's household.

In the male-oriented model, resources were allocated in favor of sons and other patrilineal relatives. Rice fields were divided among the sons. Because of his ritual obligations toward his parents after their deaths and to other patrilineal ancestors, the most senior son was entitled to inherit the parents' house and possibly a larger share of the parents' land than the other sons. Other sons might receive branch houses, as in the case of Bằng's father (B2). In Bằng's family, branch houses were bequeathed according to a strict inheritance rule. When Bằng's father returned to the main house of the family as the surviving senior male member of his generation after the death of a senior half-brother, the branch house was passed on to his junior half-brother's married son (C7), the most junior and married member of the C generation. When C7 moved into the main house, the branch house was given to Bằng, the most junior son, after Bằng's marriage. In the male-oriented model, daughters might receive some property in the form of a dowry.

As a reflection of the strength of the male-oriented model in the village of Sơn-Dương, among Bằng's relatives the distinction between patrilineal and matrilineal kin was emphasized to the extent that D1 referred to his mother's siblings' sons (D7 and D12) not as *chú* (father's younger brothers and junior male cousins) but as *cậu* (nonpatrilineal male relatives of one's parents' generation). The distinction between patrilineal and nonpatrilineal relatives corresponded to the formal organization of the local kinship network into patrilineages, the larger of which had their own ancestral halls and were divided into lineage branches *(chi).* Male lineage (branch) members attended the annual rituals of worshiping the founding couple—a ceremony that the lineage (branch) authorities prepared with the assistance of other members and their spouses.

The male-oriented and class-structured model of the kinship system exerted its influence beyond the male elite to affect many women of lower socioeconomic strata. The elderly Thanh related with pride her critical role in raising the children of her husband's junior wife:

> [Because] I worked so hard that I could not bear any children, I managed to persuade my husband's junior wife to have six children, four sons and two daughters. Altogether, I directly raised eight children, my younger brother, six children by my junior cowife, and my husband's brother's son [who, as the secretary of the Communist Party in the village in 1987, occupied the most powerful position in Sơn-Dương].

In colonial and precolonial Sơn-Dương the kinship system was also partly structured by the class dimension through a process of class-based marital alliances that occasionally overrode the preference for village endogamy. These are partially illuminated in Bằng's narrative of his and his siblings' marriages:

> I got married at the age of fourteen, when I still attended school in Hưng-Hoá. My marriage was arranged between two families of the same status, between the son of the presiding official of one village and the granddaughter of his counterpart in another [Dụng-Hiền]. The marriage was arranged with concern about the social standing of the two families as the primary consideration.
>
> The girls whom I had truly loved and who wanted to marry me, I could not marry: Lư, Duyên, and Thọ. Lư was such a beautiful lady. However, her parents were poor. Her father had joined the native guard; her uncle lived at the pagoda. She herself tended buffalo for my godfather. She wanted to marry me.... I had known Lư while attending the village school at the communal meeting house, that is, before my schooling in Việt-Trì at the age of twelve. She frequently teased me in those days. I ended up engaging in sex with

her and deflowering her with reluctance.... On the occasion of my half-sister's marriage to Hồ, later a village mayor, a classical opera *(chèo)* was performed for days as a part of the wedding celebration. It was the wedding of the daughter of my father and his second wife to the son of another wealthy family. As the bride's brother, I had the honor of sitting on a raised platform in the courtyard during the opera performance. Lư happened to sit on the floor by my side, and she whispered to me: "Would you let me know when you want to go home? I would like to leave together with you." At one point during the performance I stood up, but only to go outside to urinate. Lư joined me and kept me from returning to the courtyard. I did not know much of anything about sex then. I did it with great reluctance.... My senior sisters helped to communicate to my parents my preference to marry Lư, as I did not dare to speak too often to my father, let alone to state my desire to marry Lư. In our system it was the parents who expressed opinions and made the decisions. As soon as my father learned of my preference to marry Lư, he called me in immediately. He said that it was a matter of matching wealth and status. He asked me: "How could you dare to think of a marriage to a buffalo tender whose father works as a lowly soldier in the native guard and whose uncle is so poor as to live at the pagoda?" I stood quite embarrassed and silent like a stone....

My two [half-] brothers, Gia and Tăng, got married at an even earlier age, that is, at the age of thirteen. Just as my wife was sixteen, two years older than I was, at the time of our wedding, they married slightly older women so that the latter could help with household chores. Mrs. Gia's father, elder brother, and elder brother's son all held the title of deputy mayor at one point or another, although they owned only a few *mẫu* of land. Tăng's first wife also came from a landowning family with a few *mẫu* of land. The man whom my eldest sister, an adopted daughter of my parents, married was a son of the president of the neighboring village Dụng-Hiền and a brother to a canton chief. Her husband was actually my father-in-law's younger brother.... All of us were married through parental arrangement with utmost concern for the social standing of the involved families.

However, even among the elite of colonial Sơn-Dương, the male-oriented model was to some extent countered by a non-male-oriented system. Bằng's four-generation, patrilineally extended family had, through somewhat fortuitous circumstances, reached the culminating point of its

remarkable formation by 1928. Around the turn of the century the first
two wives of Bằng's grandfather established two separate households in
the same village.[10] The grandfather's patrilineally extended household had
split into at least two units. The first household included the grandfather
(A1), his first wife, their son (B1), their daughter-in-law, and their granddaughter (C1). The grandfather's second wife (Bằng's father's mother)
resided in a separate house with her son (B2) and the son's family. It
was only through a fortuitous combination of circumstances that Bằng's
father (B2) moved to the main house as the senior male descendant of his
generation (ca. 1905–1910). Those circumstances included the death of
the senior male descendant (B1) around the turn of the century, the lack
of male descendants in the senior branch of the family, and the death of
Bằng's father's mother (his grandfather's second wife). Bằng's junior
cousin did not move into the main house until shortly before 1928. In the
predominantly patrilineal system of northern Vietnam, with its partible
inheritance rule, the process of household fission, as exemplified by the
half-brothers in the second generation of Bằng's family, points toward the
significance of male descendants' matrilateral linkages to the founder's
different wives and toward the operation of an alternative kinship principle long observed by analysts of patrilineal systems (M. Wolf 1972; Kelly
1977). In colonial Sơn-Dương the non-male-oriented kinship principle
was weakly manifested in the tradition of establishing the second son's
ceremonial membership not in his father's *giáp* but that of his mother's
father. This incorporation of a bilateral descent principle also underlay the
wedding offerings not only to the bride's and groom's patrilineal ancestors, but also to their respective maternal grandfathers' and grandmothers'
ancestors (see Luong 1989). Among the poorest village households the
non-male-oriented model was also manifested in the relatively egalitarian labor contribution of both men and women. In these households both
men and women engaged directly in manual labor. Because of poverty
the men married late, and most remained monogamous. For example,
Bằng's cousin Tế (born in 1921) did not marry until he was twenty-seven
because of the dramatic downward mobility in his family in the aftermath
of the Yên-Báy uprising. In general, however, the non-male-oriented
model was overshadowed by its male-oriented counterpart in the colonial
period. I suggest that both the division of labor within Bằng's household
and the limited visibility of Sơn-Dương women in the local revolution
in general relate to the dominance of a kinship-centered, male-oriented,
and class-structured model in the local universe of the colonial social
formation.

On the eve of the Yên-Báy uprising, the structure of Sơn-Dương village involved a tension between a model of hierarchical relations on the one hand, and a heightened consciousness of the village as a collectivity bonded by extensive kinship, communal, and ethnic ties within a corporate framework on the other. In this context, despite the ideology of equality in the French metropolis, French colonialism both reinforced the hierarchical model within the microcosm of Sơn-Dương village and reconstructed the hierarchy of the colonial social formation in the form of a racial diarchy (Woodside 1976).

In the French colonial period, the model of hierarchical relations in rural communities was partly reinforced by the formation of the Lineage Representative Council in the 1921 French administrative reform. This reform heightened the role of the patrilineage in village structure. More important, status within the community were highly commoditized since male villagers paid progressively higher fees in exchange for honorary village ranks or actual village rank recognition in their progress through the ranking system: in Sơn-Dương men paid 15 piasters for an honorary village title *(xã tiền or xã Chính)*, 50 piasters for the deputy mayor title *(phó lý tiền or phó lý quyên)*, 70 piasters for the collective recognition of a mayor title *(lý trưởng)* (Sơn-Dương 1942, article 76); in Dụng-Hiền, 15 piasters for a Literati Association membership *(tư văn)*, 23 piasters for an honorary village title *(xã dịch)*, 29 piasters for the recognition of an honorary mayor title *(lý trưởng quyên)* (Dụng-Hiền 1942, article 14); and in Thuy-Sơn, 25 piasters for an honorary village title *(xã xử)*, 40 piasters for an honorary deputy mayor title *(phó lý quyên)*, and 50 piasters for an honorary mayor title *(lý trưởng quyên)* (Thuy-Sơn 1942, article 75).[11] Funds raised from the sale of honorary titles were used for village projects. The renovation of Sơn-Dương pagoda in 1901, for example, was funded through the sale of such titles (TTLTQG1-PT–535). Ordinary male villagers *(bạch đinh)* who could not afford honorary titles were either excluded from the feasting system, as in Dụng-Hiền, or assigned to peripheral positions in communal house ceremonies, as in Sơn-Dương and Thuy-Sơn. They were also obligated to provide the state-imposed corvée labor. They had constantly to refer to both honorary and actual officeholders, as well as their spouses, with the names of these notables' offices (for example, Ông Chánh Côn, grandfather Canton Chief/Village President [father of] Côn). Among relatives, the commoditized titles had to be added to the kinship terms of both the titleholders and their wives to mark the addressor's due respect (for example., Bác Lý Mai, senior uncle/aunt Mayor [father of] Mai). Even in referring to titleholders and their spouses in their absence, poor villagers had to avoid personal pronouns, because in the dominant discursive practices of their universe, these linguistic forms presupposed and implied a lack of respect for the referents. In contrast, the poorer villagers were addressed either in terms of their kinship positions or, more contemptuously, with personal pronouns. Although they could participate in lineage ceremonies on the basis of their age and kinship status, it was the village titleholders who, regardless of their kinship ranks, became the lineage spokesmen. Formal public rank became an obsession among villagers with some land ownership: after achieving middle-peasant status through the purchase of land and the co-ownership of an ox, the elderly Thanh saved and borrowed enough money to purchase titles for both her husband and his brothers and to give banquets for relatives, neighbors, and other titleholders on the occasions on which these titles were conferred. In the encounter between the local universe and French capitalism, commoditized status seemed to become more important, although academic achievement and national-level bureaucratic ranks still took precedence. In Sơn-Dương and numerous other northern villages, the importance of academic achievement in the local status hierarchy reflected the widely accepted Confucian view that education essentially involved moral cultivation and that educated men played a vital role in societal leadership. However, in general, commoditized status pervaded the entire structure of social life in the villages of Sơn-Dương, Dụng-Hiền, and Thuỵ-Sơn.

## The Rise of Modern Anticolonial Movements

Beyond the microcosm of the village, the colonial social formation was structured by a racial diarchy of colonial masters and colonized indigenous masses (Woodside 1976:17). At the top were approximately 10,000 Frenchmen who filled important positions in the government, in professions, and in industrial, commercial, and agricultural enterprises. Within the governmental structure the French managed to absorb 60 percent of the general personnel budget, although they held only 20 percent of all positions (Marr 1981:24). They ruled over the indigenous masses, most of whom lived in agricultural communities and whose livelihoods were sustained within a subsistence-oriented framework. The racial diarchy of colonial Vietnam is described particularly well in the French-educated novelist Nhất-Linh's account of his journey to France:

The farther the ship got from Vietnam and the closer it got to France, to the same degree the more decently the people aboard the ship treated me. In the China Sea they did not care to look at me. By the Gulf of Siam they were looking at me with scornful apprehension, the way they would look at a mosquito carrying malaria germs to Europe. When we entered the Indian Ocean, their eyes began to become infected with expressions of gentleness and compassion...and when we crossed the Mediterranean, suddenly they viewed me as being civilized like themselves, and began to entertain ideas of respecting me. At that time I was very elated. But I still worried about the time when I was going to return home! (translated in Woodside 1976:4)

Mediating between the colonial masters and the indigenous masses was the emerging Western-educated native intelligentsia that, even with the minimalist criterion of three years of French education, made up at most 0.8 percent (150,000) of the native population by the late 1930s. With the termination of the Confucian examination system in Tonkin in 1915, this French-educated native elite was trained to fill low- and middle-ranking positions in the colonial public and private sectors (as clerks, interpreters, and elementary school teachers, among other positions). Among this Western-exposed elite the conceptual distinction between insiders and outsiders, nurtured in the native communal framework, combined with the French ideals of equality and liberty to sharply heighten the consciousness of racial inequality (see also Emerson 1960:54–57). This emerging French-educated elite saw themselves as the vanguard of the new era and as the new leaders of the native masses. Their aspirations rose higher than ever when, during World War I, the French promised them a more active role in colonial affairs and when a socialist governor general (Varenne) arrived in Hanoi in 1925. Many were subsequently disappointed by the considerable persistence of a colonial order rooted in the reality of racial inequality dressed in the discourse of benevolent association. As repeatedly remarked by both French colonial analysts and leading scholars of twentieth-century Vietnam, from 1925 onward many of these French-educated members of the intelligentsia, who had been nurtured by the symbols of anticolonial activism in the preceding four decades, filled the ranks of new anticolonial parties, both Marxist and non-Marxist (GGI-DAP, 1930–1933). Nguyễn Đắc Bằng spoke of the reasons for his political activism:

[During my school years in Hanoi in the mid-1920s] I was strongly
inspired by discussions with [the future VNP leader Phó Đức] Chính
and other progressive students on the many injustices perpetuated
by the French colonizers against the colonized, some of which I had
witnessed myself. For example, on one occasion a Japanese friend
of mine and I took a train from my home district to Hanoi. Reading
French books on the train, we talked to each other about them in
French. A French train conductor made a contemptuous comment to
the effect that Vietnamese like us could not—I no longer remember
the exact comment, but it was contemptuous regarding the Vietnamese race. The Japanese told him to shut up and simultaneously slapped
the racially arrogant conductor. The conductor pulled out his pistol.
"He is Japanese," I had to shout to the French agent. The French obviously did not dare to bully a Japanese. Told to leave by my Japanese
acquaintance, the Frenchman simply left. The Japanese dared to slap
the French conductor in response to the insult because of the emergence of Japan as a power after her victory over Russia in 1905. The
French had to treat the Japanese with some respect. As a Vietnamese, I was boiling with anger at being insulted and not being able to
respond at all. What could a Vietnamese do, given the power of the
French conquerors? I felt deeply humiliated.

   That incident was only one example of the injustice imposed by
naked power. In my Hanoi school days, Chính, Lập [my friend from
Kinh-Kệ village], other progressive students, and I often commis-
erated about the powerlessness of a conquered race and about the
contemptuous treatment of Vietnamese by the French on a daily basis.
I was also inspired by French books regarding the noble ideals of liberty, democracy, and civil rights by Rousseau and Montesquieu. The
flame of patriotism in my heart was kept alive through my participation in the tumultuous student demonstration in Hanoi against the
life imprisonment sentence of Phan Bội Châu, a leading anticolonial
activist in the first quarter of the century, and the memorial service
on the shore of West Lake for Phan Chu Trinh, a reformist and well-
known patriot of the same era. These events kindled and nurtured the
patriotism of Vietnamese youth. French injustices had destroyed the
basis for any peaceful coexistence.

The new French-educated political activists became conscious not
only of the racial diarchy of colonial Vietnam but also of the impact of
French capitalism on the indigenous social formation, as is indicated in the

following manifesto of the Vietnamese Nationalist Party on the eve of the Yên-Báy uprising.

Proclamation to the people of the nation: Compatriots! Countrymen!
A duty it is to demand back a conquered country; an obligation it is to take collective vengeance against a common enemy. A calling it is to help one's countrymen in misfortune and to rescue one's own race from danger. They are all responsibilities of human beings.

For over sixty years, the French have called themselves a protector in order to appropriate our country and oppress our people. Their intention is to eliminate our race. In face of this common knowledge, how can we sit still? We all know without saying how barbarous and disreputable their policy is in this country. Power they monopolize, treating our people like animals. Schemes they devise, in order to imprison our patriots. This is to silence our countrymen in the face of oppression and injustice. Monarchy they extol, corrupt officials they tolerate, and lackeys they protect. This is to encourage brothers and sisters and fellow countrymen to kill one another off. Education they limit, free speech they prohibit, association they constrain, and mobility they restrict. Our fellow countrymen cannot learn albeit possessing brains, cannot speak although having mouths, cannot hear despite their ears, cannot move in spite of their legs, and cannot plan to work together, even among brothers and sisters. They increase taxes, exploit the mines, destroy the forests, build factories, open plantations, and use a thousand other means to carry off the wealth of our people. Our fellow countrymen are deprived of food and shelter, suffering the misery of hunger and cold. They distill poisonous alcohol and open opium shops to sell to our fellow countrymen. The health of our people declines steadily; diseases spread gradually. They deceive our fellow countrymen into leaving for New Caledonia and places with unhealthy climates so that our race is weakened. In a word, it is impossible to enumerate all the brutal acts of the French and the visible threats to the survival of our people.

Alas! In view of the wild ambition of the French and the present conditions of our country, unless we carry out a revolution soon, our race may not survive the elimination process at work. Unless we eliminate the French [from this land], they will annihilate us. In accordance with heaven's will and the people's wish, on the basis of justice and humanity, for the sake of the country of Vietnam, eighteen million compatriots, and the Hồng-Lạc [Viet] race, our party makes the first sacrifice, takes the initial step forward in order to lead the revolution and to capture towns and destroy citadels. We are determined to expel the French to France, to demand Vietnam back for the Vietnamese, and to found a democracy so that the people can escape miseries and live in happiness. We hope that all our compatriots will understand our obligations, will share the sacrifice, will work together with us to eradicate the French pirates in order to wash away the shame from our land and rescue our race. Dear compatriots! Dear countrymen! The opportunity has arrived. The movement has started. Our revolutionary forces have risen up. The success of the revolution depends on the contributions of our compatriots and countrymen. Let us stand up and risk our lives in order to eliminate the enemy. As you make sacrifices for the country, please shout "Long Live Vietnam! May the Vietnamese Revolution Succeed!"

Central Committee of the Vietnamese Nationalist Party

The proclamation of the Vietnamese Nationalist Party (AOM-AP-I, 7F–4) sought to increase solidarity among the native population through a heightened collective consciousness of the French threat to the Vietnamese race and nation. In this respect it bore a remarkable thematic resemblance to the nineteenth-century anti-French exhortation to the indigenous population discussed in Chapter 1.

> Because the court's officials were cowards and excessively anxious to save their lives, they hurriedly surrendered to the enemy.
> Given that advantage, the enemy now moves freely and kills our people with impunity.
> But people like us must try to preserve the country in which we live.
> Shall we just stare at our decay?
> Since we are determined not to live with the enemy, we shall not be deterred by their overwhelmingly superior forces,
> Since we believe that success rests upon the people's will, we shall not fret over our futile efforts…
> (translated in Trương-Bửu-Lâm 1967:113–115)

The proclamation by the VNP built on the powerful and evocative symbols of the precolonial native tradition that had served to unite most of the indigenous population in the earlier decade-long anti-French resistance. It echoed a recurrent theme in the life of Sơn-Dương village—a theme manifested in the annual ceremonies honoring the two tutelary deities who had played important roles defending the country against foreign intruders. Perhaps as a sign of the times, the VNP proclamation reflected a heightened sense of nationhood, that is, it appealed to all the indigenous ethnic groups, all eighteen-million people within the boundaries of the country, with a specific reference to the Hồng-Lạc race. Beyond the foremost objective of national independence, the VNP program combined a Western discourse on justice and civil liberties (freedom of speech, association, and mobility) with a socialist vision of political economy. Bằng elaborated in his discussion of the three principles of the party:

> The first principle is nationalism. Vietnam is to be liberated from foreign domination. All Vietnamese people, including all ethnic minorities, are to become citizens of an independent and sovereign Vietnam. The second principle is democracy. Every citizen is entitled to four fundamental rights: the right to vote, the right to impeach elected officials, and the rights to ratify and to abolish laws. The third principle involves the livelihood of the people. It would entail imposing severe limitations on capitalism through the nationalization of industries, the improvement of workers' working conditions, and an egalitarian distribution of land to the peasantry. It aims at increasing productivity and at reducing the gap between the rich and the poor to guarantee the livelihood of each citizen.

Bằng's recollected interpretation of the third principle was not necessarily influenced by his later exposure to Marxism and the rise of Marxist power in Vietnam. He reported intense debate as early as the late 1920s between party ideologues favoring communism and collective ownership and those defending the principle of private property. The debate indirectly echoed the potentially discordant voices of village institutions: those rooted in the longstanding collectivist tradition of communal land and communal tutelary deity worship and those rooted in the class-structured hierarchy of village social life. In many northern and central villages, communal land was distributed to all adult male villagers, which reinforced a strong sense of collectivity. The collectivist vision of communal life was not restricted to the communal rites of passage: on two separate occasions in the nineteenth century, Nguyễn emperors actually ordered the appropriation of private land in certain parts of the country in order to increase the amount of communal land available for distribution (Nguyễn-Thế-Anh 1971:111–112; Nguyễn-Thiệu-Lâu 1951). With clear precedents in Vietnamese history, the official VNP position on the people's livelihood (the third principle) envisioned an active use of state power to guarantee the welfare of the working masses.

In order to achieve the dual objectives of national independence and socioeconomic welfare, the VNP leadership sought to combine both the activist and reformist traditions of the first quarter of the twentieth century. They hoped not only to overthrow the colonial state but also, like most other members of the French-educated native intelligentsia, to strengthen the Vietnamese system through systematic reforms. Although the official VNP program did not strongly emphasize socioeconomic reforms, the VNP leadership actively pushed for them at the local level, as Bằng discovered in the preparation for the funeral of his father's senior mother in Sơn-Dương in 1929:

> According to custom, relatives both within and outside the patrilineage met for the entire night to discuss the funeral arrangements and to prepare for the funeral. Since I had joined the Vietnamese Nationalist Party by then, [the deputy VNP leader] Chính suggested that I cancel the big [wasteful] funeral feast. Following this suggestion, at the gathering to prepare for the funeral, I took the position that on the date of burial, villagers should simply accompany the deceased to the burying field and that they simply be offered drinks and native cigarettes. No more than that. When the idea of skipping the funeral feast was proposed, my paternal aunts strongly opposed it. They said: "If there is no funeral for the old lady, how will you have your wife claim the [feast association] debts afterwards? How will you get the rice and other contributions that the members of those associations owe us? We can only claim the debts on the right occasions." Only a senior relative [Tế's father's elder brother] had a sufficient sense of the modern era to support my idea. My brothers Tăng and Gia had also seen the new light on the issue by then. But all other male relatives supported the old ladies, forcing the organization of a funeral feast. Chính expressed a great deal of displeasure with me about this funeral. He complained about the waste of money for the funeral.

In post-1925 colonial Vietnam, the Vietnamese Nationalist Party proclamation could have been made by either of the two other anticolonial parties of this period in northern Vietnam—the virtually moribund New Vietnam Revolutionary Party (Tân Việt Cách mạng Đảng) and the rapidly ascendant communist movement. Despite the differences in their vision of a postcolonial societal order, as well as in revolutionary tactics and organizational bases, all three parties were formed in the political ferment of the

1925–1927 period. They all attracted members of the modern-educated intelligentsia, and they shared both the perception of French "brutalities" and the objective of national independence. They also had in common the search for a synthesis of the activist and reformist traditions.

Formed in 1925 and unable to transcend either an elitist network or regional ties, the New Vietnam Revolutionary Party (Tân Việt) recruited most actively among students and the low-ranking civil servants in northern central Annam.[12] It was in this part of the country that thirty of the forty-two party cells were located in 1928.[13] By the end of 1928, in the province of Phú-Thọ, the New Vietnam Revolutionary Party had formed only one cell, in the town of Hưng-Hoá (Cao-Tiến-Phùng et al. 1985:34). The New Vietnam Revolutionary Party was gradually absorbed by the Vietnamese Revolutionary Youth League (Việt Nam Thanh Niên Cách Mạng Đồng Chí Hội), which was formed by Hồ Chí Minh in Canton in 1925 and which had a considerably wider regional and class organizational basis.

Like the two other anticolonial parties of the post-1925 period, the Vietnamese Revolutionary Youth League recruited 90 percent of its original membership among the educated "petite bourgeoisie" within which the intelligentsia played a dominant revolutionary role in relation to small shopkeepers (Nguyễn-Công-Bình et al. 1985:224). However, in accordance with Marxist-Leninist doctrine, the Vietnamese Revolutionary Youth League emphasized the revolutionary potential of the industrial proletariat and launched a successful "proletarianization" campaign among its better-educated members to strengthen its roots among the emerging working class. The percentage of bourgeois revolutionaries consequently declined over time, although they were still well represented in the Communist Party membership, as partially reflected in the membership data for the provinces of Nam-Định and Hà-Nam, later merged into Nam-Hà (see Table 3).

**Table 3.** Backgrounds of Communist Party members, provinces of Nam-Định and Hà-Nam

|           | Workers | Peasants | "Bourgeois" | Landlords | Other | Total |
|-----------|---------|----------|-------------|-----------|-------|-------|
| 1927–1929 | 39      | 30       | 77          | 12        | 3     | 161   |
|           | (24%)   | (19%)    | (48%)       | (7%)      | (2%)  |       |
| 1929–1931 | 91      | 80       | 45          | 9         | 4     | 229   |
|           | (40%)   | (35%)    | (20%)       | (4%)      | (2%)  |       |

*Source:* Quốc-Anh 1975:46.

The proportion of Communist Party membership from the bourgeoisie in Nam-Hà in 1927–1931 was considerably higher than the percentage of bourgeois in the native population (3 percent) in the late 1930s (Marr 1981:31). Furthermore, the percentage of "bourgeois" Communist Party members in northern Vietnam may be underrepresented by the data from Nam-Hà. The percentage of Communist Party members from the working class in Nam-Hà probably exceeded that in most other northern provinces, because Nam-Hà included one of the three major industrial centers in the north. But even at 20 percent, Party members from the bourgeoisie played an unusually important role within the ranks of anticolonial party leadership. The overwhelming majority of the Party leaders came from the Western-educated intelligentsia that, even by the minimalist criterion of a three-year formal education, made up only 0.8 percent (150,000) of the population by the late 1930s.

Communist Party membership, although still strongest in northern central Vietnam, was widespread throughout the country. By 1930, despite its temporary split in Hồ's absence into three regional parties, the Communist Party had emerged as a powerful alternative to the Vietnamese Nationalist Party even within the VNP's stronghold in north Vietnam where, within slightly over one year of its formation in December 1927, the VNP had built up a network of 120 cells and 1,500 activists (GGI-DAP 2:12).

National independence constituted the first and foremost objective of the Vietnamese Nationalist Party, which derived its ideological inspiration directly from the Chinese revolutionary leader Sun Yat-sen's Three People's Principles (nationalism, people's welfare, and human rights) and indirectly from both Western democratic ideology and the indigenous collectivistic tradition.[14] The VNP was led by Nguyễn Thái Học (born 1901), a graduate of the École Normale and a native of Vĩnh-Yên province. As a student at the Advanced School of Commerce in Hanoi at the time of Phan Bội Châu's trial and Phan Chu Trinh's death, Học was swept up in that period's tidal wave of student activism. Initially, Học had hopes for the possibility of reforms within the colonial system under the principle of French-Vietnamese association: in 1926 he submitted proposals for reforms in Vietnamese industries, commerce, and agriculture to the new French governor general, who came from the ranks of the French Socialist Party. But he received no response. When his subsequent application to publish a monthly magazine to promote practical education was denied, his last hope for reform within the colonial framework was also extinguished. Học and numerous friends embarked on the path of revolutionary militancy and linked up with other groups in the provinces of Bắc-Giang, Bắc-Ninh, and Thanh-Hoá to form the Vietnamese Nationalist Party.

The primary objective of nationalism in combination with a Confucian-based elitism shaped both the VNP recruitment methods and the course of its development at this major juncture in Vietnamese history. The VNP leadership recruited members mainly among the nationalist and activist elements of the native elite: the modern-educated young intelligentsia, the traditionally oriented rural notables, and, for tactical purposes, the warrant officers in the colonial armed forces (cf. GGI-DAP 2:12). The party leadership in the Sơn-Dương area was no exception in this regard: it included the Confucian teacher Toại and the French-educated Nguyễn Đắc Bằng. The VNP regional committee was chaired by an elderly notable, the mayor of Sơn-Dương's neighboring Dục-Mỹ village. Of the 223 Vietnamese Nationalist Party members convicted at the 1929 criminal tribunal in Hanoi, 40 percent (91) came from the Western-educated intelligentsia (GGI-DAP 2:13). With few exceptions, other members of the native society (for example, women, soldiers, students, workers, and peasants) were organized simply into party-affiliated associations (ibid.: appendix 2; Hoàng-Phạm-Trân 1949:87).[15]

The Vietnamese Nationalist Party briefly and unsuccessfully explored the possibility of a political merger with the other two parties in order to strengthen the cause of national independence and the base of Vietnamese anticolonialism (Hoàng-văn-Đạo 1970:41–43; Hoàng-Phạm-Trân 1949:39–43).[16] In the town of Hưng-Hoá it succeeded in absorbing the only New Vietnam Revolutionary Party cell in the province (Cao-Tiến-Phùng et al. 1985:34).

The momentum of the party, however, screeched to a halt in February 1929, when local party activists assassinated Bazin, a chief labor recruiter for the plantation coolie trade, on the occasion of the New Year. The French arrested over 200 party members, initiating a phase of strong repression.[17] The assassination reportedly was attempted with the hope of demonstrating VNP activities and power among commercial and industrial workers in the face of an active, competing recruitment drive by the Marxist Vietnamese Revolutionary Youth League (Hoàng-văn-Đạo 1970:54–58). Betrayals by certain party members in the face of French manipulation compounded the VNP's problems in its long-term planning for the uprising (Hoàng-Phạm-Trân 1949:73–80). Deeply concerned about the· further erosion of VNP strength by French repression, the party leadership decided, after a turbulent debate in mid-1929, to expedite the insurrection timetable, to intensify the recruitment of new members and the mobilization of local populations, and to actively prepare for an uprising. They realized the small odds of success but won over the objections of a moderate minority with a well-known phrase predicated upon the native cultural logic: "Even if victory is not achieved, we will fully mature as human beings with our [heroic] efforts" *(Không thành công cũng thành nhân)*. It is a logic that evaluates human achievements at least as much on the basis of moral nobility as in terms of concrete results.

Within the village of Sơn-Dương, as preparation for the insurrection intensified, local leaders who came from the ranks of the native elite made extensive use of the hierarchical structure of the village as well as kinship and communal ties in order to mobilize other villagers. Nguyễn Đắc Bằng discussed the process of political mobilization and the responses of Sơn-Dương villagers:

> Revolutionary tasks required a lot of energy and a heightened activism. Starting in November 1929, I received instructions from the party to look after many fugitive comrades who came to my village to help with the production of bombs and hand grenades. I arranged for their food and shelter at my relatives' homes in the daytime. In late December 1929, when the party traitor Dương brought secret service agents to a leadership meeting in Võng-La village to arrest the party president Học and ended up wounding [his deputy] Chính, I had to organize the transportation of Chính to my village by sampan on the Red River. Chính stayed in my village, actually at the Confucian teacher Toại's house next to mine, to recover from the wound. As a result of Chính's rehabilitation in my village and the concomitant shift of the regional party headquarters to Sơn-Dương, party activities in Sơn-Dương further intensified from that point onward.

> *Why did everybody move to your village?*
> They came to my village because the Confucian teacher Toại and I provided an active local leadership. Some villagers joined as party members and party-affiliated association members. The mayor and the administration in my village simply turned their eyes away from our activities. They understood. Their relatives were party members. On the eve of the uprising the village looked like a festival day. Village administrators like Deputy Mayor Kiểm and Acting Mayor Di took the oath of loyalty to the movement at my house in a ceremony

administered by teacher Hợp, a relative of mine from Xuân-Lũng. The mayor and his people had high regards for us. They respected me personally for my education. Furthermore, my family, although not a big-landlord family, was well off. My father had been involved in the anti-French Tonkin Free School movement. It was thanks to my standing and relations with village officials that they connived at our activities and alerted us to any potential problem.

The local party membership amounted only to five, but we had approximately ten activists in a party-led association, and villagers were quite sympathetic.[18] The Sino-Vietnamese teacher Toại and I were leaders in the local party organization. No party member [in Sơn-Dương] came from the local notable ranks. We also organized an association with approximately ten members. In contrast to party members, the latter came from the manual-labor class and therefore did not provide leadership.

*Were you related to many of the party and association members?*
The Confucian teacher Toại and I were related. His mother, my mother-in-law, my paternal grandfather's first wife, and the mother of another party member, the Deputy Mayor Thanh, were all sisters. A fourth member of the party, Tín Quẩy, was related to the Confucian teacher Toại. His younger brother was a pupil of mine. Another party member, Tập, was a distant relative of mine. His mother was a native member of my patrilineage.... Within my patrilineage, a few uncles and other relatives of mine actively assisted us on the eve of the uprising. Even my brothers Tăng and Gia joined in the preparation for the uprising without any mobilization efforts on my part.... The teacher Toại had persuaded Gia to participate. Tăng joined the Student Association through his own network, asking his friends to join him in the propaganda talks to other young people and in the distribution of leaflets in many places. It was through Tăng's organizational efforts that I, as the propaganda commissioner on the regional committee, went to Hưng-Hoá for a talk with prospective young party supporters. We discussed, for example, the patriotic movements of Japan and other countries, as well as the Three People's Principles of the Chinese revolutionary leader Sun Yat-sen. I discussed this doctrine because I knew nothing about Marxism and because it was impossible to find any book on Marxism then. The discussion aimed at inspiring in these young participants patriotism and progressive political attitudes.

*How did other wealthy families in the village respond to the movement?*

It was mainly my relatives and relatives of the teacher Toại who got actively involved at the beginning. But financial contributions were provided by quite a few wealthy families in the village, especially those with literati backgrounds and with some connections to the Tonkin Free School movement. The wife of the wealthiest villager, the late canton chief Chi, contributed a few hundred piasters to the party fund for the purchase of pistols and other weapons. The second wealthiest Sơn-Dương villager, called Mrs. Village Mayor Ân [wife of the late village mayor An], and other well-off families also patriotically responded to our requests for assistance. The father of the wife of the late Mayor Ân, Mr. Đội Bốn [Squad Leader the Fourth], had joined the anticolonial movement earlier, in the late nineteenth century. A matrilineal relative of the teacher Toại, she [Mrs. Village Mayor Ân] was the most devoted matron of the anticolonial movement in Sơn-Dương.

The local party membership was small. However, thanks to the sympathy of village officials and other villagers, bombs and leaflets were produced with little difficulty in Sơn-Dương every night for over a month in early 1930. As school was still in session, I had to neglect my teaching from time to time. During the intense preparation for the uprising, although leaflets and bombs were produced mainly at night, the school was even closed down at times in the daytime.

Indeed, the VNP activities in Sơn-Dương could not have taken place at all within a close-knit rural community without at least the passive support of village authorities and other villagers. Because of the virtually impenetrable bamboo hedge that surrounds each village, fugitive political activists had to enter Sơn-Dương through the village gate under the watchful eyes of many villagers. A secret report to higher authorities would have led to the arrest of many anticolonial activists. The bomb-manufacturing team included approximately twenty people working under the supervision of fugitive VNP members and with the sympathy, if not the support, of certain elderly members from the elite families of Sơn-Dương. As Bằng narrates:

In my capacity as propaganda head of the Phú-Thọ-Yên-Báy local committee, I assisted Chính in writing, printing, and distributing leaflets to French, legionnaire, and Vietnamese soldiers, as well as to the Vietnamese populace at large. Chính and I also took charge, starting in late 1929, of the production of hand grenades in preparation for the uprising. The well-educated party members, such as Học and Chính, had learned the bomb production techniques from books. We produced two kinds of bombs. One had a cast-iron shell that was manufactured in the neighboring province of Vĩnh-Yên and transported by sampan at night to my village. The other kind of shell was adapted from cement opium containers that were bought openly on the market. The purchased gun powder was simply added to these shells.

It was actually in my housing compound, in an uninhabited cottage reserved for me and my wife, that the bombs were produced. It was the branch house occupied first by my father and then by my cousin "Uncle" Mai before he moved in with my father. It was moved onto our land for me, but I never lived in it.

*Did your family learn in advance about the production of bombs in your own house?*

After the French break-up of our regional revolutionary center at Võng-La village on the other side of the Red River, the teacher Toại cleverly found a way to obtain my senior mother's approval to turn my house into a bomb-manufacturing center. She was the senior person in the house, because my father had died of a gastrointestinal disease in 1928 and because my grandmother had died of old age in early 1929. The teacher Toại worked through Ngân, a fugitive female comrade who had been the obstetrical nurse at the Hưng-Hoá hospital and who occasionally came to meetings with Nhu at the teacher Toại's house during the intense preparation period. Earlier on, when my brother Gia had been hospitalized in Hưng-Hoá, my senior mother had taken care of Gia there and got to know Ngân. The teacher Toại asked Miss Ngân, also called Miss Secretary, to make a visit to my mother on behalf of the party. So glad to see an old acquaintance, my mother invited the visitor to stay overnight. Needless to say, Miss Ngân accepted the invitation in order to talk to my mother at length about the need to gain independence from the French. That was how my mother became sympathetic to progressive causes. And that was how bombs could be produced in my house. Every day when bombs or leaflets were pro-duced, my mother plus one or two additional household members had to serve meals to about twenty people.

*Did your senior brothers participate?*
My brother Gia did, but without enthusiasm. My other younger brother, Tăng, a sixteen-year-old student at the Franco-Vietnamese school in Hưng-Hoá at the time, was a member of the Youth Association.

*Did your wife and your brothers' wives object to it?*
They did not dare to object to it as my senior mother supported our activities. Nobody in the household dared to raise any objection under the circumstances. For our wives the Confucian maxim applied: "When at home, obey your father; after marriage, obey your husband; after the death of your husband, obey your sons."

Bombs and weapons were manufactured not only in Sơn-Dương, but also in the villages of Cao-Mại and Xuân-Lũng of Lâm-Thao district (Nguyễn-văn-Khánh 1997: 166–167), During the bomb-production period, Bằng was summoned by the French *résident,* Colas, to the provincial capital of Phú-Thọ. Colas advised Bằng that Bằng's name had been put on the secret police blacklist of revolutionary suspects and that he should not engage in underground activities. Bằng reported on a subsequent meeting with the Vietnamese chief of Lâm-Thao district:

On my way home from the provincial capital, I also stopped at the office of the Lâm-Thao district chief to submit my monthly school activity report. This district chief told me that the leaders of the party, Học, Nhu, and Chính, were reported to be hiding in the district. He told me: "If you can help the government to find them, you and I will be well rewarded. The Vietnamese, having no capacity and resources for modern warfare, will never succeed in opposing the French government, a great Western power, with its modern weaponry and its military might." He obviously knew neither of my party membership nor of the presence of two of these top party leaders in Sơn-Dương. I simply smiled and nodded my head in reply. But I told myself, "This idiotic bastard knows little of Vietnamese history. We will simply capture French weapons to kill the French themselves. A day of independence will arrive, enabling us to put behind us the shame of losing our country. If everybody thought in the same cowardly way as he does, the Vietnamese would remain forever enslaved, and independence would be a completely lost cause."

Bằng's perspective and that of the Lâm-Thao district chief on the colonial system represented opposite positions in the resistance-collaboration continuum among the native intelligentsia. Although only a minority of the native elite embarked on the path of active resistance, owing to its high cost and small probability of success, many were not reluctant to lend it at least passive support, as they did in the village of Sơn-Dương during the preparations for the uprising.

The uprising in Phú-Thọ and Yên-Báy took place on February 10, 1930, as Học's order to postpone the armed insurrection for five days arrived only after the departure of Phú-Thọ civilians and the transportation of additional arms to Yên-Báy. Because of a lack of VNP coordination and the previous repressive moves of the French, the movement fizzled. With the subsequent destruction of the VNP infrastructure in north Vietnam, the Vietnamese Nationalist Party ceased to play a significant role in Vietnamese anticolonial politics. The failure of the Yên-Báy uprising reinforced the prominence of the competing Indochinese Communist Party, which was unified by Hồ Chí Minh in February 1930, in the making of modern Vietnam.

The failure of the Yên-Báy uprising notwithstanding, the rise of the Vietnamese Nationalist Party and other modern anticolonial movements from 1925 onward was deeply rooted in the structure of the colonial encounter, that is, in the disjuncture between the metropolitan discourse of liberty, equality, and fraternity and the racial diarchy of the colonial periphery as well as between the capitalist imperialist system and the indigenous precolonial framework. The formidable coercive power of the colonial masters, their selective rewards to native collaborators, and their rhetoric of a civilizing mission and benevolent Franco-Vietnamese association brought an end to the active resistance by the majority of the indigenous population in the first three decades of the twentieth century, and even generated an exploratory accommodation of French colonialism (see Emerson 1960:10–11). However, in this process of exploratory accommodation many Vietnamese both within and outside the French-educated intelligentsia became acutely aware of the contradictions of French capitalistic colonialism in and of itself and in its relationship to the native sociocultural framework. For many revolutionary leaders after 1925, the contradictions became increasingly salient between the colonial racial diarchy and political economic transformation, on the one hand, and the official French discourse on the other.

In the period from 1925 onward many members of the French-educated intelligentsia, who were descended from the traditional elite, embarked

on an active search for national independence. Through their exposure
to the West, their world view was partly shaped by the Western ideological emphasis on liberty and civil rights, as seen in the VNP proclamation
and as emphasized by Emerson (1960:212–237). However, in accordance
with the local tradition, the ideas of equality and liberty were understood
not in terms of individual benefits, but as collective rights in the relations
between the Vietnamese and their colonial masters.

The influence of the indigenous tradition was also reflected in the considerable attention the VNP proclamation gave to the capitalist exploitation of the indigenous socioeconomic formation as well as in the party's
socialist vision. Shaped by the doctrine of Sun Yat-sen, this collectivistic
vision would not have formed strong roots in the Vietnamese landscape
if the native soil had not supported its growth. In northern and central
Vietnam, this vision was nurtured by fairly strong institutions of communal land and communal tutelary deity worship, even though the tradition
of communal land was considerably weaker in Sơn-Dương than in many
other villages and even though the significance of both institutions was
slowly being undermined by increasing class differentiation.

The tradition of the precolonial north also intensified the negative
reaction of many native actors to foreign domination because of the sharp
distinction that traditionally obtained between insiders and outsiders in the
native conceptualization of kinship, communality, and ethnicity. On one
level modern Vietnamese anticolonial movements capitalized heavily on
this salient conceptual dichotomy between Vietnamese and non-Vietnamese "races" as well as on the symbols of active native resistance against
foreign intruders in previous centuries. They also built extensively on the
structure of particularistic relations within the native precapitalist framework. For example, the Vietnamese Nationalist Party recruited members
through school bonds among the sons of the traditional elite forged in the
new context of the colonial educational system. Reproducing the dominant male-oriented and elite-centered model of the local tradition, the VNP
found its leadership among men from relatively privileged backgrounds.
Inside the bamboo hedges dotting the rural landscape, VNP leaders relied
heavily on kinship and village-bound hierarchical ties in the mobilization
process. In Sơn-Dương, for example, educated VNP members from the
privileged social stratum made extensive use of the traditional respect for
education and their rural kinship networks. The rise of modern Vietnamese
anticolonialism can be separated neither from the fundamental inequali-
ties and contradictions within capitalist imperialism nor from the salient
features of the native sociocultural framework.

CHAPTER 3

# In the Name of "Liberty, Equality, and Fraternity"

In the aftermath of the Vietnamese Nationalist Party uprising in February 1930, the French undertook quick and strong repressive measures. In Yên-Báy French troops maintained a careful check on the population. They prohibited the movement of wood rafts down the Red River from the highlands and hindered other normal economic activities, causing a loss of 10,000 piasters in revenue in March alone. As a collective punishment, the defensive bamboo hedges of Sơn-Dương and many other villages were leveled, exposing the internal landscape, "shamefully" in native perception, to the entire outside world. A large number of Sơn-Dương houses were burnt down. French planes also bombed the village of Cổ-Am in Hải-Dương province. In the province of Phú-Thọ, by February 20, 1930, 200 persons had been arrested, among whom 60 were considered to have directly participated in the insurrection and 140 to have been accomplices. The number of arrests increased to 340 by February 26 and reportedly remained in that range into and beyond March (*Trung-Bắc-Tân-Văn*, February 26 and March 30, 1930). Eighty-two political activists were subsequently sentenced to death. Other political prisoners were deported to less-accessible parts of Vietnam and other corners of the French empire, where the colonial masters planned to use their labor to exploit the resources of different regions at the periphery of the world capitalist system.

On a personal level, the repression temporarily traumatized countless villagers and further radicalized many political activists. On the national scale, the Vietnamese Nationalist Party was virtually destroyed within the country; the Indochinese Communist Party (ICP) subsequently emerged as an even more powerful anticolonial force and eventually led the indigenous northern population in a violent and successful resistance to colonialism.

On the theoretical level, the Millean approach to political action encounters an anomaly in the lack of a complete French success in extinguishing the flames of Vietnamese anticolonialism in spite of their generous cooptation rewards and the severe punishments imposed on anti-French activists. In the structural tension between French colonialism and the indigenous system, the impact of the dominant ideology of the capitalist core on the native elite of the periphery was amply reflected in the emphasis on liberty and equality in the discourse of Vietnamese anticolonialists in the aftermath of the Yên-Báy uprising (Emerson 1960). However, in the context of their little direct exposure to Western Marxism, the collectivistic vision of the political economic framework advocated by many VNP members suggests that local tradition also played an important role in shaping revolutionary ideologies.

Among the convicted political activists was the native son of Sơn-Dương village Nguyễn Đắc Bằng, who received two death sentences for his role in the uprising. More fortunate than his comrades, he was eventually granted a commutation of both. Bằng related at length his experiences in the aftermath of the VNP uprising:

> [On the night of February 11, in the aftermath of French soldiers' encirclement of Sơn-Dương] I sneaked back home from neighboring Ngũ-Xã village, where I had attended a teacher-honoring banquet hosted by the parents of my pupils. Upon seeing me, my elderly senior mother broke into tears: "Tăng hasn't come back. Gia was arrested this morning. Your name, together with many others, was called. The district chief warned that if you or any of the absentees didn't report to him within two days, the absentee's house would be burnt to the ground!"
>
> I stood there, speechless. Hundreds of depressing thoughts swept through my mind. I told myself: "Tăng and Gia have been arrested. They will certainly be tortured. They will end up with prison terms because, unable to suffer through all the torture to the end, they will probably end up confessing their affiliation with the party. Who will take care of my elderly senior mother? She is not my blood mother. However, since my own mother's death when I was five, my senior mother has given me even more love and care than she has given to her own two sons, Tăng and Gia. Whatever it is, clothes, books, tuition, or a bicycle, she has taken care of my needs first. And she even went out of her way to take care of the meals and the daily needs of those who came here to make bombs! She is a truly exemplary

senior mother! What will happen to her now that my two brothers and I will be gone?" During that sleepless night, the more I thought of the country, the party, and my family, the more anguish I suffered. I was also extremely anxious for further news from Yên-Báy and other fronts.

The following morning, I finally learned that the French forces had reoccupied Yên-Báy and that a number of our fighters had been captured, while others had fled. Our major front of Yên-Báy turned out to be a total rout!

Bằng's filial concern for his senior mother highlights the persistent conflict in the native system between the kinship duties defined within a male-oriented model and the obligations within a larger collectivistic framework.

At the urging of relatives, friends, and neighbors, Bằng decided to report at district headquarters on February 12. However, unlike many Sơn-Dương villagers, who were allowed to return to their village, Bằng was arrested: a chief of the district native guard contingent had mistaken Bằng for a comrade who had called upon the guards to surrender during the VNP's earlier attack on the district headquarters.

Bằng's retrospective account of his torture in prison highlights the contradiction between the dominant ideology of the capitalist core calling for "liberty, equality, and fraternity" and the political reality of the colony. Bằng's prison experiences and death sentences were particularly ironic because the Vietnamese Nationalist Party had adopted France's core ideology of "equality, liberty, and fraternity" as a motto in its official program (GGI-DAP 2:47).

The following morning [February 13], I was brought outside the district headquarters and ordered to line up in the street with approximately thirty other prisoners, many of whom I had long known from the villages surrounding Sơn-Dương. We were all tied up in a line with a big rope, left standing in the sun for over an hour, and eventually ordered to walk to the provincial capital about 13 kilometers away under the supervision of a native guard detachment. We were herded into a small hot and humid room at the police station, where we had to stand waiting for another hour for a clerk from the *résident*'s office to come for a basic identity investigation. We were then led to a big hall in the provincial prison, where at last we were at least untied and allowed to walk around. But even this big hall was gradually filled up the following day by newcomers, many of whom were my close comrades.

On the fifteenth I was removed from the group to an isolated cell where my legs were shackled in a wooden yoke. Somebody had provided additional information about me, because I was called not by my full name as earlier provided but as Giáo [Teacher] Bằng. In the early afternoon, in handcuffs, I was escorted by two European legionnaires armed with rifles and bayonets to the interrogation room about five hundred yards away. Two burly French interrogators had been waiting for me in this room full of torture equipment. The big one with a moustache signaled the guards to remove my handcuffs and then asked me in very good Vietnamese:

"You are Giáo [Teacher] Bằng, aren't you?"

"Yes."

"You are a member of the Vietnamese Nationalist Party, is that correct?"

"No."

"How did you get that blot?" He pointed to the small ink blot on my white trousers. I wore at the time not Western clothes but white Vietnamese mourning clothes.

"[As a teacher] I work in the classroom with ink. It happens not infrequently that ink spills on my clothes."

"That is not classroom ink. It is leaflet-printing ink. Now, tell me the truth! Who else was involved in this?"

The mustached investigator showed me a pile of leaflets in both French and Vietnamese on which I immediately recognized the handwriting of my pupils. We produced leaflets by first making a firm jelly and putting the original handwritten copy of the propaganda text on the firm jelly block—a text that I had asked students with beautiful handwriting to copy over at the school. Pieces of blank paper were then pressed against the original copy, one by one, in order to produce dozens of leaflets.

"I know nothing of the printing of leaflets," I replied.

A reeling blow from the mustached interrogator exploded in my face. Then punches and kicks rained down on my head, my back, and all over my body. "The evidence is that ink blot! If you do not admit it, I will beat you to death," roared the torturer. My blood began oozing out. I was almost unconscious, lying on the floor, when he stopped.

I did not know exactly how long it was before the other burly secret service inspector pulled me up and told me in French:

"You are a member of the Vietnamese Nationalist Party. You have printed all these leaflets. We have the evidence. You'd better admit it and tell us all the names of the party members in your cell and of those involved in the printing of the leaflets. You don't want us to torture you, do you?"

"Sir, I am not a member. And I know nothing of the printing of leaflets."

A blow immediately followed my reply, only to be followed by others. I was knocked down on the floor and totally lost consciousness this time.

It was still early in the afternoon when I regained my senses and was taken by two French soldiers back to the cell, where my legs were shackled again. This dark and windowless cell had only a small ventilation hole in the ceiling. There was no furniture except one hard wooden bed about one yard wide and a portable toilet bucket with no cover. Blood still oozed out from the swollen wounds all over my body. In deep pain and with hundreds of bed bugs crawling around me, I could not lie still in bed. I spent the rest of the day killing them with my fingers.

Bằng reported being tortured three more times in the next four days for having steadfastly denied any involvement in and knowledge of the uprising in the local area.

In late February, together with three fellow political prisoners, Bằng was escorted in chains by four French soldiers to Yên-Báy, the major site of the VNP uprising. Confronted with the testimonies of fellow activists, Bằng admitted his party membership, his authorization of the use of his house for grenade production, and his role in the printing of leaflets. However, in his narrative, he emphasized his success in hiding the names of his student assistants as well as in not admitting to all the transportation and communication tasks that he had carried out together with his comrades. He was also reportedly tortured for denying his participation in the VNP Central Committee meetings in Võng-La and La-Hào villages in Phú-Thọ.

On March 23, 1930, the second formal trial of movement participants took place in Yên-Báy, following the first trial on February 27, 1930.[1] The responses of the defendants during this two-day trial ranged from acceptance of all responsibilities, including taking responsibility for the actions of other participants; to acknowledging certain actions but denying responsibility for them by emphasizing the authoritarian nature of the VNP chain of command or coercion and deception by party members; to untruthful denials of their roles in the uprising and its preparation. The answers of the party president, Nguyễn Thái Học, fell into the first category: he claimed to be a revolutionary by profession and assumed all responsibilities for the uprising, even if certain tasks were not carried out directly under his orders. Some defendants, such as the Phú-Thọ native Nguyễn Như Liên, also valiantly emphasized that it was the duty of a citizen of a conquered country to liberate his fatherland by participating in the uprising. Within the Sơn-Dương party membership, Confucian teacher Toại's response fell into the first category, Bằng's into the second, and Phó [Deputy Mayor] Thanh into the third (*Trung-Bắc-Tân-Văn* March 30, 1930; *L'Avenir du Tonkin,* March 28, 1930). Bằng recalled the court proceedings in greater detail:

> One morning, a platoon of French soldiers came into the prison yard. Each of us was called out and handcuffed, and we were lined up in pairs. Walking in two lines along the road and escorted by the soldiers with rifles and bayonets, we were led to a long brick house on top of a hill. Our trials were to be conducted in barracks temporarily converted into a court house.... Approximately ten minutes after our arrival, there was a sudden loud command, and the soldiers stood at attention and raised their rifles in salute. The judges arrived. Total silence reigned over the court house. One defendant after another was called before the tribunal, handcuffs removed. Most memorable to this date were Nguyễn Thái Học's answers:
>
> "Are you the leader of the Vietnamese Nationalist Party?" the prosecutor asked.
>
> "Yes, I am the leader of the Việt Nam Quốc Dân Đảng," Học replied in Vietnamese. He forgot to say revolutionary *(cách mạng)* party.
>
> "What is the doctrine of your party?"
>
> "We fight against the French colonialists for the independence of our country and for the freedom and the welfare of the people of Vietnam."
>
> "You organized the uprising to kill the French, didn't you?"
>
> "Yes. For years we followed a nonviolent policy, making petitions for our independence and freedom. But it was to no avail. To achieve our goals, we had no choice but to resort to violence...."
>
> Học went on and on speaking about the principles of freedom, equality, and so on, but the judge stopped him.

"This is not a place for your propaganda. You can answer only questions concerning the uprising."

"If this is not the place for us to talk about reason, justice, and freedom, I wish to say no more."

I was called before the judges in the afternoon, after a brief ceremonial proceeding and a cursory formal questioning of five other defendants:

"Are you a member of the Vietnamese Nationalist Party?"

"Yes. I just do the duty of a member of a conquered country."

"Did you organize the printing of leaflets?"

"Yes. I did so to mobilize my people into supporting our movement and our struggle to liberate the country."

"You allowed the production of grenades in your house, didn't you?"

"Yes. It was an obligation of every member in accordance with the oath of membership: 'I will sacrifice my own life and my own property, if required, and I will obey absolutely the instructions of the party.' The production of grenades in my house was thus the collective responsibility of the party and not my personal fault."

"Did you assign members to join the Yên-Báy attack and the murder of officers and warrant officers there?"

"I was only a low-ranking member. I had no authority to assign members to Yên-Báy. Only Xứ Nhu, a member of the Central Committee, had this authority in my locality." With this statement, I was ordered to withdraw.

In a clear sign of the times, the discourse of many VNP activists reflects not merely an element of defiance derived from the legends of Vietnamese anticolonialism, but also the strong influence of French education on their thought process. For example, according to a Sûreté report (report 4213, AOM-AP, 7F–37), the teacher Nguyễn thị Bắc, a sister of party leader Học's fiancée, declared in the final round of statements that if she was not judged with justice, the statues of Joan of Arc in France might as well be destroyed. Nguyễn Thái Học's testimony constantly referred to "equality" and "liberty," although given racial diarchy and the dominant collectivist emphasis in the local tradition, the ideas of equality and liberty were understood not in terms of individual benefits, but as collective rights.

The following morning the French Criminal Commission sentenced thirty-nine political activists to death, thirty-three to hard labor for life, nine to twenty years of hard labor, four to life deportation, and one to five years of imprisonment. Among the death-row convicts were six natives of Sơn-Dương village, including Bằng and the teacher Toại (AOM-AP-I, 7F–37).

In the hope of saving the lives of many comrades, VNP President Học first appealed the sentence to the Council of the Protectorate (Conseil de Protectorat) and after its negative decision Học requested clemency. All the convicted political activists reportedly followed his lead, with the exception of his deputy, Chính (AOM-AP-I, 7F–37; Hoàng-văn-Đạo 1970:158). Bằng does not recall having either appealed or requested clemency himself.

Consideration of the clemency requests in Paris and the French measures in the aftermath of the uprising gave rise to diverse reactions and heated debates in colonial circles. With few exceptions, French colonialists in Vietnam advocated strong punitive measures and broader power for French colonial authorities. The authorities in France defended the colonial government in Indochina, but because it was susceptible to liberal pressures, it tended toward a more moderate stand. Most Vietnamese officials took strong exception to the colonialists' view. After the metropolitan government commuted nine of the thirteen death sentences in the first Yên-Báy trial in early March, M. Borel, the delegate from north Vietnam to the High Council of Colonies in Paris, called a meeting of elected representatives in order to pressure the government into empowering local French officials to use all the measures necessary for the maintenance of the *pax colonia*. In a Vietnamese preparatory forum the native members of the Tonkin Chamber of Representatives unanimously agreed to make concerted efforts at the official meeting to protest both the bombing of Cổ-Am village in Hải-Dương and the decrees of the Criminal Commission. They argued that capital punishment must not be handed out to political prisoners. At the official meeting on March 11, they filibustered various resolutions, including one that modified the 1927 decree and advocated extending the powers of the governor general and the provincial *résident*s. They refused to vote on a motion of confidence in the government's measures following the uprising. The native representatives also took the opportunity to air various grievances. They called for a greater role for Vietnamese soldiers in the colonial armed forces. They also suggested rescinding previous government orders that expelled participants in the 1926–1927 student strikes from school and barred them from the administrative apparatus of the colony (Sûreté report of March 14, 1930, AOM-AP-I, 7F–56). The only resolution that received the support of native representatives had to do with a "rational organization of the defense of Indochina along metropolitan lines" (that is, the reinforcement of metropolitan troops in Indochina). The indigenous representatives subsequently boycotted the meeting en masse. In their absence the French voted for a resolution calling for an extension of the powers of the governor general, granting him the power to decide on capital punishment cases himself without having to obtain the opinion of the metropolitan government in Paris, in order to suppress the current movement quickly (AOM-P-NF, 323–2625). The resolution was subsequently sent to France and received wide coverage in the French press in Indochina.

Bằng elaborated on the sympathy of many native authority figures with the VNP uprising when he recalled his investigation in Phú-Thọ after he returned from the Yên-Báy prison:

> Returning to the Phú-Thọ prison from Yên-Báy, we were imprisoned, this time together, in a large empty hall with hardwood platforms built along the wall. I was questioned again about the assassination of the teacher Kính in neighboring Kinh-Kệ village. This investigation, however, was conducted by a sympathetic Vietnamese provincial judge, Bùi Thiện Căn. After being served tea, I declared having no knowledge of the case, because we had returned from the Hưng-Hoá post not by the village of Kinh-Kệ but by the village of Ngũ-Xã. The native judge whispered to me: "I do not think that much information is [that is, should be] revealed during this investigation. . . . Your declaration does not need to be in depth. I also want to let you know that without my intervention, your house would have been burnt down under the orders of District Chief Ngọc." It turned out that the Lâm-Thao district chief had learned through the complaints of Sơn-Dương villagers that my house had not been burnt down, whereas their houses had been unjustly burned, despite their lack of participation in the uprising.

> *Why had your house been spared?*
> My house had been spared thanks to Canton Chief Con, a nephew of my father's second wife, the husband of my senior mother's younger sister, and at one point my gambling partner. His son had also attended my school. He told my mother: "I am going to point to a neighbor's house and tell the French that it is Bằng's house." What a disaster it would have been if they had burned my four- or five- room house! Initially, I was told, only the houses of the movement participants were burned, but the fire spread quickly because

most houses were constructed of highly flammable thatch. Because of the complaints by villagers, the district chief subsequently ordered the native guards to burn down my house. Mr. Bùi Thiện Căn reportedly scolded the district chief: "The French have burnt down two-thirds of the village. If you order the rest burned, where will people find shelter? You should realize your luck in not being captured and killed the other day. No more such orders!" My house remained intact thanks to this intervention. This judge, like the highest-ranked Vietnamese administrator *(tuần phủ)*, was sympathetic to our cause. When Dương betrayed the party and opened fire, supposedly on Học but actually hitting Chính, he reported that Học had been killed. Mssr. Lê văn Định [the head mandarin, *tuần phủ*] and Bùi Thiện Căn [the provincial judge] scolded Dương: "You are a troublemaker. What is the evidence that Học is dead? Where is his body?" Dương was very upset by this question from these mandarins, both of whom knew French despite their Confucian backgrounds. Only the Lâm-Thao district chief was loyal to the French. Later on, this district chief was relieved of his position and imprisoned for extorting money from local families in the aftermath of the Yên-Báy uprising.

In France itself liberal organizations such as the Human Rights League, leftist politicians, and a large number of Vietnamese residents openly protested against the executions of movement participants and the Cổ-Am bombing (AOM-P-NF, 323–2623; AOM-AP-I, 7F–57). The government of metropolitan France responded to the peaceful May 22, 1930, demonstration in Paris by summarily deporting approximately twenty Vietnamese, mostly students, to Indochina, even though a Paris court had earlier dismissed the government's charges against them. The deportation reinforced the strong critique of the government's Indochina policy by Socialist and Communist National Assembly representatives in their tumultuous debate with cabinet members and conservative representatives on June 13, 1930 (Records of the Chambre des deputés, AOM-P-NF, 267–2328). The government of metropolitan France defended the Cổ-Am bombing by citing the historical precedents of 1912, 1917, and 1920 and their effectiveness in restoring order with minimal cost to the colonial forces. The defense essentially reiterated an argument that the French *résident supérieur* in Tonkin had articulated with a degree of rhetorical excess:

In the attack on armed rebels, did I have to risk the lives of our own men in order to avoid striking a population whose hostility to France had long been confirmed and that had aided the assassins at Vĩnh-Bảo. Instead of an easy success, did I have to risk a failure that could provide encouragement to the rebels recently suffering losses—conditions that would allow them to drag the timid and undecisive masses into their revolt?...

In my reasoning, it was important to inflict on the bandits and those sheltering them a quick and exemplary lesson. I judged that only a punishment capable of terrifying those tempted to participate in the rebellion could totally reassure the sane and peaceful elements of the population regarding our will to defend French sovereignty in that land and to stop the movement cold. (Robin report, 1930:18–19, AOM-P-NF, 323–2626)

...The moral effect of the Cổ-Am bombing was immense [according to all the province chiefs] and sufficient for us to straighten out the serious situation in which we found ourselves. (Ibid.:21)

On the basis of the information available from its Hanoi section, the French Human Rights League raised the issue of the legality and wisdom of burning houses in Sơn-Dương village with the Ministry of Colonies. The league considered the legionnaires' act in Sơn-Dương unjustifiable, noting that the VNP destruction of the district administrative building a few weeks before the burning of the Sơn-Dương houses had been, according to Sơn-Dương village authorities, undertaken by the residents of communities on the other side of the Red River. The league also emphasized that the burning of inhabited houses was punishable with capital punishment under both the Vietnamese and French legal codes. After repeated inquiries by the league, the Ministry of Colonies eventually responded in August 1932 that considerable seditious activity had taken place in the village of Sơn-Dương with the complicity of village notables, and—powerfully illuminating the inequality in the relations between the capitalist core and the colonies— that the Sơn-Dương punishment was just and even humane in a situation where European conceptions of justice would have been misplaced. The letter of response concluded in the same spirit as the *résident supérieur*'s defense of the Cổ-Am bombing: "Any other method would have been considered a sign of weakness...it would have led us not to the destruction of a few thatch houses, but to the use of arms and the sacrifice of a much larger number of people under our protection who might have been drawn into that movement" (AOM-P-NF, 323–2623).

Within the village of Sơn-Dương, residents were shaken by the destruction of their homes and the apparently indiscriminate arrests of their rela-

tives by French forces. According to a favorite student of Bằng's (Lê văn
Tiềm), who had helped copy the propaganda leaflet and who later became
a president of the local Communist Party cell: "A small number of villagers, especially women, cursed the revolutionaries for inviting disaster on
the village. The more knowledgeable people, however, understood that
the loss of their houses meant little compared to the sacrifice of imprisoned and beheaded revolutionaries [from Sơn-Dương]." Bằng also spoke
of people falsely incriminated:

> Many local officials were arbitrarily or mistakenly arrested in those
> days, like my friend the canton chief Côn. Although not initially
> imprisoned with other local officials, Canton Chief Côn was later
> arrested because of the accusation of a distant patrilineal "uncle" of
> mine, the teacher Thẩm. My uncle taught in the neighboring province
> of Sơn-Tây, near the Phú-Thọ town of Việt-Trì. Participating in the
> Lâm-Thao attack, my uncle was wounded but initially not captured.
> After being arrested, my uncle, the teacher Thẩm, suspecting Canton
> Chief Côn of being a French collaborator, maliciously denounced the
> canton chief as a party member to the French. The accusation was
> made purely out of vindictiveness. Canton Chief Côn was imprisoned.
> He ended up with a deportation sentence and died in the Poulo Con-
> dore prison [off the coast of South Vietnam] later on.

On May 26, 1930, Bằng and the Confucian teacher Toại were tried
for the second time at the Phú-Thọ session of the Criminal Commission.
With the exceptions of Toại, Bằng's brother Tăng, and a few activists,
most of defendants attempted to deny some of their acts or to shift responsibility for them by citing coercion and deception by others. According
to a newspaper report at the time, at the Phú-Thọ trial, Bằng admitted
his VNP membership, participation in bomb production, and the recruitment of a number of villagers for the Yên-Báy front at Xứ Nhu's orders.
However, Bằng insisted that because of an eye problem, he had excused
himself from the Hưng-Hoá attack group after participating in the discussion at the teacher Toại's house (*Trung-Bắc-Tân-Văn,* May 28, 1930;
Roubaud 1931:120ff.). Despite this denial, the commission sentenced
Bằng, Toại, and eight others to death, twenty-seven to hard labor for life,
thirty-seven to life deportation, and ten to sentences ranging from deten-
tion in reeducation centers to twenty years of deportation. Bằng's brother
Tăng received a twenty-year deportation sentence for his assistance in the
bomb-production process and for distributing propaganda leaflets. Their

brother Gia was sentenced to life deportation despite his minimal role in the movement. The lack of any substantiating evidence notwithstanding, Bằng's friend, Canton Chief Côn, received the same sentence for purportedly offering a gift of 100 piasters to the teacher Toại, who reportedly refused it. The canton chief's cousin Quyên, the president of the Dụng-Hiền notable council, was also sentenced to life deportation on the basis of accusations by three other defendants that he had contributed 200 piasters to the Vietnamese Nationalist Party. Although French authorities stated that they could not independently confirm his party membership, he still received the sentence for being a part of the plot to "destroy or change the government of Indochina and to incite inhabitants to arm themselves against authority" (AOM-AP-RST, 53–427). A total of eighteen villagers from Sơn-Dương and Dụng-Hiền were convicted by the French Criminal Commission. Six were sentenced to death, nine to hard labor from twenty years to life, and three to deportation. Many local officials were also given shorter sentences in the native court for failing in their duties.

Bằng provided an account of his prison days after the Phú-Thọ trial, including his reaction to the news of the assassination attempt on the party traitor Phạm Thành Dương on May 30, 1930, in Hanoi:

> Returning from the Phú-Thọ trial, those of us with death sentences were kept in solitary cells, with our legs shackled in wooden yokes. However, in those three weeks at Phú-Thọ, we were treated much better than before. By that time the provincial authorities had resumed the management of the prison that had earlier been under the control of the colonial armed forces. French Résident Colas allowed our relatives to make prison visits and to bring in clothes, food, paper, pens, and ink. My wife and other family members visited me quite a few times and brought me food, since the death-row inmates in particular were allowed under Colas's orders to receive food from relatives and, under supervision, to see our close relatives. On the daily trip to the septic tank to empty my toilet bucket, I was also allowed by the prison warden (a fellow Lâm-Thao district native) to chat briefly with some other inmates and to exchange food gifts—gifts that they had also received from their families.
>
> Our main pastimes in those days were writing poetry and letters, both to our relatives at home and to such progressive organizations in France as the Union of Vietnamese, the French-Vietnamese Friendship Association, the Secours Rouge Internationale, and the French Communist Party. Our letters strongly denounced the unjust,

inhuman, and barbarous acts of the French colonialists in Vietnam. With suggestions from all of us, the inmates who were well versed in Sino-Vietnamese literature, especially the Confucian teachers Toại and Điếc, wrote long poems describing the events of our uprising. In our prison poetry was one poem that we planned to recite publicly just before the execution, our "Guillotine Poem," which I still remember very well to this day:

*Một bầu nhiệt huyết bấy lâu nay*
*Tô điểm non sông giọt máu này*
*Kẻ khuất người còn xin chớ ngại*
*Kém thua hơn được cũng từ đây*
*Nợ đời gánh vác, đàn sau đảm*
*Công cuộc gian lao, bước trước chày*
*Kết quả sau này mong lắm tá*
*Suối vàng hưởng được tiếng thơm lây.*

The flame [of patriotism] burns in my heart to the very end,
I am now going to shed blood beautifying the Fatherland,
Don't feel sorry that I must go and you remain,
This sacrifice is simply a test, distinguishing cowards from great men,
It is now yours, the sacred duty to liberate our beloved land,
Success or failure will be in your hands,
Your victory in the future is my hope and my dream,
I want to share it in the golden stream.[2]

The most memorable event of my days in Phú-Thọ prison occurred when the interpreter of the chief of the Tonkin Sûreté informed us one day that a major traitor of the party and a former member of our Central Committee, Squad Leader Dương, had been assassinated on Leather Street (Hàng Da) in Hanoi. (He had been promoted to the position of Sûreté inspector for his betrayal of the party and active collaboration with the Secret Service.) He had attended the Hưng-Hoá school at the same time I did, when his father worked as the Hưng-Hoá school principal, although he was a few classes ahead of me then. When I attended school in Hanoi, I had even paid a visit to his teacher father, who resided in the Hồng-Phúc neighborhood. The father was assassinated by party members [on January 22, 1930] before the son was [on May 30, 1930]. [In reality, the son was only seriously injured, but did not die.] Knowing without much difficulty who was behind

the son's assassination, the French Sûreté chief and his interpreter
came to Phú-Thọ for an investigation among the imprisoned party
members. We learned that Dương's guts were ripped apart by a bullet
that went through his abdomen. We were delighted at the news. And
in mock pity for him and his earlier-assassinated instructor father, we
wrote satirical parallel sentences, supposedly to pay respect to them:
"Pity with a Broken Heart, Oh, the Elderly Teacher in the neighborhood of Phúc, / In pain and Twisted Guts, Oh, the Mandarin Inspector
on the street of Da."

The satirical word play involves the subject in the first part of each
phrase: was it the writer or the assassinated victims who were, in the Vietnamese idiom, so heartbroken and in such pain?

During this prison period, as a teacher fluent in French, Bằng had the
opportunity to engage in a few brief conversations with Résident Colas,
a sympathetic socialist administrator. Centering on the familiar idiom of
a civilizing mission, the encounter highlights the challenge to the French
colonial myth that many members of the French-educated intelligentsia
presented:

French Résident Colas visited the death row inmates [in the Phú-Thọ
prison] one day around five o'clock. Sitting in a small chair under the
arjun tree in front of our building, he ordered the guards to unchain us
and bring us out to a long bench facing him. My two well-educated
comrades Councilor Vĩ and Doctor Đào, who were imprisoned in
Phú-Thọ at the time serving their 1928 sentences, suggested that I
come forward for a discussion with Colas. It was to be a casual conversation to allow Colas to learn more about us:

"Giáo Bằng, you have repaid us with ingratitude. The protectorate government has built schools, hired teachers, and educated you in
the French system. And yet you have repaid us by participating in a
movement that involved the murder of Frenchmen and attempted to
overthrow the government," the French *résident* said with a smile.

"Mr. Résident, I think that deep in your heart you know the truth
despite what you have said," I replied. "It is the French who should be
grateful to us Vietnamese. You couldn't govern this country without
the help of the natives. It is for this reason that you have built the
schools, hired the teachers, and trained the native people. And it is
with our labor and hard-earned tax money, Mr. Résident, that schools
are constructed and teachers are paid!"

"But look at your country before the arrival of the French: there were neither modern buildings, nor modern highways, nor modern means of transportation. Don't you agree that these achievements have been brought about by the French?"

"Sir, the most beautiful buildings are built not for the Vietnamese but for the French; the highways have been constructed for French cars; by the same token, all the modern means of transportation have been introduced because of your own administrative and military needs. The economic development has taken place for the benefit of the French, who adopt a policy of exploiting and enslaving the Vietnamese. In the light of developments in Japan, it is not far-fetched to say that Vietnam would be much better off without French colonialism!"

Smiling and not replying, Colas just said good-bye.

On June 17, Bằng and his three fellow death-row inmates learned of the commutation of the capital punishment sentences they had received in Yên-Báy. (Bằng had been given a second death sentence in Phú-Thọ, however, and that was not commuted at this time.) Early that morning thirteen death-row inmates sentenced at the same tribunal, including party leader Nguyễn Thái Học, were executed by guillotine in Yên-Báy. Later that day Học's fiancée and a key liaison agent committed suicide.

On June 20, Bằng and other Phú-Thọ death-row inmates were brought in chains to the Phú-Thọ railway station for a transfer to Hanoi. In Hanoi, Bằng and the others were initially confined to individual cells in the Hoả-Lò prison (later nicknamed the Hanoi Hilton by American prisoners-of-war). However, within a few weeks, the prison ran out of death-row cells as more and more political prisoners with death sentences were transferred there from other provinces. Bằng was transferred to a large prison hall, where he learned more about the internal party politics on the eve of the uprising. He was also a witness to the continuing debate among VNP ideologues concerning their vision of a postrevolutionary order, a debate that did not merely echo ideological conflicts in the West, but also reflected the tension between the hierarchical model and the collectivist framework in the indigenous communal system:

Probably in August, we were transferred to a nearby and similar hall, where we were joined by several other comrades who had just been sentenced to death at the Hanoi session of the Criminal Commission. All in all, there were about twenty-five of us, chained one by one along two wooden platforms on the two sides of the hall. Because conversation was a main pastime for all of us, I obtained information about many other comrades. I learned for the first time from the new death-row inmates of the debate and conflict within the Central Committee regarding the armed uprising of early 1930. Chairman Nguyễn Thái Học, Xứ Nhu, and numerous others had wanted to organize the uprising immediately, even under difficult circumstances, out of fear that the continued repression and arrests by the French would eliminate the top leadership and destroy the entire party. A few party members had insisted that the uprising be planned only after a long intensive propaganda and recruiting campaign throughout the entire country had awakened the majority of the populace into supporting and participating in the revolution. In the meantime, according to the suggestion of the second faction, the party leaders who were actively hunted should limit their activities to advising other comrades and writing books and propaganda pamphlets in a safe hideout in the mountainous province of Hoà-Bình, where the head native mandarin, Mr. Quách Vỹ, was in considerable sympathy with the movement. I also learned from Độ, a fugitive comrade arrested in China and transferred to the Hanoi prison, that Hồ Chí Minh, upon learning of the planned uprising, had intended to meet Học in Vietnam to advise its postponement but was without success.

This intense debate within the party was not limited to the timing issue but also extended to the question of ideology and postrevolutionary program. During this period in the Hanoi prison, our discussion went on day and night. At times the debate became violent between those favoring communism and collective ownership and those defending nationalism and private enterprise. Nguyễn văn Liên of the former group, a Phú-Thọ native, and Đặng Trần Nghiệp of the latter were the two adversaries most active in the debate. On several occasions their heated arguments were followed by an exchange of flying milk cans or clothing parcels. We had to separate the two and calm them down.

In late 1930 Bằng learned that his second death sentence had been commuted:

One fall night, past midnight, in the death-row hall in the Hanoi prison, I heard distinctly the heavy pounding of the boots of soldiers coming into the prison courtyard. Suspecting that it was our time of execution, I wakened my comrades, who were sleeping shackled on the two sides of the hall. There were about twenty-five of us in this building. "It is the time of our execution," I shouted to my comrades. Given the large number of soldiers, what else could it be but the arrival of the guillotine hour? I was quite sure that my life was coming to an end, given my two death sentences. The light was turned on, the metal gate to the hall was opened, and the soldiers and prison guards came in with handcuffs and heavy chains. As I was located right by the gate, they had to pass by my place before getting to other inmates. Seeing the deputy warden, Cagino, I looked him straight in the eye and pointed at myself in a questioning gesture: "Is it my turn?" He had come to talk to me now and then because of my speaking ability in French. He shook his head, moving on to pick other inmates to take to the guillotine. As my comrades passed by my place on the way to the guillotine, I was truly overcome by a feeling of ecstasy. I felt as if I had been in a dream, an incredible dream. I was choked with emotion. Tears were fast pouring down my face. I lay down on the floor, repeatedly talking to myself: "I am not beheaded. Two death sentences, and I am not beheaded." I then lapsed into a strange and short sleep. When I awoke, other comrades applauded noisily.

Rushing through my mind was my mother's earlier declaration that I would not die. It was such a powerful emotion! I had thought that my execution was certain. I did not believe my mother's statement, made even after my second death sentence, that I would escape capital punishment... I had written to bid my mother farewell.

After realizing my luck with the second clemency, I thought immediately of my senior mother's prescient statement that, despite the two death sentences, I would not be executed. After learning the news of my two death sentences, my senior mother had come to visit me at the Phú-Thọ prison. Seeing me, she broke down in tears: "Don't be afraid. You will not be beheaded. Wherever you go, write me; whatever you need, tell me, and I will send it to you." When her statement was translated into French for the investigator Riner, he laughed: "An escape from death by a convict with two death sentences?" My senior mother emphasized that our family had accumulated a lot of merit through our compassionate Buddhist acts. It was touching for me to learn later that [after seeing me] my senior mother had submitted a petition to request the substitution of one of her own two sons for me at the guillotine, reenacting the story of Tôn Trọng and Tôn Mãng in the folk tradition of China. In the classical opera there was a theatrical performance concerning the case of a stepmother who petitioned the court to execute her own child Tôn Mãng instead of her husband's son Tôn Trọng. Her petition was so moving that the court reconsidered the case and spared Tôn Trọng's life. My senior mother's request was turned down. According to French law, it was a matter of individual responsibility. Her gesture, her sacrifice for me, and her loving care given to my comrades during the preparation of the insurrection will forever live in my heart. My senior mother... she was the only one of her kind in the world. . . .

In retrospect I cannot help finding my secret revolutionary activities in this period laughable and regrettable, because the great task to be undertaken was well beyond my capacity. It was inevitable that the uprising suffered a crushing defeat. First of all, the propaganda, training, and recruiting tasks, which were difficult and complicated, were not carried out with sufficient planning or in the absolute secrecy required. Party organizations in the delta were discovered in large number, partly because of the treason of certain party members. Second, the party leadership was less than fully able and enlightened to lead the revolution to a successful end. Even the critical order to postpone the uprising from Học and Chính arrived too late in my village, as [the VNP vice president] Nhu had already ordered the movement of party members to Yên-Báy. Finally, the population had not been sufficiently "educated" and mobilized... However, the uprising can still be considered a wakening call for the Vietnamese people at large.

On July 26, 1930, before Bằng learned of the commutation of his second sentence, the French governor general had analyzed in a report to the Ministry of Colonies in Paris the reasons why he did not oppose a commutation of Bằng's second sentence:

Nguyễn Đắc Bằng: twenty-one years old, private instructor, born and residing at Sơn-Dương (district of Lâm-Thao). He already received his first death sentence under the March 28, 1930, decree of the Criminal Commission. He was convicted of having (1) joined the Vietnamese Nationalist Party; and (2) been an accomplice to the assassinations committed at Yên-Báy on the night of February 9 by providing arms, scimitars, and bombs for those assassinations.

In my report of April 14, 1930, numbered 30–CS ... I reiterated that Bằng had confessed to having joined VNQDD [VNP], to having had bombs produced at his house, and finally, to having assigned three members of his group to take part in the Yên-Báy attack. I added [in that report] that, although the role of Nguyễn Đắc Bằng was not insignificant, I did not oppose granting him his clemency request.

In accordance with that suggestion, the June 10, 1930, decree [of the French president] commuted Nguyễn Đắc Bằng's March 28 death sentence to that of hard labor for life.

Nguyễn Đắc Bằng received a second death sentence on May 27. He was convicted of (1) having willingly supplied arms (bombs) to armed bands that had attacked and invaded the Hưng-Hoá and Lâm-Thao posts, (2) having gathered and organized these bands, (3) having participated in the Hưng-Hoá event, (4) having fulfilled various duties in the bands that had attacked and invaded the aforementioned posts, and (5) finally, having attempted to assassinate French and indigenous people in the post of Hưng-Hoá at the time of the attack.

He has been denied the privilege of attenuating circumstances.

At the beginning of February 1930, Nguyễn văn Toại, called Đồ [Confucian teacher] Thuý, received an order from the Central Committee to have bombs produced in connection with the planned insurrection. Đồ Thuý knew that Nguyễn Đắc Bằng, a member of the Sơn-Dương cell, owned an isolated house at Cao-Mại [sic!] where one could undertake this clandestine production. Nguyễn Đắc Bằng was consulted, and he readily lent support to the party. Two or three days later, Đồ Thuý and Lý [Mayor] Mai brought to his house about 100 bomb shells, [gun] powder, and all the materials needed for the production of bombs. They notified Bằng that it was necessary to work hard: Xứ Nhu would like to have the bombs ready by February 6 at the latest.

Assisted by his relatives and certain conspirators, Nguyễn Đắc Bằng began the task. As the bombs became available, they were hidden in the rice fields.

On February 6 three parcels containing the bombs and scimitars were sent to Yên-Báy.

On February 9 Bằng attended the gathering at Đồ Thuý's house with a full load of bombs and gasoline. He brought along with him a small group of followers whom he had been assigned to recruit.

Bằng claimed that his role [in the uprising] was limited to his participation in this meeting and the assignment of certain recruits and that, because of an eye problem, he returned to his house after having excused himself from taking part in the attack. Bằng's statements on this point were contradicted by the available information. It has been repeatedly reported that after the departure of the group in charge of the Lâm-Thao attack, Bằng was still with the group that left for Hưng-Hoá a few moments later. Nobody stayed behind. Discipline was extremely strict. No defection could have been tolerated. Đồ Thuý, whose testimony Bằng invoked, actually and formally contradicted Bằng. He affirmed that Bằng complained of an eye problem, but Bằng never expressed any intention to part company with the group. Bằng told him [Đồ Thuý] on the contrary that it would be shameful of him [Bằng] to abandon his comrades at the moment of attack. There is little doubt that Bằng participated in the Hưng-Hoá attack. But even if his exact role during this attack cannot be determined, he must still assume a heavy responsibility: being an active member of the party, he recruited followers. It was at his house that hundreds of bombs were produced. And it was these bombs that were used by the rebels to attack Yên-Báy, Hưng-Hoá, and Lâm-Thao.

Nguyễn Đắc Bằng has received two death sentences, but without clear evidence of his [direct] act of violence, it seems that his clemency request can be granted. (AOM-AP-I, 7F–56)

On November 22, 1930, the teacher Toại of Sơn-Dương village and four other death row inmates convicted in May by the Criminal Commission at Phú-Thọ were led to an open guillotine in the provincial capital of Phú-Thọ. They had arrived by train from the Hanoi central prison the previous day. The executions started at 6:00 a.m. on November 22, and followed one another in quick succession, ending only fifteen minutes later. A few shouted "Long Live the Vietnamese Nationalist Party!" just before being guillotined (Report from Résident Passano of Phú-Thọ to the *résident supérieur*, AOM-A-RST, 53–436).

Bằng was soon sent to the notorious Poulo Condore prison off the coast of South Vietnam. An increasingly large number of VNP and Communist Party members were concentrated in this penal colony in the aftermath of the Yên-Báy and ICP-organized Nghệ-Tĩnh movements, the latter of which involved half a million Vietnamese in twenty-five provinces (see Luong 1985). In late April 1931, approximately 100 political prisoners from both parties and over 400 other convicts were herded onto the steamship *La Martinière* for a thirty-five-day journey to French Guiana in South America. They joined a small number of Vietnamese prisoners who had been sent there in 1922 for having participated in the 1917 anti-French uprising in Thái-Nguyên (north Vietnam). In this sparsely populated French colony, the French National Assembly had, in May 1930, created a special territory called Inini. They hoped to open up the vast hinterland for exploitation and to pull the colony out of a serious recession that had resulted from the collapse of the world market for many Guianese forest product exports (Ballof 1979:3–5). Three special prison camps were set up in the interior for Vietnamese convicts to expand the reach of French capitalism. A group of 523 prisoners arrived in the French Guiana capital of Cayenne on June 3, 1931, including Bằng and three other native sons of Sơn-Dương.

Back in the village of Sơn-Dương, the French continued repressing incipient resistance to their colonial order. Bằng's former favorite student Tiềm, later the first president of the Communist Party cell in Sơn-Dương, was briefly detained because he had written a ballad on Sơn-Dương history describing in positive terms the VNP uprising and the destruction of the house of a corrupt Lâm-Thao district chief. The colonial administration also closely monitored and even banned voluntary village organizations in many parts of the country in order to hinder anticolonial activities (Ngô-Vĩnh-Long 1978b: 546–562). These efforts by the colonial government further suggest that local tradition could provide organizational resources for revolutionary activities.

Community members attempted to rebuild their lives after the devastating French repression. Many villagers whose sons and husbands had been sent as prisoners to various corners of the French empire lived in great anguish. Desperate to reconstruct their familial social world, a few dozen households, including Bằng's own family, turned to Catholicism. They hoped that the French Catholic priests could exert their influence on the colonial administration to gain the release of family members. The ranks of Catholics in the province of Phú-Thọ swelled to 42,000 by the early 1940s, comprising a remarkably high 14 percent of the native population (Cao-Tiến-Phùng et al. 1985:158).

Out of desperation quite a few family members of political prisoners wrote the French authorities letters that took extreme liberties with the facts. A letter from Bằng's senior mother on behalf of her youngest son Tăng, officially a juvenile at the time of the Yên-Báy uprising, is still available in the French colonial archival records (AOM-AP-I, 9–206):

Sơn-Dương, August 1934
The Governor General of French Indochina
His Excellency:
…I have a son by the name of Nguyễn Doãn Tăng. At the time of the revolutionary movement, he was a sixth-grade student at the Franco-

Vietnamese school in Hưng-Hoá. On the twelfth day of the first lunar month [in 1930], with 12 piasters from me, he went to the provincial capital to buy books and school materials. Passing through the Lâm-Thao district seat, he saw revolutionary troops in retreat and, despite his youth, ended up being arrested by accident by the mandarins. He was tortured numerous times, although he did not know anything. Suspected of having participated in the revolutionary movement, he was sentenced to twenty years in a correctional camp. I have appealed to the authorities many times without success. I learn that His Excellency has recently assumed the post of governor general.

Would His Excellency reconsider the case for the sake of justice and humanity so that this old woman may be reunited with her son and supported [in her old age] ? I will be forever grateful to His Excellency.

Mai thị Luân

In November 1935 the French Catholic priest in Hưng-Hoá also wrote a letter on Tăng's behalf (AOM-AP-I, 9–206). However, it was not until the rise to power of the leftist Popular Front in France in 1936 that Bằng's two brothers, together with many other political prisoners, were paroled. The parolees were not allowed to leave their native villages and were required to report periodically to the district government. The better-educated, junior brother, Tăng, taught briefly at a private school in Sơn-Dương. In an attempt to co-opt the better educated among the former political prisoners, the colonial authorities assisted them in searching for steady white-collar employment both within and outside of the colonial administrative apparatus. Tăng worked at the French *résident*'s office and subsequently for the provincial land survey, while his elder brother Gia became a partner in a retail outlet for the French alcohol monopoly in Cẩm-Khê district.[3] The co-optation attempt was not totally successful. Despite his French administrative employment, toward the end of World War II, Bằng's brother Tăng resumed his political activities in the Vietminh front in the provincial capital of Phú-Thọ.

The French efforts at co-optation and the severe penalties for political activism did not succeed in completely extinguishing the flame of Vietnamese anticolonialism. For many activists, including Bằng and his brother Tăng, prison experiences eventually strengthened their resolve to continue their resistance, notwithstanding the probable severe penalties and, considering earlier failures, the apparently small odds for success. Although the opportunistic conversion of many Sơn-Dương villagers to Catholicism can be analyzed in terms of a narrow calculus of material costs and benefits, the behavior of those hardened political activists cannot be explained within the framework of logical choice. Their strengthened anticolonial resolve contributed to the meteoric rise of the Indochinese Communist Party, which, against serious odds, eventually triumphed in the cause of both national independence and socioeconomic revolution.

PART II

# The Revolution in the Village

CHAPTER 4

# The Rise of Marxist Power

On September 2, 1945, to a tumultuous crowd of half a million Vietnamese in Hanoi as well as to the nation and the world at large, Hồ Chí Minh declared the formation of the Democratic Republic of Vietnam:

> "We hold truths that all men are created equal, that they are endowed by their Creator with certain unalienable Rights, among these are Life, Liberty, and the pursuit of Happiness."
>
> This immortal statement is extracted from the Declaration of Independence of the United States of America in 1776. Understood in the broader sense, this means: "All peoples on the earth are born equal; every person has the right to live to be happy and free."
>
> The Declaration of Human and Civic Rights proclaimed by the French Revolution in 1791 likewise propounds: "Every man is born equal and enjoys free and equal rights."
>
> These are undeniable truths.
>
> Yet during and throughout the last eighty years the French imperialists, abusing the principles of "freedom, equality and fraternity," have violated the integrity of our ancestral land and oppressed our countrymen. Their deeds run counter to the ideals of humanity and justice.
>
> In the political field, they have denied us every freedom. They have enforced upon us inhuman laws. They have set up three different political regimes in northern, central and southern Vietnam (Tonkin, Annam, and Cochinchina) in an attempt to disrupt our national, historical and ethnical unity.
>
> They have built more prisons than schools. They have callously ill-treated our fellow compatriots. They have drowned our revolutions in blood.

They have sought to stifle public opinion and pursued a policy of obscurantism on the largest scale; they have forced upon us alcohol and opium in order to weaken our race.

In the economic field, they have shamelessly exploited our people, driven them into the worst misery and mercilessly plundered our country.

They have ruthlessly appropriated our rice fields, mines, forests and raw materials. They have arrogated to themselves the privilege of issuing banknotes, and monopolized all our external commerce. They have imposed hundreds of unjustifiable taxes, and reduced our countrymen, especially the peasants and petty tradesmen, to extreme poverty.

They have prevented the development of native capital enterprises; they have exploited our workers in the most barbarous manner.

In the autumn of 1940, when the Japanese fascists, in order to fight the Allies, invaded Indochina and set up new bases of war, the French imperialists surrendered on bended knees and handed over our country to the invaders.

Subsequently, under the joint French and Japanese yoke, our people were literally bled white. The consequences were dire in the extreme. From Quảng-Trị up to the north, two millions of our countrymen died from starvation during the first months of this year.

On March 9th, 1945, the Japanese disarmed the French troops. Again the French either fled or surrendered unconditionally. Thus, in no way have they proved capable of "protecting" us; on the contrary, within five years they have twice sold our country to the Japanese....

In fact, since the autumn of 1940, our country ceased to be a French colony and became a Japanese possession.

After the Japanese surrender, our people, as a whole, rose up and proclaimed their sovereignty and founded the Democratic Republic of Vietnam.

The truth is that we have wrung back our independence from Japanese hands and not from the French....

For these reasons, we, the members of the Provisional Government of the Democratic Republic of Vietnam, solemnly declare to the world:

"Vietnam has the right to be free and independent and, in fact, has become free and independent. The people of Vietnam decide to mobilize all their spiritual and material forces and to sacrifice their lives and property in order to safeguard their right of Liberty and Independence." (reprinted in Porter 1981:28–30)

Hồ Chí Minh's independence speech bears a striking resemblance to the proclamation of the Vietnamese Nationalist Party on the eve of the Yên-Báy uprising fifteen years earlier. Both demonstrate the large degree to which the Western axiomatic emphasis on civil rights (liberty and equality) shaped the discursive practices of a new generation of Vietnamese revolutionary leaders, even though, as earlier noted, this occurred within the native sociocultural logic that redefined these terms primarily as collective rights of the Vietnamese in relation to their colonial masters. More important, both Hồ's speech and the VNP proclamation of 1930 appealed to the native population through evocative symbols of unity in a national framework and the fundamental right to socioeconomic welfare within a collective whole. They attempted to respond to both the nationalist aspirations and the concrete needs of the native population. Reflecting historical contingencies and the indigenous political culture, Hồ also emphasized how the French had lost their mandate as "protector" through their subservience to Japan and their partial responsibility for the death of up to two million Vietnamese.

Hồ Chí Minh's declaration of independence in 1945 marked the rise to power of the previously underground Indochinese Communist Party and a major turning point in Vietnamese history. The declaration had been preceded by the seizure of administrative power in August by the Marxist-led Vietminh movement in virtually all Vietnamese provinces, including the province of Phú-Thọ.[1] In the ensuing armed conflict with the French (1946–1954), the Vietminh would strengthen its legitimacy as a party of national independence and gain the allegiance of Vietnamese from all walks of life, including a large segment of the French-educated elite. Furthermore, in the name of national solidarity and building on the reformist sentiment among many members of the Western-educated intelligentsia, the local Vietminh leadership would launch subtle attacks on certain ceremonial manifestations of the class-oriented and male-centered world view.

## The Underground Resistance

The success of the Indochinese Communist Party and the Vietminh movement in 1945 was no small feat, for in both Phú-Thọ and the neighboring provinces of Vĩnh-Yên and Phúc-Yên ICP membership totaled only eighty at the time of the seizure of administrative power in August 1945 (Cao-Tiến-Phùng et al. 1985:112). In the entire district of Lâm-Thao, Party membership seems to have been restricted to Sơn-Dương's neighboring village of Kinh-Kệ. In fact, the ICP did not establish its first cell in the province of Phú-Thọ until 1939 (Cao-văn-Lượng 1960:143).[2]

However, from its inception the ICP had succeeded in building and, after each repression, resiliently rebuilding numerous mass organizations as recruitment channels for the Party and bases for its activities. In accordance with the ICP emphasis on a nationalist and anti-imperialist struggle and its policy of broadened class alliance in the 1939–1945 period—a policy formulated under Hồ Chí Minh's influence—ICP cadres in Phú-Thọ in 1939 began organizing "anti-imperialist" associations *(hội phản đế)*. By late 1940 these organizations had approximately 200 members in seventeen localities in Phú-Thọ (Vĩnh-Phú 1971:28). They operated under the guidance of the provincial ICP membership, whose five cells in Phú-Thọ at this point had nineteen members (ibid.). Following the Japanese invasion of Indochina in September 1940 and Hồ Chí Minh's formation of the Vietminh (Việt Nam Độc Lập Đồng Minh Hội, or Vietnam Independence Alliance League) in May 1941, these associations were transformed into "national salvation" *(cứu quốc)* associations in October 1941.[3]

The ICP's Vietminh mass organization strategy touched the Sơn-Dương area for the first time when a national salvation association was formed in the village of Kinh-Kệ in the fall of 1941 (Lê-văn-Thụ 1973:163). This strategy aimed at identifying the ICP and its associations with the nationalist aspirations of the indigenous population and the concrete needs of the working classes in particular. Depending on the conditions in particular localities, the local associations organized protests against the Japanese coercive purchase of rice at fixed low prices and their requirement of jute cultivation in lieu of secondary food crops,[4] against the draft of young men into the colonial armed forces and the coercive recruitment of laborers for the construction of military facilities (for instance, roads, the Phú-Thọ and Nội-Bài airfields, and armament factories and warehouses), as well as against French and Japanese imperialism in general.

The Vietminh-led protest campaigns increased the visibility of the Vietminh as a rallying point for disaffected people in many localities. However, these campaigns also attracted the attention of the colonial regime to the mass organizations and drastically increased the risk of a French suppression. In Phú-Thọ, for example, four Party members and thirty-seven association members were arrested and tortured in a November 25, 1941, crackdown. Many suspects were required to report periodically to the local colonial authorities (Cao-văn-Lượng 1960:144). As a result, ICP-affiliated organizations survived only in Kinh-Kệ and six other localities in the entire province, and the coordination among them became difficult (Cao-Tiến-Phùng et al. 1985:75; Lê-văn-Thụ 1973:163).

However, the ICP possessed remarkable organizational resiliency— clearly more than that of the VNP and other political groups. In 1942, the Vietminh's national salvation associations in Phú-Thọ rebounded. Communist Party cadres even succeeded in establishing new national salvation associations in such industrial enterprises as the tea cooperative plant and the bullet factory (Lê-Tượng and Vũ-Kim-Biên 1981:164). In the village of Kinh-Kệ, national salvation membership increased from five to forty-three between December 1941 and September 1943.

At this juncture the Vietminh began its organizational efforts in Sơn-Dương with the activities of a student from a middle-peasant family, Bùi Kim Lĩnh. One of Lĩnh's early recruits, a Sơn-Dương student and the son of a Guiana-exiled VNP activist, briefly related Lĩnh's conversion to the revolutionary cause:

> Lĩnh studied at one point at the Thăng-Long school in Hanoi [where the well-known Vietnamese military strategist Võ Nguyên Giáp had taught in the 1930s]. Among his teachers was the elderly Thục, who possessed a strong revolutionary spirit. Through his teaching, Mr. Thục succeeded in heightening the political consciousness of many of his students, Lĩnh among them. Receiving special guidance, he returned to Sơn-Dương at a time when [Vietminh] cadres were also making efforts to raise the political awareness of people in this area [that is, in Kinh-Kệ village].

In regular consultation with the Vietminh leaders in Kinh-Kệ, Lĩnh began to explore the possibility of organizing a national salvation association in his native village, based on a Vietminh motto "investigate, propagandize, train, organize, and [lead to] struggle" (Sơn-Dương 1987; Lê-văn-Thụ 1973:164). In the investigation phase a Vietminh activist would target poor young peasants and family members of executed or imprisoned Vietnamese Nationalist Party members (Lê-văn-Thụ 1973:164). Informal and individual discussions would then be held with prospective political activists on local, national, and international issues, particularly the high cost of living and the protest movements against the draft, the corvée, and high taxes. In Sơn-Dương Lĩnh also transmitted ballads critical of gambling and large expensive village ceremonies, which were reminiscent of the VNP leader's critical comments regarding the large funerals in Nguyễn Đắc Bằng's household in the late 1920s.

Progressive elements would be recruited, trained, and organized into three-member Vietminh cells, each composed of an established member and two new recruits (Sơn-Dương 1987; Lê-văn-Thụ 1973:165). They would be taught covert-operation methods and how to deal with the enemy when under arrest, and then they were assigned, among other activities, the task of leaflet distribution. In this manner Vietminh activities spread from Kinh-Kệ not only to Sơn-Dương, Bản-Nguyên, and other villages in Lâm-Thao district, but also to other communities in Thanh-Thuỷ and Tam-Nông on the other side of the Red River.

Once organizational momentum was achieved, struggles against foreign capitalists began flaring up in certain localities. In Đoan-Hùng district in May 1942 peasants under Vietminh guidance successfully demanded a rent reduction and the return of appropriated land from a French plantation owner. In the same year workers at the Việt-Trì paper factory successfully demanded overtime pay, a wage increase, paid holidays, and protection against wartime inflation through the purchase of such basic commodities as rice and cloth at fixed prices (Cao-Tiến-Phùng et al. 1985:76).

In a by-now familiar pattern, French suppression quickly followed these campaigns, resulting in the arrest of almost all the provincial Party leaders (Lê-Tượng and Vũ-Kim-Biên 1981:165). On October 2, 1943, the repression reached the villages of Kinh-Kệ and Sơn-Dương, and one ICP member and seven national salvation association members were arrested. The top Vietminh organizer in Sơn-Dương, Lĩnh, was arrested together with two recruits on information provided by a previously imprisoned VNP activist (the executed Confucian teacher Toại's younger brother) and another recruit (Sơn-Dương 1987:16). Four other Vietminh recruits in Sơn-Dương were arrested within a few days (ibid.:17).[5] Bằng's cousin Tế, a landless laborer, talked about his life and his brief assistance to Lĩnh in Sơn-Dương during this period:

> In the early 1940s, after six years in the village of Vĩnh-Lại, my job as an annual live-in worker was terminated. I returned to Sơn-Dương to live with my mother. I went to work as a seasonally employed laborer (from the third to the eighth lunar month every year) for the wives of [the late] Canton Chief Chi. No longer receiving any payment in kind as in the earlier position, I was fed and paid 15 piasters a month.

> *How much did paddy cost in those days?*
> Paddy cost about 30 piasters a quintal [100 kilograms].During this period as a seasonally employed laborer, I became well acquainted

with Brother Lĩnh in the village. On one occasion, without dwelling on the reason, Brother Lĩnh asked me to accompany him to Kinh-Kệ and then asked me to serve as a sentry for a meeting once we got there. One day a number of Kinh-Kệ villagers were arrested. On learning of this development, I hurried to see Lĩnh to make inquiries, only to be entrusted with a stack of printed materials, including a map, books, and magazines with the hammer-and-sickle emblem. I knew that Mr. Kiều Hiển, a student at the Thăng-Long school in Hanoi, had recently brought back to the village a huge stack of propaganda leaflets. Moving the entrusted materials from one corner of the house to another for hiding, I eventually decided to burn them out of concern about being arrested. I was scared because I had earlier witnessed the torture of Mr. Kiều Hiển by the authorities.

Another Sơn-Dương native, Lê văn Tiềm, Bằng's favorite student, who had assisted him with leaflet printing in 1930 and who later became the president of the Sơn-Dương Communist Party branch, spoke of his teaching background and his peripheral activities in the incipient Vietminh organization of Sơn-Dương:

After obtaining the Certificat d'Études Primaires at the age of eighteen and working as a private tutor in neighboring Phùng-Nguyên village for three years, I managed to obtain an official teaching position. I taught for eight years in the village of Quỳnh-Lâm, approximately 6 or 7 kilometers from Sơn-Dương. In the early 1940s, in a switch with me, a native of that village who taught in the village of Ngũ-Xã neighboring on Sơn-Dương requested a transfer back to his native village.

In 1942, soon after my assumption of the Ngũ-Xã teaching post, Bùi Kim Lĩnh, a former student of mine, recruited me into the local Vietminh organization. I was the first recruit. Vietminh activities in Sơn-Dương at the time were limited mainly to building up the local organization to a dozen members so that activities could begin. Other Vietminh members in Sơn-Dương secretly distributed anti-French leaflets from time to time. However, the activity was limited in scale, as villagers had whispered concerns about attracting French attention.

Less than a year after I became a Vietminh member, Lĩnh was arrested. I escaped imprisonment only because Lĩnh refused to reveal the local Vietminh membership. However, with a revolutionary spirit not yet too strong and being concerned about my family's livelihood at the time, I became inactive.

Thanks to the discipline of Lĩnh and other arrested activists under torture, the Vietminh organizations in both Sơn-Dương and Kinh-Kệ were protected. Lĩnh was given a three-year sentence and died in the central prison of Hanoi in August 1944. The momentum of the organization in Sơn-Dương slowed down considerably when the mayors of Sơn-Dương and the tiny village of Thuy-Sơn (later a part of Sơn-Dương) were removed from office for not reporting on Vietminh activities and one of the two informants was appointed deputy mayor. A number of activists and sympathizers either fled to other villages or, like the teacher Tiềm, became immobilized out of concern about future arrests. With the repression of the early 1930s obviously still vivid in the mind of many villagers, the crackdown in 1943 temporarily halted overt anticolonial activities.

In contrast, in neighboring Kinh-Kệ, where ICP members were protected by village authorities, the development of the Vietminh organization went forward. The village became the coordinating point for anticolonial resistance in the entire province. The Vietminh membership in Kinh-Kệ (est. pop. 850) increased from forty-three in September 1943 to eighty-seven in early 1945 (Lê-văn-Thụ 1973:165). Under Vietminh influence the village became increasingly defiant toward the colonial authorities, refusing to pay taxes in 1944.[6] Visiting cadres from Kinh-Kệ reestablished contacts with Vietminh organizations in Đoan-Hùng, Phù-Ninh, and Tam-Nông districts. They succeeded in recruiting into national salvation associations young students, soldiers, and even civil servants in provincial offices such as the court, the French *résident*'s office, the treasury, the post office, the geographical survey, and the ammunition warehouse (Cao-Tiến-Phùng et al. 1985:76–77; Cao-văn-Lượng 1960:145, 153). In Kinh-Kệ on January 7, 1945, 300 Vietminh members from four districts (Lâm-Thao, Thanh-Sơn, Thanh-Thuỷ, and Cẩm-Khê), including those from the village of Sơn-Dương, were exhorted to mobilize local populations at the appropriate moment chosen on the basis of particular local conditions in order to widen the Vietminh's appeal. As a sign of the intensified preparation for the anticipated conflict, a self-defense militia team was organized in Kinh-Kệ after the January 7, 1945, meeting in order to provide support for future mass struggles.

The Vietminh gained further momentum when the Japanese overthrew the French colonial administration in Vietnam on March 9, 1945, and proceeded to become very unpopular with their continued tax collection and coercive rice purchases despite the poor fall crop of 1944. Famine spread throughout north Vietnam, including the village of Sơn-Dương. This catastrophe was estimated to have claimed from half a million to two million lives in northern Vietnam. Despite the smaller magnitude of the famine in the province of Phú-Thọ compared with other locations, one of the three mass graves of famine victims in the provincial capital contained more than 500 bodies (Lê-Tượng and Vũ-Kim-Biên 1981:172). In Sơn-Dương the Japanese removal of approximately 100 tonnes of paddy led to a famine among numerous poor peasant families. Although the famine was alleviated to a certain extent by large paddy loans from the wealthiest villager, the wife of the former canton chief Chi, almost ten families left their native village in search of food, and three or four villagers reportedly died (Sơn-Dương 1987:17). The landless cultivator Tế reported on his struggle for survival at this critical time:

> In 1945, because of the scarcity of rice, my family had to mix
> banana-tree bulbs with steamed cereal in order to fill our stomachs.
> To increase our food supply, I had to carry ashes to the mountainous
> region of Thanh-Sơn on the other side of the Red River to exchange
> for manioc—two baskets of ashes for a three-liter basket of manioc. I
> even had to collect discarded lichee seeds, which we cooked, peeled,
> and pounded in order to add flavor to the manioc used as a rice substi-
> tute in soup. Even so, I considered my family fortunate because many
> people starved to death in the area.

The Vietminh accordingly intensified the campaign to denounce the Japanese and their collaborators and launched a movement to seize public rice stocks in response to the concrete needs of poor peasants. They also formed guerrilla units in preparation for local insurrections and for the seizure of district and provincial administrations as soon as conditions turned favorable (Lê-Tượng and Vũ-Kim-Biên 1981:166).

Throughout the spring and summer of 1945, either orally or in leaflets, Vietminh cadres denounced the Japanese and their Vietnamese collaborators at large gatherings such as the Hùng King shrine festival in Lâm-Thao district; certain periodic local markets in Thanh-Thuỷ, Tam-Nông, and Lâm-Thao; and even at a pro-Japanese youth gathering in the provincial capital in August (ibid.: 167; Cao-Tiến-Phùng et al. 1985:89; Cao-văn-Lượng 1960:150).[7] Starting in May 1945, Vietminh cadres in Phú-Thọ also mobilized the poor to seize rice stocks in various locations and to resist tax collection by the pro-Japanese government: "Keep the rice! Destroy the enemy's granaries! No need to pay taxes on our land. Do not tolerate the theft of our rice! Fellow countrymen, join the Vietminh!" (Lê-Tượng and Vũ-Kim-Biên 1981:166). In Lâm-Thao district, from their Kinh-Kệ village stronghold, Vietminh cadres led peasants to seize rice stocks in the villages of Bản-Nguyên, Thạch-Sơn, and Tiên-Kiên as well as in the town of Hưng-Hoá on the other side of the Red River (Lê-văn-Thụ 1973:169). Large meetings were convened in Thanh-Sơn and Thanh-Thuỷ districts in May to exhort the local populace to prepare for an uprising (Cao-Tiến-Phùng et al. 1985:90).

The growing intensity and success of the Vietminh-organized activi-ties increased the significance of the Vietminh as a rallying point for the local population. After the Japanese coup in March, a small number of Vietminh members in Sơn-Dương, together with scores of other activists from the rest of the province, were sent to the Hiền-Lương guerrilla base in Hạ-Hoà district for training.[8]

The Japanese made numerous efforts to repress the movement. In the village of Kinh-Kệ, where the Vietminh leadership was planning a large regional meeting for early May, the Japanese, with the collaboration of informers, arrested twenty-four activists (Lê-văn-Thụ 1973: 170). In the provincial capital, the Japanese arrested and tortured twenty-four young activists in June in order to crack down on the distribution of tax protest leaflets and the covert financial and arms-purchasing activities of the Viet-minh. However, Vietminh strength was solid enough that this repression, although it briefly disrupted Vietminh activities, did not succeed in dis-placing the Vietminh organizations in either place for long.

In July and August, in order to expand their guerrilla forces in the province, the Vietminh made several seizures of arms from lightly guarded administrative posts (such as Phù-Ninh on July 30, Hạ-Hoà on August 2, Đoan-Hùng on August 8, Thanh-Sơn on August 11, Thanh-Thuỷ on August 15, and Lâm-Thao on August 17). The self-defense unit of Kinh-Kệ village participated in the last two events in coordination with its counterparts from three villages of Thanh-Thuỷ and four other villages of Lâm-Thao.[9] The Vietminh even succeeded in enlisting the support of the provincial security forces in preparation for the seizure of administrative power (Cao-văn-Lượng 1960:155–156).[10]

After the Japanese unconditional surrender on August 15, mostly through mass demonstrations supported by armed guerrillas and village self-defense forces, the Vietminh officially took over district administra-tions in Phù-Ninh (August 15); Cẩm-Khê, Đoan-Hùng, and Thanh-Ba (August 17); Tam-Nông and Yên-Lập (August 18); Hạc-Trì and Lâm-

Thao (August 20); and Thanh-Thuỷ (August 22). One district chief joined the Vietminh (in Hạ-Hoà), two surrendered (in Lâm-Thao and Phù-Ninh), another was assassinated (in Thanh-Thuỷ), and others abandoned their posts for refuge in the countryside.

Many Sơn-Dương villagers participated in the demonstration that culminated in the transfer of the Lâm-Thao administration to the Vietminh, although quite a few participants were less than fully aware of the nature of their action, as is clear in the account of the landless laborer Tế:

> In August 1945, when the area was flooded because of a broken dike,
> I saw a large gathering of people with flags in the fields preparing
> to leave for the district seat. Not understanding politics and simply
> looking for fun, I asked to join them and heard a few speeches in the
> district seat. It was [during this demonstration] that the Vietminh took
> over the administration of Lâm-Thao.

Riding the wave of success in various Phú-Thọ districts and taking advantage of the highly symbolic seizure of administrative power in Hanoi on August 19, on August 21 the Vietminh delivered an ultimatum to the Japanese authority in Phú-Thọ demanding the disarmament of Japanese troops, the transfer of the provincial administration, and several other items.[11] On August 22, armed guerrillas and peasants marched from across the province to the provincial capital of Phú-Thọ in order to exert indirect pressure on the Japanese and pro-Japanese Vietnamese officials. Despite some complications and tense negotiations, on August 25 the pro-Japanese provincial administration officially transferred power to the Vietminh.[12] On the same day, under pressure, Emperor Bảo-Đại in the puppet Huế court abdicated, and in the village of Sơn-Dương, under the guidance of the Lâm-Thao district Vietminh leadership, a new village administration, called the People's Provisional Revolutionary Committee, was established. The colonial era formally came to an end when Hồ Chí Minh declared the formation of the Democratic Republic of Vietnam in Hanoi on September 2, 1945.

## The War of National Liberation

From a historical perspective, the seizure of administrative power represented only the first in a series of victories for the Vietminh. For nine years challenges would come not only from outside forces in the international arena, but also from a minority of the indigenous population who would collaborate with foreigners, both Chinese and French, in their opposition to the Marxist-led Vietminh. In response, the Vietminh would rely heavily upon their legitimacy as the first government of national independence and would skillfully combine the reformist and activist traditions represented by Phan Bội Châu and Phan Chu Trinh in the earlier generation of anti-colonial leaders. Historical events in both the village of Sơn-Dương and the country at large would be shaped by the violent encounter between the forces of capitalist imperialism and the growing momentum of a national-ist Marxist movement.

In north Vietnam the first major challenge came with the arrival of approximately 150,000 anticommunist Chinese troops in September 1945 under an Allied agreement to disarm the 30,000-strong Japanese army.[13] Following the Chinese troops came a challenge from Vietnamese carpet-baggers: Vietnamese Nationalist Party remnants and other anticommunist politicians returning from exile in China. By this time the VNP had been reduced to a relatively small contingent. They no longer had a base among the peasants and workers in the country, and their socialist cause had been shed in the search for power under the shadow of Chinese troops. A more serious challenge, however, was the French attempt to reincorporate Indo-china into their colonial empire and the ensuing Franco-Vietminh war from 1946 to 1954.

In the province of Phú-Thọ anticommunist Chinese troops occupied the two major towns of Phú-Thọ and Việt-Trì. An official Communist Party source claims that they also connived with, if not actively supported, the VNP in its attacks on the Vietminh forces in these two towns in November and December 1945 (Cao-Tiến-Phùng et al. 1985:119).[14] The VNP occu-pation of Việt-Trì and its presence in Phú-Thọ lasted until June 1946 in a local modus vivendi. This understanding stemmed from Hồ Chí Minh's efforts from October 1945 onward, in preparation for a possibly protracted conflict with the French, to find a peaceful end to the Chinese occupation and to include the indigenous opposition in a new national coalition gov-ernment.[15] In the village of Sơn-Dương the Vietminh-VNP conflict had lit-tle bearing on the support of the local population for the Vietminh, despite the flight of the two Franco-Japanese-era informers on Vietminh activities and the later "elimination" of these two individuals by the Vietminh (Sơn-Dương 1987:16). The banner of nationalist socialism in Sơn-Dương had long been captured by the Vietminh owing to a decade-long absence of VNP activities in the community, the activism of local Vietminh cadres in response to the nationalist aspirations and concrete needs of the local population, and the legitimacy of Hồ Chí Minh's government as the first national independence government in almost a century.

In the spring of 1946 Chinese forces gradually withdrew from Vietnam in accordance with a February 28, 1946, Franco-Chinese agreement in which the French would return to northern Vietnam as replacements for the Chinese troops.[16] In an atmosphere of worsening relations between the Vietminh on the one hand, and the VNP and allied parties on the other, the withdrawing Chinese troops were quickly followed by many anticommunist VNP and allied party leaders. In June 1946 the Vietminh mobilized 3,000 troops to attack VNP armed forces in the towns of Phú-Thọ and Việt-Trì and succeeded in driving the troublesome VNP opposition permanently out of the province (Cao-Tiến-Phùng et al. 1985:135; Hoàng-văn-Đạo 1970:400, 403–406).

The conflict with the VNP notwithstanding, the Vietminh theme of national unity and Hồ's ideologically powerful declaration of independence captured the hearts and minds of virtually all Vietnamese. The Vietminh had reinforced the theme of national unity in November 1945, when it *formally* dissolved the ICP in a tactical move, despite the Party's continuing behind-the-scene operations. No less significant were its well-polished mass organizational skills, its ability to co-opt traditionally influential Vietnamese, and its involvement of local populations in the cause of "national salvation" and socioeconomic reforms. In late 1945 the Sơn-Dương village administration organized young activists into *cứu quốc* (national salvation) associations (youth, peasant, and women's) under the umbrella of the village Vietminh organization. In early 1946, as the need arose for a broader coalition and wider participation by all progressive elements in preparation for possibly protracted struggle with the French, additional *cứu quốc* associations (Catholic and Buddhist) were formed in the village as a part of the larger Liên Việt (Viet Alliance) front. Although membership figures are not available, these associations, together with the association of combatants' mothers formed soon after the outbreak of the Franco-Vietminh war, seem to have involved virtually all adult villagers.

Influential villagers were co-opted to serve as leaders either within the *cứu quốc* associations or in the village, district, and provincial administrations. The political activist Tăng, Bằng's brother and a roommate of the first chairman of the Vietminh provincial administration, reportedly became the director of the provincial economic office and later on the head of military supplies for the provincial defense police *(cảnh vệ)* battalion in 1946. Despite his lack of formal Communist Party or Vietminh affiliation, Bằng's former student Lê văn Tiềm, himself a teacher, was drafted to become the vice chairman of the People's Provisional Revolutionary Committee (deputy district chief) in Lâm-Thao and later to fill the position of president in the local Communist Party cell:

> It was by accident that my activity in the movement resumed in August 1945. At the time, I was seeking refuge in the Lâm-Thao district seat since the area was flooded. The Red River dike had been broken. On the evening of my arrival, I joined the crowd as the Vietminh took over the district seat. They drafted me to serve as vice chairman [deputy district chief] of the People's Provisional Revolutionary Committee in Lâm-Thao district, under Mr. Trần Quốc Sảng of Thạch-Sơn village, because they found me a competent person of integrity. I was nominated despite my lack of desire for the position.
>
> One of my main tasks as vice chairman was to take charge of dike repair from Phú-Thọ to Việt-Trì. I informed prospective contractors and subsequently supervised the work of the one chosen to ensure a high quality of the work. The other major task involved judicial duties because there was no court at the time. Wherever I went, people listened to my reasoning. They respected me as a teacher, and local problems got solved quickly. I was well liked at the local level.
>
> *Did you and the committee encounter any major insoluble problems in those days?*
> I do not recall any. All the litigations got resolved. I did well as vice chairman, thanks to my prestige in the district as a teacher.
>
> *Was there any opposition to the Vietminh?*
> Fortunately, it became inactive, although we also had to assure them that there would be no recriminations.

The first president of the People's Provisional Revolutionary Committee in Sơn-Dương was also a Sino-Vietnamese teacher and a former mayor. He was succeeded by three French-trained teachers from privileged backgrounds. Among the successful and Vietminh-supported candidates for the village people's council in 1946 was the third-wealthiest villager, the wife of the late mayor Ân. Similarly, *cứu quốc* associations in the village were led by well-educated, progressive villagers from the more privileged social strata. In other words, in mobilizing the local population, the Vietminh relied heavily on the respect for education in the indigenous sociocultural framework. However, in order to broaden their bases through *cứu quốc* associations, they also sought to include women and peasants in public activities. In the 1946 elections to the National Assembly, the provincial people's committee, and the village people's committee, women could, for the first time, participate in official political activities. The broad-based membership of both the Vietminh front and local governmental bodies dramatically increased the participation of Sơn-Dương villagers in the search for solutions to major short- and long-term problems both within the village and beyond.

In search of solutions to short-term problems, the new Vietminh government made powerful appeals to Sơn-Dương villagers for unity and national salvation. In the face of persistent hunger caused by the August flooding in the district, the village administration and *cứu quốc* associations mobilized well-off families to donate rice to other villagers, organized the population to repair the damaged dike system, and encouraged peasants to assist one another in planting fast-growing secondary staple crops in order to replace the lost rice harvest. Starvation was averted as the local food supply in the fall of 1945 reportedly increased by 150 tonnes over the preceding year (Sơn-Dương 1987). The national government also canceled poll, market, and ferry taxes (Cao-Tiến-Phùng et al. 1985:124). Villagers responded enthusiastically to the appeals of the new national government for donations to the "Independence Fund," "National Defense Fund," and "Gold Week" in order to finance basic administrative operations and the expansion of the armed forces for the cause of national independence. Well-off villagers donated money to arm the new thirty-man self-defense force in Sơn-Dương at the same time that a provincial defense police force *(cảnh vệ)* was created. Although Sơn-Dương's population amounted to less than 0.4 percent of the 500,000 inhabitants in Phú-Thọ and Vĩnh-Yên, Gold Week donations from Sơn-Dương in the fall of 1945 totaled 0.5 kilogram of gold and 1 kilogram of silver, amounting to one-third of gold donations from Lâm-Thao district and a significant 2 percent of the gold donations from the two provinces (cf. Cao-Tiến-Phùng et al. 1985:125; Sơn-Dương 1987:21; Phong-Châu 1989: 52).

In the name of national salvation, the *cứu quốc* youth association and the village administration in Sơn-Dương also launched campaigns to increase the physical activities of young villagers, to raise the literacy level of community members, and to eradicate such problems as gambling, theft, and superstitious practices among certain quarters of the local population. With the slogan "Be Strong for the Fatherland," *cứu quốc* activists organized sports teams and daily soccer practices in order to channel the physical energy of Sơn-Dương youth during the slack seasons. Responding to

Hồ Chí Minh's nationwide appeal to "destroy illiteracy as an enemy," the Sơn-Dương village administration and the local *cứu quốc* youth association launched a literacy campaign that employed not simply ideological exhortation ("It is patriotic to become literate") and social pressure (invitations by beating drums at specific households), but also indirect negative sanctions (conducting literacy tests at the village gate to embarrass less eager villagers). Within a year the movement had expanded from a single class in the communal meeting hall to fifty classes with a total of 1,250 students, including women and the elderly. This enrollment amounted to 2.4 percent of the total provincial literacy enrollment (53,324), even though Sơn-Dương comprised only 0.6 percent of the Phú-Thọ population of 290,000. By the end of 1946, 70 percent of illiterate villagers had been certified as having passed the literacy tests (Sơn-Dương 1987:22). In addition, with popular support, the village administration adopted strong measures to eradicate gambling, theft, and "superstitious" practices. Gamblers were forced to attend funeral processions for their playing cards and to publicly shout "down with gambling." Second-time theft offenders were required to hang stolen objects (for example, cucumbers or fruit) from their necks and march in procession through the village. Shamans had to report to the communal meeting hall, where they were firmly asked to destroy their altars and to abandon their practices.

Young *cứu quốc* activists also took a leading role in instituting major long-term reforms, although this occasionally triggered acrimonious debates within the community. In order to forge a greater sense of unity and to overcome territorial parochialism, the local Vietminh front, under the leadership of modern-educated young activists, pushed the hitherto separate villages of Sơn-Dương, Dụng-Hiền, and Thuy-Sơn to organize a joint worship of their identical village-guardian deities. The administrative divisions also broke down, as they were subsequently merged into one village. For the cause of stronger communal unity within an egalitarian framework, local young activists attempted to undermine the class-oriented, male-exclusive institution of communal house feasts through public criticisms and satirical ballads. With input from the district-level Communist Party leadership, this reform campaign started with young activists' critique of the unegalitarian tradition of food distribution according to which higher-ranked male villagers received the more honored portions of sacrificial animals (for example, the cockscomb was distributed to the highest-ranked notable), lower-ranked male villagers had to crowd onto a lower communal house platform around fewer food trays, and in Dụng-Hiền, villagers without titles simply could not participate. Later demands were made for the abolition of the feasting system altogether and for the division of communal land among the poor families in the village (cf. Hunt 1982:153). In response to a question on opposition to the reform processes, a major village leader at the time reported:

> Under the general guidance of Party authorities and with the agreement of other villagers, we also distributed communal land to landless cultivators. Through discussion in the district seat among village representatives, we decided to mobilize people to simplify such ceremonies as funerals and weddings and to scale down wasteful village feasts. We did not encounter any opposition even from the former notables, because they did not dare to raise any objections to such widely supported ideas in public meetings.

In the name of national salvation, the Vietminh's reform campaign eventually emerged triumphant over century-old institutions, although not without a cost to village harmony. The first president of the People's Revolutionary Committee, a former Sino-Vietnamese teacher and a mayor during the colonial period, resigned in protest. In fact, a total of four villagers, all teachers, succeeded one another in this office within a sixteen-month period (Sơn-Dương 1987:25–26).[17] Still, the hierarchical model was gradually weakened in favor of collective welfare. The relative success of the local Vietminh front in its equality-oriented reform campaign may have been facilitated by the three universal suffrage elections of 1946, in which voting rights were no longer restricted to men of wealth and education and in one of which a woman (the third wealthiest villager in Sơn-Dương) was elected as a Vietminh candidate. The themes of unity and national salvation and the Vietminh's organizational successes reinforced each other. They not only laid the groundwork for the formation of a local Communist Party branch in Sơn-Dương, but also enhanced the legitimacy of the Vietminh in preparation for the protracted Franco-Vietminh war, during which the support of local populations would prove critical for the success of the Vietminh's guerrilla warfare strategy.

French troops returned to north Vietnam in March 1946 under the provisions of a Sino-French agreement. Relations between the French on the one hand, and the vast majority of the Vietnamese population and the Vietminh on the other, were unusually tense, despite numerous negotiation sessions between the two sides throughout 1946.[18] The First Indochina War broke out on December 19, 1946, when Hồ Chí Minh issued a call to the people, urging them to join the national resistance against the French following French provocations in Hải-Phòng, Lạng-Sơn, and Hanoi in November and December:

> For the sake of peace, we have made concessions [to the French]. But the more conciliatory we are, the more aggressive the French colonialists become. They are determined to reconquer our country. No! We would rather sacrifice everything. We are determined not to lose our country and not to be enslaved. Dear compatriots, we must rise up. Male and female, old and young, regardless of religion, political party, ethnicity, all Vietnamese must rise up to fight French colonialists and to save the fatherland. Those with guns will fight with guns. Those with swords will fight with swords." Those without swords will fight with picks, shovels, and sticks. Everybody must do his or her best to oppose colonialism and to save the country! (Cao-Tiến-Phùng et al. 1985:144)

Like the Aid-the-King proclamation that King Hàm Nghi issued six decades earlier as he fled from the capital, Hồ's call for resistance against foreign invaders struck a deep emotional chord among the indigenous population. As Vietminh forces launched counterattacks on French troops in Hanoi and other towns in North Vietnam, Hồ's government and the Vietminh military command withdrew gradually toward the base of resistance in the mountainous area of Thái-Nguyên, Bắc-Cạn, and Tuyên-Quang in order to lead the resistance against the French attempt to reestablish a colonial system. The Vietminh also dispersed equipment and supplies among resistance bases. Quite a few printing plants, major warehouses, and a military hospital were moved to the province of Phú-Thọ (Cao-Tiến-Phùng et al. 1985:177).

During the first phase of the resistance (1947–1950), in order to slow down technologically superior French troops while building up their own forces, the Vietminh relied on a "scorched earth" tactic, a strengthened rural defense system, and a strategy of guerrilla warfare. The Vietminh destroyed roads, bridges, and rail lines; created obstacles to the movement of the French navy and paratroopers; and, to eliminate facilities for French garrisons, burned barracks and large buildings in provincial towns, including Phú-Thọ, Hưng-Hoá, and Việt-Trì in the province of Phú-Thọ. Within a year, according to Vietnamese sources, the Vietminh had heavily damaged 530 kilometers of roads and 2,585 buildings in Phú-Thọ and the neighboring provinces of Vĩnh-Yên and Phúc-Yên (Cao-Tiến-Phùng et al. 1985:182). As defensive measures in the large area under their control in Phú-Thọ, the Vietminh strengthened village defenses with elaborate systems of hedges and trenches, organized the hiding of food, launched a "three noes" policy among the rural population (hear nothing, see nothing, and know nothing in response to questions from strangers), as well as temporarily dispersing the population (ibid.: 191–194). In the village of Sơn-Dương, besides a thirty-man self-defense squad, two militia squads were formed of female and elderly volunteers. Gates were erected at the entrances to even small alleys, and trenches five feet deep were dug throughout the village (Sơn-Dương 1987:38). By 1948 the village had also trained a competent village guerrilla platoon. The training was sufficiently good so that during the period from 1947 to 1950, eighty Sơn-Dương villagers joined the regular Vietminh forces *(bộ đội)*. Donations were solicited, partly through the association of combatants' mothers *(hội mẹ chiến sĩ)*, in order to provide food and purchase weapons for both local guerrillas and regular soldiers. The wife of the late mayor Ân donated a few *mẫu* of rice fields for the village guerrillas to cultivate their food supply. Thanks to strong popular support, the provincial regular forces increased to one battalion (approximately 300 soldiers), not counting companies at the district level (Cao-Tiến-Phùng et al. 1985:161–164).

The first phase of the Franco-Vietminh war (1947–1950) was highly reminiscent of the first war of resistance against the French in the late nineteenth century: the Vietminh relied primarily on guerrilla warfare to disrupt the logistics of the French in the latter's offensive campaigns in Phú-Thọ and elsewhere. In contrast, the French attempted to take maximum advantage of their tactical mobility and superior fire power. In Phú-Thọ, the two sides clashed for the first time in May 1947, when 600 French paratroopers landed in Phú-Thọ and Việt-Trì. They damaged the Vietminh forces in both towns but withdrew within five days under the constant harassment of Vietminh guerrillas.

The real test of the Vietminh guerrilla warfare strategy came in the fall of 1947, when the French launched a major campaign, with 12,000 troops, in an attack on the Vietminh headquarters in the mountains. The colonial forces hoped to destroy the Vietminh quickly by capturing the Vietminh government and military command and heavily damaging the Vietminh's regular army in the process. On the western front of this campaign, the French occupied the strategic town of Việt-Trì and, in October 1947, moved their troops to Tuyên-Quang along the Clear River (Sông Lô) (Phạm-Gia-Đức 1986:160–190). In conjunction with this major offensive, the French swept through the districts of Thanh-Sơn, Thanh-Thuỷ, and Yên-Lập in southeastern Phú-Thọ (Cao-Tiến-Phùng et al. 1985:185–189).

The Phú-Thọ campaign was aimed at disrupting a major line of communication between central Vietnam and the Vietminh headquarters in the northern mountains (through the midland provinces of Hoà-Bình and Phú-Thọ). After successfully taking a number of target towns in the provinces of Bắc-Cạn and Thái-Nguyên with limited Vietminh resistance, French troops faced insurmountable logistical problems in the mountainous area of northern Vietnam, where Vietminh guerrillas constantly harassed them in a pattern reminiscent of the nineteenth-century resistance. Because of the adept use of guerrilla warfare and the grassroots support for the Vietminh, within two months the French had to withdraw their troops without achieving their objectives. Their illusion of a quick and easy reconquest of northern Vietnam was shattered.

Over the next three years, the French launched numerous military campaigns in the province of Phú-Thọ. These had four basic objectives: to hold on to the occupied territory as a source of manpower and food supply, to damage the Vietminh economic and military buildups, to strengthen the defense of the ethnic Mường province of Hoà-Bình and the Red River delta, and to disrupt Vietminh communications with north central Vietnam. In November 1948 the French launched a paratroop attack on the strategic town of Việt-Trì, which they were able to hold for the next six years. After a 1,500-soldier campaign in the districts west of the Red River (Thanh-Sơn, Thanh-Thuỷ, Tam-Nông, and Cẩm-Khê) in February 1949, the French launched a 2,600-troop operation two months later into the more economically important eastern districts (Hạc-Trì, Lâm-Thao, Phù-Ninh, and Đoan-Hùng) in order to damage an important Vietminh economic base, seize the Vietminh regional command, and destroy part of the Vietminh regular forces. French forces swept through the area of Sơn-Dương in both of these operations, and on both occasions the village guerrilla unit laid ambushes for the French troops. The first involved coordination with the provincial forces and reportedly resulted in two French and one Vietminh casualty in the rice fields of Kinh-Kệ village (Sơn-Dương 1987:39). In the second operation, in April 1949, the French did not engage Sơn-Dương's guerrilla force and quickly retreated after seizing ten cattle and burning one house (Sơn-Dương 1987:40). The elderly and children of Sơn-Dương village subsequently moved to safer areas in Thanh-Ba and Phù-Ninh districts.

Although they were unable to expand their control into much of the province, by early 1950 the French had set up pro-French administrations in thirty-one villages in the southeastern districts (Thanh-Sơn, Thanh-Thuỷ, Tam-Nông, and Hạc-Trì) and were able to exert significant influence on forty-four others, either arresting or forcing into the underground ICP members as well as Vietminh guerrillas and cadres in these localities (Cao-Tiến-Phùng et al. 1985:206, 208). In these villages the French also instituted a draft and recruited heavily among native Catholics for local intelligence and administrative services. However, the French presence in southeastern Phú-Thọ and occasional military forays into the area had no direct impact on village life in Sơn-Dương and the local support for the Vietminh, as a village leader at the time reported:

> In defense the village was well protected with a strengthened bamboo hedge and fortified gates that once closed were simply impenetrable. The French conducted two or three mop-up operations through this area during that time, once even doing a house-to-house search in the village [in August 1950]. During this search, I had to hide under the water lentils in a village pond.

*Were you informed by villagers at the ferry landing point in Bản-Nguyên of incoming French operations?*
We got sufficient warning from the skittish French soldiers themselves, who fired noisily into the air when approaching the village. Armed with only a few guns, local guerrillas might also follow the French firing with a few more shots to give additional escape warnings to one another. Our communication network did not exist then. However, the French did not really disrupt village activities since they seldom spent more than a few hours here. Area markets were held less frequently in those years, but Sơn-Dương did not specialize in marketing activities. As an agricultural village, we simply resumed our work in the fields after their departure.

Despite these French operations, villagers maintained their full confidence in the Party and the Vietminh. Supported by their families, Party cadres worked willingly without any salary in those days. When we needed men for the armed forces, villagers volunteered without any complaint. The number of volunteers always exceeded the quota from higher authorities. When regular armed Vietminh units passed through Sơn-Dương, villagers donated food. Whenever the district or local administration needed financial contributions, as we levied no taxes at the time, we simply asked for assistance from well-off families, especially from the third wealthiest villager, the most generous and enthusiastic Mrs. Ái Ân [mother of Ái and the wife of the late mayor Ân]. These families would contribute anything from rice to the sizable sum of a few hundred piasters. Support was widespread, from both the rich and the poor. We held large public meetings where the Party members in attendance easily reached one hundred, just like at a public festival, without any need to be concerned about security.

With the strong support of local populations and by means of guerrilla warfare as well as the occasional deployment of the newly formed regular forces, the Vietminh succeeded in inflicting casualties upon the French, at times heavy casualties, thus containing the effects of the French "pacification" campaign and politically destabilizing the area under temporary French control. In order to further complicate the logistics for the French in the southeastern districts, a partial trade embargo was imposed with a prohibition on rice, corn, and cattle exports to the area under French control.[19] Prefiguring the guerrilla warfare in the South Vietnam of the late 1950s and 1960s, the provincial Vietminh leadership also organized armed underground propaganda and assassination teams in occupied territory; they assassinated 67 pro-French local officials and arrested 255 others in fifty hamlets in the period from December 1949 to March 1950 (Cao-Tiến-Phùng et al. 1985:210). These small-scale offensives were occasionally combined with the use of the Vietminh regular forces, as during the April 1949 campaign, when the Vietminh mobilized one regiment and six battalions to eliminate almost one-third of the French attack troops (ibid.:197). This pattern of armed activities partially succeeded in limiting French influence to the southeastern districts and at times returned control of communities to the Vietminh.

Throughout this period, as well as through the second phase of the Franco-Vietminh war (1951–1954), the village of Sơn-Dương lent solid political and military support to the Vietminh and remained firmly under Vietminh control. The firm support for the Vietminh in Sơn-Dương and the general success of the guerrilla strategy in the province of Phú-Thọ were intimately linked to the in-depth organizational efforts of the Vietnimh and more generally to their successful mobilization of the population through nationalist appeals and reforms of political economy. Bằng's cousin Tế, the landless laborer, discussed his life during the first two years of Vietminh power and the reason for his decision to join the local regular Vietminh forces:

After the revolutionary forces had seized power, I joined the village self-defense unit and became a squad leader in 1946. I also eventually managed to get married around this time, in early 1947, at the age of twenty-seven. The marriage was certainly quite late because of our poverty. Our fortune improved slightly because my wife brought to our family 1.2 *sào* of rice fields and my mother also received an inheritance of 1.8 *sào* from my maternal grandmother. However, I still had to work for an additional year after my marriage as a live-in laborer, because I had to pay off the wedding debts and also because we had a total of only 3 *sào* in those days. The wedding costs had been substantial, including a bride price of 40 or 50 piasters plus a wedding banquet. Despite the contributions from relatives at the banquet, I still had to borrow to pay for half of the expenses. I repaid the debts with my income from another year's work as a laborer.

In late 1947 I volunteered for the regular army because my wife could take care of my mother at home then. Although I was the only son of my parents, I volunteered for the armed forces anyway out of the desire to end the oppression by foreigners. The citizen of a conquered country suffers many miseries.

*How did your mother and wife react to your decision?*
Inspired by patriotism, they were quite supportive, albeit not without some concern for my safety.

One year I was assigned to cut the telephone line on the other side of the river in the Hưng-Hoá area. I was also instructed to wait in an alluvial soil area after completing the task for transportation across the river. But after finishing the assignment, I waited for almost the entire night without seeing anybody. Getting scared at the approach of morning and running out of other solutions, I decided to cut down three banana trees and tie the trunks together with the telephone wire, and I also made sure to bring along a roll of telephone wire as evidence of my successful completion of the assigned task. Knowing neither how to swim nor how to navigate, I ended up being swept away by the current and only reached the other side at Bản-Nguyên. Boiling with anger, I decided to skip my company command and reported at the battalion headquarters. Putting down the telephone wire, I told the battalion commander: "I am quitting the army now to return to my home village!" They inquired, and I told them: "Yesterday, they [the company command] assigned me to cut the telephone wire on the other side of the river. However, they failed to pick me up as promised and abandoned me to the mercy of the enemy patrol. My mother had only one son. If I die, it will be the end of the line! I am not going to stay in the army!" The battalion commander asked me to stay on there and sent a representative to my company to ask whether all the company's soldiers were present. The company commander [reportedly] replied: "Yes, except for those on vacation and on assignment." A specific inquiry was made about me, and he reported that I had left for assignment only earlier in the day! The battalion officer retorted: "You lie! Having completed your assignment last night, he is now with the battalion! How could you take him to the other side of the river for the assignment and abandon him there?" The battalion commander consoled me and allowed me to stay with them for three days before returning me to the company.

After that event, I returned and fought alongside my fellow soldiers. In those days, I was quite brave, and at times even foolhardy. Once, during a reconnaissance mission of the enemy's mop-up operation in Cao-Mại [Lâm-Thao district seat], I saw a black enemy soldier fall asleep with his machine gun next to him. I made the offer to my squad leader to snatch the machine gun. He prevented me from doing that out of concern for my life. After two battles with the French forces, in recognition of my bravery, I was admitted as an official member of the Party. That was in 1948. Despite the occasional confrontation with French troops, I managed to take literacy classes during my four years as a soldier, finishing the equivalent of three grades and learning how to do calculations.

Around 1947, Bằng's politically conscious brother Tăng was transferred to the supplies department of the Vietminh's military medical services. Bằng's nephew by his elder half-sister, who had grown up in a wealthy family, discussed the context in which he, too, had joined the Vietminh armed forces:

I joined the People's Army in 1949, when the Vietminh came to our class to urge us to make our contributions [to the cause of anticolonial resistance]. Teacher and students, we all went. We all felt strongly about the cause of national independence. I was sent to China for training as an officer candidate. As soldiers, we had no shoes, wore latania leaf hats, received no salaries, and walked all the way to China.

Upon inquiry regarding her participation in the local guerrilla force, the elderly Thành explained:

No, I did not participate in the guerrilla forces, because I only knew
how to work the soil and provide for my family. However, my
younger brother, at that point still single, volunteered for the armed
forces. Determined to join, he did not dare to tell me. Although
he saw me when I went around searching for him, he did not even
respond to my call. He returned three years later and got married at
my suggestion.

In the first phase of the Franco-Vietminh war, the village of Sơn-
Dương sent eighty of its own sons to the Vietminh regular forces. Villagers responded enthusiastically to the Vietminh's call to arms, even though
their own tangible benefits were negligible or nothing (cf. Popkin 1979).
They also made voluntary contributions amounting to 15 tonnes of rice
and over one million piasters in resistance bonds in the 1946–1950 phase
of the resistance alone (Sơn-Dương 1987:38).

In the village of Sơn-Dương, in order to strengthen mass support in
the context of guerrilla warfare and the trade embargo by the French, the
Vietminh began initial steps toward greater economic self-sufficiency
and improving the long-term economic well-being of the peasant masses.
Toward the goal of self-sufficiency, the village administration encouraged the growth of cotton and the development of a cottage textile industry to meet the needs of the population and the growing armed forces in
the Vietminh area. Cotton was consequently grown on approximately a
dozen *mẫu* of Sơn-Dương land; 60 percent of village households spun
thread, and 15 percent of the households engaged in weaving with over
100 looms.

More significant were the long-term efforts to improve the welfare of
the peasants and to strengthen their support in the long war of resistance.
Enacting the government's July 1949 land decree, the Sơn-Dương village
administration officially lowered the land rent by 25 percent to 37.5 percent of the crop and abolished secondary rents (gifts to landlords at New
Year's and other occasions).[20] It also sold communal land to poor peasant
households with less than half a *mẫu* of rice fields and in 1949, under the
guidance of the new local Party branch, formed one of the seven experimental agricultural cooperatives in the province (Cao-Tiến-Phùng et al.
1985:247). In May 1950 the Vietminh government took further steps in the
collectivist direction by decreeing an upper limit of 18 percent interest on
cash loans and 20 percent on loans in kind as well as the abolition of peasants' pre-1945 loans and loans for which the interest payments had doubled

the principal (Hoàng-Ước 1968:67). Although the cooperative experiment
failed within two years because of internal conflict regarding the use of
cooperative resources and the distribution of the crop yield (Sơn-Dương
1987:33–34), the limited socioeconomic reforms of the 1947–1950 period
generally improved the well-being of lower-strata Sơn-Dương villagers
and strengthened their support for the Vietminh in the prolonged conflict
with the French.[21]

In the province of Phú-Thọ, the Communist Party apparatus expanded
rapidly at the local level after the outbreak of the war, probably in an
attempt to provide a stronger and potentially independent local leadership,
given the context of guerrilla warfare and a possible disruption of communication with higher authorities. Sixteen Sơn-Dương villagers were
recruited in the second half of 1947 into a joint seventy-member Party
branch dominated by members of neighboring Ngũ-Xã village. In 1948
a separate Sơn-Dương branch was formed when Sơn-Dương was recon-
stituted as an independent administrative unit and renamed Việt-Cường
(Strong Viet). The recruitment was aimed at all prospective contributors
to the cause of national salvation regardless of their class backgrounds, as
related by the teacher Lê văn Tiềm, president of the Sơn-Dương Party cell
from 1948 to 1950:

> Despite my success in the district administration, I did not continue as
> a vice chairman beyond the [two-year] term because of a conflict with
> Party members in Kinh-Kệ village. Because I had not become a Party
> member, they wanted me to follow their advice on numerous issues.
> I was considered junior to them in terms of revolutionary knowledge
> and experience. I refused to continue on for a second term in the
> administration despite their draft. It was because of this conflict that I
> was not admitted into the Party organization at the district level.
>
> I returned to Sơn-Dương, where we were supported by our daugh-
> ter from her weaving job, and I joined the village administrative
> council, though I declined the invitation to become chairman. I was
> among the first admitted into the [separate] Sơn-Dương Party orga-
> nization in August 1948—an organization that had earlier been a
> part of the Ngũ-Xã Party cell. I had not been invited to join the Party
> earlier because, given my prestige as the teacher in Ngũ-Xã and with
> my network of pupils and their parents, I would have become Party
> secretary. Ngũ-Xã Party members did not want to lose the position to
> a member from another village. Throughout the years, the people of
> that village were more concerned about village positions than about

education. That was why only one Ngũ-Xã villager obtained the Certificat d'Études Primaires.

In December 1948 I became the Sơn-Dương Party secretary. Party membership expanded rapidly in the village under my leadership. Under the guidance of higher Party authorities and on the basis of the gender equality principle, we recruited a number of active female villagers, like Mrs. Cảnh [the first wife of Tăng, Bằng's half-brother], who later became the secretary of the Party's women's cell. However, the top Party leaders were all male, because, if nothing else, being encumbered by children and family obligations, female members could not deal flexibly with wartime conditions and could not quickly escape from the French if necessary.

In retrospect, the expansion was not conducted with sufficient attention to the Party's criteria of membership, because we did not have a firm understanding of those [class background] criteria. We did not understand well the Party authorities' suggestion of targeting poor and landless peasants for Party membership. Out of poverty and the lack of both education and good public speaking skills, many members of these social strata did not at all aspire to become Party members. In contrast, former notables all wished to join the Party, but we selected only the few who could make the best contributions to our cause. Like we invited the wife of [the late] Mayor Ân, who had contributed generously to the revolutionary cause, to join the Party. She declined, citing her old age and her prayer sessions at the pagoda.

The three members of the modern-educated intelligentsia still in the village, those with the Certificat d'Études Primaires like myself, all became Party members because, with our prestige, our advice to other villagers was frequently followed. Similarly, many teachers were also recruited into the Party because of their education, their speaking skills, and the prestige that they commanded as members of the teaching profession. I can recall only a few cases of teachers who were not invited to join the Party: one because of his competitive and argumentative style of interaction and two others because of their distance from other villagers.

In those days we simply recruited the most active, energetic, and hardworking villagers, including certain former notables. The only restriction was that present and former members of other parties could not be admitted without the approval of higher authorities. Whatever background people might have, once admitted into the Party, they were devoted and conscientious members. Whatever class-based ideological differences there might be, they seldom mattered because even those former notables among Party members contributed significantly to Party activities.

Communication with higher authorities in general was limited. Meetings were convened in the district seat on the average once every quarter for the Party guidelines to be transmitted and for us to report on local conditions. The guidelines were usually quite general. As a result, we simply did our best at the local level. With some luck, the local implementation would conform to the Party policy. Without luck, we might err. District Party leaders were understanding, because our errors arose not out of bad will but out of enthusiasm.

It has to be said that nobody in the Party had a good understanding of class analysis in those days, myself included. I did my best at leading introductory-level discussions among Party members on Marxism, dialectics, and historical materialism from what I learned in district-level Party meetings. The understanding, however, was not in depth.

Under Tiềm's leadership and with quarterly membership targets from higher authorities, by October 1950 Party membership in Sơn-Dương had quickly expanded to 143, including 23 women. The Communist Party membership in Lâm-Thao district also increased from 2 in January 1946 to 1,160 in March 1949, while that in the province of Phú-Thọ increased from 36 in January 1946, to 130 by the end of that year, and to approximately 16,000 by the end of 1949 (Cao-Tiến-Phùng et al. 1985:112, 138, 147, 210, 237; Phong-Châu 1989: 56, 58, 71). The local expansion paralleled the increase in national Party membership: from 5,000 in 1945 to approximately 700,000 in 1950 (White 1983:193).

Within the framework of national salvation and in a radical departure from tradition, a fairly large number of Party members were recruited among the more dedicated activists from landless and poor peasant backgrounds in the mass organizations and in the guerrilla campaigns. However, thirteen former mayors, deputy mayors, and landlords with progressive attitudes and significant local influence were also admitted in this recruitment drive (Sơn-Dương 1987:30). The percentage of Party members from landlord, rich, and upper-middle peasant families well exceeded 46 percent. In general, the Communist Party and the Vietminh leadership in Sơn-Dương were more committed to national liberation than to the logic of class conflict within the Vietnamese social formation. Their ranks were dominated by young male activists, generally from privileged backgrounds; they carried out limited village reforms in order to strengthen the war of anticolonial resistance rather than out of a full understanding of dialectical materialism. With only limited communication from the national and provincial Party leadership, the local Party apparatus provided direct policy guidance for the Sơn-Dương village administration and mass organizations.

Because of a combination of national and international developments, the course of the Marxist-led national independence struggle and socioeconomic transformation took a sharp turn after the third national Party congress in January 1950. In the international arena, the nature of the Franco-Vietminh conflict became submerged in the international Cold War. Mao's triumph in China in October 1949 had reinforced U.S. concern regarding the spread of communism. As the Vietminh received increasing military aid from China, the United States intervened more forcefully with direct financial and logistical support for France to defeat the "communist" Vietminh movement.[22] By 1954 U.S. aid had increased to cover 78 percent of the cost of the war to the French side. Within Vietnam, under U.S. pressure the French granted the Bảo-Đại government (1948–1955) limited autonomy in order to compete with the Vietminh on nationalist appeals.

The Vietminh socioeconomic policy also became increasingly class-oriented. With its expanded armed forces and the need for regular revenues in order to sustain the war effort, the Vietminh reintroduced land taxes with a progressive tax schedule in 1951. Taxes varied from 6 to 10 percent for poor peasants to 30 to 50 percent for large landholders, with a tax surcharge of 25 percent on land rent (Hoàng-Ước 1968:70ff.). Large landholders resorted to various evasive measures: cultivating the land directly with hired labor, reducing or even eliminating the official land rent in exchange for covert rent payments or free labor, selling less fertile land at depressed prices, and dispersing holdings through bequests to children or other relatives (ibid.:70–81). Many landholders in Sơn-Dương divided up their properties as a result of the Vietminh land tax structure in the 1951–1954 period. Within the Party, under the December 1951 directive of the Central Committee of the officially reemerging Communist Party (now called the Vietnamese Workers' Party), the local Sơn-Dương Party branch launched a critical self-examination campaign in 1952–1953. It expelled fifteen members for not having a sufficiently clear understanding of class and for not fulfilling their Party obligations with sufficient devotion (cf. White 1983:193). Twenty-four other Party members were expelled for a variety of reasons in minor purges from December 1950 onward, resulting in a decline in Party membership from 131 in the fall of 1950 to 91 in 1953.[23] In September 1952 the local Vietminh front conformed to Party-imposed quotas in its slate of candidates for the village council: landless, poor, and lower-middle peasants made up two-thirds of the Vietminh-endorsed candidates; Party members and women, respectively one-third and one-sixth of the endorsed and elected candidates to the council. Although these class-oriented moves undoubtedly caused some anxiety among the upper strata of the village, they further consolidated support for the Party among the peasant masses and contributed to the recruitment of soldiers for the Vietminh's offensive military strategy in the second stage of the war (1950–1954).

On the battlefield the Vietminh, reinforced by Chinese supplies, began launching more conventional attacks on French posts along the Vietnam-China border in 1950, routing the French troops in Cao-Bằng and Lạng-Sơn in September 1950. According to Vietnamese sources, 8,000 troops in the French colonial forces, mostly African and European, were killed, wounded, or captured in this campaign, together with 3,000 tonnes of ammunition and military supplies (Phúc-Khánh and Đinh-Lục 1986:143). As a result of this serious defeat and the strong Vietminh counterattack in Phú-Thọ, the French withdrew from minor posts in the province in order to consolidate their positions in Hạ-Nông and Việt-Trì. At the same time, however, the French launched occasional large search-and-destroy operations as well as more regular air attacks and ground bombardment of Vietminh positions in the province, especially in late 1951 and in 1953 (Cao-Tiến-Phùng et al. 1985:219). Toward the end of the war, in 1953, commando teams were sent in to destroy Vietminh economic and military installations.

The village of Sơn-Dương was part of this military conflict. In late August 1950, for example, the French launched a ten-day, 2,000-troop campaign, called Chrisalide, into Lâm-Thao, Thanh-Ba, and Hạ-Hoà districts. Although they encountered strong resistance and suffering 160 casualties, the French apparently inflicted heavy damages with their reported policy of killing all, burning all, and destroying all (Cao-Tiến-Phùng et al. 1985:217–218). In Sơn-Dương a French force swept through part of the village, arrested twelve villagers, and shot one. They withdrew, however, after meeting strong protest against their rape attempts, before they got to an ambush set up by the Sơn-Dương guerrillas (Sơn-Dương 1987:40). Sơn-Dương suffered most heavily during the indiscriminate bombing and terror campaign of 1951—it was bombed once in April, twice in May, and once in December—during which seventy-eight houses were destroyed, the communal meeting house was partly damaged, and over thirty civilian villagers died (Sơn-Dương 1987:44). Tế, formerly a landless laborer, then a soldier, described the situation after the heaviest bombing on May 23, 1951:

> In 1951 the village was bombed a few times. Particularly horrible was the May 23 napalm bombing. It was spring harvest time in the village. Since my company was stationed in [nearby] Son Vi village at the time, I requested a quick visit to the village, only to see many deaths. The village had built an extensive system of trenches, which were unfortunately full of water [from the rain]. As a result, many villagers had not taken advantage of the trenches and bomb shelters during the bombing. I bought a wounded cow for my company and had to ask for a ten-day leave to take care of my family, since my house had been burnt down. During my leave, [there were so many corpses that] I had to bury relatives even at night. Being unable to locate their whole bodies, we buried only their intestines, which we found on trees in their gardens. We even found in our yard the head of a neighbor whose body could not be found. Many villagers also died from profuse bleeding from not-so-serious wounds because of the lack of medication and bandages. The scene and the smell of death were so horrible that after burying two or three villagers on the same day, I could no longer swallow food.... When I left the village at the end of my leave, I worried quite a bit about the members of my family, because we had not been able to rebuild our house, and they had to stay in the pagoda temporarily. Later that year I was granted a release from military service. I returned home. However, because of my well-known bravery as a soldier, I was drafted by the village in 1952 to command the village guerrillas for two years.

Fortunately for the Sơn-Dương villagers, the bombings of 1951 caused the last direct destruction that the village suffered in the Franco-Vietnamese war. Although the French launched the Lorraine operation in October 1952, the biggest French operation of the entire eight-year conflict, Sơn-Dương escaped damage.[24]

Despite casualties, Sơn-Dương managed to fulfill its fiscal and manpower obligations toward the state. It sent the provincial government 150 tons of paddy in 1951, the first year of Vietminh land taxes, to support the growing Vietminh armed forces. The taxes amounted to an estimated 30 percent of village paddy production at the time. One hundred of its sons joined the armed forces and left for the front in the 1951–1953 period, increasing the number of men to 180 for the entire war. A large number of villagers also served as civilian porters for Vietminh military campaigns throughout this period: 50 or 60 were porters for the fall-winter 1950–1951, June 1951, October 1952, and upper Laos 1953 campaigns; and 200 for the Hoà-Bình campaign in November 1951 (Sơn-Dương 1987:45). In the winter and spring of 1954, Sơn-Dương provided 270 civilian porters, both male and female, for up to six months in order to transport military supplies through difficult terrain for the historic Điện-Biên-Phủ campaign. For this final campaign the populations of Phú-Thọ and Vĩnh-Phúc were mobilized en masse and reportedly provided 73,000 civilian porters (28 percent of the porters for this campaign), 4,789 cattle, 500 tonnes of pork, and more than 5,000 tonnes of rice, peas, peanuts, and sugar, and other commodities (Cao-Tiến-Phùng et al. 1985:324). The Vietminh mobilized 49,500 combat soldiers and 55,000 support troops for this campaign to attack a garrison held by 16,500 French troops near the Vietnam-Laos border. Despite their massive 23,000 casualties (including 8,000 dead), the Vietminh inflicted 5,500 casualties (1,500 dead) on the French and forced the surrender of the garrison on May 7, 1954 (Harrison 1982:124).

In Phú-Thọ, under constant Vietminh sniping and bombardment and as a result of the Điện-Biên-Phủ defeat, the French decided to withdraw from their Việt-Trì and Hạ-Nông posts the following month. This withdrawal marked the end of the French colonial presence and the Franco-Vietminh war in Phú-Thọ. During the costly military conflict the Vietminh in Phú-Thọ claimed to have inflicted 4,800 casualties on the French and pro-French Vietnamese forces; destroyed 54 trucks, 8 tanks, 34 boats, and 2 planes; and captured a large number of guns, over 2,000 land mines, and 26 tonnes of ammunition (Nhân Dân, Feb. 25, 1955). The population of Phú-Thọ reportedly contributed 64,000 tonnes of paddy, the cash equivalent of 42,600 additional tonnes, over 700 tonnes of meat, 18.5 million labor days (to destroy communications in the early period and rebuild them later on), as well as more than 10,000 soldiers for the People's Army (ibid.). Of these contributions, the village of Sơn-Dương made good its share, sending hundreds of tonnes of paddy as taxes, 15 tonnes of paddy for military supply, 1,500 labor days for the destruction and subsequent reconstruction of roads, and 180 soldiers for the war of national independence itself (Sơn-Dương 1987:44–45). Twenty soldiers died and thirteen were invalided during the war of 1946–1954 (cf. Kiều-Hữu-Xuân 2001: 27)

On July 21, 1954, the Geneva Agreements and Final Declaration temporarily divided Vietnam into two zones at the seventeenth parallel:

the north as the Democratic Republic of Vietnam under Hồ Chí Minh's government and the south as the Republic of Vietnam under the former emperor Bảo-Đại of the Huế court. The accords banned the introduction of foreign troops and called for a referendum on the unification of the country within two years. The village of Sơn-Dương enjoyed a decade of peace as it underwent probably the most fundamental socioeconomic transformation in its history.

*     *     *

The Marxist-led Vietminh movement enjoyed overwhelmingly strong support from Sơn-Dương villagers as well as from the broader Vietnamese population during the course of its conflict with the French from 1945 onward. Villagers readily lent support to Hồ Chí Minh's government despite the high cost of their action, the few foreseeable tangible benefits in the early years of the conflict, and the small odds of success. Vietminh supporters faced potentially severe losses because of superior French military technology, and the material benefits to poor villagers were restricted to the elimination of taxes and a small share of the village's limited amount of communal land. Their choice, then, was not reducible to a narrow and universal matrix of material costs and benefits. Even the utilitarian theorist Samuel Popkin remarks that "the Vietminh mobilization is a clear case of the importance of contributions, some of which were not stimulated by any expectation of future selective payoff. It emphasizes how important internalized feelings of duty or ethic can be" (1979:223).

At this critical juncture of modern Vietnamese history, from 1940 to 1954, national independence constituted, for the overwhelming majority of both Sơn-Dương villagers and the larger Vietnamese population, an objective of utmost importance. In the first decade of this period the objective was pursued against serious odds at an incredibly high cost and with practically no concrete benefits. Within the framework of national independence, the revolutionary leadership sought to enact democratic ideals such as universal suffrage as well as to move slowly toward a socialist, collectivist vision of political economy with rent controls, progressive land tax schedules, and in Sơn-Dương the experimental formation of an agricultural cooperative. It can be argued that along with the Vietminh's nationalist appeals and their legitimacy as the first government of national independence, their close attention to the concrete subsistence needs of the people and the political economy of reform made a major difference in the strength of their support. It constituted a fundamental difference between the abortive VNP uprising in 1930 and the successful Vietminh

movement in 1940–1954. The dynamics of the Vietnamese revolution cannot be understood exclusively in terms of nationalism, although national
independence did constitute the primary objective for the majority of Vietnamese in the 1946–1954 period. Nor can they be seen as a concomi-
tant search for democracy among the Western-educated elite (cf. Emerson
1960: chap. 13). They cannot be analyzed primarily as a reaction by the
peasantry to the violation of the subsistence ethic by the colonial regime
(cf. J. C. Scott 1976). Although a massive violation of the subsistence ethic
existed in 1944–1945 in northern Vietnam, it did not necessarily lead to
agrarian unrest. Despite massive starvation, unrest rarely broke out in
localities without the organizational efforts of the Vietminh (see also Ngô-
Vĩnh-Long 1978b).

Despite certain Western Marxist analyses, the objective of national
independence was no less important to the native intelligentsia than to
the worker and peasant masses (cf. Murray 1980:36–37; Ngô-Vĩnh-
Long 1978b). In fact, as can be seen both in the village of Sơn-Dương
and beyond, the leadership that played a critical role in mobilizing and
coordinating the revolutionary potential of the population came largely
from the Western-educated intelligentsia (see Woodside 1976:303; Emerson 1960). As Chapter 2 emphasizes, in order to understand the roots of
the modern Vietnamese revolution, it is necessary to examine both the
inequality and contradictions within the capitalist imperialist system and
the local tradition itself. I will return to the importance of local tradition
in the conclusion of this book when I undertake a systematic discussion of
the spatiotemporal variations in local tradition and revolutionary strength
within Vietnam in the past century. The importance of local tradition is
also reflected in the persistence of certain structural tensions into the present period, which constitutes the focus of the following chapters.

# CHAPTER 5

# The Revolution in the Village, 1954–1988

On June 30, 1987, the village of Sơn-Dương organized a formal ceremony to receive the Third-class Labor Medal from the national government. The village was commended for a wide variety of achievements, ranging from agricultural production and a rapid decline in birth rate to measures of economy in the life-cycle rituals. Invited to the ceremony were not only the incumbent high-ranking cadres from surrounding villages, the district, and the province, but also retired high-ranking cadres from Sơn-Dương and the oldest villager from each of the four hamlets to represent the rest of the population. In a departure from local tradition during the colonial era, the four elderly villagers were chosen solely on the basis of age, regardless of gender and class background. The squealing of hogs was heard from early in the morning, when they were brought from all over the village for butchering and distribution to village households. Each villager, child or adult, was to receive 300 grams of pork as part of the celebration.

The celebration marked the culmination of a long process of revolutionary transformation. Significant progress had been achieved despite the painful memories of a small number of villagers, occasional policy reversals, and the hardships of the American war.

Agricultural productivity had increased dramatically from 430 kilograms of paddy per *mẫu* per crop (1.2 tonnes per hectare) in 1954 to an average of 1.4 tonnes per *mẫu* (3.9 tonnes per hectare) for most of the 1985–1988 period.[1] Experiments with a new variety of rice promised to increase the yield to 2 tonnes per *mẫu* (5.55 tonnes per hectare per crop). Equally significant was the considerably more intense use of land, thanks to the completion of the Lâm-Thao-Hạc-Trì water-control project and the construction of feeder canals starting in 1957. Before the canals were constructed, village fields had yielded only one staple crop annually. By 1988 most of the land yielded three crops. The crop-rotation index, which indicates the average number of staple crops on agricultural land, had accordingly increased to 2.6. Since 1985 the village had added the important cash crop of peanuts to the annual cycle. Grown mainly for foreign markets, the peanut crop provided villagers with sizable cash incomes. The peanut acreage correspondingly grew from 50 *mẫu* in 1985 to 151 *mẫu* in 1988.

Depending on altitude, four main crop rotation patterns existed on the 744 *mẫu* of village fields managed by the agricultural cooperative in 1988 (see Figure 2). In fields at the highest altitude, two rice crops were grown between the first and the eighth lunar months, followed by a corn crop for the remainder of the year (crop rotation pattern 1). In other high fields (199 *mẫu*), rice was cultivated from the beginning of the fifth month to the end of the eighth month of the lunar calendar *(lúa mùa),* corn and vegetables from the beginning of the ninth month to the end of the year, and peanuts from the beginning of the first month to the beginning of the fifth month (crop rotation pattern 2). To the extent that crop cycles might overlap, as in the case of the corn and rice crops in the fall of each year, the seeds of the second crop were sowed for germination on a layer of soil in the yard until the completion of the harvest of the other crop. In low-lying fields, rice was cultivated twice a year: from the beginning of the eleventh month to the middle of the fourth month for the winter-spring crop *(lúa chiêm)* and from the beginning of the fourth month to the middle of the ninth month for the summer-fall crop *(lúa mùa)* plus whatever villagers could grow within a month and a half on the land (crop rotation pattern 3). The first and third crop patterns were used on 311 *mẫu* of village fields. In the lowest fields (190 *mẫu*), rice was grown only once a year in the spring and summer (from the first to the sixth lunar month). For the rest of the year the flooded fields supplied villagers with fish as another food source (44 *mẫu* were reserved for the cultivation of rice seedlings). Corresponding to the intensification of land use, the average amount of chemical and organic fertilizers invested in each *mẫu* increased to 3.5 tonnes a year (9.7 tonnes per hectare), including 200–250 kilograms of chemical fertilizers purchased from state enterprises and 3.25 tonnes of organic fertilizers from water lentils, and human and animal waste.

The intensification of land use came hardly a moment too soon. The acreage under cultivation had declined by 19 percent between 1954 and 1988 (from 1,009 to 820 *mẫu*) because of the conversion of agricultural fields into residential land, water-control canals, cooperative stockhouses, collective livestock farms, and paddy-drying courtyards. (Of the 820 *mẫu* of cultivated land in 1988, 744 were collectively owned, and 76 consti-

### LUNAR CALENDAR MONTH

| | 1 | 2 | 3 | 4 | 5 | 6 | 7 | 8 | 9 | 10 | 11 | 12 |
|---|---|---|---|---|---|---|---|---|---|---|---|---|

Crop rotation pattern 1     |← *rice(chiêm)* →||← rice*(mùa)* →||← corn →|

Crop rotation pattern 2     |← peanuts →||← rice*(mùa)* →||← corn →|
(Alternative pattern 2)                                                          [vegetables]

Crop rotation pattern 3     *(chiêm)* →||← rice*(mùa)* →|          |←rice

Crop rotation pattern 4     |← rice →||← fish →|

**Figure 2.** Main crop rotation patterns in Sơn-Dương

tuted the so-called five-percent land allotted to individual households as garden plots.) Throughout the same period, Sơn-Dương's population had increased from 2,144 to over 4,000 people, 3,828 of whom resided in the village. The rest were mostly male villagers who had temporarily left for the armed services or other government work. In the face of growing demographic problems, in 1961–1962, 1973, and 1976, the village had sent members to clear new land in the mountain valleys of Thanh-Sơn district on the other side of the Red River as well as to the Yên-Báy region of neighboring Hoàng-Liên-Sơn province. All these attempts at opening new land had failed within a year, however, because of material hardships and the pain of family separation.

In the search for a more balanced food-population ratio, the village of Sơn-Dương was more successful in increasing crop yield and slowing village population growth. The village birth rate dropped from 3 percent in 1980 to 2.3 percent in 1986 and the first half of 1987. The annual population growth stood at a relatively modest 1.5 percent for this eighteen-month period. The secretary of the Sơn-Dương Communist Party branch discussed the mobilization of village women in the campaign for birth control:

Before 1983 Sơn-Dương couples had an average of five or six children each. A couple usually had their first child within a year of marriage. The large number of children resulted partly from villagers' desire to have sons to continue their patrilines. Newlywed couples rarely waited before conceiving, because most of the grooms were soldiers on short vacations for their weddings. In 1983, under orders from above, we encouraged population planning: ideally, a couple would wait five years before their first child, and births would be spaced at five-year intervals. On the one hand, we worked with the village clinic staff in setting the numerical target for intrauterine device placements and with the pediatrician at the district hospital regarding more technical matters. On the other, we asked the labor teams to examine the family situations of team members and to visit the families in need of better population planning in order to persuade the appropriate child-bearing-age wives to go to the clinic for IUDs. For our part, we have decided to grant a one-month leave and a waiver of corvée labor to any woman who has had an abortion and has an IUD inserted. She is also given 25 kilograms of paddy, the amount a delivering mother would receive from the cooperative. Any woman who gave birth to a fourth child would neither receive the food assistance nor be granted the waiver of corvée labor after delivery. The only exception is when the devices are defective, like on one occasion when the Saigon IUDs in use here had a 70 percent defective rate.

Villagers now understand the need to restrict the number of children to two or three for their own benefit and for society at large. When the plan is not followed, it is most often because a couple has had no son by the third or fourth birth. It is also difficult to enforce the rule of a five-year waiting period. Young couples want to have children within one to two years of marriage, especially because their parents exert pressure on them. It is the rural folk mentality. And once they have the first child, a couple wants other children all in a row. Despite these problems, the birth rate has declined from 3 percent in 1980 to 1.7 percent in 1986.[2]

Public facilities in Sơn-Dương had considerably expanded even before 1983, when the crop yield began to rise sharply. Village roads, although still unpaved, had been widened and were properly drained during the rainy season. In 1987 cars and trucks could pass through the main village road on a shortcut route to the industrial town of Việt-Trì, although it still took a lot of concentration to avoid the large potholes in certain parts of the road. Older villagers frequently remarked to visitors how the roads had improved from the pre-1945 period, when during a heavy rain they had had to hold on to the branches from the bamboo hedges along the roads and to wade in muddy water up to their knees to get from one point to another. In 1987 the village clinic, which was first set up during the war of resistance against the French, was staffed by two physician's assistants, a pharmacist's assistant, a nurse, and an administrator. It also included an oriental medicine room. The staff readily made house calls on request. The village school, which began offering junior high school classes as early as 1958–1959, was the third in the district to do so. By 1987, with forty-two teachers, it offered classes up to grade twelve and had enrolled 1,001 male and female students.[3] The three nursery schools in the village also enrolled 120 pupils. The equal access to education for boys and girls stood in sharp contrast to the almost all-male enrollment of 35 students in the three-grade village school on the eve of the August 1945 uprising.

Beyond public facilities, most Sơn-Dương villagers emphasized the significant physical improvements in their living quarters as part of the revolution in the village. As easily observed from the village roads in 1987–1988, almost all the houses in the 675 housing compounds were constructed of brick and tile. The Sơn-Dương Party branch gave a figure of 98 percent for the proportion of brick houses in 1987. As the village credit cooperative offered mainly short-term loans and loans for collective projects, these new houses were constructed with bricks produced in the villagers' backyards and paid for by the villagers' considerable savings and informal loans through credit associations, as discussed by Bằng's cousin Tế:

> In 1977 we completed the construction of a new brick house. We began planning for it as early as 1975, when I organized a ten-member rotating credit association to provide a financial cushion for members' unexpected funeral and wedding expenses. My fellow members suggested that I take the credit first. It cost me only cigarettes and tea, not a dog for a meal for them as I had thought. I received half a tonne of paddy and used it the following year to buy timber. My wife and I carried sand from the river bank on baskets hanging from a shoulder pole because we did not possess an oxcart then. We also molded and kiln-dried most of the bricks ourselves. When somebody unexpectedly offered to purchase our removable house for the asking price of 1,100 piasters, we decided to go ahead with the construction of the new house.

> *How many members does your household have?*
> We have nine members altogether: my wife and myself; our eldest son, his wife, and their three children; and our second son and his wife. Our daughters moved out upon marriage. Our eldest son and his family stay in the same house with us, and our other son and his wife stay in the thatch house just over there on the same piece of land.

Most village houses in 1987–1988 were equipped with their own wells, and many had brick outhouses and outdoor bathing rooms. In 1985, according to the village administration, the percentages of houses with wells, brick outhouses, and outdoor bathing rooms had reached 94 percent, 71 percent, and 49 percent, respectively. For transportation, village households possessed on average two bicycles each (before 1945 the entire village had only one bicycle). Most also owned oxcarts for the transportation of grain and construction materials, instead of having to employ the traditional method of carrying materials in two baskets hanging on a pole. The physical improvements within household compounds were significant in comparison to conditions on the eve of the August 1945 uprising, when there existed only five brick houses, six private wells, and no outhouses and bathing rooms in the entire village. In a message to what he perceived to be a hostile Western world, a former president of the Sơn-Dương agricultural cooperative emphasized to me that since 1954 the new brick houses in the village had required an estimated investment of 26 million bricks, 402,500 tiles, 1,820 tonnes of timber, 6,600 tonnes of coal, 3,432 tonnes of firewood, and 338 tonnes of lime.

Beyond the physical improvements and the considerably better access to public services, the village Party leaders emphasized to visitors the radical reforms to life-cycle ceremonies that they had instituted in 1986. The village prohibited the serving of cigarettes at wedding and funeral receptions, restricted the servings at funerals to tea and areca palm nuts, limited the number of wedding banquet trays to ten (sixty guests), and placed a ban on villagers' butchering of their own hogs for weddings. In order to reduce the costs of these life-cycle events and to simplify the complex sequence of rituals, the village administration specified that: (1) wedding rituals were to be held in the village office; (2) engagement ceremonies should require no more than five packs of cigarettes, half a kilogram of tea, and a few dozen areca palm nuts, instead of virtually unlimited demands by the bride's family for items to be distributed among its relatives and acquaintances; and (3) in the case of death, the corpse was to be buried within half a day. In return, the village cooperative provided free of charge a coffin, ten packages of incense, and burial services for any deceased member. The village performing arts group provided free entertainment at the brief wedding ceremony at the village office. The rationale for the reforms, according to the local Party secretary, was to avoid the extraordinarily high costs of traditional ceremonies, which included status-oriented banquets and the distribution of elaborate engagement gifts.

A well-off family probably managed a traditional ceremony all right. However, many others went heavily into debt on wedding and funeral occasions. If we take a small family with two children, in the old days, six major costly banquets would have to be given: the wedding banquets for the two children, the funeral banquets for the parents, and two reburial banquets three years after each funeral. The costs were quite burdensome, especially if we take into account most parents' efforts to build houses for their junior sons. [Both in the past and the present, the parents' house is bequeathed to the first son.]

In the summer of 1987, although the regulations regarding ceremonies seemed to be generally observed in Sơn-Dương, many villagers attempted to circumvent the rules by conforming to them in letter but not in spirit. They would restrict the number of wedding banquet guests at any one moment to sixty by having only ten food trays, but they would give two or three consecutive banquets. Or they would not butcher their own hogs themselves, but sell a hog to the village marketing cooperative for butchering on condition that most of the meat be sold back to them. Religious services were also simplified to two monthly prayer sessions held by approximately 200 devoted elderly women at a dilapidated local Buddhist pagoda. The only village nun had passed away in 1971, and most village Catholics had abandoned their religion as early as the late 1930s, well before the rise of Marxist power in Sơn-Dương. Worship of the village guardian deities had long been abandoned, ever since the French bombing of the communal house in Sơn-Dương in 1951 and the subsequent destruction of the remainder of the building. In addition, the Dụng-Hiền communal house was partially dismantled in 1958 and the one in Thụy-Sơn was converted to other uses around 1956–1958. All these changes were authorized by the village leadership. After the destruction of the Sơn-Dương communal house, the statues of tutelary village deities were moved to the ground of the house for deceased Buddhist nuns and subsequently, around 1987–1988, to the village shrine where another deity was worshipped. The neighborhood groups *(giáp)* had also ceased to exist in their capacity as ritual-centered units.

Although the twenty production teams of the agricultural cooperative were formed on the basis of residential proximity like the *giáp,* they functioned as production units, not as ritual-centered ones. Of all the village organizations dating from the colonial period, only the credit associations, the patrilineages, and the elderly Buddhist group survived into the late 1980s. Most important among the new village institutions were the agricultural, sales, purchasing, and credit cooperatives, all of which reflect the rise of the collectivistic ideology. These changes in the village are all the more remarkable as many young male villagers had been absent for at least three years in connection with the intensified U.S. war in Vietnam (1964–1975) and then the Sino-Vietnamese and Cambodian armed conflicts of 1978–1989. Three hundred sixty young men joined the armed forces during the 1965–1975 period, and another 350 joined between 1976 and 1984. After the period of intense destructive warfare between 1965 and 1972, when over one million tons of bombs were dropped by the U.S. Air Force on North Vietnam alone, and the triumph of the Marxist-led movement in the south in 1975, bringing the independence and national unity that had been out of reach for two decades, Vietnam invaded Cambodia in December 1978 to put an end to the reported armed intrusions by the China allied Khmer Rouge forces. Then in February 1979, partly in retaliation for Vietnam's armed intervention in Cambodia, China invaded Vietnam with over 100,000 troops. Although Vietnam quickly routed the Khmer Rouge from most of Cambodia, and China withdrew after one month of intense fighting along the Sino-Vietnamese border, the continuation of conflict with both the Khmer Rouge and China required the imposition of a draft and constant Vietnamese vigilance, which remained in effect in 1988.[4] Young male villagers were required to spend three years in the armed forces. Although many veterans returned to the village to fill the top positions in the Party, the village administration, and the cooperatives, many others did not come back because new opportunities were made available for veterans elsewhere and because many died in the wars. As a result, the active local labor force—predominantly an agricultural labor force—was lopsided with women, as can be seen in Table 4. The imbalance in the sex ratio in 1987 was also quite significant for the village population as a whole, albeit not as great as for the agricultural work force (see Table 5).

Underlying those concrete changes in Sơn-Dương was a fundamental transformation in the village political economy. The transformation involved a destruction of the dominant classes of the colonial social formation and the emergence of the Communist Party, the "representative of the proletariat," as the dominant force in communal affairs. The means of agricultural production were mostly collectivized, except for draft animals and the household garden plots. The rigid class-structured distinction between mental and manual labor was no longer maintained, because many university-educated cadres, mostly retirees, were also engaged in

**Table 4.** Demography of the active agricultural labor force in Sơn-Dương, 1987

| Age Range | Males | Females | Total |
|---|---|---|---|
| 16–17 | 25 | 47 | 72 |
| 18–27 | 126 | 234 | 360 |
| 28–40 | 150 | 318 | 468 |
| 41–45 | 50 | 130 | 180 |
| 45–retirement* | 130 | 302 | 432 |
| Total | 481 | 1,031 | 1,512 |
| | (32%) | (68%) | (100%) |

*Note:* The retirement age in 1987 was 55 for women and 60 for men.

**Table 5.** Sex ratios in four hamlets of Sơn-Dương village, 1987

| Hamlet | Males | Females | Total |
|---|---|---|---|
| Chung-Chính | 582 | 627 | 1,209 |
| Đại-Đình | 350 | 480 | 830 |
| Đại-Tụ | 396 | 474 | 870 |
| Dụng-Hiền | 403 | 498 | 901 |
| Total | 1,731 | 2,079 | 3,810 |
| | (45.5%) | (54.5%) | (100%) |

animal husbandry, among other things, in order to improve the living conditions of their households. Some female villagers played an active role in the public arena. At the height of the egalitarian, collectivistic ideology in 1954–1958, a female villager had occupied the powerful Party secretary position. In 1985 the local Party membership stood at 186, including 37 women (20 percent). Overall, however, it was an aging membership. The average age of Party members had risen to 53 in 1985, since only 15 new members had been admitted in the 1975–1985 period. There were 80 retirees among Party members in 1985 and 87 out of a total of 196 in 1987. The Party membership elected a 17-member leadership committee *(đảng ủy),* of which 2 members (11.8 percent) in the summer of 1988 were women, cadres in charge of women's affairs and birth control. However, real power at the local level lay with the all-male five-member Executive Committee of the Party branch (Thường vụ Đảng ủy). The committee included a secretary, an assistant secretary (the president of the village administration), and three other members (the vice-president of the administration in charge of village security, the president of the agricultural cooperative, and an assistant to the local Party secretary). The local Communist Party branch provided policy guidelines for the village administration and for the agricultural, credit, and sales and purchasing cooperatives. Comprising only village residents, the Party executive committee had a considerably greater input into the daily affairs of the village than a board of directors does into the administration of a North American corporation. It was no coincidence that the most important public space in the village was the meeting hall of the local Communist Party organization.

In Sơn-Dương, despite the rise of collectivism and the greater participation of women in the public domain, the male-centered hierarchy of the colonial and precolonial eras persisted both within the communal framework and in the kinship system. The narrative on birth control quoted in this chapter discusses the villagers' preference for sons, which points toward the persistence of a male-centered model in kinship and gender relations in the village. The model of hierarchical relations also structured both the internal organization of the local Communist Party and the dominant relation of the Party to the rest of the community. As a reflection of this, the linguistic form *đồng chí* (comrade), originally restricted to Party circles, has become a term of address selectively used to convey respect and formality among the larger population both within the village of Sơn-Dương and beyond.

*        *        *

The process of transformation that took place in the village of Sơn-Dương between 1954 and the late 1980s was not free of tension. The tension arose from a dialectical relation between the principle of radical collectivism espoused by the Marxist state for most of this period and, despite the elimination of the colonial class structure, a hierarchical sociocultural model that centered on the kinship unit. The official collectivist ideology of the state emerged dominant in the northern social formation during this time. It underlay the radical transformation of the village political economy that occurred through the land-reform program and the subsequent collectivization of the means of production. However, the pace of change was not uniform, and the path of transformation was not unidirectional.

In June 1954, just as the French were to withdraw from their last two military posts in the province of Phú-Thọ following the Điện-Biên-Phủ defeat, a land-reform team arrived in Sơn-Dương to accelerate the momentum of the Vietminh's egalitarian socioeconomic policy. It included no village member so as to minimize the impact of the extensive village network on the reform process. The team arrived with a specific directive from higher authorities: "Reliance on landless and poor peasants, solidarity with middle peasants, alliance with rich peasants, and gradual and discriminate destruction of feudal exploitation, all to enhance production and strengthen the armed resistance" (Hoàng-Ước 1968:141).[5] In a radical departure from tradition, the team did not stay with well-off households as other important visitors did, but instead based itself, through *ba cùng* (eat, live, and work together), with landless and poor peasants. It sought to raise the consciousness of the poor villagers and to conduct a classification of village households into five categories: landlords, rich peasants, middle peasants, poor peasants, and the landless (see White 1983). Among the poor villagers the team approached was Bằng's cousin Tế:

> In 1954 the rent-reduction team arrived in Sơn-Dương. They initially inquired of me who the landlords were in the village. I replied: "I do not know how to determine whether somebody is a landlord or not." The team then asked for my assistance in gathering information in the village of Vĩnh-Lại [on the rent conditions there for its future work] at a time when the enemy was stationed exactly on the other side of the river. I did not succeed in requesting the transfer of the assignment to somebody else, because nobody dared to accept this dangerous assignment.

The classification of households involved two main criteria: the size of landholding and the degree of exploitation through usury, hired labor, or land rental:

1. Households were classified as landlords if they owned sizable amounts of land and exploited others through usury and nonhousehold labor in the cultivation process (that is, through sharecropping and hiring labor). Labor was considered to come primarily from external sources if more than two-thirds of the manual labor on family land came from "outsiders." The category of outsiders included not only workers beyond the household concerned, but also secondary wives, adopted children, and sons-in-law who had been treated as landless laborers (Hoàng-Ước 1968:146ff.). Depending on their support for the Vietminh during the Franco-Vietminh war and their treatment of laborers, sharecroppers, and debtors, landlord households were further differentiated into brutal landlords, neutral landlords, and resistance-supporting landlords.[6]

2. Rich peasant households relied primarily on household labor in the cultivation of their fairly sizable landholdings but still regularly exploited other people through usury, hired labor, and land rental.
3. Middle peasant households had sufficient control over the means of production for their livelihood and relied primarily on their own labor. They only occasionally hired labor or rented land to or from others.
4. Poor peasant households did not have sufficient means of production. They were exploited through usury, land rental, and employment by members of other classes.
5. Landless peasant households had no land. They were heavily exploited by other classes, primarily through usury and employment.

The arrival of the land-reform team was the harbinger of turbulent times ahead for the large landholding families of Sơn-Dương. The team sought to destroy the exploiting classes through the redistribution of their holdings to poorer peasants and to purge the local Party branch of members with "exploiting" class backgrounds. In the context of the Franco-Vietminh war, these steps aimed at further consolidating the support for the Marxist-led Vietminh government among the peasant masses and at weakening the landlord stratum—in the Party's analysis, the indigenous class most sympathetic to colonial control (Hoàng-Ước 1968:86–95). The policy sought to destroy the class differentiation process in order to strengthen national unity and collectivism in the long term, but its method of overt class struggle was not rooted in the local tradition.

The first measure of the land-reform campaign in Sơn-Dương required landlords to reimburse their sharecroppers for the difference between the actual rents and the government-specified rent (at 37.5 percent or a 25 percent reduction from the pre-1945 period). Their loans to other villagers were canceled if these dated prior to 1945, if interest payments had doubled the principal by April 1953, or if they had been made to villagers who had sacrificed their lives during the Franco-Vietminh war. Since the government's rent-reduction policy was not applied in Sơn-Dương until 1949, landlords had to reimburse their tenants and sharecroppers for rent differentials primarily in the 1945–1949 period. A total of two tonnes of rice and over one million piasters were redistributed to 1,600 villagers in the first phase of the campaign.

In the subsequent land-reform period, in the public denunciation sessions organized by the local peasant association, four households were classified as brutal landlords, twenty-two as landlords, and ten as rich peasants. This classification was based on landholdings and labor condi-

**Table 6.** Household classification during land reform, in percentage

|  | Landlord | Rich peasant | Middle peasant | Poor peasant | Landless laborer | Nonagricultural |
|---|---|---|---|---|---|---|
| Phú-Tho | 4.06 | 2.66 | 30.40 | 37.05 | 17.11 | 7.36 |
|  | 6.72 | | 30.40 | 54.16 | | |
| Sơn-Dương | 5.65 | 2.17 | 21.97 | | | |
|  | 7.82 | | 21.97 | 70.00 | | |

Source: M. Lambourg. L'écomomie actuelle du Vietnam Démocratique, reprinted in White 1981:432.

tions in 1949 in order to discount any landowners' "illegitimate" dispersal of properties or change in land-exploitation methods in response to the government's rent-reduction and progressive-land-tax policies. Dispersals were considered legitimate if they involved bequests to children or main heirs, sales to meet family needs during disaster, or transfers to commercial and industrial ventures (Hoàng-Ước 1968:169). Little evidence was available that showed any major or systematic efforts by landlord and rich peasant households in the village of Sơn-Dương to undermine the land-reform classification through kinship or patron-client ties with poorer villagers (cf. White 1981: chap. 7).

The thirty-six households in the landlord and rich peasant categories comprised 7.82 percent of the village households. The percentage of landlord households in Sơn-Dương (5.65 percent) exceeded the 4 to 5 percent guideline suggested by higher authorities to land-reform teams (Hoàng-Ước 1968:157). At the other end of the spectrum, 70 percent of Sơn-Dương households were classified as poor or landless. These figures indicate a greater polarization in wealth differentiation and land-reform classification in Sơn-Dương than in the province of Phú-Thọ as a whole (Table 6).

The brutal landlords in Sơn-Dương were imprisoned after trials in the People's Court. All their property was confiscated. The son of one colonial-era mayor who was classified as a brutal landlord fled to the south at this point, his longstanding Communist Party membership notwithstanding. The son of another "brutal landlord" related his traumatic experiences during land reform:

My father did not own enough land to rent to anybody. We had only 3 mẫu. However, he was classified as a brutal landlord because of his land management for one of the wealthiest villagers and his occasional beatings of other villagers during his term as a village administrator. I was a Vietminh cadre at the time of this land-reform campaign. I was ordered to return to the village, although fortunately my wife and I had been considered a separate household and classified as a poor peasant family. The land-reform cadres told me to advise my father to reimburse the excess rent that he had collected. I went to see my jailed father in the communal house. I did not have the courage to address him with the pronouns *mày* (thou) and *tao* (I/me) [which implied the total denial of kinship relation], as the land-reform cadres thought I should have done. Looking away from my father, I said quietly: "Sell whatever possible for the rent reimbursement." [The deletion of the subject implied great disrespect.] I was crying hard inside at the time. On the trial day, under pressure from the land-reform cadres, my close relatives and even my wife denounced my father and addressed him with the pronouns *mày* and *tao*. He was subsequently imprisoned. In this entire episode, the physical loss meant relatively little in comparison to the emotional trauma and the damage to the social fabric. After my wife passed away, in my absence, my children moved her tomb away from my father's because of the bitterness in their relationship after her public denunciation and her indirect rejection of their kinship tie by the terms of address used during the trial. Even nowadays, I still do not feel comfortable in the presence of the relatives who denounced my father and addressed him with the terms *mày* and *tao* on that trial day more than three decades ago. It is still embarrassing for us to interact.

The wife of the late mayor Ân, the third wealthiest villager who had strongly supported the Vietminh since 1945 but who had declined an invitation to join the Party in 1948, was classified as a regular landlord instead of a resistance-supporting one. Her property was appropriated together with that of other landlords.[7] As quite a few villagers whispered to the field researchers in 1987, she committed suicide at this point, even though the land reform guidelines specified that the state would purchase the land and other means of production of regular and resistance landlords with payments over a ten-year period and 1.5 percent annual interest on the purchase price (Hoàng-Ước 1968:163–164). Resistance landlords would be allowed to donate land to the state if they wanted to escape the tension of denunciation sessions [ibid.: 166–167].) Bằng's half-sister's husband, a mayor in the colonial era and a Communist Party member during the Franco-Vietminh war, was classified as a regular landlord. Although his two sons had served in the Vietminh armed forces, all his property, except for a buffalo stable, was appropriated. One of the sons reported on his family conditions during and following the land reform:

> My father had been an active Party member during the war. My house had been a frequent meeting place for the Party leadership, and my father had been elected treasurer because of our wealth.... I volunteered for the People's Army in 1949 and was sent to China for training. We all felt strongly about the cause of national independence. As soldiers, we had no shoes, wore latania-leaf hats, received no salaries, and walked all the way to China.... When I observed the land reform in China, I wrote to my father to warn him to get rid of some land.... I was not home during the land reform, but it was reported that our property was all appropriated except for a buffalo stable. The stable was returned to our family only after some villagers had commented that my younger brother and I had been serving in the armed forces. My family was given a tiny piece of land in a village cemetery, where they grew corn. My younger sisters collected manure on the village roads and sold it to provide a supplementary income for the family. Yet after the sale they were stripped of the money by the authorities and reportedly told: "Manure belongs to peasants." Few people dared to see my family in those days. My brother, at the time stationed not too far from Sơn-Dương, had to sneak back to see my family at night. A few villagers who took a pity on my family hid small bags of rice and a few corn cobs under their shirts. They reportedly called in from outside, "Is the bastard landlord home? He'd better be home!" and discreetly threw the food inside if no other villagers were around.... We were later reclassified as rich peasants and eventually down to middle peasants. Even so, in 1958, when I was granted a vacation, I did not dare to return to Sơn-Dương. I spent my vacation elsewhere.

Bằng's brother Gia, who still owned 2.4 *mẫu* and cultivated an additional *mẫu* as a "gift" from his wealthier half-sister, was classified as a rich peasant. Most of Gia's land, like that of other rich peasants, was purchased by the state for redistribution to other cultivators. As a reflection of the intense struggle during the land reform, Gia's senior daughter-in-law and his sister-in-law, the leading female Communist Party member in the village, reportedly denounced and strongly insulted Gia in public denunciation meetings by their use of the personal pronouns *mày* and *tao* with him. Bằng's other brother Tăng and his wife, respectively an army officer and the leading female Party member in the village, were not adversely affected by the land reform because, ironically, they had lost their share of the family rice fields through Tăng's gambling in the early 1940s.

In accordance with land-reform guidelines, the confiscated, appropriated, and coercively purchased lands from landlord and rich peasant households in Sơn-Dương were distributed to landless, poor, and middle peasants. Cadres, soldiers, and workers serving the revolution—whether deceased, invalid, or on active duty—were counted as peasants if their families resided in the countryside and qualified for land as landless, middle, or poor peasant households (Hoàng-Ước 1968:172). The poor peasant Tế, who had been recruited as a land-reform cadre and assigned to work elsewhere in the province, received over 1 *mẫu* for three adult family members:

> We received 1 *mẫu* for three adults, on the basis of about 0.3 *mẫu* for each adult in our category. We received neither grain, because as a cadre I did not dare to ask for it directly, nor cattle, because we had bought one earlier.

The family of the former Communist Party secretary Tiềm was classified as "petit bourgeois." However, because his wife worked on the land, his household was considered a part of the agricultural workforce. As his large family owned only over 1 *mẫu,* they received slightly over 1 *mẫu* of rice fields to bring their total cultivated acreage to over 2 *mẫu.* The elderly Thành, whose property had increased to 2.2 *mẫu* by this time, was classified a middle peasant family. She received no land:

> At the time of the land reform, we received no land because we had been classified as a lower-middle peasant family with our 2.2 *mẫu.* I told the land reform cadres that we should be classified as poor peasants. Our holding had increased to 2.2 *mẫu* only shortly before the land reform because another family had sold us 0.11 *mẫu* out of concern about the land-reform program. We received only a large copper tray with a hole, which I returned to the original owner upon the reclassification of her class background.

An estimated 300 *mẫu* of rice fields from landlord households were redistributed to landless, poor, and lower-middle peasants on the basis of the number of adult workers in households and the current household

**Table 7.** Rice-field holdings before and after land reform, Sơn-Dương, 1954

| | Adult villagers (percent) | Holdings before land reform (in *mẫu*) | Holdings after land reform (in *mẫu*) |
|---|---|---|---|
| Landless peasants | | 0.033 | 0.4 |
| | 70 | | |
| Poor peasants | | 0.2 | 0.48 |
| Middle peasants | 22 | 0.4 | 0.57 |

holdings. According to village statistics, the average rice field holdings of landless and poor peasants increased significantly after the land reform (Table 7).

Working from its base in the peasant association, the outside land-reform team also organized a drastic purge of the local Party branch in order to bring an end to its domination by the landholding class. Within the framework of the land-reform program, the team had been authorized to educate Party members on class perspective, to purge the local Party membership of elements from the landlord and rich peasant categories still engaged in exploitative practices, and to recruit actively among landless and poor peasants. Party members from landlord and rich peasant families who had firmly carried out Party policies could be spared in the purge. However, according to Party directives, they would have to be transferred outside the community in order to mimimize their impact on the relations between the Party and the masses at the village level. In the village of Sơn-Dương, forty-two Party members were expelled in an indiscriminate purge (cf. Đặng-Phong 2005: 86–88). In other words, 46 percent of Party members were purged because of their landlord and rich peasant back-grounds, although by the least stringent criteria, at the time of land reform the landlord and rich peasant households made up no more than 13 percent of the local population. The high percentage of Party members from these backgrounds after the earlier class-oriented Party purge in 1952 clearly indicates the dominance of landlords and rich peasants in the village sociopolitical structure and in the support for the war of national liberation from 1946 to 1954 (cf. E. Wolf 1969:292). Thirteen new Party members were admitted from the ranks of villagers with landless and poor peasant backgrounds in 1954. And in another departure from the male-oriented, and class-structured model of hierarchy in the colonial era, a female Party member became the Party leader (Party secretary) from 1954 to 1958. As a result of the land reform, not only did the radical egalitarian and collectivist ideology emerge dominant within the communal framework of Sơn-Dương, but it also restructured household relations, especially among the elite, because many daughters-in-law played a major role in denouncing their husbands' parents for exploitative practices.

The Party purge and the land-reform program totally shattered the unity of the earlier years of the Franco-Vietminh war. Like their counterparts in other communities, many Sơn-Dương villagers from landlord and rich peasant households had joined the Vietminh in the cause of national independence and had been consequently admitted to the Communist Party. A North Vietnamese authority on land reform has analyzed Party conditions throughout North Vietnam in 1953 as follows:

> In terms of ideology, a large number of Party members possessed a nationalistic spirit, actively participated in the anti-imperialist movement, but did not have a sufficient class awareness and did not understand the division between landlords and peasants. The influence of landlords' and rich peasants' world views was still fairly strong among many Party members. In terms of organization, Party cells still had members from exploiting classes [3 to 4 percent], some of whom occupied positions of authority in the Party branch and village administration in a number of localities. (Hoàng-Ước 1968:180)

In the aftermath of the land-reform campaign, the tension in Sơn-Dương was extraordinarily high between embittered landlords, rich peasants, and expelled Party members, on the one hand, and their denouncers and the remaining Party members, on the other. When Bằng's brother Tăng, reportedly a Điện-Biên-Phủ veteran, returned to Sơn-Dương on a short vacation in 1955 and suddenly died, his god-brother (the chairman of the village Vietminh front during the war) and his brother Gia were accused of poisoning Tăng and three other Sơn-Dương villagers. Gia was reclassified a "reactionary rich peasant" and his adopted brother, a reactionary landlord. Both were imprisoned. Although allowed to keep his thatch house and garden land, Gia lost all his rice fields. The high tension in the local community reverberated beyond the communal framework, because many high-ranking Party members and cadres at the district and national levels came from relatively well-off families in the countryside.

In 1956 the Communist Party and the government of the Democratic Republic of Vietnam launched a rectification program throughout North Vietnam to correct the excesses in the earlier local implementation of the land-reform policy. In the summer of 1956, as the leading advocate of the class-alliance policy in the Vietnamese Communist Party, Hồ Chí Minh lent his personal prestige to the rectification of land-reform excesses. On August 18, Hồ took the initiative by writing to the rural populace:

> The status of those who have been wrongly classified as landlords or as rich peasants should be reviewed [rectified].
>
> Party membership, rights, and honors should be restored to Party members, cadres, and others who have been wrongly convicted....
>
> Unity is our invincible force. In order to consolidate the North into a solid base for the struggle to reunify our country, our entire people should be closely and widely united on the basis of the worker-peasant alliance in the Vietnam Fatherland Front. It is all the more necessary for veteran and new cadres of the Party and Government to assume identity of ideas, to be united and single-minded, and to compete to serve the people. (translated in White 1981:430)

In an unprecedented forty-day session in September and October of 1956, the rectification program was ratified by the Party Central Committee (White 1981:432). Among the specific measures was the reclassification of demobilized or active-duty soldiers who had served more than one year in the People's Army as revolutionary soldiers (*quân nhân cách mạng*), even if they were landlords or children of landlords (*Nhân Dân nguyệt san,* November 1956: 53). No longer considered as landlords were households that had to rent out land or rely primarily on hired labor because household members were actively participating in the resistance against the French, engaging in other occupations, or were unable to work the land for health reasons, *and* that had cultivable land per capita no more than three times the average amount of land per capita in the community (ibid.: 58). Local governments and peasant associations would no longer interfere in the visits of ordinary villagers to landlord households or in the way that these villagers addressed the members of landlord households (ibid.: 68). As an affirmation of the principle of religious freedom, cultivable land belonging to pagodas, shrines, Christian churches, and ancestral halls that had been appropriated was to be returned in amounts sufficient to sustain the activities of these religious entities and the livelihood of monks, nuns, priests, and ancestral hall caretakers associated with them (ibid.: 54).

In Sơn-Dương, because of his absence from the village during the land reform, Party member Tế, in his capacity as the assistant secretary of the peasant association, was appointed to rectify the earlier excesses. Of the twenty-six families originally classified as landlord households, seven remained in the landlord category, but five and fourteen were reclassified as rich and middle peasants, respectively. The wife of the late mayor Ân, who had committed suicide, was posthumously reclassified as a resistance landlord. The ten originally classified rich peasant households, including that of Bằng's brother Gia, were reclassified as middle peasant families. Seventy-three percent of the landlord households and 100 percent of the rich peasant households in Sơn-Dương were thus reclassified in their favor, as compared with 66 percent and 82 percent, respectively, in North Vietnam as a whole (Đặng-Phong 2005: 85). In Sơn-Dương, the households reclassified as rich and middle peasants had some of their previously appropriated property returned. Gia and the nominally adopted son of his father were released from prison. However, redirecting pent-up hostility toward his earlier denouncers, Gia reportedly almost resorted to physical violence. Each member of a reclassified household was granted rice fields approximating the holding of a middle peasant. He or she regained the right to vote and to stand for election to the village people's council. However, despite Party guidelines on alliance with rich peasants, rich peasants were not allowed into peasant associations, administrative committees, village guerrilla forces, or security forces. Members of brutal and regular landlord households continued to suffer the consequences of their land-reform classification for years, since brutal and regular landlords' children, no matter how bright, were not admitted to institutions of higher education, although they could be employed in nonsensitive positions in the state apparatus. Starting in 1957, as a result of the Party Central Committee's rejection of class background as the primary criterion of Party membership (White 1981:435), the local Party branch gradually readmitted twenty-nine of the forty-two expelled Party members, which brought the number of Party members to ninety-six. Over time, ten of the thirteen new members admitted during the land reforms were dropped from the Party branch for "unethical conduct" and insufficient political knowledge.

Despite the rectification of land-reform errors, the land reform radically transformed the colonial class structure as a strategic step toward a collectivistic political economy. It also consolidated the position of the Communist Party among the rural masses and led to concrete improvements in the lives of the vast majority of peasants. These gains were further strengthened in 1957, when a major irrigation system, with feeder canals, was built in the Lâm-Thao-Hạc-Trì delta, increasing food production in the village by 14 percent from 1953 to 1957. The land reform and the water-control project transformed the peasant masses in more than material terms: from an attitude of resignation, many came to have a positive outlook on the larger world. This new outlook was reinforced by the state in its labor mobilization slogan during the 1957 canal construction: "Squeeze water from the earth, and replace heaven in making rain." The overt deferential behavior of peasants toward landlords, of which the pattern of addressing men of wealth by their formal titles constituted an intrinsic part, was eliminated as well.

By 1957 the socioeconomic structure of Sơn-Dương in particular and of northern Vietnam in general had been fundamentally transformed with the elimination of the colonial landholding class and with the supremacy of the Communist Party as the representative of the proletariat. The traditional male-oriented, kinship-centered, class-structured model of hierarchy was seriously undermined in favor of a radical egalitarian and collectivistic ideology.

The village Party history concluded the following about the land-reform program:

> The rent and land revolution achieved significant results in (1) overthrowing the feudal landlord class, the objective of the people's nationalist democratic revolution; and (2) eliminating forever the feudal land ownership by landlords and distributing land to poor and landless peasants.... In the process of land reform, we made serious errors (1) in not having sufficiently educated the masses, leading to people's and many cadres' loose understanding of the Party's policy; (2) in not differentiating the enemies in accordance with Party policy, creating anxieties and disunity in the countryside; and (3) in not relying firmly on the guidelines of Party reorganization, causing upheaval in the local apparatus with an emphasis on the expulsion of Party members and not on their education as well as with the reliance on the peasant association and "correct background" cadres at the expense of the village administration and the local Party leadership. (Sơn-Dương 1987:48–49)

Radical collectivist principles truly gained ascendancy the following year when the Vietnamese Workers' Party and the government of the Democratic Republic of Vietnam launched the cooperative program in 1958. On the one hand, the program was aimed at solving the problem of a resurrected socioeconomic differentiation within the peasantry. On the other, the Party and the state were also seeking to increase agricultural production and procure resources for an accelerated industrialization process within a centrally planned and collectivist political economy. In Sơn-Dương the cooperative program was launched with the formation of labor-exchange teams, whose membership ranged from three to eighteen households. However, because of an emphasis on voluntary participation, membership in the program had its ebb and flow, with many members withdrawing at one point (Sơn-Dương 1987:51). In 1959, under Party guidance, Party members were instructed to take the lead in persuading their families to join a cooperative as well as in convincing their relatives and other villagers. Two hamlet-level cooperatives were established in 1959, followed by two others the following year. All the means of agricultural production (rice fields, draft animals, and farm instruments) were pooled, except for the 5 percent of cultivable land that could remain in the possession of cooperative members for household use as residential, gardening, and animal husbandry land. Cooperative members initially received their share of the crop according to both their labor input and their contribution of land and draft animals.

The process of cooperative formation was not completely smooth. Although not overtly resisting collectivization, quite a few Sơn-Dương villagers were less than enthusiastic. Most eventually joined the cooperatives, but up to 15 percent of the members withdrew at one point (Sơn-Dương 1987:52). The elderly Thành, who had moved from a landless laborer to a middle peasant position by the time of the land reform, commented on the process:

> We were better off after the land reform. Within a few years, a cooperative program was launched because they said: "Otherwise, many poor and landless peasants may sell their land and end up destitute again." We were among the first to join. We did not waver at all, unlike some other families that withdrew and rejoined. My husband headed the inspection team for the cooperative, which left us no choice. We had some difficulties at the beginning. On the one hand, villagers who did not want to join cursed us behind our backs: "Those Party members are crazy!" We also had some difficulty with village criers, who took grain from cooperative land without permission and were ready to beat up those making an issue about it.

The former landless laborer Tế, the first president of the Chung-Chính cooperative, elaborated on the process of cooperative formation:

> When the rectification program was completed, I was recruited to head a labor exchange team. It was 1957–1958 then. I exhorted peas-

ants to join on the basis of mutual assistance. Each team had fifteen to eighteen households. Those with cattle helped those without. It was also at this time that I was selected as a member of the Party leadership committee in the village.

When the village started establishing an agricultural cooperative, the Party committee asked me to become the president of a cooperative. I replied: "I do not know how to do it. I know neither how a cooperative functions nor what it means being a cooperative president." But they told me: "You should accept the responsibility. The district administration will provide the necessary guidance."

*How were the living conditions of your family at the time?*
Honestly, we were doing well economically at the time when I was drafted to head a cooperative. We owned a head of cattle and more than 1 *mẫu* of land. Although our house was not big by any standard, after receiving the land from the land-reform campaign, we managed to save enough money for bricks and to pave our courtyard for drying paddy. However, the Party initiated the cooperative program to increase agricultural production. The Party also actively promoted [formerly] poor and landless peasants to more important positions at the time. As Party members, we had to clear the path with enthusiasm in order to provide a good example for other villagers, no matter how we actually felt in our hearts. Practically no choice was available on the matter. I ended up being the president of Chung-Chính cooperative, the biggest one in the village both in terms of membership and the amount of cattle and land, for three years.

The cooperative had no office at the beginning. My house became the cooperative office where even the general meetings for all cooperative members were held. My wife and my mother had to serve tea for cooperative members for about three years, until I stepped down from the president's position. Despite my lack of knowledge, fortunately it was not too complicated to run a cooperative in those days, because villagers were quite honest. We assigned people to carry paddy to drying courtyards, to take it in overnight, and eventually to check it into the cooperative warehouse, all without weighing the paddy before or after. If members had been greedy, we could have lost quite a bit with such a loose system of control. But believe me, members were not at all devious.... We did well as a whole. I remember a request one year from a district cadre for the paddy consumption of households within the cooperative and whether production met members' needs. I estimated monthly consumption at 33 kilograms of paddy for each adult. [We did well by this standard. . . .]

Our family received over 1 tonne per crop, although my job as the president of the cooperative was considered the equivalent of only fifteen labor days and thus earned me only 90 kilograms of paddy per crop. A labor day was worth 6 kilograms of paddy when the crop was divided in those days. The rest of our paddy share came from our land and cattle stocks in the cooperative. We received 25 percent of the crop yield from our land, and a four-labor-day credit for every 0.1 mẫu plowed by my buffalo. Our share of the paddy crop was quite good in those days, because we simply divided the crop among ourselves according to a labor-day credit system after reserving the seeds for the next crop and fulfilling the paddy obligations to the state. We made no provision for future investments. As a sideline, with a 0.3 mẫu garden, my family also grew vegetables and raised pigs. My mother was able to enjoy the fruits of the revolution for a few years before passing away in 1962. In general, my job turned out to require more activism and devotion than sophisticated formal training.

In all those years the only major complication arose when a number of villagers decided to resign their membership in the cooperative. They were calculating middle peasants who wanted to leave the cooperative after a not-so-great harvest, even though each of those families had a paddy reserve of easily half a tonne to 1 tonne. The higher authorities initially dragged their feet on the return of the land and cattle to those peasants. Village militia even intervened when those peasants tried to get back their cattle and cultivate their land. We also attempted to estimate their grain reserves and made debt claims on the reserves after leaving those peasants just enough for their survival. They were allowed to leave the cooperative, but they eventually reapplied for membership. Their new membership applications were accepted after they agreed to our condition that if they ever left again, they would lose all their land and animal contributions to the cooperative. It was certainly a triumph for the principle of collective labor over that of individual labor. By 1962 every villager had joined a cooperative.

A member of the Chung-Chính cooperative described his background and explained why he withdrew from the cooperative and reapplied for membership:

My grandparents had six children, three sons and three daughters. Until 1951 my father and two uncles all lived in the same wooden house with their mother and their own families, except for a period when an uncle of mine lived in Yên-Báy. They split up and built three separate houses only when our house was destroyed by French bombing in 1951. Before 1954 our livelihood came from cultivation and weaving. Our family was poor. When my family and those of my uncles still shared the same house, we sharecropped 0.3 *mẫu* of rice field. We split the crop half and half with the landlord because we provided the seeds and the draft animal ourselves. We did not have enough to eat. My mother and my uncles' wives had to collect cow dung and human excrement for sale as fertilizer. My father also worked as a shaman, although he earned only his food and contributed little to the family budget. I went to school for one year only.

At the time of land reform, we were classified as a poor peasant family and received a few *sào* of rice field. Our lives improved considerably because we no longer worked for other people. We joined the Chung-Chính cooperative because the entire village joined one cooperative or another at the time. But we resigned our membership, as many other families did, because we found cooperative work too restrictive. We had to show up at a certain hour. Although we got back the land, we lost our cow with this resignation because of some change in cooperative management personnel. We managed to buy a buffalo with small loans from relatives. We rejoined after one agricultural season and contributed the buffalo to the cooperative. We eventually adjusted to the work hours in the cooperative. Despite the numerous debates at one point among cooperative members about how many points a task should be given, we were pleased as cooperative members, especially in the earlier days, when a labor-day credit yielded 4 to 5 kilograms of paddy.

In general, the cooperative program proceeded fairly smoothly in Sơn-Dương, as in most northern villages. Over the next fifteen years, the principle of collectivism gained further ascendancy with the establishment of the credit and purchasing cooperatives and the further collectivization of the means of production. In 1966 village authorities merged four hamlet-level cooperatives into two larger ones. Two years later these two cooperatives merged into a village-wide one in order to plan and utilize resources better. It was a relatively smooth process, as is highlighted in Party member Té's continued narrative:

When the cooperatives were merged, I headed the inspection team and joined the management committee of the new cooperative. In the context of war, the higher-level cooperative in Sơn-Dương had fewer problems than cooperatives elsewhere. I told members of another village: "Your village [cooperative] has three fathers, while we have only one. Despite the earlier division of Sơn-Dương into three villages [before 1945], we had the same customs and worshiped the same guardian deities. The earlier administrative division in Sơn-Dương merely resulted from the conflicting interests of village notables in the past [in the nineteenth century]. In your case, you had three different contests at the annual village festivals: rice cooking, wrestling, and group singing. You had three different traditions; hence the problems with a higher-level cooperative."

The idiom of kinship in Tế's discussion of the smooth merger process in Sơn-Dương suggests that far from being submerged in the egalitarian and collectivist ideology at the time, the hierarchy-centered kinship ideology still persisted as a relatively important parameter of the village structure.

As part of the concentration of production resources, smaller livestock farms were concentrated into a large one. By 1971 the collective farm had increased its stock to 300 breeding ducks and 3.000 for meat and eggs, as well as 20 breeding sows and 300 regular pigs. Hog husbandry annually produced 300 piglets, 1.5 tonnes of pork, and a large quantity of manure for the rice fields. The labor system was changed from working-day credits to credits for specific tasks. The shares of cooperative members in the harvest depended only on their labor contributions and no longer on their contributions of land and draft animals as it had at the time of hamlet-level cooperative formation. By 1965 the yield per crop had increased from 500 to 700 kilograms per *mẫu* (that is, from 1.4 to 1.95 tonnes per hectare), where it remained stable throughout the duration of the U.S. war. Thanks to the increase in double-cropped acreage, paddy production increased from 780 tonnes in 1965 to 940 tonnes in 1972. As a result, despite the population increase, paddy production per person remained approximately 310 kilograms throughout this seven-year period. The village was able to contribute 3,140 tonnes of paddy to the war effort from 1965 to 1975 through its tax obligations and through low-priced sales to the state.

However, partly because of the need to minimize the risk to human life in large gatherings during the intensive U.S. bombing of the north (1965–1968), the production process was decentralized through a contract system. After the merger of smaller cooperatives, although planning became increasingly centralized and resources were concentrated, the agricultural work itself was contracted out to production brigades that corresponded to the earlier hamlet-level cooperatives. It was further contracted to inter-household task-specialized teams that, upon the completion of the work, allowed their members to take care of their own household gardens. This decentralization took place during a three-year period beginning on the very first day of U.S. bombing in Sơn-Dương and the province in June 1965; over this time 620 U.S. fighter squadrons reportedly dropped tens of thousands of tons of bombs on Phú-Thọ and neighboring Vĩnh-Phúc (*Vĩnh-Phú* 1971:108). The village rebuilt bomb shelters; organized fire, excavation, alarm, and emergency medical teams; trained the village militia to shoot at low-flying attack planes and the entire population to capture parachuting pilots; and dispersed village classes throughout the four hamlets. Wearing thick thatch hats, young students took lessons sitting half-way inside classroom trenches in order to minimize the risk to their lives. During this period, in order to gather information, sabotage the economy, and weaken the will of the North Vietnamese people, the United States reportedly sent South Vietnam-based commando teams into the province and dropped propaganda leaflets and counterfeit North Vietnamese bills (*Vĩnh-Phú* 1971:108–109). These measures by the United States were to no avail, as the solidarity among the villagers increased in support of the war effort, both in terms of resources and manpower. The state and the Party appealed to the young people of Sơn-Dương with its slogan "Three Readinesses, Three Capacities": for men, these were readinesses to fight, to join the armed forces, and to be assigned to whatever task the country deemed necessary; for women, they were the capacities to take care of the family and encourage male family members to fight in the war, to take charge of production and other tasks on behalf of departing male fighters, and to serve the war and prepare to fight. Three hundred sixty men were sent to the front between 1965 and 1975. As a result, women played an even greater role than before in the production process. Households with insufficient labor and too many consumers were sold paddy at preferential prices by the cooperative.

In early 1968, toward the end of the intensive U.S. bombing campaign, the village of Sơn-Dương became part of the new province of Vĩnh-Phú, which was created by the merger of Phú-Thọ and neighboring Vĩnh-Phúc. Toward the end of the three-year U.S. bombing campaign in 1968, certain localities in Vĩnh-Phú experimented for the first time with a system of household contracts, especially in livestock husbandry. In the Đồng-Xuân cooperative (Lập-Thạch district) households on contract with the cooperative for pig husbandry were allotted a certain amount of cooperative land to grow food for the pigs. They would receive labor-day credits for meeting production quotas (for example, twenty-three labor-day credits for a 55-kilogram pig and half a tonne of manure), 80 percent of the surplus above the quota, or a penalty of 40 percent of the deficit in case of falling below the production target (*Vĩnh-Phú*, April 12, 1968, 2–3).[8] The collective hog stock consequently increased from 3 in 1961 to almost 200 in early 1968, not counting the sizable private stocks of cooperative members. The provincial leadership extolled Đồng-Xuân's exemplary achievements. Other villages were exhorted on a weekly basis to follow Đồng-Xuân's innovation by the provincial Party newspaper *Vĩnh-Phú*, which carried a large headline: "Learn From, Catch Up, and Bypass Đồng-Xuân; Struggle to Achieve Three Major Objectives: Each laborer cultivating one hectare, producing 5 tonnes of paddy, and raising two hogs." The household contract system quickly spread to the rest of the province, including the village of Sơn-Dương, where it was adopted for swan husbandry. By October 1968, 618 cooperatives in Vĩnh-Phú (more than half of its agricultural cooperatives) had entered into production competition with Đồng-Xuân. In certain cooperatives, especially in Kim-Anh, Lập-Thạch, Vĩnh-Tường, and Yên-Lãng districts, households even contracted with the cooperative for transplanting, tending, and fertilizing both rice and secondary crops (*Vĩnh-Phú*, March 21, 1968, 1; *Vĩnh-Phú* July 30, 1968, 1). However, Party ideologues at the provincial and national levels quickly smothered the movement:

> A good contract system responds to the basic needs of socialist management: to create conditions conducive to a continuous increase in labor productivity and, most importantly, to strengthen the collective economy, as well as to perfect the new [socialist] relations of production... and simultaneously to conquer the small-producer mentality....
>
> As the Party leadership committee of Bình Xuyên district has recognized, the [household] contract system easily becomes a total contract system in which cooperative members receive paddy fields for their own cultivation of vegetables and secondary crops on contract with the cooperative.... This is a decentralized management method that weakens the collective economy and incidentally enlarges the household economy sector. It is contrary to the principle of socialist management. It is a symptom of rightist thinking. (*Vĩnh-Phú*, November 1, 1968, 2)

The ideologues suggested instead the limitation of contracts to small production teams—a method that, in their opinion, fostered both the collectivistic ideology and the exchange of technical knowledge (*Vĩnh-Phú,* November 1, 1968, 2; November 22, 1968, 1; December 13, 1968, 2). The leadership of the Party branch and the cooperative in Sơn-Dương were directly reprimanded for allowing household contracts in swan husbandry.

As a further consequence of the collectivistic ideology, the purchase price for paddy that the state commercial apparatus offered to cooperatives fell increasingly behind the inflation-prone cost of living. By 1970 the paddy price offered by the state amounted to only 25 percent of the going rate at local rural markets (Phạm-Cường and Nguyễn-văn-Bá 1976:104). The radical collectivist ideology remained dominant in the public domain as late as 1978. When the household contract system was reintroduced in 1978 for the cultivation of secondary staple crops in certain localities, the Party secretary of Vĩnh-Phú province reportedly declared in a provincial Party meeting: "It is better to let the fields lie fallow than to allow household contracts."

The local covert resistance to the radical collectivistic vision of political economy emerged strongly after the end of the U.S. war in 1975, when cooperative members increasingly turned their attention to their household garden plots. If a major war with a Western superpower had strengthened the solidarity and collectivistic orientation of Sơn-Dương villagers, agricultural production suffered a serious setback in the 1978–1981 period as the yield per hectare dropped from an average 2 tonnes in the preceding fifteen years to approximately 1.5 tonnes per crop. The declining productivity stemmed from a decline in the returns from cooperative work, which was caused by two sets of factors. First were the decrease in cultivated surface, due to various public work projects, and the absorption of the growing population (an unabated annual birth rate of 3 percent) into the local agricultural work force. The yield from the land was now divided among a larger number of cooperative members. Second were the continuing decline in the state's purchase price for paddy (as low as 12 percent of the market value) and the greater scarcity of subsidized consumer goods after Chinese aid was cut off as a result of the Sino-Vietnamese conflict (Ngô-Vĩnh-Long 1988; see also White 1988; Fforde 1989:194–197). In a vicious cycle, the diminishing returns from cooperative work led villagers to pay greater attention to their household garden plots. Despite the adoption of high-yield crop varieties, the return on a cooperative labor-day credit declined steadily to below 2 kilograms by the late 1970s from approximately 6 kilograms at the onset of the cooperative program in 1958–1960. The former cooperative president Tế noted the problems:

> In Sơn-Dương, despite the lack of conflicts rooted in tradition [among the merged hamlets and lower-level cooperatives], the yield per labor day in the higher-level cooperative dropped steadily to an average of 1.7 to 1.8 kilograms of paddy. This problem stemmed from population growth and the decrease in cultivated acreage. The village population kept increasing. At the same time, cultivated acreage had dropped owing to the construction of irrigation canals, the collective livestock farm, collective paddy-drying courtyards, and collective warehouses. [Furthermore] cooperative members received points for the work on contract [to the task-specialized teams]. They consequently showed up late and tried to finish the work as soon as possible so that they could take care of their gardens and other economic activities at home.

In the summer of 1979, for the first time in half a century, Nguyễn Đắc Bằng returned to his homeland from Canada, where he had resettled in 1976 with his new family from Guyana (see Luong 1992: 117–124, 163–167). He made a second, extended visit in early 1983 to experience again the New Year celebrations of his youth. In 1991, in his last visit to the land of his birth before passing away in 1996, he was accompanied by two daughters and a grandson. Bằng's extensive account of his encounter with the land and people of his youth after half a century of exile adds many details to the picture of life in the village in those difficult years of the radical collectivistic economy:

> My feeling was indescribable when the Aeroflot plane landed at Hanoi's Nội-Bài Airport on my first trip…the following morning, I ran into my senior brother Gia on the hotel staircase on the way down to breakfast. It was an emotional encounter after half a century of absence, as tears streamed down our faces and as we happily wept at being able to see each other again.
>
> [The following day, returning to Sơn-Dương,] I was led to our ancestral land, where I saw nothing but a poor thatch house. Like the pagoda, the meeting hall, and, as I found out later, also our ancestral hall, much of the five-room brick house of my youth had been destroyed by French bombing during the Franco-Vietminh war. The

only reminders of the house of my youth were the brick gate, the brick yard, and the house steps. From the house came joyful screams of "Grandfather Bằng is home at last." In the next half hour even more people came to the small house already full of relatives.

Visitors came forward one after another, introducing themselves as the children of such-and-such persons. The passage of the decades notwithstanding, I was still able to pass muster as I told them where I thought their parents and grandparents had lived in the days of my youth. They were quite pleased at seeing me home, able to recollect the events of the past, my advanced age and the half century of absence notwithstanding. . . .

It was an eventful first night in Sơn-Dương because of the loose village security and the dilapidated condition of my ancestral house. It rained hard during the night. In the heavy rain, water poured down through the leaky thatch roof into the house. We had to change our sleeping location from one corner to another! The house was also broken into during the rainstorm. A few hoodlums from the village anticipated a successful night, thinking that as an overseas Vietnamese from North America, I had brought back a large amount of cash. Sleeping on the same bed with me in the altar-cum-guest room, the main room of the house, my brother's grandsons were awakened by the noise and caught the burglars in the house.

Retaining his pleasure-seeking lifestyle, my brother Gia had done little to maintain our ancestral home. As the head of my branch of the Nguyễn Doãn patrilineage, [my senior brother] Gia and his wife had lived [in our ancestral home] together with his second son and the latter's family. Having been in conflict with his father, Gia's eldest son Thuy had long before moved to the village of Phú-Hộ, a former hilly plantation about 15 kilometers away, where he had a lot of children by his second and third wives. . . . The condition of my ancestral house was particularly deplorable because the majority of village houses had been constructed of bricks by the time of my visit. The living conditions in the countryside had improved a great deal over the past. The village fields were double-cropped, because the government had built a long irrigation canal from the Lâm-Thao district seat to Việt-Trì.

After my first day in my home village, I went with relatives to the Ngũ-Xã market, which was held every morning. The periodic market of the old days in my village was no longer held. In our area only the Ngũ-Xã and Cao-Mại markets had stood the test of time. The trip was not bad because [even after the heavy rain] the village roads were still not too muddy. They had been enlarged and leveled. Although it was not yet possible to drive a car all the way into the village, the roads were no longer flooded in the rainy season.

God, [even] the peasants [at the market] had started talking about my return! Marketing activities were less lively than in the old days, [partly] because there already existed a purchasing and sales cooperative in every village. The merchandise was composed simply of vegetables, frogs, fish, eels, poultry, and other small items that villagers raised, caught, or produced in the small household economic sector. It was mainly old people who sought to earn supplementary incomes [for their families] with paltry amounts of whatever it was in their baskets. The peddlers at Ngũ-Xã market still divided themselves into different areas: one for fish, eels, and frogs, another for poultry and meat, and another for vegetables.

Although the shelves of the cooperative store were virtually empty except for fish sauce, soybean sauce, other minor items, and occasionally meat, the Ngũ-Xã market was simply not as lively as in the old days. The socialist government considered private commerce exploitative in nature. The land had been collectivized, being divided only into ten large fields at the time of my first return. Such a collectivist economy only fostered passivity on the part of the people. Take draft animals. The cooperative had only a few for plowing. One member used one one day, another member the following day, and another the next. The buffalo were overworked and fed little. They could not but die one after another. At one point, the second son-in-law of my deceased senior brother Tăng even had to pull the plow in the field himself because of the shortage of buffalo. The only private land was the household garden plot, where fish, fowl, and pigs were raised and where fruit and vegetables were grown. The government allowed only small-scale private enterprises, such as [cottage] brick industries and housing contract work. For example, Gia's first son, Thuỵ, had worked as a housing contractor for some time. If you wanted to have a house built, you would call him over for measurement, design, material delivery, and construction labor. He simply hired workers for his contracted projects.

*Hiring workers?*

Yes, the government had allowed it well before my first return home. The second daughter of my other brother, Tăng, could produce bricks on order for other villagers. Noncollective economic activities were still allowed, but nowhere close to the scale of the past. I repeatedly said [in Vietnam] that with the continuation of the same collectivistic economy, the buffalo would all die in Vietnam!

The declining productivity of the collective fields in Sơn-Dương village encapsulated the problems on the national scale, since in the 1978–1980 period Vietnam suffered a severe food shortage. It resulted partly from bad weather and partly from the state's low purchase price for paddy. As a result, no sooner had the Vĩnh-Phú Party leadership declared it better to let the fields lie fallow than to allow household contracts than the national Party leadership and the state authorized the household contract system in agriculture in 1981 in a complete policy reversal. Under this system the household, under its two-to-five-year contract with the agricultural cooperative, was responsible for rice transplanting, crop tending, and harvest. In other words, the household was responsible for 70 percent of the labor input in agricultural production, for which it received labor point credit (Nguyễn-Huy 1980:11). In principle, the agricultural cooperative still provided for plowing, irrigation and drainage work, the spreading of fertilizer, seeds, and the spraying of insecticide, although in Sơn-Dương, the household also took care of plowing. Collectively owned land was allocated primarily on the basis of the household's adult work force. To ensure an equitable allocation, under this system each household received small pieces of land of varying quality in different parts of the village (ibid.).[9] The state also increased its purchase price for paddy to a level only slightly below the local market price.

The application of the household contract system in November 1982 brought about a dramatic increase in agricultural productivity and food production in Sơn-Dương, because cooperative members could retain the increased yield above the cooperative quota. Average yields reached 1.3 and 1.5 tonnes per *mẫu* (3.6 and 4.2 tonnes per hectare), respectively, for the summer-fall and winter-spring crops, with the quotas set at 0.88 and 0.94 tonnes per *mẫu*. Corn production averaged 1 tonne per *mẫu*, with a quota of 0.6. Peanuts yielded 0.6 to 0.7 tonnes per *mẫu*, with quotas varying from 0.3 to 0.4 tonnes, depending on the field. When the crop was damaged by natural calamity, the cooperative revised the quotas downward. For example, because the winter-spring crop in 1987 was adversely affected by a drought, and because productivity had declined by an average of one-third, the quota was lowered by 42.5 percent. Instead of 0.94 tonnes, the household on contract delivered only 0.55 tonnes on an average production of 1 tonne per *mẫu*. Similarly, in the fall of the same year, when the average yield dropped further to 0.86 tonnes, the quota was lowered by 47.5 percent to 0.46 tonnes. Members also received back part of the crop delivered on contract to the cooperative on the basis of their labor point credits for work performed on the contracted land. However, out of what cooperative members kept over and above the cooperative quotas and what they earned from the cooperative through the labor-point-credit system, they had to purchase additional fertilizer to maximize the crop yield. This complex system is illustrated in a cooperative member's description of his income sources in the spring of 1987:

> In my family my wife is counted as the only active adult member of the cooperative. I have reached retirement age. Our eldest daughter has already married outside the family. Our eldest son, a veteran, works away from home, and one of his younger brothers is now in the armed forces. Three of our children still go to school at present. With only one active cooperative member, our household receives 0.6 *mẫu* of land contracted with the cooperative. To supplement our income from the cooperative, we also contract for the care of a cooperative buffalo. Our rice harvest last month yielded only 0.6 tonnes of paddy from 0.6 *mẫu* of rice field because of the drought. The cooperative agreed to lower the quota by 43 percent, which means that we delivered 330 kilograms to the cooperative as a part of the contract. On the other hand, we earned 90 labor-day credits for the work done on the contracted 0.6 *mẫu*, on the standard basis of 15 credits for 0.1 *mẫu*. Our work involved transplanting, cultivating, crop tending, harvesting, and drying the paddy. Because of the smaller amount left to the cooperative after paying for retired members' pensions, taxes, chemical fertilizers, seeds, and irrigation water fees, the quantity of paddy for each labor-day credit dropped to 0.5 kilogram from an average of 1.2 kilograms in previous crops. The cooperative consequently owed us only 45 kilograms of paddy for the work on the 0.6 *mẫu* and 100 kilograms for our tending of a cooperative buffalo. Subtracting this amount from the revised quota on 0.6 *mẫu* of contracted land, we still owed the cooperative 185 kilograms. We therefore kept 415 kilograms.
>
> On top of our share of paddy, we also received a cash equivalent of over 30 piasters per labor-day credit from the cooperative's export of peanuts [that is, 7,800 piasters for six months for 290 credits]. On the other hand, we had to spend about 120 kilograms of paddy [about

4,800 piasters] to buy additional chemical fertilizers for our 0.6 *mẫu*. Otherwise, the yield would not have reached 100 kilograms per 0.1 *mẫu*, because the cooperative provided only 3 kilograms of chemical fertilizer per 0.1 *mẫu*. The paddy we received last spring was just enough for a family of five. Fortunately, we earn quite a bit from our hog husbandry. The piglets born of our two breeding sows are usually exchanged with the cooperative for an average of 1.4 tonnes of paddy a year, although this spring I have been selling quite a few piglets to people from other villages for cash. We also have twenty ducks. We sell eggs to villagers for 20 piasters an egg. In addition, we have a brick kiln that can bring in up to 30,000 piasters a year. The elder of our two teenaged daughters can earn quite a bit in her spare time in the summer. She takes a bus to a market about 20 kilometers away, buys wood for retail sale in the local market, and earns 500 to 700 piasters a day [that is, the equivalent of 12.5 to 17.5 kilograms of paddy at the official local price or slightly less at the open market price]. For thirty years of service in the armed forces, I also receive a small pension worth about 5 kilograms of rice a month.

After the spring harvest of 1987 the cooperative delivered 148 tonnes of paddy to the state for the annual tax bill, for an average of 200 kilograms per *mẫu*. The cooperative also owed state agencies approximately 250 tonnes of paddy for chemical fertilizers and the water-control-maintenance fee for the year ending in May 1987. According to the secretary of the local Party branch, the incomes of villagers derived from cooperative work alone averaged an equivalent of 475 kilograms of paddy per person in 1986, when the crops were reportedly average. (This figure includes the share of cash, peanuts, and corn from cooperative work.) It more than doubled the 1980 average income, which stood at 220 kilograms of paddy per person. On the assumption of no change in village obligations toward the state and state agencies between 1986 and 1987, the estimated paddy production in Sơn-Dương reached 1,414 tonnes of paddy in 1986, of which tax levies amounted to 10.3 percent.

Party member and former cooperative president Tế gave a more general overview of the development of the household contract system in the village:

[Despite the overpopulation problem] the crop yield has increased dramatically, from 600 kilograms of rice per *mẫu* at the time of the introduction of household contracts in 1982 to an average of 1.5

tonnes per *mẫu* nowadays. At present, [with the household contract system] some cultivators have even increased the yield to over 2 tonnes per *mẫu,* while the cooperative quotas are set at 0.94 and 0.88 tonnes respectively for the spring and fall crops. For example, in the spring crop of last year [1986], the yield per *mẫu* from our contracted land reached 2 tonnes. We had to hand over to the cooperative only 0.94 tonnes to meet the quota specified in the contract with the cooperative for the spring crop. However, I actually kept almost 1.5 tonnes because I also received seeds as well as paddy for the work performed on the contracted land.

*How much land does your family contract with the cooperative?*
With three main laborers, we contract 1.7 *mẫu* for the winter-spring crop, 1.3 for the summer-fall crop, and about half a *mẫu* for the winter corn crop.

We harvest 90 to 100 kilograms of corn for each *sào* and, paying no taxes to the state, keep 60 to 70 kilograms for ourselves.

I would say that nowadays of every 100 households, 10 are truly well-off, 20 possess some surplus, 50 have sufficient means to feed their members, and only 20 face the problem of making ends meet. These 20 households may have less domestic labor [because of the draft], spend beyond their means, or not want to acquire new technical knowledge. It may be necessary to group them together for collective help, because household contracts or not, they have trouble improving their lives because of their obstinacy.

With the household contract system, provincial food production in Vĩnh-Phú increased by 20 percent to 364,000 tonnes within the three-year period to the end of 1983 (*Nhân-Dân,* June 14, 1984, 2). This rebound from the nadir of the late 1970s was paralleled by similar developments across the country as the production of food crops increased to 18.2 million tonnes in 1985 from 14.4 million tonnes in 1980.

Despite the spectacular success of the household contract system in agriculture, there were minor difficulties in its implementation, both in the village of Sơn-Dương and elsewhere. A small number of villagers in Sơn-Dương complained of the decline in the yield per labor-point credit, a decline from an average of 1.2 to 2 kilograms in the mid-1980s to 0.5 kilograms of paddy in 1987. Both within and beyond the village of Sơn-Dương, the village leadership not infrequently drew upon the resources of the cooperative for public projects and the salaries of village cadres. The yield per labor-point credit diminished as the paddy stock to be divided among cooperative members dwindled. From the perspective of the cooperative management, many villagers showed a lack of responsibility in their use of collectively owned draft animals. Although the cooperative invested money to purchase sixty-four buffaloes between the spring of 1986 and the spring of 1987 in order to increase the collective plowing force, it lost approximately thirty buffaloes in 1987 because they were overworked and underfed. Because of a lack of technical knowledge, shortage of labor, or insufficient resources to purchase fertilizer, approximately 10 percent of the contracting households could barely produce above the production quotas and could not make ends meet. By early 1988, 26 percent of the 822 contracting households (214 households) owed the cooperative 110 tonnes of paddy because they had food shortages. Beyond Sơn-Dương, in the province of Hà-Nam-Ninh in the lower delta of northern Vietnam, many cultivators took the decisive step of returning the contracted land to their cooperatives after experiencing diminishing yields per labor-point credit and an increase in their production quotas. The return of the land led to a serious food shortage in this province in the spring of 1988.

To provide additional incentives for cultivators to increase crop yields and raise national food production above the 1985 figure of 18 million tonnes, the national leadership reformed the household contract system in early 1988. Party Directive 10 prohibited village administrations from tapping cooperative resources for their cadres' salaries. It also prohibited the cooperative from increasing production quotas without a technological change and a corresponding higher crop yield. Most important, it guaranteed cooperative members a long-term lease on the contracted land and at least 40 percent of the production quota for their fulfillment of the transplanting, crop-tending, and harvesting tasks. (Had this policy been applied in the fall of 1987, given the revised production quota of 46 kilograms per *sào,* Sơn-Dương cultivators would have received 18.4 kilograms per *sào* instead of the actual 6.75 kilograms for their fifteen labor points.)

In order to raise food production, the village leadership in Sơn-Dương refined the household contract system in the spring of 1988. Agricultural households were divided into three categories: poor contractors (70 households), average contractors (412 households), and good contractors (350 households). Poor contractors were defined as households whose crop yields usually fell below the norm of 1.4 tonnes per *mẫu* and who could not pay back their paddy debts to the cooperative. Average contractors usually produced within the norm, and good contracting households clearly exceeded it. With this distinction among contracting households, the village leadership planned to allow the good contractors to bid on 110 *mẫu* of the most fertile rice fields (called *ruộng tăng sản*). The objective was to reward good contractors and to increase productivity on the land. However, this contract system had to be modified to some extent in the direction of greater equality under the pressure from Sơn-Dương cultivators. Of the 273 hectares (760 *mẫu*) of reallocated land, 31.25 hectares (86.8 *mẫu,* called 10 percent rice fields) were equally divided among all residents of the village, regardless of gender and age. Each person received 72 square meters. Even retired state cadres were allocated 72 square meters each. A second pool was formed of 180.76 hectares (502.1 *mẫu*), which the cooperative allocated on an egalitarian basis to all villagers, except for industrial workers, white-collar workers, and retired state employees. The third category included 61.9 hectares (171.9 *mẫu*), many fields with less reliable yields, on which only the more successful cultivators could bid. Of these hectares, 36 (100 *mẫu*) were considered fields with more reliable yields, from which the cooperative required bidders to hand in 2 hundredweights of paddy per *mẫu* on top of what the cultivators of fields in the second pool had to submit. The cooperative promised not to raise production quotas for at least five years. Barring a change in household size and contracting status, contracting households were also guaranteed the same pieces of land for twenty years as an incentive for them to make long-term investments in the fields. In 1989, primarily as a result of reform refinements in the previous year, national food production increased to 20 million tonnes. Vietnam resumed the export of rice after a hiatus of about forty years and regained its status as the third major rice exporter in the world. Its rice exports exceeded 1 million tonnes in 1989 and 1990.

As part of the decentralization process, the agricultural cooperative in Sơn-Dương sold, in spring 1988, its entire herd of 108 buffaloes to members at the going market price of 0.5 tonne of paddy each. Any group of five cultivators without a draft animal was given priority in this program. Buyers were required to pay half of the amount after the spring crop and the other half after the fall 1988 and spring 1989 rice harvests. Including additional buffaloes purchased by individual households from other communities, the draft animal force of Sơn-Dương had increased to 382 by the end of the summer of 1988. As part of the general trend, the collective livestock farm had been abandoned since 1982. The farm buildings had all been dismantled except for the frames. The largest cooperative paddy-drying courtyard was rented to a private carpenter, reportedly the

**Photo 1.** Main village road

**Photo 2.** Old-style village house

**Photo 3.** Interior decorated in traditional style

**Photo 4.** Interior decorated in revolutionary style

**Photo 5.** Herbal pharmacist measuring ingredients

**Photo 6.** Washing dishes by the household well

**Photo 7.** Abandoned collective livestock farm marks the shift from collective agriculture to decentralized household production

wealthiest man in the village, with savings of at least 70 tonnes of paddy. The seventy poor households faced serious difficulties, since the expected monthly food supply of 15 kilograms per capita from the basic rice field allotment *(ruộng khẩu)* would have to be partially reinvested in the purchase of seeds, fertilizer, and plowing services. Secondary occupational opportunities were quite limited, except at the village market reopened in the late summer of 1988 and at the private furniture factory, which had twenty-five to thirty-five employees, mostly from outside the village. Approximately ten households also wove mosquito-net cloth. Some villagers also engaged in petty trade. A female villager who started trading rice in the mid-1980s reported having carried rice in baskets, 30–40 kilograms each time, and, due to the lack of bicycles, walked with fellow traders for almost 10 kilometers each way to the industrial town of Cao-Mại to supplement their meager agricultural incomes. Those with bicycles reportedly went to Thanh-Sơn district across the river and earned 7 kilograms of bamboo shoots for one week of trade. The socioeconomic differentiation among village households had increased markedly since 1982, although land, as the most important basis of production, was still largely collectivized. The radical collectivistic emphasis of the 1960s and 1970s had clearly shifted in favor of the hierarchical sociocultural model centering on the kinship unit.

The hierarchical model had persisted to a remarkable degree in the structuring of kinship and gender relations in Sơn-Dương village. Within the communal framework, despite the equal access of female villagers to educational opportunities and their significant role in the agricultural production process, the executive committee of the local Party branch included no female Party member. The enlarged Party leadership committee counted only two women out of seventeen members (11.8 percent), in comparison to the high proportion of 31 percent (four of thirteen) in 1977. None of the five members of the cooperative management committee *(ban quản trị)* was a woman, and only 40 percent of the production team leaders were female, in contrast to 20 percent and 70 percent, respectively, in 1977. The percentage of women rose to 22 percent on the People's Council, which, however, possessed only nominal power in the system. Village leaders explained the decline of women's public status despite their significant labor contribution in terms of women's lack of rhetorical skills and the return of war veterans in the 1980s.

In the familial context, junior adult males were visibly present at the central table in front of the ancestral altar at the expense of their senior female relatives (mother and paternal aunt), who either sat at the side of the room or ate separately in a side room of the house. The only exception involved the frequent insistence among guests and hosts that a widow of truly advanced years, most often the mother of the household head, join the men for the meal at the central table. The desire to have sons for the continuation of the patriline still formed a fundamental part of villagers' sociocultural reality, as pointed out by the secretary of the local Communist Party branch in his earlier discussion of population control. Similarly, patrilocal residence was taken for granted as part of the local reality. In order to reduce the rate of conversion of rice fields into residential land, for example, the Sơn-Dương village administration specified that it would no longer grant a request for residential land unless a household head had more than three daughters-in-law in residence within the same compound. The percentage of patrilineally extended families in Sơn-Dương was estimated to exceed 44 percent in 1987 (see Luong 1989:750). Polygamy still existed, despite its prohibition in the 1960 legal code. One of Bằng's nephews (his half-brother's son) had three wives in 1987–1988, following Bằng's father and grandfather in their tradition of polygyny. After giving birth to a daughter, the nephew's third wife daily entrusted the baby to his second wife when she went to work at the office of the local agricultural cooperative (see also Luong 1989:749–753). By the early 1980s, many patrilineally related households had reconstructed lineage genealogies and collected contributions to re-establish the male-centered patrilineages and the worship of lineage-founding ancestors.

Bằng's narrative on his extended visits to the land of his youth opens another window on the continuity in the texture of the village fabric:

> On learning of my visit to the Ngũ-Xã market and my presence in the area, my former wife Lan, who had been living in the village of Ngũ-Xã, hurriedly left for Sơn-Dương to see me. She had been remarried to a man in Ngũ-Xã. She had done so in 1936 only at my suggestion. I had written to her earlier from South America with this suggestion, because I was not released with my two brothers and many other political prisoners during the first year of the Popular Front government in France. By this time, our second son had also died in infancy.

> *Did your three adopted sons stay on in your household after your deportation to South America?*
> My wife could not raise all three by herself. They all returned to live with their parents. Lan had bad luck in life. Her [second] husband did not live long. Neither did her child with him. She has since lived with the daughter of her second husband in a very big house. She wept all the time during our first encounter after half a century.

> [During my two visits to Sơn-Dương in 1979 and 1983] the news of my return traveled far and fast. My adopted children, those among my pupils who had been adopted because of the poverty of their families, came immediately from other villages in the district on hearing the news of my return. The descendants of some of my comrades who had passed away in South America also invited me to come over so that they could learn more about the lives of their ancestors in that land. I also saw former schoolmates, especially during the second Vietnam visit, and even former gambling partners. During my week-long visit to Phú-Hộ, one of my nephew's daughters also rode me on her bicycle to my maternal land in Xuân-Lũng by the Red River, where I had many emotional encounters with my cousins on my mother's side. I was invited to many banquets by relatives within my patrilineage, by my adopted children, and especially by my former pupils, dozens of whom were still alive at the time and some of whom had achieved high-ranking provincial and district positions in the socialist government. I received so many invitations, at times as many

as three on the same day, that I told a nephew of mine to handle my social calendar. Otherwise, the specially prepared food would remain untouched and be wasted.

I organized together with my senior brother Gia a family reunion on the anniversary of our father's death.... "This year on father's death anniversary, you can tell our nieces and nephews or their children that I will pay for the entire anniversary event. They simply need to come to help with the purchase and the preparation of foods," I told Gia. Normally, the sons and daughters of the deceased make financial contributions to the gathering held on the anniversary of a parent's death. The deceased's grandchildren would make the contributions on their parents' behalf if the latter had passed away. A few days before the anniversary, the children or grandchildren would have to contact the chief of the patrilineage branch to inquire about how he planned to organize the anniversary and what they needed to contribute. The contributions were usually in the form of uncooked rice, regular or glutinous. If the anniversary was small, only chickens and ducks were cooked. In the case of a bigger anniversary, a pig might be slaughtered. [At my father's anniversary] my senior brother Gia had to kowtow first three times before the altar, praying to my father as the head of the lineage branch and asking him to enjoy the food offerings. Other relatives and our close associates followed him before the altar. We then divided ourselves up four to a tray, with the four senior relatives in the middle. Although large banquets [to which all relatives could be invited] were no longer given, there still existed a spirit of kinship, at least within the branch.

During my second Vietnam visit, as it had been planned to coincide with the New Year, my senior brother's eldest son, as the branch chief, and I had to bring offerings to the altar of our patrilineage-founding ancestors. The genealogies of my lineage and my branch are still maintained and updated. In my father's branch, genealogical records with the listing of both sons and daughters and descendants through sons date back at least four generations. During the second visit I even returned [to Xuân-Lũng] for my maternal grandfather's death anniversary in my mother's patrilineage. Attendance at the Xuân-Lũng anniversary easily totaled fifty to sixty, because my maternal grandfather had quite a few children.

In other words the process of transformation in the village of Sơn-Dương from 1954 to 1988 was not free of tension. It involved a dialectical relation between the principle of radical collectivism espoused by the Marxist state and a hierarchical model for sociocultural reality centering on the kinship unit. The official collectivist ideology of the state emerged dominant in the northern social formation and underlay a radical transformation of the village political economy. However, the pace of change was not uniform. These fluctuations notwithstanding, the sense of progress in Sơn-Dương village was unmistakable, especially to the poor villagers of the darker colonial days. The sense of gratitude and optimism that pervaded the narrative of the former landless laborer and Party member Tế summed up well the views of many less articulate villagers:

> After thirty-two years of public service, from the days in the armed forces to my final year as a credit cooperative president, I think that our victory over French imperialism in spite of our primitive weapons had to do with our strong will to free ourselves of foreign oppression and enslavement as well as with the leadership of Uncle Hồ and the Party. Other fellow countrymen had risen up before then, but their vision did not appeal as well to the masses.
>
> Having gone through the struggle for national independence and the revolution, I see clearly what it has brought to people, especially to the poor. Before the revolution we had to wade in the mud on the village roads during the rainy season, because many young men had to work elsewhere for the entire year and could not stay long enough in the village to repair the roads. In terms of health care, in the old days we had to rely on traditional medicine and prayers. As far as education was concerned, the village school had thirty or forty pupils, and continuation beyond the third grade was possible only for the children of well-off families. Personally, I still remember so vividly the famine of 1945, when we had to substitute manioc and sweet potatoes for rice. I still recall how for ten piasters owed to a village landlord, a relative and an acquaintance of mine had to mortgage the services of their children as live-in domestic servants and dung-collecting and grass-cutting services for two or three years until the loans were paid off. Nowadays we have widened roads, a village clinic staffed by nurses and physicians, and a village school through to the secondary level with a thousand students. Some villagers have rising expectations and feel discontented with their present conditions: having bicycles, they demand motorcycles, and they will eventually want automobiles. But it is simply greed.

Personally, I feel content with having my own house, my own bicycle, my own cow, and an oxcart. After the harvest, we can transport the grain back to the house in the oxcart and have it polished with the cooperative's machines. Although our house does not have much furniture, I do not care as long as we have warm clothes and sufficient food. It is more important to foster in one's children collectivism and ethical standards. I only wish to see my sons fulfill well their military duties to the state and their moral obligations to the community. As our traditional proverb puts it: "A monument will be eroded within one century. A reputation will last for millennia." I do not agree at all with some brothers in the village who are better off and who still grumble about their living conditions. I find the present expectations of young people unreasonable. In the old days, even at the Hùng King shrine festival, we did not dress as fancily and colorfully as the youth do nowadays. We worked hard and saved pennies in our day. The youth of today spend almost without limits, hundreds of piasters for a shirt and a pair of trousers. We care about sufficient food and warm clothes, while they think of good taste and a nice appearance. They simply take for granted what we had to struggle so hard for. They do not even want to believe our stories of the old days. Our country is still poor. However, compared with my youth, we have come a long way. On the ceiling of my house up there are parallel sentences carved at the time when our house was built in 1977. It sums up my thoughts: "Owing to ancestors, the new house is constructed; thanks to the Party and Uncle [Hồ], the present conditions are achieved" *(Ơn tổ tiên xây nhà mới, nhờ bác đảng có ngày nay).*

# PART III

# Market Economy and Local Dynamics

CHAPTER 6

# The Market Economy and
# Socioeconomic Differentiation

In 2006 the village of Sơn-Dương was more integrated into the Viet-namese market economy and the global capitalist system than at any point since the consolidation of power by the postcolonial Vietnamese state in 1954. This integration was partly facilitated by a better road and transport system. Living standards had significantly improved as a result of agricultural decollectivization and market economy participation, the greater vulnerabilities of the poor notwithstanding. The relatively egalitarian class system during the command-economy era had also become gradually restructured as a result.

Two decades earlier, a Sơn-Dương villager wishing to get to Hanoi had to ride a bicycle to the provincial capital of Việt-Trì in order to take a state-run train or boat to the national capital. This sixty-mile trip had normally taken seven hours. Starting in 2001, a bus run by a private entrepreneur in neighboring Kinh-Kệ commune passed through Sơn-Dương at about 6:00 a.m. every day to pick up passengers going to Hanoi. Villagers missing that bus could go to neighboring Tứ-Xã commune (formerly called Ngũ-Xã, see Map 3) or to the district seat to catch buses that departed twice daily for Hanoi. Despite many stops along the way, the trip to the capital of Vietnam was reduced to about three hours. Villagers could also take an alternative, fairly quick route on the other side of the Red River, going through Sơn-Tây to Hanoi, thanks to the construction of two new bridges in 2003 and the significant improvement in the road system. From the provincial capital, villagers could also take a bus direct to the southern province of Bình Dương, a rapidly growing light-industrial center next to Hồ Chí Minh City. Many villagers had joined the migrant workforce, finding employment not only in the provincial capital of Việt-Trì, but also in Hanoi, southern Vietnam, and overseas.

Sơn-Dương villagers participated in the market economy not simply through selling their labor and products elsewhere. The market economy had penetrated deeply into the daily lives of those remaining in Sơn-Dương through the commodification of residential land. During the command-economy era, village government allocated residential land on the basis of need. In 1994 the village government sold 8.4 hectares of residential land at the price of 40,000 VND (US $3.65) a square meter along the main village road. Ten years later the price of property along this road had skyrocketed to an average of 850,000 VND (US $54). It even reached 1 million VND (US $64) a square meter near the center of the village. The decade saw an average increase of fifteen times the price in 1994 along the main village road; partly this was because the road had been paved and officially designated as a part of provincial highway 324. Numerous private businesses had sprung up along the road.

By 2006 most of the village streets had been paved in concrete, replacing the paths that used to be muddy in the rain. But the physical improvement in the village went far beyond the road system. Visitors to Sơn-Dương could not help but notice the beautifully renovated elementary and junior high schools at one end of the village or the more elaborate tombstones in the cemetery nearby (see Photos 8 and 9).

**Photo 8.** New elementary school

**Photo 9.** Renovated tomb

Villagers had also extensively renovated the village pagoda, and they reconstructed an imposing communal house by April 2006 (see Photos 10–13). The changes in physical infrastructure had reached deeply into village households: electricity had come to the village over a decade earlier, and piped water since 2002. While there had been only two two-storied houses in the village in 1987 and four in 1995, by 2006 numerous two-storied houses had sprung up in different parts of Sơn-Dương (Photo 14). All of these improvements had been funded with private money, reflecting a rapid rise in household wealth in Sơn-Dương. My 2004 survey of 283 Sơn-Dương households reveals a net per capita income of 3.55 million VND (US $228) a year for the period from July 2003 to June 2004.[1] This was equivalent to 1,739 kilograms of paddy and was 3.9 times higher than the estimated net per capita income a decade and a half earlier (see Luong 1993:268–269). The living standards in Sơn-Dương had improved significantly in less than two decades following Sơn-Dương's incorporation into the market economy of Vietnam and the global system, and thanks to state investment in the village infrastructure during the 2001–2006 period.

**Photos 10 and 11.** Communal houses

**Photos 12 and 13.** Village pagodas

**Photo 14.** New two-storied house

# Village Economy

Income sources for village households had diversified significantly since the end of the collectivized economy in the late 1980s. By 2004 agriculture accounted for only 42.5 percent of the net incomes in the 283 surveyed households in Sơn-Dương. Of this, 35.5 percent came from local nonagricultural sources and 22 percent from remittances and private monetary gifts.

### Land and Agriculture

In 1994 the agricultural land in Sơn-Dương was reallocated for twenty years in a total decollectivization of agriculture. Villagers had total freedom in the production process and in their use and marketing of agricultural products. The agricultural cooperative which had played the dominant role in the command-economy era was transformed into an irrigation-water and crop-protection provider on contract with agricultural households. The twenty production teams in the village were no longer directly involved in production; instead they represented team members in negotiations with the service cooperative and collected fees and taxes for the cooperative and the local government.

Cultivated land was divided into three categories:

1.  "Garden" land: 76 *mẫu* (27 hectares, slightly over 10 percent of the
    cultivated acreage), which local authorities had designated as garden
    land, were not reallocated in 1994. Each villager retained the 72 square
    meters of garden land allocated in 1988.
2.  Reserve land: 55 *mẫu* (19.8 hectares, over 7 percent of the cultivated
    acreage) were transferred from the agricultural cooperative to the vil-
    lage government in order to deal with an anticipated increase in the
    need for residential land and other local needs in the future, In Sơn-
    Dương, village authorities sold off 8.4 hectares (23.3 *mẫu*) in 1994 in
    order to bring electricity to the village from a major provincial road
    about two kilometers away. They rented out the rest through auction
    in order to obtain supplementary income for village expenses.
3.  The rest of cultivated land (about 600 *mẫu* or 216 hectares) was divided
    among villagers on an egalitarian basis. The majority of those in the
    agricultural labor force received 468 square meters each. Each child
    born between the issuance of the national land decree (Decree 64)
    in 1993 and its implementation in Sơn-Dương in 1994 received only
    120 square meters. Households with tax arrears (192, almost 20 per-
    cent of village households) received only 192 to 298 square meters for
    each person born before the issuance of Decree 64, depending on the
    amount of the tax arrears. The twenty production teams formed dur-
    ing the era of collective agriculture still retained the land that would
    have been distributed to those households and rented them out to other
    households in the same teams.

The decollectivization process in Sơn-Dương differed from that in
most localities in the Red River delta in that the former villages of Sơn-
Dương, Dụng-Hiền, and Thụy-Sơn did not reclaim their pre-1954 land,
whereas villages *(thôn* or *làng)* elsewhere reclaimed theirs from the commune *(xã)*-level cooperatives and allocated that land to their own members
(cf. Kleinen 1999:10, 13, 14).

As a reflection of an egalitarian ideology and in order to ensure an
egalitarian distribution, given the varying quality of land, a household typically received eight to twelve parcels of cultivable fields in different parts
of the village. From 1994 onwards, villagers had to pay only agricultural
taxes, irrigation and crop-protection fees, and other fees imposed by the
village government and collected by the agricultural cooperative. The villagers had total control over the production and marketing of their final
products. In 2002 the national government also eliminated agricultural
taxes. In 2004 the village cooperative collected annually 33.5 kilograms of

paddy for each *sào* (360 square meters), or 930 kilograms for each hectare, 63 percent of which went to the irrigation authorities. The rest was retained in the village to cover various services provided by the cooperative. Important for villagers was the principle that land would no longer be adjusted for family size and that children born after this land reallocation would not be eligible to receive any land, at least not until 2014. Because it was possible that land might be reallocated in 2014, and because numerous villagers considered agricultural production to yield only a modest income, no market developed for agricultural land in Sơn-Dương. Households that migrated elsewhere usually rented their land to close relatives. In contrast, an active market had developed for residential land. It was due to villagers' continuing demand for residential land and the collective need to fund village infrastructure projects that the village government continuously sold off reserve land between 1993 and 2006. The biggest residential land sale took place in 1993–1994 when, in order to cover the cost of bringing electricity from a major provincial highway to Sơn-Dương, the village government sold off 8.4 hectares of reserve land. In 2004, when higher authorities required the village to shoulder 60 percent of village infrastructure costs, the local government decided to sell off an additional 1,350 square meters for 810 million VND (for an average of 600,000 VND or US $38 per square meter).[2] The acreage of reserve land had dropped from 55 *mẫu* (19.8 hectares) in 1994 to 39 *mẫu* (14 hectares) a decade later.

Agricultural diversification toward cash crops had taken place very slowly in Sơn-Dương despite the village's relative proximity to a major industrial town with a factory workforce in 2003 of 4,743, as well as to the provincial capital of Việt-Trì, a major industrial center of north Vietnam with a 2003 population of 136,123. Only nineteen of the surveyed households (6.8 percent) in the village regularly cultivated vegetables, and an additional twenty-two (7.8 percent) cultivated vegetables for a part of the year. The amount of land used for vegetable cultivation averaged 464 square meters among those forty-one households. They planted a variety of cash crops, including green beans, pumpkins, soy beans, onions, and tomatoes, but they faced wide fluctuations in price for their produce. One village official commented: "Villagers plant cash crops on almost ten hectares of land. But to whom can we sell garlic, cucumbers, chili pepper, and peanuts? In the neighboring village of Sơn-Vi, chili peppers fall all over and make the ground red, as the prices are too low."

In 2003–2004 the average net income from vegetable cultivation was only 4.1 million VND (US $261) a hectare, which was not at all higher than that from paddy. Yet according to all interviewed villagers, vegetable cultivation required considerably more household labor for crop watering

**Table 8.** Paddy yield per hectare (in tonnes)

|                | 1986 | 1987 | 1988 | 1989 | 1990 |
|----------------|------|------|------|------|------|
| Chiêm (spring) | 4.2  | 2.8  | 3.2  | 4.1  | 3.9  |
| Mùa (fall)     | 3.6  | 1.7  | 2.9  | 3.7  | 2.2  |

and protection than growing rice. As an exception, a former Communist Party secretary reported in 1998 a net earning of 20–25 million VND (US $1,500–$1,860) a year on 1,080 square meters of cash crop land. His strategy involved a careful timing of cultivation and harvest, and his family harvested the crop in small quantity at different times in order to avoid having to sell a large quantity at a time of market oversupply. The village president noted that this success also resulted from his access to irrigation water and his ability to protect his crop better because his home was at the edge of the village close to his land.

In 2004 most households in the village adopted the pattern of two rice crops and one winter crop of corn (crop rotation pattern 1 in Figure 2, Chapter 5). Of the households surveyed, 240 (86 percent) cultivated this winter crop, for an average of 1,231 square meters among the corn-cultivating households. This crop yielded an average net profit of 5.36 million VND (US $344) per hectare in the winter of 2004.

In the twelve months preceding our June 2004 survey, paddy yield varied from 4.3 tonnes a hectare for the fall 2003 crop to 5.3 tonnes for the spring 2004 one. Figures from village authorities for the period from 1995 to 2003 indicate that paddy yield varied from 3.3 tonnes a hectare (fall 1997) to 5.8 tonnes a hectare (spring 2003), for an average of 4.4 tonnes a hectare for this nine-year period. Despite these fairly significant variations, the figures show an improvement and a lesser variation than for the 1986–1990 period, when the paddy yield varied from 1.7 tonnes to 4.2 tonnes a hectare, for an average of 3.2 tonnes a hectare (see Table 8).[3]

The increase in paddy yield in the decade and a half since the late 1980s resulted from the adoption of higher-yield varieties and more investment in chemical fertilizers. Of the average cash investment of 3.82 million VND (US $245) per hectare per crop, the major expenses were chemical fertilizers (44.3 percent), irrigation water fees (13.1 percent), land rental (12.9 percent), seeds (12.7 percent), and insecticides and herbicides (6.3 percent). The remaining fairly important costs were plowing fees and labor (3.4 percent), transplanting labor (3.1 percent), harvesting labor (1.5 percent), and transportation from field and drying (1.3 percent). The labor costs were modest because of the average 249 labor days invested per crop in a hectare of paddy field, only 5 percent involved hired labor. All these cash expenses amounted to an average of 40 percent of the paddy yield value in a good harvest season, and 56.5 percent in a season with a mediocre yield. Sơn-Dương villagers retained an average of 300 kilograms of paddy (about 210 kilograms of rice) per person per year for their own consumption and sold off 49 percent of the crop to cover expenses.

Within agriculture, most major risk-takers among the Sơn-Dương villagers invested not in vegetable cultivation, but in hog and fish farms. Household 139 was one of the wealthiest in Sơn-Dương, with a per-capita annual income of about 16 million VND (about US $1,000). The household had rented 1.66 hectares of land from the village since 1995 at an annual rate of 1.6 tonnes of paddy per hectare. This land was turned into a fish farm, which the household had established by borrowing 100 million VND (US $6,400) in 2003;50 million VND ($3,200) was still owed to the Bank of Agriculture in 2004. Like other cash crops, fish suffered a wide fluctuation in market price. The 0.11 hectares (3 *sào*) of shrimp cultivation suffered from a precipitous drop in price (almost 50 percent) between the time the household began raising its shrimp to its harvest of them in 2004, permitting it to only break even with regard to cash expenses and bring in no compensation for household labor. Luckily for this household, fish brought in higher prices in the twelve months preceding my fieldwork in 2004 because the avian influenza in Vietnam caused many consumers to switch from fowl to fish.

Besides the risk of price fluctuations, fish-farm owners risked social conflict with paddy cultivators over access to water and the paddy cultivators' use of fertilizers and insecticides that affected the fish. The head of the fish-farming household 139 reported that he was willing to enlarge his aquaculture business if he could rent a much larger area in order to reduce the risk of fertilizer and pesticide leakage from the paddy fields. The paddy cultivators, on the other hand, complained about the fish and shrimp farms of which the operation affected the flow of irrigation water for their crops. Mediating this conflict, the commune leadership considered zoning as a strategic solution for the development of aquaculture, which they considered an important part of the strategy to diversify the local economy. They planned to increase aquaculture acreage from 7 hectares in 2004 to 11 hectares in 2006.

However, the zoning solution immediately encountered the problem of villagers' highly fragmented land holdings, a problem rooted in their demand for an egalitarian distribution of fields of varying quality located in different parts of the village. During my fieldwork in summer 2004, the village authorities launched a campaign to persuade their fellow villagers to consolidate their holdings by exchanging land with their neighbors, if they held any piece under 240 square meters. Of the village households with agricultural land, 70 percent had one or more fields under 240 square meters. Many villagers were not enthusiastic about this plan and cited the future division of fields among their children. No matter how consolidated their fields might be to begin with, they would ultimately fragment again. But the village authorities persisted and reported that by the end of 2006 they had essentially completed the voluntary land-exchange program.

### Industrial Employment and Commerce

Most villagers sought to increase their income not from agriculture and aquaculture, but through the sale of their labor, among those who were short of capital or risk-averse, or, by opening new businesses, among those with capital and willingness to take risk.

In 2003–2004, 184 village residents in 283 surveyed households had nonagricultural earnings of at least 70,000 VND a month. Of these villagers seventy-eight commuted to work: twenty-four to the provincial capital, twenty-six to the former district seat 8 kilometers away, and fourteen to nearby communes in the same district or across the Red River. One important employer of commuting Sơn-Dương villagers was the state fertilizer and chemical factory in the old Lâm-Thao district seat. With its 4,353 workers by the end of 2003, it was the largest industrial employer in the province of Phú-Thọ (Phú-Thọ-Statistical Office 2004:189). However, the relatively modest expansion of this state firm during the 1994–2004 period led a number of villagers to seek work further away, in the construction industry in Việt-Trì or in the new industrial zone on the border between Lâm-Thao district and Việt-Trì township.[4] A number of commuting villagers worked in a cement factory set up in 2002 by a Sơn-Dương native in this new industrial zone. This factory, which by 2004 employed 380 workers, produced over 100,000 tonnes of cement and reportedly had annual revenues of more than US $5 million (*Phú-Thọ,* 28 July 2005).[5] Workers here earned an average of 1 million VND (US $65) a month. Four of the seventy-eight commuting Sơn-Dương workers also worked in the growing foreign sector in the Việt-Trì area. In Việt-Trì and Sơn-Dương's own district the construction industry had been booming due to rising personal incomes and business investments, and employed many villagers.

The increase in employment opportunities in Việt-Trì, however, was both recent and inadequate to meet the needs of many Sơn-Dương households for additional incomes. By the end of 2004 the province of Phú-Thọ had attracted only forty-three foreign investment projects, with US $310 million in capital, and this had occurred mostly during the 2001–2004 period. This amounted to less than 1 percent of the approved foreign capital in Vietnam by that time, a modest result despite the fact that the province of Phú-Thọ had aggressively sought foreign investment. The province had offered many local incentives such as rent-free land for the first eleven to sixteen years of operation and corporate tax rates of 10 percent-20 percent for the first ten to fifteen years, depending on location, instead of the 28 percent levied by the national government (www .phuthotrade-tourism.gov.vn).[6] According to official statistics, the labor force in the foreign and private industrial sector grew only modestly in Phú-Thọ, from 46,109 in 1995 to 56,333 by the end of 2000 and 66,308 by the end of 2004 (Phú-Thọ, Statistical Office 2001:141–142; Phú-Thọ, Statistical Office 2006:115–116). This led many young Sơn-Dương villagers to migrate beyond the province, many moving as far as the southern part of Vietnam.

Of the 934 surveyed Sơn-Dương villagers above the age of fifteen and no longer in school, 303 (32.5 percent) had been migrant workers for one month or more in the preceding twelve months. Entire families in 38 of the surveyed 321 households had left Sơn-Dương, although they still had houses and agricultural land in the village. Of the villagers absent from Sơn-Dương at the time of our survey, 63 percent were male; 65 percent were 16–35 years old; 16 percent, in the 36–45 age range; and 11 percent, below the age of 16. The most popular destinations were Hanoi (21 percent), elsewhere in Phú-Thọ (19 percent), Bình-Dương province (near Hồ Chí Minh City, 13 percent), Hồ Chí Minh City (9 percent), and Kiên-Giang province (southern Vietnam, 8 percent). The majority of those migrating to Hanoi were construction workers, while those in Bình-Dương worked mainly in foreign enterprises, and those moving to Kiên-Giang worked in commerce. In 2005 and 2006, twelve villagers also left for work in Malaysia and Taiwan. Remittances from villagers working elsewhere averaged $195 a year per household, which amounted to 22 percent of the average household income in Sơn-Dương.

Long-term migration also entailed many costs, however. One was the education of the children who accompanied the workers, since some localities gave low priority to the children of nonresidents for admission to local schools (see Luong and Vũ Văn Ngọc 2009). One villager cited the limited education opportunities for his children in Kiên-Giang province as the reason for his return to Sơn-Dương. Another cost was the lack of people to care for family members back in Sơn-Dương village, especially the sick and the old. From the surveyed households, 29 percent of those who had left the village after 1986 had returned to Sơn-Dương to live, although 40 percent of the returnees mentioned that their return was only temporary. The rest of the returnees, citing among other reasons the difficulties of living in their chosen destinations and the need for their presence at home, joined the resident nonagricultural workforce, despite the lower incomes they could earn at home.[7]

The resident nonagricultural workforce of Sơn-Dương included both wage laborers and shop owners. Resident wage laborers worked for construction contractors, carpentry shop owners, and other village entrepreneurs. In 2004 village authorities listed 160 entrepreneurs in the village, 113 of whom had their own shops, including 18 variety stores, 15 rice mills, 11 furniture/carpentry shops, and 10 agricultural supply stores. Other entrepreneurs engaged in rice trading, construction work, rice wine distillation, tailoring, and motorcycle and bicycle repair. However, this official list of 160 entrepreneurs and shops did not include many small businesses that had no store fronts but were known to villagers through word of mouth. These included many small rice traders, of whom there were approximately fifty to sixty in Sơn-Dương. These traders sold about 150–200 tonnes a month altogether to a growing number of nonagricultural households in the province of Phú-Thọ. There were also thirteen large-scale rice traders in Sơn-Dương who reportedly bought paddy all over the Red River delta and sold altogether about 160 tonnes a month at a major rice market in the provincial capital. Numerous rice traders came from the two hamlets of Sơn-Dương into which a number of women from the neighboring Tứ-Xã commune, long known for their trading skills, had married. The number of businesses in Sơn-Dương in 2004 had thus significantly increased from 1991, when there had been only ten rice-milling machines, a small number of rice traders, and two transportation carts in the entire village.[8]

Most local businesses served the production and consumption needs of Sơn-Dương villagers, many of whom had increasing disposable incomes since the decollectivization of agriculture. The ten agricultural supply stores, for example, met the burgeoning need for chemical fertilizers and for supplies relevant to the growing animal husbandry sector. The four construction-material stores and the eleven carpentry shops provided bricks, tiles, cement, and doors and windows for the booming construction of housing for the living and tombs for the dead. From 1999 to 2004, 64 (23 percent) of the 283 households surveyed had new houses constructed either for themselves or for children forming new households or had their current houses renovated.[9] The carpentry shops also provided furniture for local houses, as well as benches and tables for schools in Sơn-Dương and some of the surrounding communities. Construction contractors in Sơn-Dương estimated in 2004 that the reconstruction of ancestral tombs and the construction of new ones, mainly from 1998 onwards, had cost over 1 billion VND (over US $70,000).

Village entrepreneurs experienced a major problem because most local customers purchased goods on credit. According to business own-ers, many villagers could easily pay off their purchases, but did not do so. A large store selling both fertilizers and construction materials reported outstanding debts of about 100 million VND (US $6,400) in the summer of 2004. The most successful variety store owner in Sơn-Dương reported a regular outstanding credit of 20 million VND (US $1,300) to customers. Households relying on agricultural income normally paid off part of their debt after each harvest season, while those on salary paid on a monthly basis. A store owner selling agricultural supplies reported an outstanding debt of about 20 million VND by his approximate 200 customers and two or three cases of bad debts over a ten-year period. He said: "About 90 percent of my fertilizer customers buy on credit. Only about 10 percent of consumers buying on credit have a cash-flow problem. The rest, despite their ability to pay right away, still buy on credit. The credit has to be paid up after the harvest." Store owners were able to reduce the large amount of debt only on the eve of Lunar New Year due to the Vietnamese belief that one's condition on the first day of the New Year will have a lasting impact for the rest of the year.

Sales on credit reflect both the competition among businesses and the way they are embedded in the tight social network of a community where villagers are related through kinship, neighbor relations, and association ties, and where trust is emphasized as a major indicator of a good social relation. Debt defaults were rare, but the widespread practice of purchase on credit strains the financial resources of business owners. Fortunately, the extension of credit by banks for those with land as collateral has eased the problem for business owners. The Vietnam Bank of Agriculture and Rural Development increased its loan portfolio more than ten times between 1994 and 2004 (from 9,275 billion VND [US $872 million] in 1994 to 142,293 VND [US $9.02 billion] in 2004) (Đỗ-Tất-Ngọc 2006: 82).[10] In addition to the Vietnam Bank of Agriculture and Rural Development, the government-sponsored Social Policy Bank also extends low-interest loans for poverty alleviation to the poor directly, to employers who generated

**Table 9.** Loans, July 2003 to June 2004 (in million VND)

|  | With interest | Without interest | Total |
|---|---|---|---|
| Banks | 1,501.0 |  | 1,501.0 |
| Kin | 37.0 | 261.75 | 298.75 |
| Rotating credit associations |  | 171.36 | 171.36 |
| Informal money lenders | 102.8 |  | 102.8 |
| Friends |  | 56.0 | 56.0 |
| Store owners (buying on credit) | 47.7 |  | 47.7 |
| Mass organizations | 27.0 |  | 27.0 |
| Other sources | 39.0 |  | 39.0 |

employment of the poor, to poor students in technical or higher education, and to adults with overseas work contracts.

In 2004, according to the commune president, about 600 households in Sơn-Dương owed the Vietnam Bank of Agriculture and Rural Development about 4 billion VND (US $254,000). This figure is congruent with the figure of 951 million VND (US $60,304) borrowed from the Vietnam Bank of Agriculture and Development by the 283 surveyed households that made up 26 percent of Sơn-Dương households. Fifty-eight (20 percent) of those households also received low-interest loans from the Social Policy Bank, totaling 275 million VND (US $17,440, 18 percent of the amount owed to banks by surveyed Sơn-Dương households). Although banks were the most important source of credit, they were only one among many (see Table 9).

Of the 283 surveyed households, 119 (42 percent) participated in rotating credit associations, contributing on the average 120,000 VND (US $7.60) a month. Of the 163 contributions that those 119 households made, 13 were on a monthly basis (mostly among salaried workers, cadres, and merchants), 12 on a bimonthly basis, 18 on a quarterly basis, 66 every four months, 47 every half a year, and 7 on an annual basis. The most common contribution interval (every four months) reflects the agricultural economy of Sơn-Dương, for there is one harvest every four months. The median size of these associations was six. Among the surveyed households, the credit from the savings of participating households thus amounted to 171.36 million VND (US $10,860) a year, which was the third most important source of credit after loans from banks and relatives. They were a useful source of credit, since they were interest-free, like just most loans from friends and relatives. Rotating credit was mobilized most often for occasions requiring major expenditure, such as a wedding, house construction, or the purchase of a motorcycle or color television.

The easier access to formal credit as well as to informal loans due to higher disposable household incomes encouraged not only agricultural production and business investment, but also housing and tomb construction, ritual expenditures, and the purchase of consumer durables, especially from 2000 onwards. For example, two-thirds of the 98 motorcycles and 57 percent of the 158 color televisions in the 283 surveyed households were purchased after the beginning of 2000. The increasing expenditures in turn led to a boom in private businesses and the rising importance of nonagricultural income sources in the village. Among the surveyed households, nonagricultural earnings (excluding remittances, government transfers, and interhousehold transfers) amounted to US $90,000 in the twelve months preceding the survey and averaged US $316 per household (35 percent of the average household income).

## Socioeconomic Differentiation and Class Structure

Households in Sơn-Dương had not only gained higher incomes in general, but had also become more sharply differentiated in wealth and vulnerabilities since decollectivization. Among the 283 surveyed households, villagers in the bottom income quintile had a per capita income of 1,072,000 VND (US $68) a year, as compared with the top quintile's 7,845,000 VND (US $497). The bottom income quintile earned 6.1 percent of the total income, while the top one earned 44.3 percent (see Table 10).

It should be noted that land holdings did not vary significantly among households in different socioeconomic strata: there were 2022 square meters of cultivated land and 366 square meters of residential land per household in the bottom quintile, and 2025 and 409 square meters respectively in the

**Table 10.** Per capita income by source, 2004 (in 000 VND)

|  | Total | Agriculture | Nonagriculture | Remittances & cash gifts |
|---|---|---|---|---|
| Bottom quintile | 1,072 | 718 | 194 | 156 |
| Below-average quintile | 2,073 | 1,028 | 549 | 270 |
| Average quintile | 2,957 | 1,365 | 1,186 | 397 |
| Above-average quintile | 3,839 | 1,625 | 1,431 | 679 |
| Top quintile | 7,845 | 2,495 | 2,949 | 2,668 |

top one. Even when adjusted for the slightly larger average household size in the bottom quintile, the difference in agricultural land holdings was not significant at all.[11] The differences in agricultural income between the bottom- and top-quintile households resulted to some extent from the top quintile's larger amount of rented land (an average of 1,114 square meters per household in the top quintile versus an average of 395 square meters in the bottom one), but primarily from the greater role of animal husbandry and agricultural service provision among the top-quintile households. However, even so, the top quintile earned only 3.5 times more than the bottom quintile from agriculture. This difference pales by comparison with the fifteen-times difference in nonagricultural income and the seventeen-times difference in remittances and cash gifts.

In general, the richer households in Sơn-Dương had more members migrating for nonagricultural work or engaging in local nonagricultural work. Among the largest resident income earners in Sơn-Dương were successful entrepreneurs, workers in large companies, and active or retired state cadres serving in education, the armed forces, and the security apparatuses. Primary and secondary school teachers in Sơn-Dương earned an average of 1 million VND a month from the state (US $63, equivalent to 5 hundredweights of paddy or 350 kilograms of rice). This average salary was in the same range as that of chemical-fertilizer factory workers who had long been considered among the highest earners in the village, receiving almost twice as much as the top commune officials. My former host in Sơn-Dương earned the equivalent of 5 kilograms of rice a month of his thirty years of armed service in the late 1980s. A decade and a half later, his pension had increased to the equivalent of 160 kilograms of rice. In Sơn-Dương, the richer households also generally had more members migrating for work. Among the surveyed households, the bottom quintile had on average 4.7 person-months of migration per household a year, while the top quintile was more than double that, at 9.8 person-months.

Despite the increasing socioeconomic differentiation brought about by national and global market integration since the late 1980s, the egalitarian land distribution in 1994 had so far prevented the emergence of either a landless peasantry or a sharply polarized class structure in Sơn-Dương as had occurred in the southern part of Vietnam. When a new household was formed, parents typically gave the members of the new household their shares of agricultural land. No Sơn-Dương villager had to rely exclusively or primarily on selling his/her labor to agricultural employers for livelihood, although a number of Sơn-Dương villagers did work for wages, mainly in construction projects. Only 25 of the 934 surveyed Sơn-Dương villagers above the age of fifteen and no longer in school worked for wages in agriculture; and all but one worked for less than fifteen days a year in this kind of work. In contrast, in the Mekong delta, the export-oriented agricultural area in southern Vietnam, the percentage of landless people in 2004 stood at 23 percent (Ravallion and Van De Walle 2008:198), many of whom had to work as floating agricultural laborers for a good part of the year.[12]

In Sơn-Dương, even among those who worked full time for wages in factories, in small furniture workshops, or on fish farms, most either had access to agricultural land or belonged to households with access to agricultural land. In the 1994 land distribution in Sơn-Dương, only industrial workers and full-time permanent state employees like teachers and career officers in the armed forces were not allocated land. In contrast, in the southern third of rural Vietnam, there was no collective ownership, and thus no land distribution. Those Sơn-Dương villagers left out of the land distribution did not have land because of their career choices, not because they had been dispossessed of the means of production.

While Sơn-Dương villagers, like most rural dwellers in northern and northern central Vietnam, were guaranteed some land for their livelihood, they also had to shoulder larger shares of their educational and health-care expenses and of infrastructure construction costs. This came about partly as a result of decollectivization and the principle of cost-sharing *(xã hội hoá)*. Officially, there was no tuition at the primary and junior high school levels. However, parents were charged various small fees, including fees for school renovation and construction: when the junior high school was reconstructed in 2005, each student had to pay 150,000 VND (almost US $10) to cover the cost of furniture and other classroom materials. Starting at the senior high school level, tuition was charged, and the amount increased to about 1,800,000 VND (US $114) a year at the university level.[13] While this amount is very modest by international standards, the additional room-and-board costs in Hanoi could add up to at least four times that amount in 2004. This was a heavy burden for Sơn-Dương households except for those in the top quintile. In health care, the national government began charging user fees for major services in 1989 and introduced health insurance in 1992. In 2004, in Sơn-Dương, only a small number of villagers had health insurance: (retired) civil servants and career soldiers, (retired) workers at state or major private firms, students under quasi-compulsory health-insurance coverage, and sixty-two households with health cards under the poverty-alleviation program. Few villagers bought voluntary health insurance. As a result a major illness requiring hospitalization would cause a

**Table 11.** Poverty-reduction loans, Sơn-Dương, 2003–2004

|                                  | Income quintile | | | | | |
|                                  | 1  | 2  | 3  | 4  | 5  | Total |
|----------------------------------|----|----|----|----|----|-------|
| Poverty-reduction loan—Yes       | 5  | 8  | 4  | 7  | 8  | 32    |
| Poverty-reduction loan—No        | 48 | 43 | 54 | 48 | 58 | 251   |
| Total                            | 53 | 51 | 58 | 55 | 66 | 283   |

*Note:* 1 equals lowest income quintile; 5 equals highest.

major financial hardship for the majority of villagers.[14] In many cases the need to pay educational or major medical expenses prompted one or more household members to migrate in search of additional income or to rely on their social networks for interest-free loans or gifts.

In order to alleviate the social burden on the poor, the village government targeted sixty-two households for poverty alleviation in 2004 and exempted them from school fees and infrastructure levies. However, my survey data indicate a considerable leakage of these benefits to the non-poor and a considerable number of poor households unable to receive these benefits. In 2004, according to the government's criteria, a household in the rural lowlands was considered poor if its annual per capita income fell below 1.2 million VND (US $76). (This poverty line was raised to 2.4 million VND, or US $150, as of 2006.) By the 2004 criterion, 40 households in the survey sample, with 169 persons (12.9 percent of the surveyed population), were poor in 2004. However, only 2 (6 percent) of the 32 reported antipoverty loans in our survey sample went to these officially poor households. The remaining 30 loans (94 percent) went to the nonpoor by government criteria, many of whom were in the top income quintile (quintile 5) in Sơn-Dương (Table 11).[15] Similarly, of the 18 households reporting special material assistance on the occasion of the New Year occasion only 4 (22 percent) met the government's poverty criterion.

Despite the considerable socioeconomic differentiation that has emerged among the Sơn-Dương households and their relative vulnerabilities, the principles of collective ownership of agricultural land and egalitarian (re-)distribution prevented the re-emergence of a landless peasantry in the first decade of total decollectivization, reflecting the socialist legacy in the northern half of Vietnam.

# CHAPTER 7

# The Intensification of Social
# and Ritual Life

With the contraction of economic space under state control and increasing private wealth, villagers in Sơn-Dương intensified their ritual activities and relations in their social networks, both through gift exchanges and through the establishment of numerous voluntary associations. Social relations intensified mainly among the villagers of Sơn-Dương, in parallel with the considerable persistence of village endogamy, despite the stronger integration of Sơn-Dương into the national economy and the global capitalist system. The male-oriented, and class-structured model of Vietnamese society also gradually reasserted itself and strengthened both within the kinship domain and beyond.

Of the 382 married couples in the 283 surveyed households in Sơn-Dương, 80 percent were endogamous marriages. Of the 74 exogamous marriages, 21 spouses came from the neighboring commune of Tứ-Xã and 13 from other communes in Lâm-Thao district. Although the percentage of commune endogamy declined during the 1996–2004 period, it still remained at 72 percent (see Table 12; cf. Krowolski 1999:142–145; Krowolski 2002, Luong 2009a).

Whether endogamous or exogamous, marriages in Sơn-Dương were strongly embedded in a system of patrilocal residence, patrilineal descent, and a male-centered division of labor, despite the state's emphasis on gender equality. Sơn-Dương villagers still took patrilocal residence as a given part of sociocultural reality, even though, beginning in 1994, the local government no longer required the coresidence of three daughters-in-law as a condition for granting additional residential land. The overwhelming majority of newlywed couples still resided with the husband's parents for at least a few years after marriage (see Table 13). This percentage declined to less than 75 percent in the decade of 1986–1995 in connection with the commune's large-scale sale of residential land at modest prices in 1994.

**Table 12.** Commune endogamy and exogamy (in percentage)

|  | Before 1955 | 1956– 1965 | 1966– 1975 | 1976– 1985 | 1986– 1995 | 1996– 2004 | 1923– 2004 |
|---|---|---|---|---|---|---|---|
| Commune endogamy | 86 | 80 | 66 | 80 | 89 | 72 | 80 |
| Commune exogamy | 14 | 20 | 34 | 20 | 11 | 28 | 20 |
| wife marrying in | 9 | 18 | 27 | 14 | 9 | 21 | 15 |
| husband marrying in | 5 | 2 | 5 | 6 | 1 | 7 | 4 |
| both spouses from outside |  | 2 |  | 1 |  |  | 0.5 |
| N of cases | 44 | 44 | 41 | 90 | 96 | 67 | 382 |

**Table 13.** Post-marital residential pattern (in percentage)

|  | Before 1955 | 1956– 1965 | 1966– 1975 | 1976– 1985 | 1986– 1995 | 1996– 2004 | 1923– 2004 |
|---|---|---|---|---|---|---|---|
| Patrilocal | 89 | 84 | 76 | 80 | 68 | 76 | 77 |
| Neolocal | 9 | 16 | 20 | 18 | 32 | 21 | 21 |
| Matrilocal | 2 |  | 4 | 2 |  | 1 | 2 |
| Other |  |  |  | 1 |  |  | 0.3 |
| N of cases | 44 | 44 | 41 | 90 | 96 | 67 | 382 |

A number of young couples formed their own households on newly pur-chased land instead of staying with the husband's parents, which increased neolocal residence to 32 percent. But the percentage of newlywed couples in patrilocal residence rose above 75 percent again in the following decade (cf. Luong 2003b; Luong 2009a; Nguyễn-Hữu-Minh 1998:176–235; and Nguyễn-Hữu-Minh and Hirschman 2000).

In a family of many sons, the eldest son and his wife normally stayed with the parents, while younger sons eventually moved out to form their own nuclear family households. Nuclear families made up 67.2 percent of village households, 17.4 percent involved two or more related nuclear families under the same roof (for example, parents and a son's nuclear family, forming a "joint" family household), and 14 percent had one or more relatives who did not form a nuclear family residing with a nuclear family (for example, a nuclear family with one of the husband's parents in addition, thereby forming an "extended" family).

The desire for sons to continue the patriline and conduct ancestor wor-ship underlay the social tolerance for polygamy in Sơn-Dương, despite its illegality. It seems to have been practiced more openly in this market-economy period than it had been in the command-economy era. In 2004 the head of the Women's Association in Sơn-Dương could easily cite five cases of polygamous relations, including one man with three wives who lived in separate households, and another in which two wives resided with the husband in the same household. In the Đỗ lineage, if a couple did not have a son, and if the wife agreed to the husband's polygamy and made a ritual offering through the lineage head, the lineage would accept the husband's mistress or second wife and the sons from the second wife as official lineage members. In a household without a son, it was the husband's nephew (a younger son of his younger brother or of his closest junior patrilineal male cousin), not his daughter, who carried out official ancestor worship for him after he died. In many cases, this also means that the nephew inherited the man's house at the expense of his daughter. However, if a daughter and her husband were residing in the house at the time of the death of the last member of the senior couple, they could remain in the house and *personally* commemorate the daughter's parents on the death anniversaries of the parents. It was common to hear villagers bemoan the sad fate befalling one of their close relatives who had no sons.

In 2004, within the household, the division of labor was still structured to the advantage of men, despite the active participation of women in the labor market. Among villagers aged sixteen to sixty-five, women played a considerably more important role than men in domestic work (see Table 14)

These male-centered households formed the fundamental building blocks for the resurgence of patrilineages and ancestor worship since the 1980s in Sơn-Dương. By 2004, most of the twenty-seven patrilineages had been re-established. The few patrilines that did not have formal organizational structures originated in three handicapped veterans who were welcomed to the village after the 1946–1954 Franco-Vietnamese war as a matter of official policy and who married village women. Some patrilineages had been reconstructed as early as 1980, during the command-economy era. The main functions of a patrilineage remains the same: it organizes rites of solidarity (ancestor-worship ceremonies, ancestral tomb reconstruction and maintenance); it transmits ethical values as well as knowledge about the patrilineal kinship hierarchy and the wider socioeconomic roles of the members of the patrilineage for the mobilization of kinship ties among members in need; and it facilitates mutual assistance and promotes formal education among its members.

The patrilineages of Sơn-Dương had been most active in the reconstruction of ancestral tombs. A construction contractor in Sơn-Dương

**Table 14.** Gender and household division of labor, 2004 (in percentage)

| | Buying food Male Female | | Cooking Male Female | | Dishwashing Male Female | |
|---|---|---|---|---|---|---|
| Frequent (more than half) | 4.3 | 65.8 | 13.8 | 51.4 | 8.9 | 51.2 |
| Occasional (less than half) | 3.2 | 6.4 | 20.0 | 25.5 | 3.4 | 9.7 |
| Not at all | 92.3 | 27.3 | 65.9 | 22.5 | 87.3 | 38.4 |

| | Laundry Male Female | | Sweeping house Male Female | | Looking after children Male Female | |
|---|---|---|---|---|---|---|
| Frequent (more than half) | 14.3 | 70.4 | 13.9 | 44.2 | 6.2 | 14 |
| Occasional (less than half) | 16.3 | 14.6 | 10.7 | 16.1 | 5 | 11.2 |
| Not at all | 69.1 | 14.1 | 75.1 | 39.1 | 47.3 | 31.1 |
| Not applicable | | | | | 41.1 | 43.0 |

estimated in 2004 that over 1 billion VND (US $65,000) had been spent on reconstructing the tombs in the two village cemeteries in the preceding decade. The two largest patrilineages in Sơn-Dương (Nguyễn Đình and Nguyễn Trọng) had also restored or reconstructed their ancestral halls by 2004. Banquet gatherings on the death anniversaries of ancestors were organized either annually in small patrilineages or once every few years in big ones. These events largely celebrated the anniversaries of male ancestors. Female ancestors were usually commemorated with small offerings made by a few elderly lineage members. In a small lineage, all the adult male members and their spouses who were in the village attended, while in a big lineage only household representatives would attend the ceremony. Among the 283 surveyed households in Sơn-Dương, 260 (92 percent) reported regularly attending the death anniversaries of the founding ancestors of their patrilineages. The expenses for these gatherings were reportedly covered by levies on participants (in 57 percent of surveyed households), on male members of a patrilineage (in 34 percent of households), or on households in the patrilineage (in 6 percent of households).

Many lineages also established funds for mutual assistance on special occasions (sickness, funerals, weddings; and, in one lineage, also for longevity celebrations). Levies were commonly imposed either on households or on male members *(đinh),* although some lineages required contributions from all members, male and female. Seven patrilineages had also set up education-promotion funds by 2004. These funds were used as awards for male and female lineage members who had succeeded in university/college entrance examinations, A successful entrepreneur, a former teacher, in the Nguyễn Trọng lineage, started this initiative in 1990 by donating a bicycle imported from Hungary to each university graduate in his lineage. This lineage was still in the local educational vanguard in 2004, for it had organized an annual ceremony to give symbolic awards to all of its members who had excelled in their studies at any level. Because these education-promotion funds were disbursed to excellent students regardless of gender, they were raised through levies either on households or on all lineage members, male and female.

The worship of immediate ancestors (parents, grandparents) also had a strong patrilineal orientation. In the 283 surveyed households, among the 221 immediate ancestors to whose death anniversaries guests were invited, only 8 were wives' ancestors or relatives; 192 were husbands'; and 21 were the spouses of the senior surviving members of involved households, who were also parents or grandparents of the more junior members in these households. Typically, the eldest son or grandson was responsible for worshipping his parents and grandparents. He would normally specify the financial contribution to be made by his siblings and their descendants. One eldest son in Sơn-Dương explained the organization of the death anniversary of his father:

> The gathering of relatives . . . is only partly maintained nowadays. It is mainly a gathering of siblings, some of whom live far away. On the upcoming death anniversary of my father, my younger sibling in Hanoi will have to come back here for the ceremony. I will not grant any exemption. His presence is required in commemoration of our father. He may say that I am feudal, but I do not mind the criticism. Without this requirement, I may not see him for a long time, and our bond will be weakened. For this anniversary, I invite only my siblings and a few elderly senior relatives, and tell my children and their spouses to come.

In 2003–2004 a death anniversary for an immediate ancestor (parent and grandparent) or a close family member/relative (spouse, sibling, child, aunt/uncle without surviving child) involved an average of thirty-four people who partook of the anniversary meal. The size of a death anniversary meal/banquet depended partly on the wealth of the household (see Table 15). For example, for the death anniversary of a husband's parent, the

**Table 15.** Average size of death anniversary banquet, 2003–2004

| Income quintile | Spouse | Death anniversary for Husband's parent | Husband's grandparent |
|---|---|---|---|
| Lowest | 32 (n=10) | 26 (n=20) | 13 (n=7) |
| Below average | n/a (n=1) | 36 (n=23) | 17 (n=6) |
| Average | n/a (n=1) | 33 (n=21) | 18 (n=2) |
| Above average | 44 (n=4) | 34 (n=34) | 60 (n=7) |
| Highest | 42 (n=5) | 42 (n=48) | 46 (n=14) |
| Total | 36 (n=21) | 35 (n=146) | 36 (n=36) |

size of the banquet increased from an average of twenty-six participants among the lowest-quintile households to forty-two among the highest-quintile ones.

While women of Sơn-Dương played an important role in the preparation of annual death anniversaries for the ancestors of their husbands' patrilineages and for their own parents, ancestor worship had a strong male and patrilineal orientation. Given this, many elderly women of Sơn-Dương village found mutual support in the Buddhist association for the elderly *(hội Phật giáo, hội chư bà, hội vãi),* which was composed mainly of elderly women aged sixty or above. A small number of younger women in special circumstances (mainly widows, divorced women, and spinsters) and a few men also belonged to the association. However, while its few elderly male members helped with pagoda renovation projects, they did not participate in regular prayer sessions at the Buddhist pagoda or in those for the deceased. Nonetheless, with approximately 370 members in 2004, the Buddhist association was one of the largest spontaneous associations in Sơn-Dương. The Buddhist elderly women's association held well-attended bimonthly prayer sessions (on the first and fifteenth day of each lunar month) in the renovated pagoda. About 200 women reportedly attended these prayer sessions. In addition, the association also organized special ceremonies on Buddha's birthday, on the lost-soul day (the fifteenth of the seventh lunar month), on the first and fifteenth of the first lunar month, and on the anniversary of the last presiding nun's death in 1971. Attendance at these special events reportedly reached 300 or more (see Photos 12 and 13 in Chapter 6). The operating expenses for the pagoda were covered by revenue from 1,344 square meters of rice fields as well as by modest charges on members who partook of meals at the pagoda on major ceremonial occasions.

In the Sơn-Dương pagoda, the elderly women divided themselves into three groups, *vãi mới* or *vãi em* (new elderly women), *vãi thứ* or *vãi trung* (middle elderly women), and *vãi thượng* (senior elderly women). The most senior group was seated in the central wing closest to the altar, and the most junior, away from it in the two side wings. Age and the date of entry into *hội chư bà* determined seniority (see also Luong 1993:272, 284). A male Party member in Sơn-Dương remarked on this strict seating order and the impressive female organization:

> The elderly ladies form one of the strongest organizations to be found anywhere. Their discipline is impressive. On the first and fifteen days [of the lunar month], the ladies automatically find their seats in the pagoda, with little dispute on the issue. If somebody is in the wrong seat, she will be asked to move and will automatically comply with the request. The voice of the most senior lady carries more weight with other members of the association than that of an agency head with his workers. Nobody takes any mat or bowls from the pagoda. On the ritual days, a few ladies voluntarily clean up the pagoda before the ceremonies. The ladies have a strong sense of their own obligations at the pagoda, perhaps because of the belief in religious virtues. At other forums the attendance is not good because people engage in disputes. Many villagers consider these meetings a waste of time. I have suggested to the local leadership that the bimonthly meetings of the elderly constitute a good forum for the dissemination of government policies and directives, such as on family planning. Those of us retired cadres who know a bit about Buddhism and can talk in a simple language relate easily to the elderly ladies. They listen quietly and attentively, unlike the audience elsewhere.

The Buddhist elderly women's association offered free prayer services for deceased villagers and led funeral processions (except processions for Catholics) (see Photo 15). (In 2004, there were nine Catholic households in Sơn-Dương.) The family of the deceased routinely offered a donation to the association, ranging from a low of 200,000 VND (US $13) to a high of 1 million dongs (US $65), depending on family income. The association reportedly also received about $650 in donations in 2004. Since the local government had allocated the association 1,344 square meters of rice fields, the income from which was used to cover regular pagoda expenses, donations to the association were put into the pagoda renovation fund. This fund was also enriched by the successful fund-raising efforts of association members, since virtually all the female elderly in the village joined this association, and since association members were also mothers, grandmothers, aunts, and grand-aunts of virtually all the villagers, including the village officials. It was the elderly Buddhist women who spearheaded the local movement to renovate cultural and religious monuments with their renovation of the Buddhist pagoda in 1987–1988, 1993, 2000, and 2001. (The Buddhist pagoda in Sơn-Dương, like numerous village pagodas in northern Vietnam, included for worship not only buddhas and deities in the Buddhist pantheon, but also many other deities, including the child-guardian deity [đức ông] and tigers, to which meat was offered.) [1] In fact, the elderly Buddhist association was the only association not associated with the Marxist Party-state that had had a continuous existence since the French colonial period.[2] Since Buddhist mantras were chanted as an essential component of all funerals except among Catholics, it was no coincidence that the elderly Buddhist women's association had survived since 1954 (cf. Kleinen 1999:167). Even in the heyday of socialist reconstruction, the elderly women could not be stopped from attending their monthly worship sessions at the pagoda. In 2001, after the renovation of the worship house for the nuns who used to be in charge (nhà tổ), the provincial authorities recognized the Buddhist pagoda in Sơn-Dương as a provincial cultural heritage, and villagers organized a big ceremony to celebrate this designation. The elderly women's Buddhist association has been the most resilient nongovernmental organization in Sơn-Dương since the consolidation of Marxist power in north Vietnam in 1954.

The successful renovation of the Buddhist pagoda as the site for elderly women's activities prompted a number of elderly men to raise the possibility of reconstructing the Sơn-Dương communal house (đình) in the mid-1990s. However, this proposal encountered criticism from a number of influential villagers who associated the communal house with superstitious deity worship and emphasized the need to save resources for other projects. In the spring of 1999 a number of elderly men renewed the campaign after the commune administration changed its earlier position and supported reconstruction. The letter to the higher authorities on the need for a communal house in Sơn-Dương cited numerous reasons: the importance of the communal house as a symbol of people's village roots and of Vietnamese culture, the lack of a home for the tutelary deities who were meritorious to the nation, the cultivation of manners (no rude speech was allowed at the communal house), and the greater importance

of spiritual life over material living conditions. The fund-raising committee also cited with nostalgia the old Sơn-Dương communal house, reportedly constructed in 1729, which had columns 1.1 meter in diameter and
was reportedly the most beautiful in Phú-Thọ province. The committee
aimed to raise 150 million VND (US $10,700), despite the fact that rela-
tively few men attended the worship of tutelary deities at a small village
shrine *(đền)*.[3] The largest attendance occurred on the first day of lunar new
year. This major occasion attracted about 20 of the 220 elderly men in
the village in 2004. The most successful activities at the communal house
were monthly poetry recitals, which drew about fifty people, and daily
morning exercises, in which twenty to thirty elderly men participated. The
communal-house-reconstruction campaign received a major boost when a
native son with a successful cement business donated construction materials worth about 900 million VND (US $56,000), more than five times the
original fund-raising target. In April 2006 the new communal house was
completed; it cost 1.7 billion VND (US $106,250) (see Photographs 10
and 11 in Chapter 6). The village organized a major celebration and feast,
to which over 500 elderly villagers, major donors, and provincial and district officials were invited. Villagers cited with pride that the reconstructed
communal house was the biggest in Lâm-Thao district. In December 2006
village officials planned to resurrect the village festival in the third lunar
month of 2007, which would include the slaughtering of pigs for the worship of tutelary deities.

The reconstruction of patrilineages, the resilience of the elderly Buddhist association, and the plan to resurrect activities around the communal
house were a part of expanded social space in Vietnam not firmly under
state control. What was distinctive about Sơn-Dương and other northern
villages, in contrast to southern communities, was the proliferation of formal voluntary associations that reflected the villagers' ardent quest for
more expanded and stronger social relations. During the command-economy era, the only voluntary associations which operated in the shadow of
state-organized associations were the rotating credit associations *(họ)*, the
elderly women's Buddhist association, and the slowly re-emergent patrilineages. In the years from 1988 to 2004, many other voluntary associations were organized without government sponsorship, including same-
class alumni associations *(hội đồng học)*, the retired teachers' association,
same-age associations among men *(hội đồng niên)*, the same-military-service association *(hội đồng ngũ)*, the association of policy-favored households *(hội gia đình chính sách)*, the same-origin association *(hội đồng*

*hương)* among Tứ-Xã natives in Sơn-Dương. Of the surveyed households in 2004, 41 percent participated in rotating credit associations, and one-third of the members of these households over the age of fifteen were in same-class alumni associations.

The majority of those associations had pre-1945 roots. The Buddhist elderly association, the rotating credit associations, and the patrilineages all constituted a major continuity with the past. Same-class alumni associations *(hội đồng học)* were conceptually linked to the alumni associations *(hội đồng môn)* of the prerevolutionary era, although the membership of a *hội đồng môn* included all the former students of a particular teacher over the years and focused on honoring a teacher, while the current associations are oriented toward maintaining ties among former classmates. Similarly, the retired teachers' association bears some resemblance to the literati association *(hội tư văn)* of the prerevolutionary era, although the literati association included all educated men, retired or not, not simply retired teachers. The *hội tư văn* was an elite association devoted mainly to the worship of Confucius, while the retired teachers' association was simply an occupation-based mutual aid society. Among the new associational forms were the same-age associations among men *(hội đồng niên),* the same-military-service association *(hội đồng ngũ),* the Southeast military-service association *(hội quân nhân vùng Đông Nam bộ)*, and the association of policy-favored households *(hội gia đình chính sách)*. In 2004 the association of policy-favored households had ninety-one members who received monthly stipends from the state, including the households of thirty-eight badly wounded soldiers, seventeen invalid soldiers, and thirty-four war martyrs.

These associations drew their memberships from the village population only, with two exceptions, the high school alumni associations and same-military-service ones, whose members were natives of neighboring villages in the same district. The members of most village-based associations provided financial assistance to one another on the occasion of major life-cycle rituals (weddings and funerals) in members' families or when members faced major expenditures (major sickness or, in a number of cases, house construction for a married son and his family).

The spontaneous voluntary associations played a role in the lives of Sơn-Dương villagers at least as important as the state-sponsored mass organizations. Among the state organizations were the Peasant, Veteran, Women's, and Youth associations, which were branches of the national Peasant, Veteran Associations, and Women's and Youth Unions. Most active were the Women's Association (in family planning mobilization campaigns) and the Veteran Association (in the organization of funeral ceremonies for members). Sơn-Dương's Elderly Association, which had 567 members in 2004, most above the age of fifty-nine, was also officially recognized by the local government and the Fatherland Front (the national party-state's popular mobilization apparatus).[4] Starting in 2004, it received a modest annual budget from the local government. Its poetry-gymnastic club organized regular gymnastic exercises and monthly meetings for poetry recitals. The Elderly Association also held annual longevity celebrations for members reaching the lunar ages of seventy, seventy-five, eighty, eighty-five, ninety, and ninety-five. It also coordinated visits to seriously sick members and to the families of deceased ones. The association also owned a four-wheeled coffin carrier that it lent free of charge to the families of deceased members.

Because virtually all Sơn-Dương villagers are related to one another, either consanguineally or affinally, due to the high rate of village endogamy over centuries, the spontaneous local associations in Sơn-Dương increased the multiplexity of social ties and intensified social networks among villagers. The reproduction and reinforcement of social ties, partly through gift exchanges at life-cycle ceremonies and in daily life, and partly through the formal structures of the associations, many of which were reminiscent of those in the prerevolutionary era, considerably tightened village boundaries and social networks in Sơn-Dương.

In parallel to the exponential increase in formal associational ties was the intensification of ritual activities. Despite the state's long-standing efforts to curtail ritual activities in order to curb "superstition" and to save resources for socioeconomic development, in Sơn-Dương as elsewhere in Vietnam, major household-centered ceremonies—rituals in a child's first year, weddings, the longevity celebrations for the elderly, funerals, death anniversaries—intensified and expanded in scope from the mid-1980s onwards. Birthdays were added to the life-cycle rituals in about 5 percent of Sơn-Dương households, according to a village official in charge of social and cultural affairs.

Of household-centered rituals, weddings and funerals, which were generally the larger and potentially more expensive ones, constituted the main focus of the negotiation between the state and local populations. The efforts of the Sơn-Dương commune leadership to make the communal hall wedding ceremony central to the wedding ritual and to eliminate or reduce the size of wedding banquets had little impact on village life. A retired cadre provided one of the reasons for this failure in 1991:

In 1987, when you were here, the leadership tried to simplify ceremonies and to organize weddings at a village hall. But the change took place due to pressure from above. If the ceremony could simply take place at the public hall and end after the entertainment there, it might survive. But in reality, in the morning, the relatives of the groom still organized a delegation to the bride's house to ask for the bride. After asking for the bride, the bride's and groom's senior relative delegations went to the village hall for the ceremony, and then had to return to the groom's house. There were many complications. The public hall was simply too small, and many people had to stand chaotically outside. The bride's relatives could not simply see her off at the public hall because it was not the final destination. Everybody left after the public hall ceremony for the groom's house where the ceremonial verbal exchange took place again. The basic steps still had to be taken. The public hall ceremony was simply an addition, a complicating addition, especially when the weather was not cooperative. When there is no longer pressure from above, villagers invariably skip this additional step.

Basic long-existing steps in the wedding also became more elaborate. For the main reception on the wedding day, the percentage of wedding receptions where only candies and cookies were served, following state recommendations, dropped from 9 percent in 1976–1985 to 2.3 percent in 1986–1995 and 2.8 percent in 1996–2004.

Although the commune government had attempted in 1986 to limit the number of wedding banquet guests to 60, the number of guests routinely exceeded this number. Among the 505 weddings taking place in the 283 surveyed Son-Dương households between 1976 and 2004, the average number of guests at wedding banquets, which were held separately on the bride's and groom's sides, increased from 120 in the 1976–1985 period to 162 in the following decade and 222 in 1996–2004. If the groom or one of the parents worked at a nearby state factory or as a senior village cadre, the number of guests might exceed 600 (100 trays of banquet foods) because coworkers or people in a senior cadre's extensive contact network had to be invited.

The wedding expenses of the bride's family rose not only due to the increasing size of the wedding banquet, but also because of the additional reception for her on the eve of the wedding, which was well attended by her numerous friends and acquaintances. The bride's dowry had also increased in size. If during the command-economy era, it had normally included clothes, pillows, a blanket, and a mosquito net, by 2004 the list of dowry items had expanded to include a bicycle, her share of the rice fields allocated to her by the commune, and possibly gold if her family was wealthy. The dowry had thus increased to the level approximating the rice-field dowry among the wealthy in the pre-1954 period.

On the groom's side, the expenses besides the wedding banquet would include engagement gifts to the bride's family (normally cakes, candies, and 200–300 areca nuts to be distributed to her relatives and acquaintances as a part of wedding announcements) and several ceremonial trays of food on the wedding day to the bride's family (one to her own family, one to her father's lineage branch head, one to her mother's original family, to be offered respectively to her patrilineal and matrilineal ancestors) and to the groom's ancestors (his father's lineage branch head and his mother's original family). If the bride or the groom was born of the second wife in a family, a tray of food had to be offered also to the ancestors of his or her senior mother (the father's senior wife). If the bride or the groom or his or her parents had godparents *(cha mẹ nuôi),* additional trays of food had to be brought to the households of the godparents. The ceremonial food trays given to the original families of senior mothers and to the households of godparents reflected the strong emphasis on kinship as socially constructed and not based simply on blood and genetic ties.

In the context of larger, more elaborate, and more expensive weddings, wedding gifts became more frequent and from the mid-1990s onward often came in the form of cash. In 1991 a retired cadre in Sơn-Dương still emphasized to me that unlike people in Hanoi and many other communities, villagers routinely refused cash gifts, except from the siblings of the newlywed couple or from very close senior relatives and only when delivered in private before the ceremony. Small gifts in kind from the couple's closest friends could be delivered on the wedding day. This elderly villager elaborated:

> If somebody offers a cash gift at the wedding, the parents would automatically plead with the guest not to do it. A very close senior relative can give cash to a wedding, but only in private and before or after the ceremony. More common are rice loans offered by close relatives. If the parents are not well off, they can also ask for loans *(đi kêu giúp)* from other relatives and close friends. A loan can be up to 100 kilograms of rice. All these loans have to be recorded and paid. Even if a close senior relative declares that the rice is a gift, it still has to be reciprocated on the occasion of his or her children's or grandchildren's weddings.

By 2004 cash gifts had become a widespread practice and were carefully recorded by recipients for the sake of future reciprocity. Gifts ranged from a low of 10,000 VND (US $0.63) from many elderly villagers to 20,000 VND (US $1.26) from regular guests to 50,000 VND (US $3.15) from those in more special relationships to the couple. These amounts were relatively modest in comparison to those in villages closer to Hanoi (see Luong 2009b). But the pervasiveness of cash gifts from the mid-1990s onwards reflects the spread of the cash economy as well as the rising income of villagers. If, in the past, wedding invitations were simply a matter of sentiment and reciprocity, with the timing of reciprocation unspecified, cash gifts which were intended to help the bride's and the groom's families to defray wedding banquet expenses added another layer in social exchanges and relations. Villagers commonly used the business idioms of *lỗ* (loss) and *lãi* (profit) to discuss the economy of weddings. They reported that cash wedding gifts were normally insufficient to cover wedding banquet expenses. Even at weddings where the monetary gifts exceeded banquet expenses (usually due to the larger number of guests from outside the village or in special relations to recipients or their families), the families of the recipients felt an obligation to reciprocate at an equivalent level at future ritual events organized by givers. A couple with six children and six wedding gifts from another family with only two children and thus two weddings normally tried to reciprocate by increasing the amount of wedding gifts they gave, so that the total gifts of both families would approximate the same amount. In the context of Sơn-Dương village, there is normally, in the long run, no real profit from a wedding (cf. Tessier 2009).

Despite the relatively modest wedding gifts in Sơn-Dương, that money still amounted to 3.3 percent of the incomes of the 283 households surveyed in 2004, ranging from 7.1 percent among the bottom quintile households to 2.2 percent among top quintile ones. Many village households had to attend two banquets for the same wedding and to present two gifts since the bride's and the groom's families organized wedding banquets separately and since 80 percent of the marriages of ever-married members of the 283 households surveyed involved commune endogamy.[5]

Among surveyed households, the average number of guests staying for meals at funerals increased from 133 in 1976–1985 to 220 in 1986–1995 and to 212 in 1996–2004. This phenomenon took place despite the 1986 directive by the commune government that restricted funeral servings to tea and areca palm nuts. While individual monetary gifts at funerals in Sơn-Dương were about the same as at weddings, 10,000 VND–20,000 VND (US $0.63–1.26), the amount spent on funeral gifts amounted to only 0.5 percent of their annual incomes. This was partly because there were fewer funerals than weddings—due to the relatively young population—and because most households did not have to make two gifts for the same event in the cases of funerals. For a poor household, funeral cash gifts helped to defray the cost of a coffin, since the days when the agricultural cooperative provided a free coffin were long gone.

The increasing number of guests at wedding and funeral meals reflects the widening relations of Sơn-Dương villagers, both kinship-based and not, as well as a nationwide trend among Vietnamese households to build up their social networks in the era of economic reforms. The widening social networks constitute an important resource, social capital that can be mobilized in time of needs.

In reaction to these increasingly elaborate ritual activities and intensified gift flows, the Communist Party and the national government issued Directives 27 and 14 in 1998 on "civilized" activities at weddings, funerals, and festivals. These directives sought to curb the increasing elaborateness of weddings, funerals, and festivals, the "superstition" associated with many rituals, and the enrichment of some high-cadre families through large wedding and funeral gifts. The subsequent Decree 04/1998 of the Ministry of Information and Culture elaborated on the directives and banned, among other things, the serving of meals at funerals. It called for the elimination of "backward" customs like lying in the path of the coffin during a funeral or throwing votive paper in the funeral route (Vietnam 2005:250–251). Given the mixed results of the 1998 directives and decree, the prime minister's office, in 2005, issued Decision 308 on "civilized" activities in such rituals, which specified what must and should be done or not done. Among the bans were those on superstition and the use of working time and state funds for such rituals unless cadres were attending certain rituals as a part of their official duties. To be encouraged were wedding-banquet simplification and savings, which were to be achieved by offering neither meals nor cigarettes at weddings; the minimizing of funeral wreaths and the gradual elimination of votive paper thrown on the streets during funeral procession; the use of music from tapes and CDs rather than funeral music performed live; cremation instead of burial; the organization of memorials in the following weeks only among family members, relatives, and close friends. The 2005 decision went further than the 1998 decree in certain aspects. For example, the 1998 decree allowed the use of a live band at funerals and did not mention anything about cigarettes, but the 2005 decision exhorted people to avoid them.

**Photos 15 and 16.** Funeral processions on main village road

In Sơn-Dương, the local administration attempted to regulate ritual activities in accordance with the national directives. In 2000 it issued regulations on a "cultured" life *(nếp sống văn hóa)*. In these regulations a cultured life involved, among other things, no more than two children per family; promotion of education, partly through the education-promotion funds of patrilineages; simple wedding meals without alcohol or cigarettes; funerals without meals, cigarettes, or live music; no walking on canes or lying in the path of the coffin during funeral processions; no gambling or drug use; and no polluting of public space. In 2001–2003 more specific regulations were developed for each hamlet which, despite some minor differences, did not deviate significantly from the commune regulations (see Appendix 1). If we take the regulations of Hamlet 5 as an example, they specified that the groom should wear a Western suit and the bride a Vietnamese long dress *(áo dài)*, but the regulations did not mention anything about the consumption of alcohol at weddings.

The commune administration in Sơn-Dương sought to enforce the regulations through a combination of material penalties and symbolic incentives. Starting in 2003, it required a 500,000 VND (US $32) deposit for a wedding. This amount would be forfeited if the family failed to comply with a few major regulations like the ban on cigarettes, on loud music or music late into the night, and the limitation of the wedding celebration to twenty-four hours. With regard to funerals, the regulations developed in Sơn-Dương had gone beyond the 1998 national decree and those in many surrounding communes by banning live bands, and so a number of villagers verbally contested the regulation allowing the use of prerecorded funeral music only. When a number of elderly villagers openly discussed hiring a live funeral band, the commune administration, which was supposed to deliver the main eulogy for the deceased, took a public stand to the effect that it would provide no eulogy, nor any assistance in the form of a coffin carriage or the organization of grave digging, if the family of the deceased hired a live band (which was reportedly going to cost about 1 million VND or US $64). The threat was apparently effective.

The government in Sơn-Dương also granted a "cultured family" or "cultured hamlet" designation to households and hamlets that complied with hamlet regulations on a cultured life. Households evaluated themselves and were evaluated by the hamlet on three major sets of criteria: material comfort (up to 30 points), harmony (up to 25 points), and progressive behavior (up to 45 points). The cultured-family certificate would be awarded to a household meeting five criteria: the family had received a minimum of 70 points on a 100-point scale; they maintained harmony within the household; they avoided conflict with their neighbors; no family members engaged in gambling, drug use, or prostitution; and they followed the policies of the Communist Party and government laws.

Hamlets were also evaluated on the basis of households' meeting the cultured-life criteria. By 2004 about 70 to 80 percent of Sơn-Dương households had received cultured-family certificates. The commune government also recommended three of eight hamlets to higher authorities for the cultured-hamlet designation (in 1994 the four hamlets of Sơn-Dương had been divided into eight hamlets). As an example of how the criteria at the hamlet level were applied, Hamlet 8 was not recommended despite its strong achievements in numerous aspects because one household in the hamlet had five children, and another, which had no undue hardships, did not pay its taxes and local levies.

In Sơn-Dương, commune and hamlet regulations since 2000 have no longer officially limited the size of wedding banquets, although the district's cultural office suggests no more than 300 guests. Local officials realize the difficulty of enforcing such a rule, however, since according to villagers, weddings in the households of some senior commune officials had as many as 600 guests due to these officials' large social networks. In 2004 a number of villagers reported that the bans on cigarettes, meals for funeral guests, and cooked food offerings for the deceased at funerals were not effective. The deceased's patrilineal nephews and many parents of the deceased's children-in-law still offered cooked sticky rice and steamed chickens to the deceased and his or her family. Villagers also reported widespread continuation of the practice of daughters and daughter-in-laws lying in the courtyard of the house in the path of the coffin as it was taken to the cemetery, although one village official said that this practice had ended in Sơn-Dương in the early 2000s.

Villagers commonly used the expression *tình cảm* (sentiment) to explain the increase in the number of wedding-banquet guests (see Malarney 2002). Sentiment exists as a part of dyadic relations as well as within the framework of the many new voluntary associations formed in the village since the early 1990s. As one observant villager suggested, the increase in wedding-banquet guests related partly to the membership of the bride, the groom, and the parents of both in voluntary associations, since they felt obliged to invite fellow association members to reaffirm their common bonds. But sentiment or an increase in association membership cannot by themselves account for the virtual doubling of the average number of wedding guests over two decades. The increase was also related to the greater capacity and willingness of the families to spend their material resources, as well as by the greater capacity and willingness of people in their networks to offer cash gifts, in order to reaffirm and strengthen social relations.

In Sơn-Dương the household-centered life-cycle rituals and the groups linked to these rituals (such as the elderly Buddhist women's association) were generally the most resilient in face of the state's attempt to restructure society and ritual life. In contrast, the ritual cycles outside the kinship domain was more fundamentally transformed. Not yet resurrected by 2006, for example, was the pre-1954 village-wide festival on the ninth and tenth of the eighth lunar month, when villagers slaughtered pigs and a buffalo for the worship of tutelary deities at the communal house and the shrine, wore new clothes, and ate special festival foods. The neighborhood *(giáp)* pig-slaughtering ceremony on the third day of the first lunar month and the ritual fight with Ngũ-Xã villagers remained a distant memory from the days of the Franco-Vietnamese war. At the regular communal house *(đình)* events, villagers sat in an essentially gerontocratic order, evidence of a more egalitarian system influenced by the Marxist state (see Luong 1993 and 1994). Among other life-cycle rituals, the practice of bride price had been discontinued. State-sponsored ceremonies in the solar calendar on the anniversary of the founding of the Communist Party (March 2), Veteran and War Memorial Day (July 27), and National Independence Day (September 2), have been added to the ritual cycles. Popular activities such as sports have been made part of National Independence Day celebrations, with some variation from one year to the next.

In Sơn-Dương, opposition to state control was strongest regarding kinship-centered life-cycle ceremonies, which the state only wanted to simplify. In any case, the most basic elements remained unchanged from the pre-1945 period. These rituals were deeply embedded in the tight kinship networks in rural northern Vietnamese communities where the pervasive use of kinship terms for address and self-reference highlighted the rights and obligations of mutual assistance (see Luong 1990: chap. 2.) The persistence of many ritual practices in the 1954–2006 period was also aided by the great degree of community endogamy in north Vietnam, which rendered more intricate the local social networks and made local cadres more susceptible to community pressures when implementing state policies. Mutual assistance among relatives became even more important since the diminishment of collective resources under the 1988 contract system prevented the agricultural cooperative in Sơn-Dương from drawing on its welfare funds to contribute a coffin to a funeral. Household-centered life-cycle rituals intensified given the increasing importance of reciprocity among relatives (see Luong 1993 and 1994; Kleinen 1999: chap. 8; Malarney 2003, Tessier 2009). Subtle widespread local resistance to certain sociocultural regulations by the state, such as those regarding wedding and funeral meals, led to a modification of state policies in the same way that the everyday resistance to radical collectivization led to a shift in economy policy (see Kerkvliet 2005; Fforde and de Vylder 1998; Luong 2003a; Luong 2007). Changes in both economic and sociocultural policies in Vietnam have been at least as much a result of pressure from the local population as policies have caused changes in local practices.

# CHAPTER 8

# The Restructuring of Local Governance

In July 1998, revisiting Sơn-Dương commune for the first time in seven years, I was startled by the profound crisis that had arisen in the relationship between the local population and the commune administration. As a reflection of its magnitude, from 1993 to 1998, under strong local social pressure, many Communist Party secretaries and presidents of the People's Committee had quickly succeeded one another. Tensions reached a boiling point during my visit: local families were reportedly refusing to pay not only their irrigation fees but also commune levies. These arrears had totaled US $18,000 for half a year. As a result the commune's cumulative debt to the state irrigation authorities had spiraled to approximately US $15,000. Peasants reported that the flow of irrigation water to the commune had slowed significantly, causing them considerable hardships during the rice cultivation season. For half a year commune cadres had also not received their salaries because of this politically rooted financial crisis. At a major meeting during which the secretary of the Communist Party branch in Sơn-Dương reviewed commune activities in the first half of 1998, a villager was reported to have asked publicly who had elected this political leader to a position of authority. Since I first visited the commune in 1987, relations between the local population and the state seemed to have undergone a fundamental transformation, in parallel to the proliferation of communal- and kinship-based local associations. Within the context of these intricately tight local social networks, the local population was clearly attempting to exert considerable pressures on the state and Party apparatuses, not simply through subtle resistance (Kerkvliet 1995 and 2005), but through open confrontation and occasionally adversarial public dialogue. Spontaneous local associations based on kinship, religious, and communal ties and constitutive of "alternative civilities" in rural northern Vietnam (see Weller 1999) can serve as a strong foundation for the mobilization for collective action in the face of growing local socioeconomic inequality. These associations have been at least as effective in strengthening the voice of local populations as bourgeois-dominated voluntary associations are in communities with a greater market penetration. Such dialogues have led to a restructuring of governance in rural Vietnam.

## The Unfolding of Public Dramas

### The Public Drama in Sơn-Dương

The public drama in Sơn-Dương began on December 13, 1996, when the family members of many war dead *(liệt sĩ)* and war invalids gathered outside the commune's cemetery for the revolutionary and war dead. Having been denied access to the commune meeting hall, those Sơn-Dương villagers chose the other officially sacred space in the commune for their meeting. The elderly president of the commune association of *gia đình chính sách* (policy-favored households) started the meeting with incense burning in commemoration of those "native sons who had sacrificed their lives for the independence and welfare" of the country. The family members of the war dead and war invalids were joined by many residents of one commune neighborhood, whose leader was a sister of one of the war invalids. The villagers were reacting with indignation to what the leaders of a spontaneous, local anticorruption movement had uncovered in the previous few days:

1. A list of eighty-three "war dead and war invalid" households, signed by the president and the main tax official of Sơn-Dương commune, had been submitted in 1996 to higher authorities for full or partial exemption from agricultural taxes, as required by the national government's tax exemption decree. However, the list contained nine households that were not eligible for the tax exemption and the commune administration had granted no exemption to a number of exemption-eligible households on the list or only a part of their exemption.

2. Of those eighty-three households, the agricultural land holdings of fifty-nine had been artificially inflated without their knowledge in order to obtain higher exemptions which, needless to say, were not passed on to them.

The leaders of the local anticorruption campaign accused local officials of pocketing the difference between the higher, province-granted exemptions and the actual exemptions received by village households.

Eighty-four villagers signed a resolution that demanded the firing of the commune's president and main tax official, a full investigation by the commune administration, the firing of any cadres found embezzling or responsible for the loss of public funds, a critical examination of the involved Communist Party members by local Party cells *(chi bộ đảng)*, and criminal prosecution of all corrupt officials.

Subsequent investigations uncovered the embezzlement of 28 tonnes of paddy in 1994 and the second half of 1995 alone (no conclusion regarding the first half of 1995). In 1994, for example, the president of the People's Provincial Committee approved a tax exemption for 127 Sơn-Dương households, but the district list contained only 83 households, and the village administration exempted only for 53. According to the two leaders of the anticorruption movement, the amount embezzled from 1994 to 1996 was 42 tonnes of paddy.

The trial of the corrupt local officials in the provincial court on November 15, 1997, inflamed local opinion. Many villagers signed a petition to the Supreme Court, alleging procedural irregularities in the trial and questioning the verdict. They accused the police and judicial authorities of lacking respect for the local population. They also alleged the following irregularities:

1. Not inviting the villagers who had discovered the embezzlement to attend the trial as well as "problematic" invitations to eight victims: four victims had died, one had moved to southern Vietnam; one was an elderly invalid; one suffered from mental illness; and the last allegedly had very limited education and understanding

2. Excluding from judicial consideration the embezzlement that took place in the first half of 1995 and in 1996 due to an "incomplete investigation" by the police and the government inspectorate

3. The court's refusing to take into account the aggravating circumstances of the crime (that is, local officials' corruption had taken place at the expense of war dead and invalid families), and using narrow legal guidelines on embezzled amounts in deciding on a relatively light sentence for the commune's former head tax official

4. Not prosecuting district tax officials

5. Not suspending the Sơn-Dương defendants at the trial from their Communist Party cells, as required by laws and regulations

6. Sentencing only the head tax official in Sơn-Dương, even though the corruption involved other commune and district officials

7.  Violating the 1993 governmental stipulation on a 50 percent penalty on
    the embezzled amount by requiring that the convicted official returned
    only the embezzled amount

The leaders of the anticorruption movement also gathered signatures
for a request to the National Assembly, the president, and the prime minister of Vietnam for further investigation. The petitioners denounced various local administrations for selling agricultural land illegally in 1994
(see Chapter 6), underdeclaring the cultivated surface in the commune
in order to lower the commune's agricultural tax bill, embezzling irrigation fee payments, and permitting no local financial transparency. The
petitioners emphasized that the district authorities, having "oppressed"
the local denouncers of corruption, could not be trusted to investigate the
charges in the petition; that a commune investigation committee should
be established on the basis of an October 1997 resolution by members of
the Commune People's Council; and that the appeal trial should be held in
Sơn-Dương for the education of villagers.

The letter from Sơn-Dương commune to the central government constituted only one instance of a massive outpouring of local grievances
received by the Vietnamese Cabinet. The central government received
105,110 letters in 1998 alone (*Công An Thành Phố Hồ Chí Minh,* July 15,
1999, p. 39).

Because the convicted official remained free in the commune into the
summer of 1998, despite having received a prison sentence in November
1997, Sơn-Dương villagers became convinced that provincial, district, and
commune officials were trying to protect many accomplices at the commune and higher levels, and treating the convicted man quite leniently
in exchange for his agreement not to expose other corrupt officials in the
case. Although in the summer of 1998 the provincial police sent two inves-
tigators from the provincial capital to the commune daily for a thorough
investigation, this did not mollify villagers because the investigation had
not yielded any concrete results. As a response, the Sơn-Dương villagers refused to pay anything to the commune administration except their
agricultural taxes, which were required by law. This threw the commune's
irrigation fees into arrears, with the debt to the irrigation authorities bal-
looning to about US $15,000 by summer 1998. This led to a reduction
of irrigation water during the summer 1998 planting season. The local
population's confrontation with the state and Party apparatuses showed no
sign of abatement by the time of my visit in July 1998. An assessment in

1999 documented that the arrears in irrigation fees by then totaled almost 500 million VND (about US $35,800) and that arrears in various other charges—including corvée labor charges *(lao động công ích)* and water-control-maintenance fees—between 1996 and 1999 amounted to another 500 million VND. Between 1996 and 1999, only a small percentage (varying between 11 and 27 percent) of local households reportedly paid these fees every year.

The anticorruption and fee-withholding movement in Sơn-Dương deeply divided the local Communist Party and its mass organizations. About half the Party members in Sơn-Dương publicly supported the anticorruption movement, and one of the two key leaders was the president of the Veteran Association, a mass organization that had come into existence at the national level in 1989, following a directive from the Central Secretariat of the Vietnamese Communist Party. From 1996 to 1999, local Communist Party and commune power holders were unable to mobilize the other mass organizations, the Women's Association, the Peasant Association, and the Youth Union, to help persuade the majority of the population to pay various local levies.

The public drama in Sơn-Dương was far from being an isolated crisis in rural northern Vietnam. In 1997 Thái-Bình province in the lower Red River delta witnessed widespread unrest that culminated in violence and destruction in quite a few localities (see Luong 2005:132–134). In his public post mortem of the Thái-Bình unrest at Thái-Bình Provincial Party Congress in 1998, Vietnamese President Trần Đức Lương attributed it to three sets of factors:

1. Onerous local levies were imposed without consultation on poor local populations in order to finance 577 billion VND (US $48 million) of infrastructure projects (roads, schools, clinics, and electric power grids) in a forty-four-month-period from January 1994 to July 1997.[1] Local infrastructure taxes amounted to 161 billion VND (US $13.4 million) in this period, while district and provincial ones totaled 15 billion VND (US $1.25 million).

2. Corruption and inefficiency characterized the use of local resources. In Thái-Bình province, in 62 of the 152 investigated communes, where investigation had been completed by early 1998, it was reported that the majority of local grievances were valid to various extents. More specifically, in a number of localities, the costs of construction and infrastructure projects had been inflated by 20 to 25 percent by corrupt officials and project bidders in collusion with each other. In some cases,

the 5 percent of land reserved at the commune level for unanticipated needs and commonly rented for additional local government revenue had been sold or leased without the public's endorsement.

3.  The authorities were unresponsive to grievances and paid inadequate attention to the discontent of the population (including the discontent of "revolutionary elders, veterans, retired cadres; and party members"). Local cadres had reportedly even challenged people to go ahead and file grievances, while the higher authorities did not act quickly in response to local grievances, and sometimes even protected commune officials and hid the truth from authorities above them.

President Trần Đức Lương's analysis suggests similarities between Thái-Bình and Sơn-Dương regarding the corruption of local officials and the unresponsiveness of higher authorities to local grievances.

On the national level, in response to this perception of onerous local levies, the government eliminated taxes on agricultural land effective 2003. The government also issued the "grassroots-democracy decree" (Decree 29) in May 1998. This decree required local governments to consult closely with the elected representatives of the local population on local finances and levies and to be more transparent regarding local finances (Vietnam 1999). Among the issues requiring direct discussion with the local population and their direct decisions by popular vote are infrastructure projects and social contributions, local custom regulations, and the establishment of inspection committees for agreed-upon infrastructure projects (ibid.:18–19). Land-use planning, hamlet-boundary demarcation, and compensation for appropriated land are also issues that require consultation with the local population before the Commune People's Committees or Councils can make decisions. Local populations can also play more prominent inspection roles regarding the activities of commune administrations, commune finances, land use, local grievances, corruption issues, and social assistance to the war dead and war invalid. This can be achieved through the Commune People's Councils, the Fatherland Fronts, or the state-sponsored mass organizations (women, peasants, youth, and veterans); or through local attendance at People's Council meetings or participation in local inspection committees (ibid.: 22–23). Hamlet chiefs (*trưởng thôn,* or in Sơn-Dương, *trưởng khu*) are to be elected directly by voters or household representatives. (In 1994, the four hamlets of Sơn-Dương were divided into eight, called *khu.*) In 2002 the national government required two candidates for each hamlet chief position so that voters could have a choice.

With the support of the government and the Communist Party, the Vietnamese National Assembly also passed a grievance and denunciation law in December 1998. This law specifies the rights and duties of those who have grievances or make denunciations, which include their obligation to tell the truth and the right of denouncers to the protection of their identities. Government agencies are obligated to respond to grievances within forty-five days and to denunciations in ninety days. Between January 1999, when the law went into effect, and March 2004, the number of letters received amounted to 878,053, averaging 167,248 a year (*Người Lao Động* online 21 May 2004). About 60 percent of the letters had to do with land, especially the rate of compensation for land appropriated in connection with infrastructure projects, as well as a perception of unfairness in local officials' implementation of compensation policies on appropriated land (*Vietnamnet* 20 May 2004).[2]

In response to the fact that a number of Communist Party members took leading or supporting roles in the agrarian unrest in northern Vietnam, the Vietnamese Communist Party issued a new set of regulations in 2002 that explicitly prohibited Party members from engaging in the sorts of activities as occurred in Sơn-Dương during the height of the unrest in 1996–1999. Under the new regulations, although Party members are allowed to file grievances and denunciations within Party channels, they are prohibited from, among other things: (1) providing information that might potentially be used by others for public grievances and denunciations; (2) organizing, inciting, or participating in public grievances or denunciations or in organizational meetings leading to public grievances or denunciations; (3) signing grievance or denunciation letters with non-Party members outside of Party channels (prohibition 3); (4) participating in public meetings or protests without the permission of party and government authorities (prohibition 6) (Vietnamese Communist Party 2004:156–192).

By 2004 the crisis of legitimacy in Sơn-Dương commune had subsided, partly because of the retrial and the imprisonment of two local cadres, and partly because of the implementation of the aforementioned national policies and considerable infrastructure investment by the state. The convicted commune tax official reportedly had his sentence increased to about five years, and another commune official, in charge of land issues, received a three-year prison term.

Authorities in the province of Phú-Thọ and the district of Lâm-Thao also forgave the irrigation fee arrears of 500 million VND (US $35,800) and provided financial support, mostly partial, for numerous commune projects, such as:

1. a commune administrative building in 2000, at a cost of about 300 million VND (US $20,260)
2. a primary school reconstruction in 2002, at 1.4 billion VND (US $92,000)
3. a piped-water system in 2002, at 1.4 billion VND (US $92,000)
4. paved commune roads, including those leading to other communes; these began in 2002, at an estimated cost of 1.4 billion VND (US $92,000)
5. a village clinic in 2004, at 170 million VND (US $10,800)
6. a junior high school in 2005, at 1.6 billion VND (US $100,870)

Although the Vietnamese government gave high priority everywhere to infrastructure improvements in order to facilitate economic development, the level of infrastructure construction in Sơn-Dương seems much higher than that in many other northern communes. By 2006 there was also active discussion at the provincial level about designating Sơn-Dương as one of four communes in the province identified for special development.

The high level of support for infrastructure development in Sơn-Dương commune may have also been facilitated by the fact that three Sơn-Dương villagers were in the provincial leadership of Phú-Thọ province in the early part of the twenty-first century. During my research in 2004 villagers related with pride the fact that two native sons were provincial department directors and one was the deputy secretary of the provincial Party apparatus (one of the three most powerful figures in the province). By 2006 this deputy secretary had become the chair of the provincial People's Committee, that is, he was then head of the provincial government and thus the second-ranked official in the provincial Party system.

However, most of the infrastructure projects in Sơn-Dương were not funded entirely by the state or international aid. The one exception was the piped-water system, which was funded entirely by UNICEF (United Nations Children's Fund). And even for this project, households had to pay 350,000 VND (about US $23) for a water meter and a connecting pipe from the household to the main system. Other infrastructure projects were implemented on the basis of cost-sharing between the commune and higher levels of government. The higher levels, for example, provided only 40 percent of the cost of renovating the primary school and initially only one-quarter of the junior high school renovation. For the commune road-paving project, the provincial and district governments provided only cement, and the commune had to provide sand, pebbles, and labor. Similarly, for the commune clinic, higher authorities covered only 60 percent of the costs. Given the cofinancing requirement for numerous infrastructure projects, the commune administration had to rely heavily on the sale of land under its control for residential purposes, as well as on levies on commune house-holds. Local levies for infrastructure projects in 2004 averaged 53,000 VND (US $3.36) per person or 240.000 VND (US $15.22) per household among the 283 surveyed households. Together with state-required cash payments in lieu of labor on public work projects and residential land taxes, as well as other local levies (for social affairs, irrigation canal construction, and kindergarten fees, among others), the levies averaged 411,000 VND (US $26) per household, which amounted to 2.9 percent of the income in the surveyed households (varying from 7.7 percent among bottom-income quintile to 1.6 percent among top-income quintile).

Nevertheless, by the end of 2006 the commune administration still owed contractors 1.8 billion VND (US $110,000), including half the cost for the commune administrative building that had been constructed six years earlier, almost a quarter of the cost of the primary school renovation built four years earlier, and two-thirds of the cost of the junior high school renovation. The construction boom in Vietnam since the early 1990s has brought many infrastructure companies a thriving business, but they also face severe financial problems due to extraordinary delays in payment by government agencies on all levels. Although projects signed by govern-ments above the commune level are normally guaranteed funding by the Ministry of Finance, the cost-sharing principle at the commune level usu-ally means no secure funding for commune projects and only a vague plan as to how the commune can raise funds. Access to bank credit, which has become easier after the mid-1990s, has facilitated the survival of many construction companies, especially state companies, but the difficulty of demanding interest on late payments and the tendency not to resort to law-suits also means that companies have had to build bank interest payments over a long period into its project costs and to cut corners or to use lower-quality materials than originally agreed. A village informant familiar with construction materials reported that infrastructure contractors routinely hired workers from outside Sơn-Dương for their work in the commune in order to minimize the flow of information about their use of lower-quality materials than specified in contracts.[3]

Even in 2003, of the 200 million VND (US $13,000) which the Sơn-Dương administration hoped to collect as a part of its own regular revenues from the local population, the commune succeeded in collecting only 70 percent. (These revenues come from the rent on the commune reserve land; local levies for social assistance, irrigation system improvement, corvée labor, school construction, nursery school teachers' salaries; and fees for birth and other administrative certificates.) Even at 70 percent, this percentage compared quite favorably with the range of 11 to 27 percent during the 1996–1999 crisis in Sơn-Dương. In order to collect arrears from households, the commune administration imposed new measures in the summer of 2004:

1.  Irrigation fee arrears, if accumulated over two or three rice-planting seasons and unrelated to serious illnesses, would lead to the cutting off of the water supply.
2.  The commune would not issue papers for temporary absences (for migration purposes), for bank loans, for new residential land, unless the arrears were paid up.

The commune administration did not require payment of arrears as a precondition for birth or marriage certificates or for the certification necessary for attendance at universities, colleges, or technical schools. This policy was implemented in June 2004, during my visit, and the village administration reported receiving 6 million VND (US $380) in arrears payments within three weeks.

Annually, in the mid-2000s, the provincial government had to provide a subsidy of about 200 million VND (US $13,000) to the commune administration for the commune's regular operating expenses, quite apart from infrastructure construction costs. One regular major expense was the full salaries for nineteen commune officials, as well as stipends for lower-level cadres. Among the officials with full salaries were the Communist Party secretary *(bí thư)* and another member of the Party's executive committee *(thường vụ đảng uỷ);* the commune president and vice-president *(chủ tịch* and *phó chủ tịch Uỷ ban nhân dân);* one ranking member of the People's Council *(hội đồng nhân dân);* the heads of the Fatherland Front, the Women's Union, the Youth Union, the Veteran Association and the Peasant Association; the cadres in charge of land records, finance (two cadres), roads and irrigation, justice (including birth, marriage, and death certification), social and cultural affairs, commune offices in general, as well as a local policeman and the head of the local militia. Among the cadres entitled to modest stipends were the eight hamlet chiefs, the deputy heads of the mass organizations, and the part-time assistants in the social and cultural affairs office.

The fact that the Communist Party secretary was considered the leading commune official reflects the dominance of local governance by the Communist Party, which had 239 members (4.9 percent of the population) in Sơn-Dương in 2006 (*Phú-Thọ* online 13 February 2006). The top officials in the commune were all Party members. The commune president *(chủ tịch Uỷ ban nhân dân)* in Sơn-Dương, as elsewhere in Vietnam, was the deputy Party secretary, a fact that reflects the subordination of the commune government to the Communist Party secretary and the Communist Party organization. The commune president was elected not directly by voters in the commune, but by the People's Council (see below).

Moreover, the political arena was still heavily male-dominated. The three members of the Executive Committee *(thường vụ đảng uỷ)* of the Communist Party organization in Sơn-Dương were all male. In the Leadership Committee of the Party (Đảng ủy), the percentage of women had not improved significantly from two decades earlier: it was 11 percent in the late 1980s and 15 percent in 2006 (two members out of thirteen). Only one of the eight hamlet chiefs, all of whom were also Communist Party cell secretaries for their hamlets, was female. The percentage of women Party members had actually dropped, from 20 percent in 1985 to 15.5 percent (37 out of 239) in 2006. This resulted from the heavy domestic duties of women as well as the importance of the armed forces as a major channel to Communist Party membership.

On the much less influential People's Council (Hội đồng nhân dân), whose members were directly elected by Sơn-Dương voters every five years, women and non-Party members had a more visible presence. In the 2004 election, of the forty-one candidates to the People's Council vetted by the Fatherland Front, thirteen (32 percent) were non-Party members and fifteen (37 percent) were women. Of the twenty-four elected council members, however, only five (21 percent) were non-Party members and seven (29 percent) were women. The percentage of women on this council increased from 21 percent in 1994–1999, to 32 percent in 1999–2004, but dropped to 29 percent in 2004–2009.[4] The head of the commune Women's Association explained the low participation of women in the commune's political life in terms of women's domestic duties, while the secretary of the Communist Party organization in Sơn-Dương emphasized that women were better in action than in speaking, and this put them at a disadvantage in the public arena.

Although the crisis in the legitimacy of the local leadership had subsided by 2004, tension still simmered below the surface. The label "traitor-rebel" *(phản loạn)* was leveled not only at the leaders of the anticorruption campaign in 1996–1999, but also at an entire neighborhood strongly supportive of the movement. During our survey and my interviews in summer 2004, one household in this neighborhood refused to cooperate, and it took considerable patience for me to get some information from its head on his family. He complained about the traitor-rebel label applied to his neighborhood and about the increasingly higher local levies as well as the requirement of local levy arrears payments as a condition for the issuance of certain kinds of paper from the commune.[5]

In Vietnam of the 1990s, the unrest in Thái-Bình as well as the crisis in Sơn-Dương and possibly in many other localities was unparalleled for its open confrontation and challenge by the local population to the Party and state apparatuses. This confrontation has led to a major national policy change that has strengthened the voice of the local population in commune affairs and has sanctioned lasting changes in state-society relations at the local level.

On one level, those developments lend further support to Kerkvliet's perspective that the Vietnamese state is "mass-regarding" and can be responsive to pressures from society (Kerkvliet 1995, Kerkvliet 2003). Kerkvliet argues that pressure can be channeled through state-sanctioned participation in state-organized mass organizations, but that most pressure comes in the domain of everyday politics and involves "trying to live within or modify the prevailing contours as well as engaging in subtle, nonconfrontational everyday resistance to slip under or to undermine the system" (Kerkvliet 1995:400).

On another level, in the rural Vietnamese landscape the social pressures to which state policies have responded can take more confrontational forms and involve more than subtle everyday resistance. From a historical perspective, the closest equivalents to the crises in Thái-Bình and Sơn-Dương in the rural Vietnamese lowlands from 1975 onwards were the open resistance of many Mekong delta cultivators to collectivization in the late 1970s and the peaceful demonstrations by former landowners in many southern Vietnamese (Nam bộ) district and provincial towns in the late 1980s regarding their land from the precollectivization period (Luong 1994). The landowner demonstrations, however, were less openly confrontational towards the state, while to my knowledge, the resistance of cultivators to collectivization was less than a concerted collective action. If the crises in Thái-Bình and localities such as Sơn-Dương were unparalleled under a Marxist state in the second half of the twentieth century, how were they triggered?

I suggest that the three factors President Trần Đức Lương discussed (onerous local levies, corruption, and unresponsive authorities) constitute important but not sufficient conditions for the outbreak. From a cross-regional and comparative perspective, local corruption was neither limited to the Red River delta nor necessarily more serious there than in other parts of the country. There is no clear evidence that local authorities in Thái-Bình were less responsive to grievances than those elsewhere. And the annual local levies at the time of 20 kilograms of paddy per person in both Thái-Bình and Sơn-Dương were not particularly onerous because the subsistence margin of Red River delta peasants as a whole had significantly improved in the 1990s.

In the 1990s Sơn-Dương villagers generally experienced a significant improvement in their standard of living, like most rural residents of the Red River delta and other parts of the Vietnamese lowlands. On the basis of village statistics and my July 1998 interviews with a good number of Sơn-Dương villagers about their various economic activities in the summer of 1998, I estimate that the *net* per capita income in Sơn-Dương had increased from 450 kilograms of paddy in 1991 to 530 kilograms of paddy in 1998. This increase took place despite the decline in per capita *net* yield from agriculture from 400 kilograms of paddy to 320 kilograms due to a 15 percent increase in population.[6] The increase in the standard of living for the average Sơn-Dương villager resulted partly from the diversification of income sources and partly from the significant rise in the official incomes of active and retired state employees. Most significant among the new income sources was the temporary or seasonal migration of up to a quarter of the local labor force for jobs elsewhere in the country. Retired state employees also enjoyed a significant rise in income: my village host's pension for thirty years of services in the armed forces increased from five kilograms of rice in 1987 to 150 kilograms in 1998. Among active state employees, those working at the nearby Lâm-Thao chemical fertilizer factory earned about US $80 a month, thanks to the high demand for fertilizers in connection with the country's agricultural export boom. From a long-term perspective, the average per capita annual income of 530 kilograms in 1998 had risen significantly from that of 220 kilograms in 1980. Socioeconomic inequality within the commune seems to have been limited, at least in comparison to that in the Mekong delta, since agricultural land was distributed in a relatively egalitarian way within the commune. Of the 1,034 households in Sơn-Dương in summer 1998, approximately

450 owned televisions, while only a few had had them seven years earlier. In the context of a notable rise in per capita incomes and living standards from 1980 to 1998, the 1998 commune taxes in Sơn-Dương, averaging 20 kilograms of paddy per person or 3.8 percent of the average net income, cannot be considered too onerous.[7]

While comparable data are not available for Thái-Bình province, the World Bank's living standard surveys in 1993 and 1998 indicate that living standards had increased most dramatically in the Red River delta in this five-year period. The percentage of the population living in poverty declined by 34 percent in the Red River delta (from 63 percent in 1993 to 29 percent in 1998), in comparison to a drop of 19 percent in the country as a whole (Vietnam and World Bank 1999:4, 15). It was also in the Red River delta that the poverty gap index, which measures the depth of poverty among poor households, was reduced by the largest margin (from 18.8 in 1993 to 5.7 in 1998) (ibid.:16). Of the seven socioeconomic Vietnamese regions, the Red River delta was also the only one in which rural household expenditures had grown by a higher percentage than those of urban ones between 1993 and 1998 (ibid.:75). Even if commune levies consumed on the average a higher percentage of rural household expenditures in the Red River delta than elsewhere (see endnote 7), there is no evidence than these levies were so onerous as to threaten the subsistence of Red River delta peasants (cf. James C. Scott 1976). From a historical perspective, these peasants' livelihoods were considerably more precarious in 1978 than in 1998. In spatial comparative terms, the 1998 poverty rate and poverty depth index were lower in the Red River delta than in five of the six remaining regions.[8] Yet unrest in the Red River delta was unparalleled in the country in the first quarter of century since the reunification of Vietnam in 1975.

How can we understand the major crisis in state-society relations in Sơn-Dương commune and Thái-Bình province, and its absence in the Mekong delta, where there was a greater depth of poverty and sharper stratification, if local taxation in the Red River delta was not so onerous, and if commune governments in the Red River delta were neither necessarily more corrupt nor necessarily less responsive to local populations? I would like to suggest that the crisis in state-society relations in rural northern Vietnam cannot be *fully* explained without a close examination of the local sociocultural framework, both in terms of the social fabric and ideological formation. Having been partly restructured by the dialogic relation among the voices of the Marxist state and the prerevolutionary era of Vietnam, the local sociocultural framework in the northern lowlands was characterized by a strong discursive emphasis on relative equality and by the extensive proliferation of kinship-, village-, and religion-based local associations that were reminiscent of the colonial social structure (see Chapter 7). How these factors played a role in the crisis in Sơn-Dương and the Red River delta in general will be discussed in comparison to their relative absence in the southern third of Vietnam in the next chapter.

CHAPTER 9

# Theoretical Reflections

The past century has witnessed violent turns in the encounter between capitalist imperialism and the social formations of agrarian societies at the periphery of the capitalist world system. The emerging social formations at the periphery, which are built on the basis of noncapitalist principles in many cases, have also been fundamentally restructured in the past half a century. In many respects the dynamics of this encounter and subsequent restructuring are epitomized in the Vietnamese revolution. The Vietnamese transformation has influenced important theoretical models embedded in the major traditions of contemporary Western social theory represented by John Stuart Mill, Karl Marx, and Emile Durkheim. In the following analysis of their relative strengths and weaknesses, I seek to make a small contribution to their refinement on the basis of empirical data on the Vietnamese revolution and the village of Sơn-Dương in particular. More specifically, I suggest that the revolutionary processes in modern Vietnam cannot be understood primarily in terms of a material cost-benefit analysis of historical agents. Rather, these processes must be situated with regard to both the structure of capitalist imperialism and the local indigenous framework.

A major problem of the rational-choice framework (Popkin 1979; Olson 1965) remains how to incorporate historically and socioculturally specific values into its model of revolutionary processes. Without such an incorporation, the framework simply projects Western utilitarian ideology onto a radically different sociocultural landscape, where it encounters numerous empirical anomalies. For example, on which matrix of material costs and benefits did a large number of young Sơn-Dương villagers from different social strata volunteer for the Vietminh armed forces in the 1946–1950 period, when Vietminh troops faced an enemy of overwhelming technological superiority and before the poor recruits could foresee any substantial socioeconomic reforms in their favor? On which universal grid of values did one-half to two million northern Vietnamese peasants accept starvation in the spring of 1945 instead of revolting spontaneously and seizing the rice that would have given them a chance of survival? It would likewise be an oversimplification to explain Son-Duong villagers' redirection of labor input to their household garden plots in the 1978–1981 period exclusively in terms of the diminishing returns from cooperative work. In the 1965–1975 period the cooperative labor input had remained high in spite of the diminishing returns to cooperative members. These low returns had resulted from the cooperative's low-priced paddy sale to the state as a part of its contribution to the war effort.

To label irrational such behavioral choices on the Vietnamese political landscape is to explain them away in the face of the inadequacy of the theoretical model. I do not deny the significance of material costs and benefits in the analysis of human action. Many behavioral choices in the course of the Vietnamese revolution are amenable to such a "rational-choice" analysis, most notably the suspension of active resistance to French colonialism and Son-Duong villagers' instrumental, short-termed conversion to Catholicism in the 1930s in the hope of gaining the release of their politically active family members. Similarly, the strengthened support among the poorer social strata for the Vietminh in the 1950–1954 period can be explained within the rational-choice framework: the Vietminh had placed greater emphasis on the socioeconomic revolution at that time to the advantage of poorer peasants. However, the needs for survival, sexual reproduction, and material well-being are always refracted to a certain extent by a historically situated and socioculturally constructed matrix of meanings. To reduce the rich texture of the native system of rules and meanings to a supposedly universal grid of material costs and benefits is to fail to explain a wide range of historical events and human acts. While appropriately stressing the dynamics of collective action in the revolutionary processes, the rational-choice framework has focused on agency at the expense of structures—structures that constrain human action both through external sanctions and through actors' acceptance of certain ideological premises constitutive of these structures (cf. Elliott 2003:5–6, 17).

Through its close attention to the dynamics of capitalism, the Marxist approach has enhanced our understanding of the encounter between world capitalism and local indigenous systems. However, because it pays limited attention to the active role of indigenous precapitalist traditions in revolutionary processes, the approach is not without its share of empirical anomalies as well.

In the Vietnamese context, as pointed out by world-system theorists (Wallerstein 1979; Murray 1980), the unequal exchange between the colonizing core and the colonized periphery constitutes a major structural parameter within which revolutionary processes in the periphery are embedded. This unequal exchange emerged in the nineteenth century as an integral part of the global competition among different states within the capitalist core, not necessarily for the immediate profits to be gained from colonial conquests, but out of concern for being denied access to possible markets and resource bases in Africa and Asia (Murray 1980:10–15). In order to recoup the costs of the colonial adventure, once a *pax colonia* was established in Vietnam, the metropolitan and colonial state apparatuses began using coercive measures to lay the groundwork for capitalist operations and to strengthen the revenue sources of the colonial state. As pointed out by Murray and as briefly discussed in Chapter 1, these measures included the concession of indigenous land to colonial settlers for the development of major cash crops; the introduction of direct and indirect taxes and the conversion of tax payments from kind to cash to facilitate capitalist growth; and the oppressive appropriation of labor through the corvée system, the maintenance of rural labor reserves (to be elaborated on shortly), and repressive labor laws to hold down labor costs for capitalist agromineral ventures.

In the interaction between capitalism and the local precapitalist sector in colonial Vietnam, the impact of world capitalism was far from uniform. It was most striking in the south, which emerged as one of the top three rice-exporting areas in the world. There approximately two-thirds of the rural population was separated from the means of agricultural production, land and labor became strictly commoditized, and classes became increasingly differentiated. In contrast, in the north and center, although the rural population was increasingly drawn into market relations, the majority still tenaciously held on to their minuscule land holdings, buffered in many communities by the small shares that they held of communal land. Although the institution of communal land in the village of Sơn-Dương was not significant in the colonial period, in northern and central Vietnam, the proportions of inalienable communal land averaged 21 percent and 25 percent respectively of the cultivated acreage. Murray suggests that the persistence of communal land in the north and the center contributed to the formation of noncapitalist labor reserves for the plantations, mines, and factories within French Indochina and beyond. Such reserves allowed workers to rely on kinship and communal ties for survival in times of recession and during their preproductive and postproductive periods (youth and old age). It has been suggested that the cost of capitalist production was consequently held down because capitalist

firms had to pay only the cost of short-term labor reproduction (the cost
to sustain workers physically during the period of employment) and not
the cost of long-term labor renewal (the cost of replacing a physically
debilitated work force with a new generation of laborers and of maintaining a temporarily idle work force during economic downturns) (Murray
1980: chap. 5; see also Meillassoux 1981; Wolpe 1972). Within the con-
fines of northern and central rural communities, the noncapitalist sector of
the colonial social formation absorbed part of the cost of labor reproduction for the capitalist sector through partially effective social insurance
mechanisms and thus contributed to the process of capital accumulation.
The noncapitalist system persisted to a considerable extent in northern and
central Vietnamese villages, since land was available for purchase primarily within communal boundaries, and since most of the mining, industrial, and plantation labor force would re-enter the communal framework
whenever possible (Gourou 1936:360–361; Vũ-Quốc-Thúc 1951:67–78).
The high turnover rate among plantation and industrial workers had to do
not merely with the vicissitudes of the capitalist world economy, but also
with the desire of many workers to return to the noncapitalist communal
framework. To world-system theorists the uneven spread of capitalism in
colonial Vietnam actually contributed to the process of capital accumulation in the colonial context, at least in the short run.

> In the Red River delta and the coastal lowlands of Annam, the social
> differentiation of village inhabitants, the disintegration of owner-
> occupancy and petty-proprietorship as the principal social relations of
> production, and the consequent growth of the home market evolved
> relatively slowly during the. colonial era. The preservation of the
> apparently "traditional" structures of northern village communities
> became an absolute requirement for the labor-force renewal of landless
> or virtually landless wage-laborers who were compelled by economic
> necessity to migrate from their natal village communities in search of
> seasonal and temporary employment at the European-dominated points
> of production. Metropolitan capital recognized the historical manner
> in which these northern agricultural village communities fulfilled the
> functions of social security for unemployed or partially employed
> wage-laborers. Hence, colonial policies deliberately aimed at the con-
> servation of particular elements of village organization as one means of
> ensuring the survival of a migrant labor system beneficial to the large-
> scale metropolitan concessionary enterprises that organized agromin-
> eral export production directly under the sway of capital.

In contrast, the historic process of native settlement and village formation had hardly begun in the Mekong delta when it was interrupted by the French colonial occupation. Consequently, the patterns of land tenure and ownership, class relations, and village organization in the Mekong delta developed in direct response to colonial rule and the politicoeconomic influences of the capitalist world economy rather than through extensive contact with traditional indigenous social and economic organization. In the Mekong delta, the spread of commodity exchange and circulation, the growth of the home market, and the dissolution of the elements of the noncapitalist mode of production evolved at a relatively rapid pace (Murray 1980:8–9).

In the long run, Murray suggests, "these 'blockages' [in northern and central Vietnam] to the homogeneous spread and deepening of the extended reproduction of capital coincided with economic stagnation, declining productivity, and the vicious cycle of rural poverty associated with the 'underdeveloped' regions of the globe" (ibid.:x; cf. Geertz 1963).

Despite the insights provided by the Wallersteinian theoretical framework regarding the macrostructure of the world system, I suggest that although class constitutes an important element in the examination of colonial policies, the native sociocultural framework also plays an important role in shaping the encounter between capitalist imperialism and the indigenous system. The dynamics of the Vietnamese revolution cannot be seen merely in terms of local class struggle (cf. Paige 1975). Neither can the remarkable persistence of the noncapitalist sector in northern and central Vietnam be analyzed primarily in terms of its contribution to capital accumulation.

First of all, active resistance to French colonialism did gain support among many members of the native elite. It can be clearly seen in the history of Vietnamese anticolonialism in Sơn-Dương, and it is attested to by the necessity of the special category "resistance-supporting landlord" in the land-reform campaign in the north after independence (cf. Murray 1980:36–37; Ngô-Vĩnh-Long 1978b). The active support of these members of the indigenous elite for anticolonial movements cannot be mechanically explained in terms of the struggle by the working classes of the periphery against the capitalists of the core. As discussed in the preceding chapters, the nationalist aspirations among many members of the native intelligentsia were rooted partly in the contradiction between the racial inequality of colonial Vietnam and the metropolitan discourse of "liberty, equality, and fraternity" and partly in the divergence between local tradition and capitalist imperialism. The sharp contrast between the actual structure of the colonial racial diarchy and the official metropolitan discourse is highlighted in the account by French-educated novelist Nhất-Linh of his journey from Vietnam to France, quoted in Chapter 2:

> The farther the ship got from Vietnam and the closer it got to France, to the same degree the more decently the people aboard the ship treated me. In the China Sea they did not care to look at me. By the Gulf of Siam they were looking at me with scornful apprehension, the way they would look at a mosquito carrying malaria germs to Europe. When we entered the Indian Ocean, their eyes began to become infected with expressions of gentleness and compassion... and when we crossed the Mediterranean, suddenly they viewed me as being civilized like themselves, and began to entertain ideas of respecting me. At that time I was very elated. But I still worried about the time when I was going to return home! (translated in Woodside 1976:4)

The liberty to which the colonial masters claimed they were uplifting the indigenous masses did not stand up to close scrutiny, as indicated by the expulsion of Vietnamese students (including naturalized French citizens) in the spring of 1930 simply for having demonstrated in Paris against the French execution of participants in the Yên-Báy movement (see Chapter 3). In Vietnam, in combination with the symbols of anticolonialism nurtured from earlier waves of resistance and the indigenous belief in racial or ethnic competition and survival, the contradictions within the colonial system as viewed through native lenses led a minority of the young intelligentsia to engage in acts of active resistance for the cause of national independence. The organizational efforts by many children of the traditional elite created a crucial link among the rural communities. As can be seen in the massive 1944–1945 Tonkin famine, discontent among the indigenous masses was seldom transformed into a major movement without a leadership that could effectively mobilize them (see Luong 1985:170; cf. James C. Scott 1976: chaps. 5 and 7). As the historian Woodside remarks:

> It does not slander the political contributions of one of the most hardworking and resourceful peasantries in all Asia to point out... that the Vietnamese revolution was led for the most part by the sons of the traditional intelligentsia, and that this was the section of Vietnamese society which found itself earlier and most often in demeaning circumstances of cultural and political conflict with the colonial power. The peasantry were also exploited by the colonial power, and cher-

ished extensive memories of a national tradition of resistance to outside aggression. *But peasants did not have to make enormous immedi-*
*ate cultural concessions* to the French colonialists in order to survive.
(Woodside 1976:303; emphasis added)

If nationalist appeals propelled many children of the traditional elite
(including Hồ Chí Minh) toward a path of political activism, their conflict
with the French masters hardened many of them and launched them on a
leftward political trajectory. Underground and prison experiences under
the colonial yoke shattered the elitism among many nonleftist activists
and began a process of transformation toward socialism, as can be seen in
the political trajectory of the exiled Sơn-Dương native Nguyễn Đắc Bằng
(cf. Zinoman 2001). Bằng's case was not an isolated incident, although
such transformation was not universal. As a contemporary Vietnamese
source remarked, "In the specific conditions of our country, the ideological and political trajectory of the majority of [Communist Party] members
involved a move from nationalism to class awareness, or the inextricable
relation between the two" (Hoàng-Ước 1968:194).

The regional variations in revolutionary strength and socioeconomic
conditions in Vietnam present the Marxist models with a second major
anomaly. In colonial Vietnam the peasantry were most heavily dispossessed of the means of production in Cochinchina (South Vietnam), where
approximately two-thirds of the rural population was landless. However,
Paige's model notwithstanding, from the mid-nineteenth century to 1975,
the armed resistance to French colonialism and capitalism was generally
more limited in the south than in the north and the center. With the sole
exception of the armed insurrection in certain areas of Cochinchina in
1940 (Nguyễn-Công-Bình et al. 1985:318–319; cf. Paige 1975:323–324),
at no point did the anticolonial armed movement in the south exceed or
even approach the intensity of the unrest in the center and the north. In
the pre-World War II period, it was in Annam (central Vietnam) that the
1930–1931 unrest posed the greatest threat to the colonial order (see Luong
1985; Brocheux 1977; and Ngô-Vĩnh-Long 1978a). During the first Indochinese war (1946–1954), the French encountered considerably greater
resistance in Annam and Tonkin.[1] During the period of direct and massive
U.S. intervention (1964–1975), it was not in the former Cochinchina but
in the southern part of central Vietnam that the National Liberation Front
developed its strongest roots (Mitchell 1968). This pattern of regional
variation constitutes a striking anomaly to Paige's model, which predicts the greatest socialist revolutionary potential in Cochinchina (with

noncultivators deriving their incomes from the land and a large class of cultivators dependent on wages and sharecropping arrangements). In the face of this empirical anomaly, Paige suggests that the more mountainous terrain of north and central Vietnam provides a more favorable condition for guerrilla warfare. Paige also argues that north and central Vietnam are closer to supply base areas (China during the Franco-Vietminh conflict and North Vietnam during the U.S. war) (Paige 1976:326–332). Although the geographical factor is certainly not insignificant, it is not as important as Paige suggests. Even if Paige's geographical explanation were adequate, his model would still encounter another major anomaly: the considerably slower pace of socialist agricultural development in southern Vietnam after the end of the U.S. war. By 1980, 83 percent of households in the coastal plains of southern central Vietnam had joined labor exchange teams and agricultural cooperatives that involved 76 percent of the cultivable acreage. In contrast, the percentages in south Vietnam reached only 31 percent and 24 percent, respectively (Nguyễn-Huy 1983:113; cf. Ngô-Vĩnh-Long 1988:165). It is a historical fact that north and central Vietnam, despite their lesser degree of class polarization, constituted the areas with both stronger resistance to Western intervention and greater socialist revolutionary potential.

I hypothesize that the precapitalist tradition of north and central Vietnam provided stronger ideological and organizational resources for the active resistance to French colonialism in particular and to capitalist imperialism in general. Despite a considerable internal tension between its class-structured hierarchy and communal collectivism, this tradition nurtured values conducive to the growth of nationalism, to collectivism in a relatively mild form, and to a hierarchical organizational framework. This tradition differs fundamentally from capitalism, which, as defined by Wallerstein, is oriented toward "the maximization of surplus creation" (1979:285).

On one level, the indigenous precapitalist framework was characterized by both class cleavages and a male-oriented, kinship-centered hierarchy. These features were reinforced through linguistic socialization within the family and by the rigid Confucian distinction between mental and manual labor in society at large. Within the family, children were (and continue to be) socialized at an early age into discursive practices that rendered salient the authoritarian structure of the kinship unit, the distinction between patrilineal and nonpatrilineal kin, and the male-centered hierarchy. For example, even in late adulthood a person must continue to use the term *"con"* (child) for self-reference when speaking with his or her parents. Such a linguistic usage highlights the hierarchical nature of the inter-action. In the village of Sơn-Dương, as part of the androcentric principles of descent, the term *chú* (paternal uncle) is used in reference only to the father's paternal junior uncle's sons (patrilineal relatives) and not to the father's maternal junior uncle's sons (nonpatrilineal kin, called *cậu*). In the sociocultural system prior to the twentieth century, in which the mastery of Confucian literature was the main route to power, it is no coincidence that the most popular male middle name, *văn*, means literature. The exclusive use of *văn* for males reinforced the legitimacy of male power in the politi-cal structure of the larger society (see Luong 1990:92–93).

Outside the family context, as the Sơn-Dương villager Bằng related, educated men could not engage in manual labor without incurring social stigma. In the village of Sơn-Dương, the class distinction was further accentuated by the pervasive commoditization of status that occurred as part of the colonial encounter—a process that exempted the exclusively male purchasers of honorary titles from corvée for their lifetimes. Villag-ers paid the utmost attention to one another's class standing in establishing marital alliances. The class-based, male-oriented hierarchical order was rendered salient both in the seating order at communal-house ceremo-nies and in daily speech interaction, in which ranking villagers and their spouses had to be addressed with their formal titles (Mr. Mayor, Mrs. Can-ton Chief) (see also Luong 1988). I suggest that the hierarchical structure of the local tradition, maintained partly through the socialization process, accounts for numerous features in Vietnamese anticolonialism and the Vietnamese revolution: the male-centered elitism in the VNP recruitment and organizational methods, the Vietminh's reliance on male members of the intelligentsia for local leadership in the early period of anti-French resistance, and the male dominance in both domestic and public relations in postcolonial Sơn-Dương.

On another level the growth of nationalism and a collectivistic vision of political economy are facilitated by important communal institutions and corresponding conceptual categories in the local tradition of the north and the center. Northern and central villages maintained sharp boundaries through the villagers' participation in the collective worship of tutelary deities, an extraordinary degree of village endogamy, the institution of communal land, and their nucleated settlement pattern. In Sơn-Dương it is no coincidence that in villagers' consciousness both of its tutelary dei-ties had played important roles in defending the country against foreign invaders. In terms of community structure, the rate of intracommunity marriages frequently exceeded 80 percent for colonial northern villages

(Nguyễn-Xuân-Nguyên 1942; Luong 1990:52–53), whereas community exogamy was preferred in the south (Hickey 1964:100). In Tonkin and Annam the percentages of communal land in total cultivated acreage remained 21 percent and 25 percent, respectively, well into the colonial period, compared with 3 percent for Cochinchina (Ngô-Vĩnh-Long 1973:15–16). Correspondingly, each northern and central rural community sharply distinguished "insiders" *(nội tịch)* and "outsiders" *(ngoại tịch)* among village residents. It might take three to four generations for the descendants of outsiders (that is, those not born in the community) to gain the full membership status of *nội tịch,* especially where communal land was sufficiently abundant to be redistributed periodically among all the adult male insiders. The categories of *nội tịch* and *ngoại tịch* constituted part of the general, sharp distinction between the members and nonmembers of a social unit, whether it was kinship, communal, ethnic, or racial. In contrast, group boundaries were considerably less rigid in southern Vietnamese communities, where settlements were nonnucleated and where significant geographical mobility existed in the frontier environment (see Rambo 1973: chap. 2). The sharp conceptual distinction between members and nonmembers in Tonkin and Annam underlies the northern and central tradition of great formality in interaction with outsiders. In the face of outside forces, it also fostered a sense of unity and collectivism among members of the same category.

Both within and beyond the indigenous communal context, the tension between interclass solidarity and class differentiation in the precapitalist framework was mediated on the one hand by the Confucian high valuation of moral cultivation at the expense of wealth accumulation and mercantile activities and on the other by the norm of noblesse oblige for educated men in their relations with other social strata. Noblesse oblige was manifested in the precolonial practice of tax reduction for cultivators in times of natural calamity (Ngô-Vĩnh-Long 1973:33–34; James C. Scott 1976:54). The tension between class differentiation and interclass unity was partly mediated, in James Scott's terminology, by a subsistence ethic constitutive of the indigenous precapitalist order (James C. Scott 1976). In Vietnam this precapitalist ideology was considerably stronger in the earlier-settled north and center than in the frontier south. It stood in sharp contrast to the rigid and onerous fiscal policy of the colonial state, which contributed heavily to the process of capital accumulation at the expense of the dominated native classes. Not only did higher taxes and state monopolies significantly increase the tax burden on the indigenous population, but in a departure from the precolonial practice and in direct violation of the subsistence ethic, the colonial state also offered no tax deferral or reduction in times of natural disaster (ibid.: chap. 4).

The precapitalist tradition of northern and central Vietnam has proved a fertile ground for the growth of both nationalism and a mild collectivism, on the one hand, and for anticolonial resistance, on the other. Through a sharp distinction between insiders and outsiders in the native conceptualization of kinship, communality, ethnicity, and nationality, the northern and central tradition has intensified the negative reaction of many Vietnamese to any foreign intrusion on the indigenous landscape and to the French domination in the colonial racial diarchy. Modern Vietnamese anticolonial movements capitalized heavily on this salient conceptual dichotomy of Vietnamese and non-Vietnamese races as well as on the symbols of active native resistance to foreign intruders in previous centuries. In northern and central Vietnam, the relatively strong institution of communal land in particular and the subsistence ethic of the precolonial period in general heightened the sense of many native actors of colonial and capitalist exploitation. They nurtured a collectivist vision of political economy among many VNP members in the 1920s, well before their exposure to Marxism. The existence of communal land and the subsistence ethic also facilitated the process of land collectivization in northern and central villages, in comparison with its slow progress in the south after 1975. Even during the difficult 1978–1981 period for the collectivistic economy in Sơn-Dương, villagers resisted a radical collectivism at the expense of their community and households but not the concept of collective land ownership per se. Finally, within the bamboo hedges of the corporate rural community, extensive kinship and communal ties have facilitated the mobilization of resources by local revolutionary leaders, especially the generally well-regarded members of the native intelligentsia.

In the modern history of Vietnamese anticolonialism two sets of factors have led to the triumph of the Marxist-led movement against major Western powers. On the surface, the conflict among the states within the capitalist core during the course of World War II facilitated the Marxists' rise to power (cf. Skocpol 1979: chap. 2). The vulnerability of the French was first exposed with the advance of Japanese forces into Indochina in September 1940 and then laid bare when the French colonial government subsequently collaborated with Japanese military authorities and then when the Japanese terminated French administrative powers in March 1945. On a deeper level, the Marxist-led anti-imperialist movement succeeded because the Vietminh effectively combined nationalism and equality-oriented socioeconomic reforms with a skillful selective use of the indigenous precapitalist tradition. In the process of revolutionary mobilization, Vietnamese Marxist leaders drew upon the symbols, discursive practices, and values of the indigenous precapitalist tradition that had been nurtured within the corporate rural communities of the north and the center. Hồ Chí Minh's Declaration of Independence on September 2, 1945, for example, appealed strongly to the indigenous conceptions of national unity and a subsistence ethic that French capitalism had severely strained. In chastising the French for their historic failure in their role as a protector, Hồ's declaration also drew upon the notion of a change in the Mandate of Heaven (see also Mus 1952). In their organizational efforts in the village of Sơn-Dương, the Vietminh often chose teachers as transitional district and village administrators, drawing upon the dominance of the distinction between mental and manual labor and the general authority commanded by the intelligentsia in the precapitalist framework. The Chinese-influenced and indigenous noncapitalist tradition cannot be ignored in any analysis of the Vietnamese encounter with French colonialism or with the capitalist world system in general (see Marr 1971:97; Luong 1985; Boudarel 1984).

In the final analysis the Vietnamese revolution involved a dynamic interplay between local tradition and capitalist imperialism in the colonial context. In the encounter between the two systems, the persistence of the noncapitalist labor reserves in north and central Vietnam did not merely contribute to capitalist accumulation (cf. Murray 1980; Mellaissoux 1981). It also provided ideological and organizational support for the anticolonial resistance (cf. Smith 1984; and Nash 1979:330). In the long run the encounter between the Vietnamese tradition on the one hand, and Western colonialism and capitalist imperialism on the other, both adversely affected capitalist accumulation and ushered in a new era in the indigenous social formation.

*        *        *

The post-independent social formation in North Vietnam was established as an antithesis to capitalist imperialism. In the 1954–1975 period, the tension with the United States and its South Vietnamese ally and the subsequent open warfare sustained nationalist fervor. They strengthened the state's call for sacrifice, its push for egalitarian collectivism, and its strong control of political, economic, and sociocultural fabric in North Vietnam. I suggest that after the reunification of Vietnam, the regional variation in sociocultural dynamics, which was conditioned by history, the environment, and political economy, powerfully shaped the course of political economy and historical events in the country. I argue that our understanding of economic, social, and cultural restructuring in Vietnam from the mid-1980s onwards, including the unrest in Sơn-Dương and many northern villages in the late 1990s, is incomplete unless we pay close attention to the regional variation in local dynamics.

The economic crisis in Vietnam in the 1975–1986 period was rooted partly in the agricultural-product procurement difficulties of the socialist state, especially in the southern part of the country. When the wage-and-price controls of the wartime period were imposed on the southern economy, with state prices for rice dropping as low as 10 percent of the black market price in 1979, peasants in the Mekong delta withheld rice from the state commercial system. The government's food procurement steadily dropped, from 950,000 metric tons in 1976 to 398,800 metric tons in 1979, not because of any significantly lower paddy or food production in 1979, but because of the declining purchase price for food and the shortage of desirable consumer goods that the government made available to agricultural producers (Ngô-Vĩnh-Long 1988:170–171; Fforde 1999:56).[2] The command economy encountered difficulties not merely in agriculture and in the southern third of Vietnam. In Sơn-Dương and many other northern agricultural cooperatives after 1975, there was a vicious cycle of enlarged cooperative membership due to population growth, lower returns on cooperative labor input, greater attention by members to their household garden plots, and declining or stagnating agricultural productivity on the cooperative land. The failure of a procurement system based on wage-and-price controls aggravated the food and paddy shortage and led to the partial replacement of rice by other cereals in urban areas in the late 1970s, which numerous urban residents of the period could still vividly recall three decades later. The state's subsequently higher procurement prices for agricultural and industrial products, higher salaries for state cadres, and increased money supply led to annual inflation rates in the 50 to 92 percent range in the 1981–1985 period. When the currency exchange in September 1985 caused a loss of confidence in the value of the new currency, inflation skyrocketed to 775 percent in 1986. The strong resistance of numerous cultivators in the southern third of Vietnam to agricultural collectivization and the socialism-oriented command economy thus contributed significantly to an economic crisis and eventually to a shift in economic policy towards a market economy in 1986 and a re-engagement with the global capitalist system in the late 1980s.

By the end of 2006, approved foreign direct investments, mostly from the global capitalist system, had reached US $60 billion. After Vietnam joined the World Trade Organization at the end of 2006, approved foreign direct investment amounted to US $20.3 billion in 2007 and exceeded US $60 billion in 2008. Although actual disbursement hovered around half of the approved amount due to the implementation time lag, foreign capital was having a visible impact in Vietnam by the end of 2006, especially in Hồ Chí Minh City, Hanoi, and surrounding provinces. Foreign factories, the largest of which employed more than 50,000 workers, were more heavily concentrated in the southern provinces around Hồ Chí Minh City. Vietnam also exported US $40 billion of goods in 2006, mostly to the global capitalist world. Within two decades of the shift toward a market economy, Vietnam had became strongly reintegrated with global capitalism at the same time that it was still a one-party nation-state and still officially committed to socialism. The commitment to socialism is retained partly through adherence to the principle of state and collective ownership of land as a means of production and the dominance of the state sector in certain industries like energy, domestic aviation, and rail transport (cf. Verdery 1996: chap. 1). However, the principle of collective land ownership is actualized only in the northern half of Vietnam and a few central coastal provinces. In the late socialist period of the current Vietnamese social formation, the one-party state mediates the relation between local populations and global capitalist forces.

In the past two decades, the considerable regional variation in local sociocultural dynamics continues to play an important role in shaping the regionally varied interaction of local populations with global forces. In the southern third of Vietnam, where the economy is heavily oriented towards the export of rice, pepper, shrimp, fish, and light industrial products, class stratification has sharply increased with the emergence of a landless rural proletariat as well as with a growing industrial working class toiling in foreign and domestic firms. Living-standard survey data indicate that the landless made up 22.9 percent of the population in the Mekong delta and 37.3 percent in the rural southeast around Hồ Chí Minh City (see Table 16). Many of the landless work as mobile agricultural workers or casual laborers, and they form a growing rural proletariat.

In the north and the northern part of central Vietnam, the collective land ownership and relatively egalitarian land distribution have helped to minimize rural landlessness. While a growing number of young northern and central villagers have migrated in search of more remunerative employment in urban areas and in the south, these migrant workers also tend to resettle in their native villages much more frequently than their southern counterparts do (see Luong 2009a). Many of those from the

**Table 16.** Percentage of landless population in rural Vietnam

|                          | 1993–1994 | 2004 |
|--------------------------|-----------|------|
| Northern Uplands         | 2.2       | 2.8  |
| Red River Delta          | 2.0       | 5.7  |
| North-Central Panhandle  | 3.5       | 6.8  |
| South Central Coast      | 9.8       | 13.3 |
| Central Highlands        | 7.2       | 3.0  |
| South East               | 21.7      | 37.3 |
| Mekong Delta             | 14.0      | 22.9 |
| Rural Vietnam            | 7.8       | 12.3 |

*Source:* Ravaillon and Van de Walle 2008:197–198

north or central regions leave their children under the care of their parents in their villages. Given the fact that migrants from the north and central regions have access to land in their native villages and can rely on kinship and other village social institutions for support during preproductive and postproductive periods, have these villages become "labor reserves" for capitalist accumulation as they did before in the French colonial period?

Starting in 1995, the Vietnamese government required social insurance contributions from employers (15 percent) and employees (3 percent) of wages or salaries. While many employers have avoided full contributions (see Luong and Gunewardena 2009), this system in principle provides a pension for workers in their old age, making them less dependent on kin for survival in their postproductive years. The remittances of migrant workers have also played a very important role in stimulating the local economy in Sơn-Dương and many other communities. The mediation by a government still officially committed to socialism has prevented communities in north and north central Vietnam from becoming simply labor reserves for capitalist accumulation.

In this late socialist period of modern Vietnam, unrest without external support has taken place in the form of wildcat labor strikes that demand timely wage adjustments—these have occurred mostly in the urban and peri-urban south—or agrarian unrest, which has occurred mainly in the northern lowlands. I suggest that the outbreak of agrarian unrest in the north in the late 1990s was strongly influenced by local ideological formation and the sociocultural fabric.

In terms of ideological formation, I suggest that the Marxist state's collectivistic and egalitarian ideology from 1954 to 1989 has strongly influenced local discourse and penetrated local consciousness throughout northern Vietnam. In Sơn-Dương, the strong discursive emphasis on relative equality has, over the years, moved the land-distribution policy in this direction despite the state's emphasis on rewards to efficient agricultural producers from 1988 onwards. For example, in 1988, when the state's Directive 10 encouraged communes to allow more efficient producers to bid for more land, the Sơn-Dương leadership planned to reserve the more fertile fields in the commune, making up 15 percent of the commune land, for bidding by more efficient producers. By 1994, under local social pressure, the 5 percent of land available for bidding was composed, not of fertile fields, but mainly of ponds.

However, the egalitarian ideology has not seemed to penetrate the consciousness of all Sơn-Dương villagers to the same degree. It has been the older members, who went through the austere, more egalitarian periods of the 1960s and the worst of the U.S. war, who were the leading voices for lesser inequality and formed the anticorruption movement in Sơn-Dương. It was veterans in particular among the older members of the local population who were emboldened, due to their wartime sacrifices on the front line, to take leading roles in the mobilization of the Sơn-Dương villagers in 1997–1998.

In the Mekong delta, however, I suggest that the local ideological formation was not dominated by egalitarianism. This came about not only because of the official ideological differences between North and South Vietnam during the Cold War and the U.S. war period, but also because of historically rooted and centuries-old regional differences. Up to the early part of the twentieth century, Vietnamese in the southern third of the country were living in a relatively new and fertile land with more spatial and socioeconomic mobility opportunities. They were less concerned about their own survival or the greater wealth of their fellow villagers. This historical condition has rendered wealth accumulation a less important issue for public debate in southern Vietnam, both in the past and in the present era.

I suggest in addition that the mobilization of the local population for collective action in Sơn-Dương and in other northern localities has been facilitated by tight social networks within strongly demarked village boundaries. In contrast, the much looser social networks in Vietnamese cities and the more open southern villages are less conducive to concerted collective action (see Luong 2005). The intricate, cross-cutting network of local associations, established in the context of a tight kinship network in northern villages, in contrast to those in cities and in the southern countryside, facilitates local mobilization for a concerted action, at times even in adversarial and open confrontation with local administrative apparatuses.

From a theoretical perspective, the numerous local associations in the village of Sơn-Dương and in other northern Vietnamese villages do not constitute a civil society as normally conceptualized in the Western social science literature, multivocal as this term "civil society" is due to its embedding in different Western theoretical and ideological perspectives (see Brook and Frolic 1997, Frolic 1997, Chamberlain 1993, Weller 1999:14–16, among others). Since these perspectives have developed in relation to Western historical experiences, as Madsen points out, for most of these theorists, "civil society consisted in the utilitarian, contractual relationships characteristic of a bourgeois society created by a modern market economy" (1993:188). In the broader meaning of the term, "civil society" refers to any institutionalized association relatively independent of the state and of such "traditional" ties as kinship and communal relations (ibid.:189).

In rural northern Vietnam, given the radically different historical trajectories of Vietnam and the West, civil society as conceived on the basis of Western historical experiences has not really emerged, since most communities in rural northern Vietnam have not yet witnessed the emergence of a bourgeois class.[3] However, voluntary associations have proliferated as the domain under state control has contracted in the past two decades. In Sơn-Dương, only two of those new associations, the veteran and elderly associations, have received some support from the state (cf. Frolic 1997). The rest are not even officially recognized by the state. While none of those new associations are political or would be tolerated as political in their orientation, the ties formed through them can be mobilized for collective action and for a concerted voice for better local governance (cf. Brook and Frolic 1997:41–42). In the northern Vietnamese rural landscape, kinship-, religious-, and village-based local associations can directly or indirectly serve as effective bases for the dialogic relations of the local population with the Party-state apparatuses.

The collective action in Sơn-Dương village and numerous other localities in the northern province of Thái-Bình and beyond in the 1990s led to a major national policy change (the grassroots democracy decree) that has strengthened the voices of local populations in community affairs and sanctioned lasting changes in local state-society relations. Spontaneous local associations based on kinship, religious, and communal ties and constitutive of "alternative civilities" in rural northern Vietnam (see Weller 1999) have served as a strong foundation for mobilization for collective action in face of growing local socioeconomic inequality. These associations have proliferated in the northern rural part of the country, where the bourgeoisie has not fully emerged after decades of collectivization. They are at least as effective in strengthening the voice of the local population as bourgeois-dominated voluntary associations are in communities with a greater market penetration. The focus on state-sanctioned, urban-based, bourgeois-dominated voluntary associations in the existing literature on Vietnam and many other non-Western societies reflects analytical assumptions that are deeply grounded in Western historical experiences and in the dominant Western social theoretical framework of the state and civil society. I suggest that without a consideration of "alternate civilities" and the differences between the historically shaped sociocultural frameworks of the Red River delta and the Mekong delta, we cannot fully explain the magnitude of the crisis in state-society relations in the northern Vietnamese rural landscape while there was a relative lack of unrest in the agrarian south despite the considerably sharper class stratification there.

# Appendix 1

## Regulations on Cultured Life in Hamlet 5

Socialist Republic of Vietnam
*Independence-Liberty-Happiness*
\*
*Sơn-Dương, 1 March 2003*

Implementing the cultured life regulations of Sơn-Dương commune, the mobilization committee works out the regulations for a cultured life in Hamlet 5 as follows:

## Part I.  General Regulations

Article 1
Building a cultured life is an important objective in the government's tasks of leadership and management and in the self-mastery of the people. It aims to promote good customs, to uphold the people's tradition of moral standards, and to spread the good tradition of the native land.

Article 2
Regulations on a cultured life aim at regulating the activities of every member of society in compliance with the policies of the Party and government; at developing the economy, raising living standards, building a life with culture, raising the solidarity in the neighborhood and hamlet, and providing mutual support for progress.

## Part II.  The Contents of the Regulations

Article 3
Every member of the hamlet and of each family actively participates in production in order to eliminate starvation and to reduce poverty. We strive for stable living standards and to achieve per capita income of 2 million VND a year. Family members should live harmoniously and provide mutual support to one another, with grandparents and parents being exemplary, and with children and grandchildren showing filial piety. We should maintain hierarchy and order in the tradition of the patriline and among matrilineal relatives; solidarity within the neighborhood and the village; and exemplary compliance with policies and laws. There should be no illiteracy, no school dropouts, no participation in "social evils," and no family with more than two children.

We mobilize every member to participate actively in social and cultural activities, to have at least 80–85 percent of the households hang the national flag on holidays and during the Lunar New Year, to encourage the patrilineages to establish education-promotion funds in order to encourage students to excel in their studies as in the Nguyễn patrilineage. We actively participate in cultural and sport activities that are beneficial to the health of everybody.

## Part III.  Weddings, Funerals, Longevity Celebrations, and Festivals

Article 4
On weddings. A wedding takes place in conformity with the law on marriage and the family and with local customs. The engagement ceremony is simple, with no more than fifteen representatives on each side, with no meals and banquets, and without cigarettes. If there are any violations of these engagement ceremony regulations, neighbors will not participate in the wedding.

The bride and the groom have to register their marriage before the wedding, in conformity with the law on marriage, and they do not get married early. If there is a deliberate violation of the law, the hamlet will criticize the violator and propose that the People's Committee of the commune render justice in conformity with the law.

The wedding celebration has to be simple and may not last more than one day. The groom's family will not go the bride's family twice to receive the bride, and there will not be a banquet in connection with the visit to the bride's family two days after the wedding *(lại mặt)*. Wedding gifts should reflect sentiment and not corruption, debts, and conspicuous consumption. Wedding clothes need to be beautiful and simple. The groom will wear a Western suit, and the bride a traditional *áo dài* [Vietnamese dress]. The wedding room will be decorated well but not elaborately. The wedding music has to be sound, played at a reasonable volume, and turned on only between 5:00 and 22:00. The wedding banquet depends on the family's circumstances, but invitations should be extended only to relatives, immediate neighbors, and close friends. Cigarettes will absolutely not be offered at a wedding.

Article 5
On funerals. A family with a member passing away needs to inform the hamlet chief and the People's Committee of the commune so that they can prepare for the funeral. The family also needs to inform the cemetery caretaker so that a plot can be reserved for the burial.

The funeral will be organized by the Cultural Office, which represents the Party and the government, and by the mass organizations.

The hamlet will assign an agricultural production team to dig the grave, push the coffin carriage, and accompany the deceased to the grave. The deceased will be buried within thirty-six hours. A person dying of an infectious disease will be buried within twenty-four hours. Funeral visits depend on the sentiment between the visitor and the deceased's family. Funeral wreaths and banners will be used only by a group. No cooked foods will be offered.

The family of the deceased will not hire a band for music but will use the funeral music tapes provided by the Cultural Office. The music will be played not too loudly and only between 5:00 and 22:00. The bad customs of lying in the path of the coffin and walking on canes are to be eliminated. The family of the deceased will offer only areca nuts and tea to guests and will not use cigarettes. The meals on the third day of the death and special commemorative days will be simple, and only close patrilineal and matrilateral relatives are to be invited.

Reburial will take place at least three years after the death. After the grave is dug up for reburial, all the wood has to be removed and the grave has to be filled. The tomb should not be too big, and should be between 1.5 and 2 square meters (for a bad [abnormal] death case). It should not be built outside the cemetery and should not trespass on the property of other people.

The family of the deceased has to take good care of the materials borrowed from the Funeral Committee. If anything is damaged or lost, the family of the deceased has to pay for the repair or the replacement.

Article 6
Longevity celebrations. A longevity celebration is a moral obligation to the elderly and needs to be organized well. It should be organized only for the elderly reaching the age of 70, 80, 90, 100, and above. The Fatherland Front and the Elderly Association will organize the celebration for the elderly in the morning of the second day of the first lunar month at the meeting room of the commune. At home the family should organize only a simple celebration, with no elaborate banquet, and involving only the descendants, close relatives and friends of the celebrated elderly.

## Part IV.  Economic Development

Article 7
Every member of the hamlet and in each family needs to have enthusiasm towards labor and production and to maximize the multiple-crop potential of the land. He/she should apply science and technology to production, plant seeds at the right time, and grow many new varieties of paddy under the guidance of the agricultural cooperative. He/she should use the land appropriately, neither trespassing [on somebody's land] nor transforming the land, nor causing damage to the surrounding fields.

He/she should develop animal husbandry, raise new species like low-fat hogs, high-egg-volume ducks, and hybrid cows…, and should give immunization shots to animals in order to avoid epidemics. Manufacturing and commerce are to be developed in conformity with the law, with no trade tricks and no trade in banned or fake goods.

## Part V.  Environmental Cleaning

Article 8
Each family needs to protect the paved streets of the hamlet and heavy trucks are prohibited from using these streets. Every family needs to have clean household facilities, with 80 to 85 percent of all households using

clean water. Animal husbandry pens need to be far from living quarters and not to pollute the neighborhood. Each family should not dump sewage water onto the streets or prepare its organic fertilizers on the streets. The family has to clear the sewage channel. It should neither tie cattle on the streets, nor dig along the streets for the flow of sewage. Any family with a pond near the streets has to build embankments and has to repair street damage due to weak embankments. A family cannot deepen a pond located right next to a neighboring house. It cannot plant bamboo or big trees right next to the street. If a big tree has existed along the street for a long time, its owner has to clear the branches so as not to affect the electric wire system. Each family has to build a water drainage channel around the gate of the house. If the animals raised by one family damage the crop or property of another, the former family has to compensate 100 percent. Any family that needs to bring water from one side of the street to the other for irrigation has to protect the street and to use water pipes; the family cannot dig up the street. Bricks and tiles cannot be manufactured in residential areas, as that will affect the residential environment. The Youth Union will clean the streets in the neighborhood and the hamlet on the twentieth day of every month.

## Part VI. On Security and Social Order

Article 9
Every resident of the hamlet has to live and work in compliance with the Constitution and the laws. He/she will neither be drunk nor engage in shouting matches or fights, which will disrupt community solidarity. Any violator will be criticized in front of the people of the hamlet. If it is a serious violation, the hamlet will propose that the People's Committee judge the violator according to the laws. The hamlet will not have any resident addicted to drugs, engaging in prostitution or gambling, playing an illegal lottery, or adopting superstitious practices.

Article 10
Every resident of the hamlet has to implement the policies of the Party and the local administration and has to pay fully his/her tax and local budget obligations as well as irrigation fees in order to make the native land wealthier and more beautiful. He/she will actively participate in the campaigns launched by the Party and the government.

# Form for evaluation of a cultured family

| | Scale (points) | Self-evaluation (points) | Neighborhood evaluation (points) | Achieved | Not achieved (reasons) |
|---|---|---|---|---|---|
| **Materially comfortable family** | **30** | | | | |
| • A stable living standard, with no shortage of food | 10 | | | | |
| • Active labor participation by all family members capable of working | 10 | | | | |
| • Careful and rational spending | 10 | | | | |
| **Harmonious family** | **25** | | | | |
| • Harmony and mutual support among family members for progress; exemplary grandparents, parents, and elder siblings [for younger family members]; children and grandchildren with filial piety | 15 | | | | |
| • Maintenance of solidarity, order, and security in neighborhood, hamlet, and village | 10 | | | | |
| **Progressive family** | **45** | | | | |
| • Exemplary compliance with policies of the Party and laws of the state; no illiterate members in the applicable age groups; no school dropouts; active participation in social and cultural activities | 10 | | | | |
| • Compliance with cultured life regulations on weddings, funerals, longevity celebrations; no superstition; no storage of explosives, weapons, obscene materials; no participation in "social evils" | 15 | | | | |
| • Neat and clean house, with well, bathroom, and toilet; maintenance of sanitation in public space | 10 | | | | |
| • Family planning, with one to two children per couple; healthy and good children | 10 | | | | |

Article 11

The people of the hamlet have to comply with the laws of the government. Any question or grievance has to be filed in accordance with the established procedures. There will be neither grievances bypassing appropriate authorities nor large gatherings, causing a waste of time of the people. The people of the hamlet will mobilize their children and siblings to follow the military draft law.

## Part VII.  Implementation of the Regulations and Awards

Article 12

These regulations are based on consultation with and the consensus of the entire hamlet and appropriate both to the customs and situation of the people in the hamlet and to current laws. Under the guidance of the government and the Party organization in Hamlet 5, the Fatherland Front committee guides people in the implementation process. [Adherence to these guidelines was monitored with self-evaluations and neighborhood evaluations. See evaluation form at left.]

Individuals and families which implement these regulations well will be publicly mentioned in hamlet meetings and recommended for merit certificates by the commune government.

Individuals and families violating these regulations will be criticized publicly in hamlet meetings and, for a serious violation, recommended to the government for a penalty.

In the process of implementation, if any regulation is not yet appropriate to the conditions of the hamlet, there will be a consultation with the people of the hamlet regarding the modification of the regulations.

# Appendix 2

## Chronology

### Vietnam to 1883

| | |
|---|---|
| 111 B.C.E.–905 C.E. | Chinese colonial rule, punctuated by numerous revolts |
| Tenth century | Independence; Vietnam still nominally under Chinese suzerainty |
| 1407–1427 | Chinese colonial rule (Ming dynasty) |
| 1427–1786 | Independence under the Lê dynasty |
| 1570–1786 | Bipartite division of Vietnam; two viceroys are still nominally under the Lê king |
| 1786–1802 | Unification under the Tây-Sơn dynasty |
| 1802 | All Vietnam under the Nguyễn dynasty |
| 1859 | First French attack on Cochinchina |
| 1861–1872 | Anticolonial resistance in Cochinchina |
| 1862 | Concession of the northern half of Cochinchina to France by the Vietnamese court |
| 1865 | Remnants of Taiping troops move to Vietnam from China after the collapse of the Taiping movement |
| 1867 | Concession of all of Cochinchina to France by the Huế court |
| 1873 | French attack on Hanoi |
| 1874 | France demands exclusive rights to Vietnamese foreign trade and establishes a commercial presence in select northern and central localities |
| 1881 | Chinese troops move into northern Vietnam to "protect" Vietnam from the French threat |
| 1882–1883 | French attack on Hanoi, Huế, and Hòn-Gay coal-mine areas |
| 1883 | Tonkin and Annam become French protectorates |

# Vietnam and Sơn-Dương Village, 1884–2006

*(Sơn-Dương events are indented and in italics)*

| | |
|---|---|
| 1884–1896 | First major wave of anticolonial resistance in Tonkin and Annam |
| | *Sơn-Dương becomes an anticolonial base* |
| 4/1885 | *Massacre of one hundred villagers by Chinese troops* |
| 6/1885 | Withdrawal of Chinese troops from Vietnam under the Tientsin agreement |
| 1890 | Birth of Hồ Chí Minh |
| 1907 | Tonkin Free School movement |
| 1908 | Tax protest movement in Annam |
| 1925 | Formation by Hồ of Vietnamese Revolutionary League |
| 1927 | Formation of Vietnamese Nationalist Party (VNP) |
| 2/1930 | VNP movement in Tonkin; formation of Indochinese Communist Party (ICP) |
| | *Participation of villagers in VNP uprising against French colonialism; massive arrests and burning of village houses by the French* |
| 5/1930–8/1931 | ICP-led Nghệ-Tĩnh soviet movement |
| 1936–1938 | Popular Front rule in France |
| 9/1940 | Arrival of Japanese troops in Indochina; modus vivendi with French colonial administration |
| 5/1941 | Formation of Communist-led Vietminh Front |
| 1942 | *Spread of Vietminh influence* |
| 10/1943 | *French repression of Vietminh influence* |
| 3/1945 | Formal end to French rule; Vietnam under Japanese influence |
| 8/1945 | Surrender of Japan; Vietminh seizes power |
| | *Formation of Vietminh administration* |
| 9/1945 | Hồ's Declaration of Independence |
| 1946 | *Merger with Dụng-Hiền and Thuy-Sơn into one village* |
| 12/1946 | Outbreak of Franco-Vietnamese war |
| 1948 | France creates "State of Vietnam" under former emperor Bảo-Đại |

|  | *Separation of Party membership of* |
|--|--|
|  | *Sơn-Dương from neighboring Ngũ-Xã; first* |
|  | *village Communist Party cell founded* |
| 1950 | Major defeat of French by Vietminh along Sino-Vietnamese border; direct U.S. military aid to French in Vietnam |
| 1951 | *French bombing (four incidents)* |
| 5/1954 | Victory of Vietminh at Điện-Biên-Phủ |
| 6/1954 | *Arrival of land-reform team* |
| 7/1954 | Geneva Agreements: temporary division of Vietnam into two parts |
| 1956 | Rectification of land-reform errors in the north |
| 1958 | *Formation of labor-exchange teams* |
| 1959 | *Formation of hamlet-level cooperatives* |
| 12/1960 | Formation of the National Liberation Front of South Vietnam |
| 1965 | Introduction of U.S. ground combat troops to South Vietnam |
| 3/1965 | Beginning of sustained U.S. bombing of North Vietnam |
| 6/1965 | *U.S. bombing* |
| 1968 | End of sustained U.S. bombing of the north |
|  | *Sơn-Dương becomes part of the new province of Vĩnh-Phú; creation of villagewide cooperative; short-lived experiment with household contracts in agriculture* |
| 4/1975 | Collapse of Saigon government |
| 1976 | Unification of Vietnam |
| 12/1978 | Vietnamese troops in Cambodia |
| 2/1979 | Chinese invasion of Vietnam |
| 1979 | Limited introduction of the household contract system in agriculture |
| 1/1981 | Directive 100 on the nationwide application of the household contract system |
| 11/1982 | *Reintroduction of the household contract system in agriculture* |
| 1986 | Economic reform policy adopted |
| 6/1987 | *Third-class labor medal awarded by the state* |

| | |
|---|---|
| 1988 | Further agricultural reforms (Directive 10)<br>*Application of Directive 10* |
| 1989 | Withdrawal of Vietnamese troops from<br>Cambodia |
| 1994 | Lift of U.S. trade embargo against Vietnam<br>*Allocation of agricultural land for twenty<br>years; division of four hamlets (thôn) into<br>eight hamlets (khu)* |
| 1996–1999 | *Local unrest* |
| 1997 | *Province of Vĩnh Phú divided into Phú-Thọ<br>and Vĩnh-Phúc* |
| 1999 | *District of Phong-Châu divided into districts<br>of Lâm-Thao and Phù-Ninh* |
| 2006 | Vietnam joins World Trade Organization |

# Appendix 3

## Significant People in Sơn-Dương Village and Anticolonial History

In Vietnamese naming practice, personal names follow family names and middle names. Most Vietnamese are referred to by their personal names. The following figures, with the exception of Hồ Chí Minh, are listed alphabetically according to their personal names. Titles used in the text are given in parentheses.

| | |
|---|---|
| Bằng, Nguyễn Đắc (Giáo) | A French-trained village teacher and a leader of the Vietnamese Nationalist Party (VNP) organization in Sơn-Dương village, exiled to French Guiana in 1930; passed away in Canada. |
| Bích, Nguyễn Quang | The Vietnamese governor of Hưng-Hóa to 1884 and a leader of the anti-French movement in North Vietnam in the late nineteenth century. |
| Bốn (Đội) | The leader of the anti-French guerrilla movement in Sơn-Dương village during the late nineteenth century. |
| Châu, Phan Bội | A Confucian scholar and leader of the activist school of Vietnamese anticolonialism in the first quarter of the twentieth century. |
| Chính, Phó Đức | Deputy leader of the Vietnamese Nationalist Party; executed in 1930. |
| Diên, Bùi Hữu | A Communist Party member and a leader of the Vietnamese inmates of Guiana prison camps. |

| | |
|---|---|
| Dương, Phạm Thành | A major traitor to the Vietnamese Nationalist Party leaders on the eve of the Yên-Báy uprising in 1930. |
| Gia, Nguyễn Khắc | Bằng's senior brother |
| Giáp, Nguyễn văn | Treasury director in Sơn-Tây to 1883 and a leader of the anti-French movement in the Hưng-Hoá area in the late nineteenth century. |
| Hồ Chí Minh | The most important anticolonial leader in post-1925 Vietnam; leader of the Vietnamese communist movement and president of the Democratic Republic of Vietnam from 1945 to 1969. |
| Học, Nguyễn Thái | President of the Vietnamese Nationalist Party, 1927–1930; executed by the French in 1930. |
| Lập, Bùi Khắc | A leader of the VNP organization in the village of Kinh-Kệ, neighboring on Sơn-Dương. |
| Lĩnh, Bùi Kim | A major Vietminh organizer in Sơn-Dương village in 1942–1943. |
| Ngữ (Đốc) | A major anti-French guerilla commander in the Hưng-Hoá area from 1888 to 1892. |
| Nhu, Nguyễn Khắc (Xứ) | A Confucian scholar and vice-president of the VNP on the eve of the Yên-Báy uprising; committed suicide after being captured by the French in 1930. |
| Tăng, Nguyễn Doãn | Bằng's senior brother; a French-trained teacher, a VNP movement participant and later a Vietminh cadre. |
| Tế, Nguyễn Doãn | A landless peasant in the colonial period, later a Communist Party member and the first president of an agricultural cooperative in Sơn-Dương. |
| Thành (Elderly) | A landless woman laborer in Sơn-Dương during the colonial period. |
| Tiềm, Lê văn | A French-trained teacher and Bằng's former student; president of the Communist Party cell in Sơn-Dương during its formative period (1948–1950). |

Toại, Nguyễn văn (Đồ)          A Confucian scholar and a leader of the
                               VNP organization in Sơn-Dương village;
                               executed by the French in 1930.
Trinh, Phan Chu                A Confucian scholar and leader of
                               the reformist school of Vietnamese
                               anticolonialism in the first quarter of the
                               twentieth century.

# Notes

## Introduction

1. The shrine to the Hùng kings is only fourteen kilometers from Sơn-Dương. The names of many villages near the present provincial capital Việt-Trì reflect the location of the capital of the Hung dynasty in this part of northern Vietnam: Vân-Đội and Cẩm-Đội were army barracks (*đội* means "soldiers"), Minh-Nông and Phù-Nông were agricultural stations (*nông* means "agriculture"), and Lâu-Hạ and Lâu-Thượng were palaces for the king's concubines (*lâu* means "palace") (Phạm-Xuân-Độ 1939:9–10). The capital of Vietnam moved farther south and east, reaching its present location, Hanoi, by the eleventh century as the Vietnamese gradually built up an extensive dike and irrigation system in the lower Red River delta.

2. The village population figure does not include a small number of schoolteachers from other communities or industrial workers affiliated with the Lâm-Thao phosphate factory residing in the village.

3. The figure of 300 mẫu represents my own estimate. It is based partly on the actual ownership of 230 mẫu by twelve households that were still classified as landlord and rich peasant households after the rectification in 1956 of earlier land-reform errors. The reclassified households had some of their previously appropriated properties returned.

4. In the past decade Vietnamese Marxist theoreticians have increasingly used the phrase *thời kỳ quá độ* (period of transition [toward socialism]) to refer to the current period of the Vietnamese social formation—a period that will, in their conception, last into the foreseeable future. The phrase highlights a departure from the earlier, decade-long emphasis on an accelerated process of socialist construction. The frequent usage of *thời kỳ quá độ* is linked to the wide-ranging economic reforms away from tight central planning toward a more open intellectual atmosphere that has emerged since 1981. This ter-

minology and the reforms notwithstanding, the northern Vietnamese social formation since 1954 is still dominated by socialism in that the achievement of socialism remains the ultimate official goal of the state. In this book the term "socialist" is used to abbreviate "oriented toward socialism" for the period since 1954 in northern Vietnam.

5. Hickey's (1964) *Village in Vietnam* is a landmark ethnographic study of a village in the Mekong delta of South Vietnam in the late 1950s. Houtart and Lemercinier's (1981) *La sociologie d'une commune vietnamienne* provides valuable statistical data on a Catholic village in the Red River delta of northern Vietnam in 1979. Phạm-Cường and Nguyễn-văn-Bá's (1976) *Revolution in the Village* focuses on the socioeconomic structure of a northern village in the socialist era, and Trullinger's (1980) *Village at War* is a historical examination of the sociopolitical processes in a central Vietnamese village through the Franco-Vietminh conflict (1946–1954) and especially the American war (to 1975).

6. Many of the forty Vietnamese provinces in 1990 were divided to create sixty-four provinces by 2004 (see Malesky 2006).

7. Dr. Vũ Huy Phúc of the Vietnam Institute of History has suggested that Vietnamese Marxists do not emphasize class conflict in their analysis of the nationalist democratic revolution (against the French), which lasted until 1954. However, in the Leninist thesis on colonialism, nationalist revolution in a colonial context constitutes an integral part of the struggle against world capitalism.

8. Wallerstein emphasizes the vital importance of semiperipheral states in the functioning of the capitalist world system. In Wallerstein's conceptual framework, semiperipheral states such as Brazil stand between the core and the periphery in terms of economic power. In the case of rapidly rising labor costs in the core, the semiperiphery serves as an alternative zone for capitalist investment. It also weakens the opposition coming from social formations outside the core of the capitalist world system, since semiperipheral formations such as Japan may emerge as core states (Wallerstein 1979:29ff.).

9. However, for Emerson, democracy in the new nation-states tends to be fragile. First, despite the dominance of nationalism, such nations are far from consolidated. Internal crises often lead to centralization of power. Second, these new nations tend to lack the preconditions for the success of democracy, which, for Emerson, include "mass literacy, relatively high living standards, a sizable and stable middle class, a sense of social equality, and a tradition both of tolerance and of individual self-reliance." (Emerson 1960:277–278)

10. To Sahlins, historically situated acts function as signs, thus existing in a dual mode of valuation: in a relation of opposition to other signs within an integrated indigenous conceptual system and in a relation of indexicality within individual social actors' varied instrumental schemes of practice (see Sahlins 1981:68; cf. Barth 1966).

## Chapter 1:  Vietnamese Anticolonialism

1.  In its reports to the Ministry of Colonies in Paris, the Indochinese colonial government initially attributed certain VNP-organized incidents of unrest to Communist involvement (cables 260 and 273 to the Ministry of Colonies, respectively on February 11, and February 13, 1930, AOM-P-NF, 322–2614). Thirty years later some analysts, including the French minister of colonies at the time of the VNP-organized revolt, still linked the Yên-Báy incident to the Communist movement (Piétri 1960:278–281).

2.  There have been numerous studies in both Vietnam and the West on the ICP-led movement of 1930–1931. Among recent Western-language sources, see Luong 1985; Brocheux 1977; and Ngô-Vĩnh-Long 1978a.

3.  Nguyễn Khắc Nhu was referred by the title *xứ*, because he ranked first in a provincial screening test for the Confucian regional examination.

4.  The final French report estimated the size of the Phú-Thọ contingent at fifty to sixty on the basis of the number of fourth-class tickets sold on February 9 for the Phú-Thọ-Yên-Báy trip (Wintrebert report, p. 11, AOM-P-NF, 323–2626; see also Nguyễn-văn-Khánh 1997:168). A VNP participant and the French *résident* in Yên-Báy at the time reported approximately 200 party members and sympathizers from Phú-Thọ (Nguyễn-Hải-Hàm 1970; Report of Résident Massimi, AOM-P-NF, 323–2626).

5.  The provision of information to the French by a ranking VNP informer, Phạm Thành Dương, dealt a severe blow to the VNP insurrection plan on the eve of the uprising. For example, in early November 1929, Dương reported fully to French military intelligence on his November 1, 1929, strategy meeting with Học, the party president, in a well-guarded locality in Bắc-Ninh province. At this meeting Học reportedly asked for the map of the Bạch-Mai airfield barracks and delegated to Dương the task of recruitment for the planned attack there. Học reportedly revealed that other centers such as Nam-Định, Bắc-Ninh, Hải-Phòng, Lạng-Sơn, and Móng-Cáy were ready, while Hanoi was not. He promised to provide Dương with 300–600 civilians for the Bạch-Mai airfield attack as well as with arms and food for this civilian contingent. He showed Dương the method of manufacturing bombs and indicated that forty could be produced every day. In a meeting of the party general assembly in the same village two days later, Học discussed his plan to hold on to the attacked localities for five or six days in order to await the arrival of the VNP emigré armed forces from China. Học reportedly emphasized the need to recruit veterans of the colonial forces as well as the necessity to launch the attack simultaneously in Annam and Cochinchina. At the next meeting on November 24, 1929, in the La-Hào area of Phú-Thọ, a provisional government was reportedly formed with the concurrence of representatives from thirteen provinces. Học was elected president; Xứ Nhu, vice-president; Phó Đức Chính, interior affairs minister; Dương, military affairs minister; and the

mayor of neighboring Võng-La village (Phú-Thọ), finance minister (AOM-AP-I, 7F–57).

6. Insurrection plans were compromised in the provinces of Bắc-Giang, Bắc-Ninh, Hà-Đông, Kiến-An, Hải-Dương, and Vĩnh-Yên (AOM-P-NF, 323–2626). After the outbreak of the movement in Yên-Báy, the colonial authorities also arrested suspects in the provinces of Hải-Dương and Bắc-Ninh, including VNP collaborators in the colonial armed forces.

7. In Yên-Báy collaboration between the military and civilian authorities did not occur because the military commander considered the base and the quarters of military personnel off-limits to the civilian police. The relations between military and civilian authorities there were also complicated by the civilian *résident*'s background as a former officer with a lower rank than the military commander (Robin report 1930, 37–39, AOM-P-NF, 323–2626).

8. The four other districts were Quảng-Oai, Quốc-Oai, Bất-Bạt, and Vĩnh-Tường (Đặng-Huy-Vận 1967:49).

9. The catalyst for the event was a list of demands sent by the French General de Courcy to the Huế court, which the Vietnamese considered both contemptuous and provocative. For example, de Courcy insisted that not only he but also his troops be permitted to enter the royal palace through the central door, an act that was a royal prerogative (Trương-Bửu-Lâm 1967: 43–44).

10. Hoàng-Kế-Viêm, the former governor general of Hưng-Hoá, Sơn-Tây, and Tuyên-Quang, was appointed troop commander (Kiều-Hữu-Hỷ et al. 1961:10). However, he played little role in the anticolonial movement from this point onward.

11. Other major centers of resistance in northern Vietnam were situated in the provinces of Hưng-Yên, Hải-Dương, and Bắc-Ninh (see Marr 1971:71ff.) An excellent general analysis of Vietnamese anticolonialism in this period is provided in chap. 3 of Marr 1971.

12. The death of over twenty villagers in 1895 may have been attributed to anti-French guerrillas in order to evoke the sympathy of the colonial authorities to whom the letter requesting a tax reduction was addressed.

13. The dates in brackets represent the dates of the original administrative formation. The dates of provincial reformation are in parentheses.

14. After the establishment of *pax colonia,* land temporarily abandoned because of warfare or flooding was granted in large plots to colonial enterprises. The commercial firm Bourgoin Meiffre, for example, was reportedly granted 8,500 hectares that had been seized from fifty-seven villages in three provinces along the Black River. The Saint Frères Company took over 523 hectares from indigenous cultivators in Đoan-Hùng district (Lê-Tượng and Vũ-Kim-Biên 1981:130). In the pre-World War I period little capital was invested in these colonial agricultural ventures.

15. In Lâm-Thao the group had its strongest base in the villages of Xuân-Lũng (Bằng's maternal ancestral village) and Tiên-Kiên (approximately nine kilometers from Sơn-Dương) (Lê-Tượng and Vũ-Kim-Biên 1981:145).

## Chapter 2: Village Structure in Revolutionary Processes

1. In terms of population, of the 8,826 villages in the northern delta and midlands in the late 1920s, 29.12 percent had populations less than 300 (5.17 percent had fewer than 100 inhabitants). Only 24.41 percent of the villages had populations greater than 1000 (Bùi-Thiết 1985:32). In terms of cultivated surface, the official history of Sơn-Dương reported that the cultivated acreage in the French colonial period was only 1,009 *mẫu,* including 600 *mẫu* for Sơn-Dương, 250 *mẫu* for Dụng-Hiền, and 150 *mẫu* for Thuy-Sơn (Sơn-Dương 1987). The 1942 village regulations for Dụng-Hiền mention 241 *mẫu* of rice fields (Dụng-Hiền 1942). It is not clear why the acreage of rice fields in Dụng-Hiền dropped from 298 *mẫu* in 1921 to 241 *mẫu* in 1942, or why the cultivated acreages also seem to have dropped for the other two villages.

2. The French-created Lineage Representative Council replaced a Council of Notables (Hội đồng kỳ mục) whose membership was based not on the principle of patrilineage representation but on past and present administrative services at the deputy mayor rank or above, equivalent honorary ranking, and academic achievements. Because the old notables were discontented with the 1921 reform, the French resurrected the Council of Notables in 1927. Important decisions made by the Lineage Representative Council were then subject to veto by the Hội đồng kỳ mục (Toan-Ánh 1969:89; Sơn-Dương 1987:7; Gourou 1936:266; Trần-Từ 1984:64).

3. Sơn-Dương, Dụng-Hiền, and Thuy-Sơn had already formed three separate villages according to the national list compiled around 1810 (Dương-thị-Thế and Phạm-thị-Thoa 1981). However, my village sources insisted that Dụng-Hiền and Thuy-Sơn did not secede until the 1830s (Sơn-Dương 1987:5).

4. Sơn-Dương villagers identified General Quý Minh as the god of Tản-Viên Mountain on the other side of the Red River. Sơn-Dương's worship of General Quý Minh started well before the colonial period. A local historian reported that in the 1830s, in preparing a royal decree recognizing the tutelary deities of Sơn-Minh village, Vietnamese court officials discovered one overlapping element in the village name and its deity's name. The overlap violated a Vietnamese naming taboo that prohibited the use of a superior party's name, and as a consequence, the name of the village had to be changed from Sơn-Minh to Sơn-Dương.

5. After repelling the Mongols, the Trần court decreed that eighteen villages in the surrounding area worship General Lân Hổ on the anniversary of his death (Ngô-Quang-Nam and Tạ-Huy-Đức 1986:191).

6. In 1907 Thuỵ-Sơn had 38.9 *mẫu* of communal land (TTLTQG1-PT–537). The rental income from Thuỵ-Sơn communal land was used at that time to cover a teacher's salary and collective ritual expenses (District chief's March 28, 1913 report to *résident,* ibid.). It is not clear why the amount of communal land in Thuỵ-Sơn declined to 1.58 *mẫu* in 1942; the figure appears in a context in which the sale of communal land was banned by the Vietnamese court and the colonial government unless it was authorized by district or provincial officials on an exceptional basis. In Sơn-Dương, in the first decade of the twentieth century, 38 *mẫu* were reserved for allocation to soldiers (called *binh điền*) in order to supplement their incomes. In 1907, with the actual allocation to soldiers amounting to only 15 *mẫu* (2.5 *mẫu* per soldier), village notables requested to convert 23 *mẫu* of communal land to education land *(học điền).* The district chief of Lâm-Thao ordered the village to increase the allocation to each soldier to 3 *mẫu* and to allocate the rest to the poor and to a teacher (1907 correspondences between Sơn-Dương village notables and Lâm-Thao district chief, TTLTQG1-PT–535).

7. At the time of my field research in 1987, elderly villagers still remembered that the former literary shrine had been located at what was then the village clinic. The shrine had reportedly been larger when Sơn-Dương was the administrative seat for Sơn-Vi district in the early nineteenth century.

8. The Phú-Thọ archives record an election in 1913 for the Sơn-Dương canton chief position in which Bằng's father, Nguyễn Doãn Thanh, was one of the three candidates. He lost badly in this election. The voters were current and former canton chiefs and deputy chiefs, current heads and deputy heads of village notable councils, and current village mayors *(lý trưởng)* (TTLTQG1-PT–473). Archival records also reveal that Bằng's father, Nguyễn Doãn Thanh, owned 22.6 *mẫu* of rice fields and 2 mẫu of residential land in 1910 when Nguyễn Doãn Thanh was first elected mayor of Sơn-Dương (TTLTQG1-PT–483). This record confirms Bằng's statement that his family owned between 20 and 30 *mẫu* of rice fields in his youth.

9. The official records of Confucian doctorate degree holders in the nineteenth and early twentieth centuries (Cao-Xuân-Dục 1974) do not list any person from Nguyễn Đắc Bằng's maternal grandfather's native village or from Bằng and the grandfather's district.

10. No information is available on the settlement pattern of the third wife and her son.

11. The commoditization of status had certain precedents in Vietnamese history. In the nineteenth century donors to public causes were either granted honorary mandarin titles or exempted from taxes for a number of years (Nguyễn-Thế-Anh 1971:141–142; Trần-Trọng-Kim 1964:477–478).

12. The Tân-Việt was formed by a group of modern-educated young men (Tôn Quang Phiệt, Trần Mộng Bạch, Ngô Đức Diễn) and Confucian scholars (such as Lê Huân) released from imprisonment for their political activism in

the 1908–1912 period. The name Tân Việt Cách Mạng Đảng was adopted only in 1928 after a quick succession of names: Hưng Nam and Phục Việt, both meaning Restoration of Vietnam; Việt Nam Cách Mạng Đảng (Vietnam Revolutionary Party); and Việt Nam Cách Mạng Đồng Chí Hội (Vietnam Revolutionary League) (GGI-DAP 1.1, 11, 15, 23, 41).

13. The other twelve party cells were concentrated in the large urban centers of northern and southern Vietnam (GGI-DAP 1.33–34).

14. In its platform the Vietnamese Nationalist Party also referred obliquely to the postcolonial construction of a democratic socialist system (GGI-DAP 2.7).

15. The main exception involved female party members, who had been given full membership in the Confucian scholar Nhu's group in Bắc-Giang and who were consequently admitted as full-standing VNP members at the time of the merger.

16. According to a founder of the Vietnamese Nationalist Party, negotiations foundered when the New Vietnam Revolutionary Party objected to what it considered the loosely organized activities of the VNP. The VNP in turn objected to maintaining revolutionary headquarters overseas, which the Vietnamese Revolutionary Youth League insisted upon, citing the minimal risk of French repression to the top revolutionary leadership (Hoàng-Phạm-Trân 1949:39–43).

17. The accounts by ranking VNP members differed regarding whether the assassination was sanctioned by the top party leadership or carried out independently by local party members despite Học's veto (Hoàng-Phạm-Trân 1949:57–59; Hoàng-văn-Đạo 1970:54–58).

18. Relying on oral historical sources in the neighboring village of Kinh-Kệ, Nguyễn-văn-Khánh mentioned that the VNP had over forty party members in Sơn-Dương (1997:164). This figure probably includes not only party members but also the members of VNP-affiliated associations.

## Chapter 3: In the Name of "Liberty, Equality, and Fraternity"

1. In the first Yên-Báy trial on February 27, 1930, fifteen defendants were convicted, thirteen of whom were sentenced to death. Four of these death-row inmates were beheaded on March 8, 1930 (Hoàng-văn-Đạo 1970:155–156).

2. The golden stream is a Sino-Vietnamese allusion to the world of the deceased.

3. In 1942 the partnership came to an end when Gia's partner killed the district chief of Cẩm-Khê. Gia returned to Sơn-Dương as a cultivator.

## Chapter 4: The Rise of Marxist Power

1. By August 1945 the Vietminh had seized all Vietnamese provinces except for four provinces in the north: Vĩnh-Yên, Hà-Giang, Lào-Kay, and Lai-Châu (listed in Huỳnh-Kim-Khánh 1982:326).

2. The Indochinese Communist Party began its activities in this region first in Vĩnh-Yên, where the ICP predecessor, the Vietnamese Revolutionary Youth League, had organized a progressive youth organization as early as 1928 (Cao-Tiến-Phùng et al. 1985:34). In Phú-Thọ, from the first cell in Cát-Trù (Cẩm-Khê district) formed in 1939, party membership expanded to three other localities (the paper factory in Việt-Trì, Phú-Hộ plantation in Lâm-Thao district, and Thái-Ninh village in Thanh-Ba) and increased to approximately a dozen cells by 1940. A provincial committee was formed in Phú-Thọ in the same year (ibid.:57).

3. In the period from September 1940 to March 1945 the Japanese occupied Indochina militarily. The French colonial administrative apparatus was left in place but subject to Japanese command.

4. See Huỳnh-Kim-Khánh 1982:299 and Ngô-Vĩnh-Long 1973:131–132 for a discussion of the economic effects of the Japanese military occupation on the Vietnamese rural population.

5. Another source reports that six Sơn-Dương villagers were arrested on October 4, 1943, and that the thirteen arrested Sơn-Dương and Kinh-Kệ villagers included three Vietminh sympathizers (Lê-văn-Thụ 1973:166, Phong-Châu 1989: 34).

6. During the tax season of 1944, administrative guards from Lâm-Thao district struck a villager, instead of the village deputy mayor, for the delay in tax submission. Kinh-Kệ villagers beat up the guards and managed not to pay taxes that year following extensive arguments with a low-ranking district official (Lê-văn-Thụ 1973:168).

7. After the Japanese-organized coup on March 9, 1945, the Japanese reportedly helped such anticommunist parties as the Đại-Việt Nationalist Party to organize in Phú-Thọ and neighboring provinces. They also set up youth associations as one organizational base for anti-Vietminh activities.

8. From 1943 to early 1945, at the instruction of the ICP Central Committee and on the basis of the organizational infrastructure from the 1940–1941 anti-imperialist youth movement, party cadres had built up an important base in this hilly area near the neighboring province of Yên-Báy. They reportedly relied on influential local notables and their own networks to provide protective cover for sixty fugitive party members passing through the area at various points and for other party activities (Cao-văn-Lượng 1960:144). Vietminh organizations such as notables' and mandarins' national salvation associations were set up in the area. A platoon of guerrillas armed with modern weapons was subsequently formed in early 1945.

9. The three Thanh-Thuỷ units came from the villages of La-Hào, Võng-La, and Thượng-Thị, the first two of which, interestingly, also constituted the earliest VNP bases in Phú-Thọ in the pre-1930 phase of the VNP. The four other Lâm-Thao units came from the villages of Cao-Mại, Bản-Nguyên, Chu-Hoá, and Tiên-Kiên (Lê-văn-Thụ 1973:172).

10. With the cooperation of the provincial security unit, the Vietminh leadership in Phú-Thọ first made a plan to seize arms, money, and medical supplies for the guerrilla bases on the other side of the Red River (in Thanh-Sơn and Yên-Lập). However, the plan did not materialize, because on the day of the uprising, most Vietminh sympathizers among the security force leaders were assigned to duties outside the provincial capital. An alternative plan by the provincial party leadership was also caught up in the chain of quickly unfolding events, beginning with the Japanese surrender in mid-August 1945 (Cao-văn-Lượng 1960:154-157).

11. Other demands included the return of arms that the Japanese had confiscated and the withdrawal of Japanese troops from the province of Phú-Thọ, which had served as a gathering point for Japanese troops withdrawn from the neighboring Yên-Báy and Tuyên-Quang. The Japanese agreed to the immediate transfer of power, promised to return the 500 guns taken from the provincial security forces and French troops, and withdrew to their barracks to await orders from higher authorities on the disarmament question.

12. On August 23, 1945, an armed conflict broke out when a Vietminh patrol was fired on while stopping a convoy of Japanese arms and troops from the neighboring province of Tuyên-Quang. With its emphasis on political and diplomatic struggle, the Vietminh leadership organized a large demonstration in the provincial capital. Mandarins in the Japanese-supported administration, who were serving as mediators at the time between the Japanese and the Vietminh, were invited to the demonstration only to encounter protests against the mandarinate and the monarchy (Cao-văn-Lượng 1960:160–161). After two days of tense negotiation, the mandarins in the pro-Japanese government officially transferred power to the Vietminh front on August 25 (Cao-văn-Lượng 1960: 158–162).

13. Stationed above the sixteenth parallel from October 1945 to April 1946, these Chinese troops reportedly averaged 125,000 (McAlister 1971:209).

14. A ranking VNP member reported that in Phú-Thọ the VNP platoon succeeded in forcing the Vietminh garrison out of its barracks only through a ruse to gain support from the Chinese. Caught in an ambush and pushed into a corner of the Vietminh barracks by Vietminh troops occupying a blockhouse, the VNP commander ordered his troops to fire into the neighboring Chinese garrison in order to provoke Chinese fire on the Vietminh barracks. The ruse succeeded, and the Vietminh blockhouse was heavily damaged by Chinese fire, and this forced the Vietminh troops to retreat from their own compound (Hoàng-văn-Đạo 1970:397–398). This source did not report any Chinese help in the VNP attack on Việt-Trì in December 1945.

15. In order to preserve national unity, the 1945 governmental decree of a 25 percent land-rent reduction was rarely carried out. In December 1945 Hồ agreed to delay elections until January 6, 1946, in order to allow for electoral participation by the opposition and, as an unusual concession, allowed

the opposition 70 nonelected seats in the 350-member National Assembly. The ten ministers in Hồ's new national coalition government in March 1946 included two Vietminh members, two from the Vietminh-allied Democratic Party, two independents, two from the VNP, and two from the rightist faction under Nguyễn Hải Thần (Hoàng-văn-Đạo 1970:294–299). The VNP troops, according to a short-lived agreement between Hồ's government and the VNP leadership, were to be merged into the army of the Democratic Republic of Vietnam. In Phú-Thọ, according to a local Communist Party source, despite the coalition agreement at both the national and provincial levels, the VNP forces still launched an attack on Vietminh troops on January 23, 1946 (Cao-Tiến-Phùng et al. 1985:134).

16. In exchange for this agreement the French gave up their special territorial rights in Shanghai, Hankow, and Canton, returned Kwangchouwan to China, sold the Yunnan rail line to the Chinese, granted duty exemption to Chinese goods in transit through northern Vietnam, modified the statute regarding Chinese immigrants in Vietnam, and created a tax-free zone in Hải-Phòng, where a sizable Chinese community existed (Hoàng-văn-Đạo 1970:300).

17. Another village president was forced to resign over abuse of the village's medical supplies. The reason for the third resignation is not known.

18. On March 6, 1946, facing the prospect of returning French troops, Hồ Chí Minh signed an agreement with France that recognized the Democratic Republic of Vietnam (DRV) in north and central Vietnam as a free state within a French Union and granted the native population in south Vietnam the right to merge with the DRV through referendum. In return, France could station 15,000 troops in northern Vietnam to complete the task of disarming the Japanese and to help with the maintenance of order for a limited period. As soon as the agreement was signed, however, it was sabotaged by the creation of a separate Republic of Cochinchina (South Vietnam) by French colonialists in Indochina and hawkish elements in the mother country. The Fontainebleau negotiations between France and the DRV broke down in the summer of 1946 over the Cochinchina issue and the nature of the relations between the DRV and the French Union.

19. The Vietminh allowed only the export of tea, wax-tree resin, bamboo shoots, and brown tubers and the import of salt, cloth, and Western medicine. In Sơn-Dương a Communist Party member was demoted for exporting cattle and another expelled for selling eggs (Sơn-Dương 1987:35).

20. In 1948 the ICP national leadership had called for the strict enactment of limited land reforms, including the appropriation of land owned by French and Vietnamese collaborators, communal land redistribution, a 25 percent rent reduction and the abolition of secondary rents, as well as the encouragement of labor exchange and the formation of agricultural cooperatives (Hoàng-Ước 1968:56ff.). In many communities, landlords exerted pressure on combative

tenants by demanding back the land and draft animals rented to these tenants in order to rent them out at lower rates to more compliant peasants; they also demanded the payment of old loans and threatened peasants with a suspension of credit extension (Hoàng-Ước 1968:66–67). In Sơn-Dương village cadres did not promptly carry out the land reform policy in 1948 out of concern that landlords would demand land back from sharecroppers (Sơn-Dương 1987:34).

21. Among other changes in the village of Sơn-Dương by the end of the first phase of the Franco-Vietminh war were the resumption of regular education up to grade three and health improvement through smallpox vaccination, a village medication cabinet, and the establishment of a maternity clinic operated by a midwife with modern training.

22. At the end of 1949 the Vietminh front was merged with the broader Liên Việt (Viet Alliance) front and was officially referred to as the Liên Việt. The Liên Việt membership in the provinces of Phú-Thọ, Vĩnh-Yên, and Phúc-Yên increased from 200,000 in 1947 to half a million by the end of 1949 (Cao-Tiến-Phùng et al. 1985:160). For the sake of simplicity, I refer to the front during the 1950–1954 period as the Vietminh.

23. Five of the thirty-nine purged members were expelled specifically for adding three kilograms of paddy to every hundred kilograms of village tax obligation during the Vietminh's first land tax season in 1951. Another member had been expelled earlier for violating the Vietminh's food trade embargo on French-occupied territory. Data are not available from the local party branch to perform an analysis of how many expulsions had to do directly with the class background of members.

24. The Lorraine campaign involved three divisions of French troops launched along major routes in Hạc-Trì, Lâm-Thao, and Đoan-Hùng districts. The Vietminh countered with a combination of guerrilla and conventional warfare, reportedly inflicting 2,000 casualties on the French (Cao-Tiến-Phùng et al. 1985:271–274).

## Chapter 5: The Revolution in the Village

1. Owing to a combination of bad weather and insect infestation, the average rice yield per *mẫu* dropped to 1 tonne in the spring of 1987 and 0.6 tonne for the following fall crop.

2. I arrived at the higher birth-rate figure of 2.3 percent than that from the raw birth data that the village cadre in charge of statistics provided for 1986 and the first half of 1987. The secretary's figure, in my opinion, involved a confusion of the village birth rate with the population growth rate.

3. Enrollment in the village school was 700 in 1960 and 980 in 1965. However, these figures include some junior high school students from neigh-

boring villages. When the school was first established, it was attended by students from six other villages in the area (Sơn-Dương 1987:52).

4. In September 1989 Vietnam officially withdrew its troops from Cambodia. The state reportedly demobilized half a million troops by 1989.

5. The land-reform campaign in the village of Sơn-Dương constituted part of the fifth rent-reduction enforcement wave and the second land-reform campaign in northern Vietnam. The policy of alliance with rich peasants was formulated in the light of experimental programs in 1953 (Hoàng-Ước 1968:97–108).

6. In the earlier rent-reduction and land-reform phases, the first category included "French-collaborating landlords." However, as the Geneva Agreements banned trials of those collaborating with the other side during the war, the focus of land reform was changed to brutal landlords who had "violated criminal and civil laws" (Hoàng-Ước 1968:105).

7. A distinction was made between confiscation *(tịch thu)* and appropriation *(trưng thu)* in the land-reform campaign in North Vietnam. Confiscation implied political punishment whereas appropriation did not. Appropriated land included that of non-French foreign landlords and village associations as well as any land illegitimately acquired by the church or the pagoda. Other religious land, according to the land-reform policy, would be purchased by the state for redistribution to landless, poor, and middle peasants (Hoàng-Ước 1968:162ff.).

8. In most of the agricultural cooperatives in the province of Vĩnh-Phú, households had long contracted with the cooperatives for the care of draft animals. However, they obtained only labor-day credits (*Vĩnh-Phú,* December 13, 1968, 2). The Đồng-Xuân innovation involved the introduction of production targets and incentives to households to exceed these targets.

9. Initially adopted in certain northern agricultural cooperatives on an experimental basis in 1977, the household contract system was sanctioned by the Party Central Committee at its Sixth Plenum in 1979. By 1983 this contract system had spread rapidly to the entire country, including already cooperativized southern central Vietnam and the two-hundred-plus lower-level cooperatives in the Mekong delta (*Nhân-Dân,* May 30,1983, 1; April 21, 1983, 1).

## Chapter 6: The Market Economy and Socioeconomic Differentiation

1. See Introduction for more information on the household survey.

2. Villagers who needed residential land could not convert their agricultural land to that purpose because they had clear usage rights for twenty years only. As to their "garden" land, over which they had permanent control, the high tax imposed in 2004 for the conversion of agricultural land to nonagricultural use deterred individual conversion. Furthermore, villagers strongly

preferred to live closely together rather than to convert distant garden land into residential land.

3. Data are not available for 1991–1994 due to the rapid turnover in the leadership of the village government in the mid-1990s (see Chapter 8).

4. The state fertilizer and chemical factory in the old Lâm-Thao district seat had 3,859 employees in 1994 and 4,353 in 2003 (Phú-Thọ, Statistical Office 2004:189; Vietnam Chamber of Commerce and Industry 1996:633). The other major industrial employer in Lâm-Thao district, the state battery company Vĩnh Phú, had its share of the national battery market cut from 40 percent in the mid-1990s to less than 10 percent in 2000. Many employees of this state battery company were temporarily laid off in 2005 (*Phú-Thọ,* November 8, 2005).

5. This cement company invested more than US $14 million in 2004 to achieve an annual production capacity of 300,000 tonnes of cement and tripled this capacity to 1 million tonnes by the end of 2005 (*Phú-Thọ,* July 28, 2005).

6. In December 2005 the Vietnamese prime minister clamped down on these additional incentives that the provinces were offering in their competition for foreign investment. Tax reduction below the national tax framework was held to be a major violation of national laws (Decision 1387/QĐ/TTg on December 29, 2005). Thirty-two of Vietnam's sixty-three provinces were cited for offering incentives in violation of national laws. For reasons not known, however, Phú-Thọ was not on this list, and Phú-Thọ provincial authorities escaped a reprimand from the national government (see also *Tuổi Trẻ,* May 30 and 31, 2005; *Người Lao Động,* May 26, 2005; *Tiền Phong,* May 23, 2005, and August 3, 2006).

7. In the summer of 2004, a worker in a local carpentry workshop earned 20,000–25,000 VND (US $1.27–1.59) a day, depending on his skill level. An agricultural laborer, regardless of gender, earned about 20,000 VND a day, an experienced construction worker (typically male), 18,000–20,000 VND; and a menial female laborer, 15,000 VND a day.

8. By 1991 the ten mosquito-net weaving looms and the wooden-furniture factory had ceased to operate due to a lack of market for their products.

9. Of the 283 houses surveyed, 281 had brick walls (251 with brick or tile floors, and 30 with earthen floors), 2 had wooden walls, and 1 had bamboo and thatch walls. If constructed in 2004, and not including the value of the land they were built on, these houses cost from a low of 2 million VND (US $127) to a high of 200 million VND (US $12,700), averaging 32 million VND (US $2,100) in value.

10. Adjusted for inflation, the loan portfolio of the Vietnam Bank of Agriculture and Rural Development increased from 9,275 billion VND in 1994 to 62,553 billion in 1994-constant VND.

11. The average household size in the top quintile was 4.32, as compared with 4.66 in the bottom income quintile. Due to the greater migration among the members of top-quintile households, the average number of actual household residents in the top quintile declined to 3.4, while the number of actual residents was 4.27 among bottom-quintile households.

12. The percentage of landless people in the Mekong delta and the southeast (around Hồ Chí Minh City) does not necessarily indicate poverty. An increasing number of rural households in the Mekong delta and the southeast no longer relied on agriculture for a livelihood, and some were relatively well off. But many landless households were also among the poorest. In the Red River delta, 5.7 percent of the population was landless in 2004.

13. University students trained in education were exempted from tuition payments.

14. Starting in 2005, the national government provided free health-care insurance for children who were six years old or younger.

15. It is conceivable that some households reporting antipoverty loans received microcredit outside the framework of the state-sponsored poverty-alleviation program and mistook a microcredit loan for an antipoverty one, even though the interviewers clearly distinguished the state's antipoverty loans from microcredit from other organizations. Such confusion on the part of interviewees may have arisen because microcredit programs outside the antipoverty program framework, such as those offered by the Women's Union, were in general also supposed to target the poor. However, it remains a fact that a significant percentage of microcredit loans went to the nonpoor in Sơn-Dương. The leakage of microcredit loans to the non-poor was much higher in Sơn-Dương in 2004 than in Vietnam as a whole two years earlier (World Bank and International Donors 2003: Table 7.1). The rather widespread leakage of antipoverty benefits in many communes became widely known in 2009 when the Vietnamese government decided to provide Lunar New Year gifts of 200,000 VND to each member of officially classified poor households, to a maximum of 1 million VND per household. The Vietnamese press reported that due to problematic classifications in numerous localities, many well-off households received those gifts, while many poor ones did not. Problematic classifications resulted from cadres' limited abilities, personal favoritism, as well as from their well-meaning efforts in a number of cases to provide free health benefits (supposedly targeted at the poor) to nonpoor households with seriously ill members, or to facilitate tuition reduction for or student loan access by nonpoor households with members attending technical high schools, colleges, or universities (*Tuổi Trẻ* March 18, 2009; *Người Lao Động* March 11, 2009; *Tiền Phong* February 25, 2009; and March 6, 2009; *VN Express* online February 18, 2009).

## Chapter 7:  The Intensification of Ritual and Social Life

1.  In Sơn-Dương, many of the non-Buddhist deities—*mẫu thượng thiên* (goddess of the upper sky), *mẫu thượng ngàn* (goddess of the highlands), *mẫu Thoải* (goddess of water), *Hắc hổ* (black tigers), etc.—were worshipped in the house for deceased nuns. A child-guardian deity (referred to as Đức ông), to whom many villagers symbolically "sold" their small children for protection, was worshipped in the main pagoda. In 2004, 160 village children were reportedly sold to this male deity for protection in a ritual that included the offering of sticky rice and chicken in the main pagoda. Villagers typically asked for their children back when the children turned twelve years old. The pantheon in the main pagoda also included non-Buddhist deities such as the Jade Emperor (Ngọc Hoàng), and southern and northern star gods (Nam Tào and Bắc Đẩu). See Diệp Đình Hoa 2000 (378–382); and Kleinen 1999 (166) regarding similarly mixed deity pantheons in two Buddhist pagodas in Hà Tây province in the Red River delta. See also Ngô Đức Thịnh 2004; and Nguyễn Quang Lê 2004 on the worship of Taoist goddesses and its relation to folk Buddhism.

2.  The local government officially recognized the Buddhist association in the late 1980s.

3.  Villagers had renovated the village shrine in the late 1980s. They moved the statue of the senior village deity, Qúy Minh, from a temporary location in the village pagoda to the shrine at that time. In 2004 villagers covered regular expenses at the shrine with the revenues from 600 square meters of rice fields, which were a significant increase from 72 square meters in the late 1980s.

4.  In 2004 the Fatherland Front in Sơn-Dương had as its constituent units the Peasant Association (780 members), the Veteran Association (219 members), the Women's Association (729 members), the Elderly Association (560 members), and the Youth Associations (560 members), the Buddhist Association (about 370 members), the Bonsai Association (15 members), the Education-Promotion Association (over 200 members), and the Red Cross Association (two rescue teams composed of students). Its executive committee was composed of the Front president and vice-president and a ranking member of the commune Party organization, who provided Party leadership to the Front.

5.  The practice of giving wedding gifts to the bride's side reportedly became widespread from the mid-1990s onwards. Before that, wedding gifts were presented mainly to the groom's family by the groom's relatives and friends.

## Chapter 8:  The Restructuring of Local Governance

1.  Of those 577 billion VND, the central government contributed less than 7 percent. Approximately 25 percent was raised directly through com-

mune levies; 42 percent was borrowed from various local sources; and 26 percent came from the sale of local land (Trần-Đức-Lương 1998).

2. The high percentage of grievances regarding land issues reflects in part the fact that official compensation rates for appropriated land have normally fallen far below market prices. Of the remaining cases, social welfare benefits (for war martyrs, war invalids, and the poor) constituted a major category of grievances (*Vietnamnet* 20 May 2004). Approximately 11 percent involved denunciations of specific officials.

3. See Phạm-Viết-Đào (1996) for an inside discussion of infrastructure projects and quality in Vietnam.

4. Data are not available on the change over time in the percentage of non-Party members on the People's Council of Sơn-Dương.

5. It is not clear whether the commune administration treated the people in this neighborhood differently than others, as this topic was too sensitive for a foreign-based researcher to ask directly.

6. The net annual agricultural incomes in Sơn-Dương averaged 550,000 VND per person (US $42) in 1998.

7. The World Bank's living standard survey in 1998 indicates that commune taxes (including "voluntary contributions") averaged 4.8 percent of the expenditures of Vietnamese rural households. Taxes reached 6.6 percent of rural household expenditures in the Red River delta, but dropped to 2.6 percent for households in the southeast region around Hồ Chí Minh City (Vietnam and World Bank 1999:97).

8. The poverty-rate index and poverty-depth index in the Red River delta were higher only than those in the southeast (provinces in the Hồ Chí Minh City region).

## Chapter 9: Theoretical Reflections

1. In Cochinchina (south Vietnam) millenarian movements such as the Hoà Hảo attempted more a restoration of the status quo ante than a fundamental transformation of the Vietnamese social formation. They hardly qualify as revolutionary movements (cf. Paige 1975: 325-326; Popkin 1979: ch. 5; Tai 1983).

2. Paddy production was 11.8 million tonnes in 1976 and 11.4 million tonnes in 1979 (Trần-văn-Thọ et al. 2000:248).

3. The main exceptions in the northern rural landscape are such communes as Ninh-Hiệp or Bát-Tràng, which have specialized in commerce and manufacturing for centuries and where members have accumulated considerable wealth since Vietnam's shift to a market economy in the late 1980s (Tô-Duy-Hợp 1997, Luong 1998).

# References

Archives nationales, Section d'outre-mer. AOM-P-NF. Paris. Indochine-Nouveaux fonds. Files 267, 322, 323.

———. AOM-AP-I. Aix-en-Provence. Indochine. Files 2, 7F, 9.

———. AOM-AP-RST. Aix-en-Provence. Résidence supérieure du Tonkin. Files 27, 53.

*Avenir du Tonkin.* 1930–1931.

Ballof, Daniel. 1979. "La déportation des Indochinois en Guyane et les établissements pénitentiares spéciaux, 1931–1945." *Équinoxe* 10:1–25.

Barth, Fredrik. 1966. *Models of Social Organization.* London: Royal Anthropological Institute.

Boudarel, Georges. 1984. "Marxisme et Confucianisme." In *Les aventures du marxisme,* ed. René Gallissot, 321–356. Paris: Syros.

Brocheux, Pierre. 1977. "L'implantation du mouvement communiste en Indochine française: Le cas du Nghệ-Tĩnh, 1930–1931." *Revue d'histoire moderne et contemporaine* 24:49–77.

Brook, Timothy, and B. Michael Frolic. 1997. "The Ambiguous Challenge of Civil Society." In *Civil Society in China,* eds. T. Brook and B. M. Frolic, 3–16. Armonk: M. E. Sharpe.

Bùi-Thiết. 1985. "Quy mô lãnh thổ, dân cư làng xã Bắc bộ đầu thế kỷ XX" (The Populations and Territories of Northern Villages in the Early Twentieth Century). *Tạp chí Dân tộc học* (Journal of Ethnology) 2:29–38.

*Bulletin économique de l'Indochine.* 1890–1940.

Cao-Tiến-Phùng et al. 1985. *Lịch sử đảng bộ tỉnh Vĩnh Phú (1930–1954)* (History of the Party in the Province of Vĩnh Phú, 1930–1954). Việt-Trì: Ban Tuyên giáo Tỉnh ủy Vĩnh Phú.

Cao-văn-Lượng. 1960. "Phú-Thọ: Thành lập chi bộ đầu tiên và sự phát triển cơ sở đảng" (Phú-Thọ: The Establishment of the First Party Cell and the Development of Party Organizations). In *Cách mạng tháng tám* (The August Revolution), vol. 1, ed. Trần Huy Liệu, 143–162. Hanoi: Nhà xuất bản sử học.

Cao-Xuân-Dục, comp. 1974. *Quốc triều đăng khoa lục* (Records of Successful Examination Candidates of This Dynasty). Trans. modern Vietnamese by Lê-Mạnh-Liêu. 2nd ed. Saigon: Trung tâm học liệu.

Chamberlain, Heath. 1993. "On the Search for Civil Society in China." *Modern China* 19:199–215.

Cố Nhi Tân. 1969. *Nguyễn Thái Học*. Saigon: Phạm Quang Khải.

*Công An Thành Phố Hồ Chí Minh.* 1999.

Đặng-Huy-Vận. 1967. "Thêm một số tài liệu về Đốc Ngữ và phong trào chống Pháp ở vùng hạ lưu sông Đà cuối thế kỷ XIX" (Additional Documents on General Ngữ and the Anti-French Movement in the Lower Đà Valley at the End of the Nineteenth Century). *Nghiên cứu lịch sử* (Historical Research) 96:45–56.

Đặng-Phong, ed. 2005. *Lịch sử kinh tế Việt Nam 1945–2000* (Tập II: *1955–1975*) (Economic History of Vietnam 1945–2000 [Vol. 2: 1955–1975]). Hanoi: Nhà xuất bản Khoa học xã hội.

Diệp-Đình-Hoa, ed. 2000. *Người Việt ở đồng bằng Bắc bộ* (The Vietnamese in the Northern Delta). Hanoi: Nhà xuất bản Khoa học xã hội.

Đỗ-Tất-Ngọc. 2006. *Tín dụng ngân hàng đối với kinh tế hộ Việt Nam* (Bank Credit and the Household Economy in Vietnam). Hanoi: Nhà xuất bản Lao động.

Dụng-Hiền. 1942. *Hương ước xã Dụng-Hiền năm 1942* (Village Regulations of Dụng-Hiền Commune in 1942).

Dương-thị-Thế, and Phạm-thị-Thoa, eds. 1981. *Tên làng xã Việt Nam đầu thế kỷ XIX* (The Nomenclature of Vietnamese Villages in the Early Nineteenth Century). Hanoi: Khoa học xã hội.

Elliott, David W. P. 2003. *The Vietnamese War: Revolution and Social Change in the Mekong Delta, 1930–1975.* 2 vols. Armonk, NY: M. E. Sharpe.

Emerson, Rupert. 1960. *From Empire to Nation: The Rise of Self-Assertion of Asian and African Peoples.* Boston: Beacon.

Fforde, Adam. 1989. *The Agrarian Question in North Vietnam, 1974–1979.* Armonk, NY: M. E. Sharpe.

———. 1999. "From Plan to Market: The Economic Transition in Vietnam and China Compared." In *Transforming Asian Socialism: China and Vietnam Compared,* eds. Anita Chan, B. Kerkvliet, and J. Unger, 43–72. St. Leonards, Australia: Allen and Unwin.

———, and Stefan de Vylder. 1996. *From Plan to Market: The Economic Transition in Vietnam.* Boulder, CO: Westview.

Frolic, B. Michael. 1997. "State-led Civil Society." In *Civil Society in China,* eds. T. Brook and B. Michael Frolic, 46–67. Armonk, NY: M. E. Sharpe.

Gammeltoft, Tine. 1999. *Women's Bodies, Women's Worries: Health and Family Planning in a Vietnamese Rural Community.* Richmond, Surrey: Curzon.

Geertz, Clifford. 1963. *Agricultural Involution.* Berkeley: University of California Press.

Gourou, Pierre. 1936. *Les paysans du delta tonkinois.* Paris: L'Ecole française d'Extrême-Orient.

Gouvernement géneral de l'Indochine, Direction des affaires politiques et de la sûreté générale (GGI-DAP). 1930–1933. *Contribution à l'histoire des mouvements politiques de l'Indochine française.* 6 vols. Hanoi.

Gran, Guy. 1975. "Vietnam and the Capitalist Road to Modernity: Village Cochinchina, 1880–1940." Ph.D. dissertation, University of Wisconsin at Madison.

Harrison, James P. 1982. *The Endless War: Fifty Years of Struggle in Vietnam.* New York: Free Press.

Henry, Yves. 1932. *L'économie agricole de l'Indochine.* Hanoi: Extrême-Orient.

Hickey, Gerald. 1964. *Village in Vietnam.* New Haven, CT: Yale University Press.

Hoàng-Phạm-Trân (pseudonym of Nhượng-Tống). 1949. *Nguyễn Thái Học.* 2nd ed. Saigon: Tân Việt.

Hoàng-Ước. 1968. "Cách mạng ruộng đất ở Việt Nam, Phần I và II" (The Land Revolution in Vietnam, Parts I and II). In *Cách mạng ruộng đất ở Việt Nam* (The Land Revolution in Vietnam), ed. Trần Phương, 1–217. Hanoi: Nhà Xuất bản Khoa Học Xã Hội.

Hoàng-văn-Đạo. 1970. *Việt Nam Quốc Dân Đảng* (The Vietnamese Nationalist Party). 2nd ed. Saigon: Nguyễn Hoà Hiệp.

Houtart, Francoise, and Genevieve Lemercinier. 1981. *La sociologie d'une commune vietnamienne.* Louvain-la-Neuve: Catholic University of Louvain.

Hunt, David. 1982. "Village Culture and the Vietnamese Revolution." *Past and Present* 92:131–157.

Huỳnh-Kim-Khánh. 1982. *Vietnamese Communism, 1925–1945.* Ithaca, NY: Cornell University Press.

Kelly, Raymond. 1977. *Etoso Social Structure.* Ann Arbor: University of Michigan Press.

Kerkvliet, Benedict J. Tria. 1995. "Village-State Relations in Vietnam: The Effect of Everyday Politics on Decollectivization." *Journal of Asian Studies* 54:396–418.

———. 2003. "Authorities and the People: An Analysis of State-Society Relations in Vietnam." In *Postwar Vietnam: Dynamics of a Transforming Society,* ed. Hy V. Luong, 27–54. Lanham, MD: Rowman and Littlefield.

———. 2005. *The Power of Everyday Politics: How Vietnamese Peasants Transformed National Policy.* Ithaca, NY: Cornell University Press.

Kiều-Hữu-Hỷ et al. 1961. *Thơ văn Nguyễn Quang Bích* (The Poetry and Prose of Nguyễn Quang Bích). Hanoi: Văn Hóa.

Kiều-Hữu-Xuân. 2001. *Tráng khúc Sơn-Dương* (Sơn-Dương Epic). Việt-Trì: Hội Văn học nghệ thuật Việt Trì.

Kleinen, John. 1999. *Facing the Future, Reviving the Past: A Study of Social Change in a Northern Vietnamese Village.* Singapore: Institute of Southeast Asian Studies.

Knudsen, John Chr. 1990. "Cognitive Models in Life Histories." *Anthropological Quarterly* 63:122–133.

Krowolski, Nelly. 1999. "Se marier au village." In *Mông Phụ: Un Village du delta du Fleuve Rouge* [Mông Phụ: A Village of the Red River Delta], ed. by Nguyễn Tùng, 137–150. Paris: Harmattan.

———. 2002. "Village Households in the Red River Delta: The Case of Tả Thanh Oai, On the Outskirts of the Capital City, Hà Nội." In *Gender, Household, State: Đổi Mới in Việt Nam,* eds. Jayne Werner and Danièle Bélanger, 73–88. Ithaca, NY: Cornell University Southeast Asia Program.

Lê-Tượng. 1967. "Góp thêm ý kiến về Đốc Ngữ và phong trào chống Pháp ở vùng hạ lưu sông Đà cuối thế kỷ XIX" (Additional Ideas on General Ngữ and the Anti-French Movement in the Lower Đà Valley at the End of the Nineteenth Century). *Nghiên cứu lịch sử* (Historical Research) 101:51–57.

———, and Nguyễn-Khắc-Xương. 1987. *Truyền thuyết Hùng Vương.* 5th ed. Việt-Trì: Hội Văn học nghệ thuật Vĩnh Phú.

———, and Vũ-Kim-Biên. 1981. *Lịch sử Vĩnh Phú* (The History of Vĩnh Phú). Việt-Trì: Ty văn hóa và thông tin Vĩnh Phú.

Lê-văn-Thụ. 1973. "Phong trào Việt Minh xã Kinh-Kệ" (The Vietminh Movement in Kinh-Kệ Commune). In *Những ngày cách mạng tháng tám: Hồi ký* (The Days of the August Revolution: Memoirs), vol. 1. Việt-Trì: Ban Nghiên cứu lịch sử đảng Vĩnh Phú.

Luong, Hy Van. 1984. "'Brother' and 'Uncle': Rules, Structural Contradictions, and Meaning in Vietnamese Kinship." *American Anthropologist* 86:290–315.

———. 1985. "Agrarian Unrest from an Anthropological Perspective: The Case of Vietnam." *Comparative Politics* 17:153–174.

———. 1988. "Discursive Practices, Ideological Oppositions, and Power Structure: Person-referring Forms and Sociopolitical Struggles in Colonial Vietnam." *American Ethnologist* 15:239–253.

———. 1989. "Vietnamese Kinship: Structural Principles and the Socialist Transformation in Twentieth-Century Vietnam." *Journal of Asian Studies* 48:741–756.

———. 1990. *Discursive Practices and Linguistic Meanings: The Vietnamese System of Person Reference.* Philadelphia: John Benjamins.

———. 1991. "Vietnamese Life-History Narratives: Discursive Practices and Ideological Oppositions." Unpublished manuscript.

————. 1992. *Revolution in the Village: Tradition and Transformation in North Vietnam, 1925–1988.* Honolulu: University of Hawai'i Press.

————. 1993. "Economic Reform and the Intensification of Rituals in Two North Vietnamese Villages, 1980–1990." In *The Challenge of Reform in Indochina,* ed. Borje Ljunggren, 259–292. Cambridge, MA: Harvard Institute for International Development.

————. 1994. "The Marxist State and the Dialogic Restructuration of Culture in Rural Vietnam." In *Indochina: Social and Cultural Change,* eds. David Elliott, H. V. Luong, B. Kiernan, and T. Mahoney, 79–117. Claremont, CA: Claremont-McKenna College.

————. 1998. "Engendered Entrepreneurship: Ideologies and Political Economic Transformation in a North Vietnamese Center of Ceramics Production." In *Market Cultures: Society and Morality in the New Asian Capitalisms,* ed. Robert Hefner, 290–314. Boulder, CO: Westview.

————. 2003a. "Postwar Vietnamese Society: An Overview of Transformational Dynamics." In *Postwar Vietnam: Dynamics of a Transforming Society,* ed. Hy V. Luong, 1–25. Boulder, CO: Westview.

————. 2003b. "Gender Relations: Ideologies, Kinship Practices, Political Economy." In *Postwar Vietnam: Dynamics of a Transforming Society,* ed. Hy V. Luong, 201–224. Boulder, CO: Westview.

————. 2005. "The State, Local Associations, and Alternate Civilities in Rural Northern Vietnam." In *Civil Society, Globalization, and Political Change in Asia,* ed. Robert Weller, 123–147. London: Routledge.

————. 2006. "Structure, Practice, and History: Contemporary Anthropological Research on Vietnam." *Journal of Vietnamese Studies* 1:371–409.

————. 2007. "The Restructuring of Vietnamese Nationalism, 1954–2006." *Pacific Affairs* 80:439–454.

————. 2009a. "Rural-to-Urban Migration in Vietnam: A Tale of Three Regions." In *Reconfiguring Families in Contemporary Vietnam,* eds. Magali Barbieri and Danièle Bélanger, 391-420. Stanford, CA: Stanford University Press.

————. 2009b. "Gifts and Social Capital in Two Rural Vietnamese Communities." In *Modernities and Tradition in Vietnam: Anthropological Approaches,* eds. Hy V. Luong et al. Hồ Chí Minh City: National University of Vietnam Press.

————, and Dileni Gunewardena. 2009. "Labor Market, Urban Informal Economy, and Earnings during Rapid Economic Growth: The Case of Hồ Chí Minh City." In *Urbanization, Migration, and Poverty in a Vietnamese Metropolis: Hồ Chí Minh City in Comparative Perspectives,* ed. Hy V. Luong, 211–256. Singapore: National University of Singapore Press.

————, and Vũ Văn Ngọc. 2009. "Education Expenses, Migration, and the Schooling of Youth in Urban Vietnam." In *Urbanization, Migration, and Poverty in a Vietnamese Metropolis: Hồ Chí Minh City in Comparative*

*Perspectives,* ed. Hy V. Luong, 192–208. Singapore: National University of Singapore Press.

Madsen, Richard. 1993. "The Public Sphere, Civil Society and Moral Community," *Modern China* 19:183–198.

Mai-Hanh. 1967. "Đốc Ngữ và lực lượng nghĩa quân sông Đà trong phong trào chống ngoại xâm của nhân dân Việt Nam thời cuối thế kỷ XIX" (General Ngữ and the Đà River Resistance Force in the Vietnamese Movement against Foreign Invasions at the End of the Nineteenth Century). *Nghiên cứu lịch sử* (Historical Research) 97:27–42.

Malarney, Shaun K. 2002. *Culture, Ritual and Revolution in Vietnam.* London: Routledge Curzon.

————. 2003. "Return to the Past? The Dynamics of Contemporary Religious and Ritual Transformation." In *Postwar Vietnam: Dynamics of a Transforming Society,* ed. Hy V. Luong, 225–256. Boulder, CO: Rowman & Littlefield.

Malesky, Edmund. 2006. "Gerrymandering—Vietnamese Style: The Political Motivations behind the Creation of New Provinces in Vietnam." Unpublished paper presented at the Annual Meeting of the American Political Science Association, Philadelphia, September 2006.

Marr, David. 1971. *Vietnamese Anticolonialism, 1885–1925.* Berkeley: University of California Press.

————. 1981. *Vietnamese Tradition on Trial, 1920–1945.* Berkeley: University of California Press.

Marx, Karl. 1963. *The Eighteenth Brumaire of Louis Bonaparte.* New York: International Publishers.

McAleavy, Henry. 1968. *Black Flags in Vietnam: The Story of a Chinese Intervention.* London: George Allen and Unwin.

McAlister, John, Jr. 1971. *Vietnam: The Origins of Revolution.* Garden City, NY: Doubleday.

Meillassoux, Claude. 1981. *Maidens, Meal and Money: Capitalism and the Domestic Community.* Cambridge: Cambridge University Press.

Mitchell, Edward J. 1968. "Inequality and Insurgency: A Statistical Study of South Vietnam." *World Politics* 20:421–438.

Mitrany, David. 1951. *Marx against the Peasant.* Chapel Hill: University of North Carolina Press.

Murray, Martin. 1980. *The Development of Capitalism in Colonial Indochina (1870–1940).* Berkeley: University of California Press.

Mus, Paul. 1949. "The Role of the Village in Vietnamese Politics." *Pacific Affairs* 22:265–271.

————. 1952. *Vietnam: La sociologie d'une guerre.* Paris: Editions du Seuil.

Nash, June. 1979. *We Eat the Mines and the Mines Eat Us: Dependency and Exploitation in Bolivian Tin Mines.* New York: Columbia University Press.

Ngô-Đức-Thịnh. 2004. "Đạo Mẫu ở Việt Nam" (Mother Goddess Religion in Vietnam). In *Đạo Mẫu và các hình thức Shaman trong các tộc người ở Việt Nam và Châu Á* (Mother Goddess Religion and Shamanistic Forms in Ethnic Groups in Vietnam and Asia), ed. Ngô Đức Thịnh, 23–61. Hanoi: Nhà xuất bản Khoa học xã hội.

Ngô-Quang-Nam, and Tạ-Huy-Đức. 1986. "Mỹ thuật dân gian" (Folk Arts). In *Địa chí Vĩnh Phú: Văn hoá dân gian vùng đất tổ* (The Geography of Vĩnh Phú: Folk Culture in the Ancestral Land), eds. Ngô Quang Nam and Xuân Thiêm, 173–209. Việt-Trì: Sở văn hóa thông tin Vĩnh Phú.

Ngô-vi-Liên. 1928. *Nomenclature des communes du Tonkin.* Hanoi: Lê văn Tân.

Ngô-Vĩnh-Long. 1973. *Before the Revolution: Vietnamese Peasants under the French.* Cambridge, MA: MIT Press.

———. 1978a. "The Indochinese Communist Party and Peasant Rebellion in Central Vietnam, 1930–1931." *Bulletin of Concerned Asian Scholars* 10:15–34.

———. 1978b. "Peasant Revolutionary Struggles in Vietnam in the 1930's." Ph.D. dissertation, Harvard University.

———. 1988. "Some Aspects of Cooperativization in the Mekong Delta." In *Postwar Vietnam: Dilemmas in Socialist Development,* eds. David Marr and Christine White, 163–173. Ithaca, NY: Cornell University Southeast Asia Program.

*Người Lao Động,* 2004–2009.

Nguyễn-Công-Bình et al. 1985. *Lịch sử Việt Nam* (History of Vietnam). Vol. 2. Hanoi: Khoa học xã hội.

Nguyễn-Hải-Hàm. 1970. *Từ Yên-Báy đến Côn Lôn* (From Yên Báy to Poulo Condore). Saigon: Khai Trí

Nguyễn-Hữu-Minh. 1998. "Tradition and Change in the Vietnamese Marriage Patterns in the Red River Delta." Ph.D. Dissertation, University of Washington, Seattle.

———, and Charles Hirschman. 2000. "Mô hình sống chung với gia đình chồng sau khi kết hôn ở đồng bằng Bắc bộ và các nguyên nhân tác động" (Post-Marital Patrilocal Residence Model in the Red River Delta and the Factors at Work). *Xã hội học* (Sociology) 1:41–54.

Nguyễn-Huy. 1980. "Về các hình thức khoán trong hợp tác xã trồng lúa." (On the Types of Contract Systems in Rice-growing Cooperatives). *Nghiên cứu kinh tế* (Economic Research) 118:9–23.

———. 1983. *Đưa nông nghiệp từ sản xuất nhỏ lên sản xuất lớn xã hội chủ nghĩa* (To Bring Agriculture from Small-Scale Production to the Large-Scale Production of the Socialist Era). Vol. 2. Hanoi: Khoa học xã hội.

Nguyễn-Khắc-Viện. 1971. "Confucianisme et marxisme." In *Tradition et révolution au Vietnam,* eds. J. Chesneaux et al., 21–57. Paris: Anthropos.

Nguyễn-Quang-Lê. 2004. "Bàn về mối quan hệ giữa Phật giáo và Đạo Mẫu dân gian" (Discussion on the Relation between Buddhism and Folk Mother

Goddess Religion). In *Đạo Mẫu và các hình thức Shaman trong các tộc người ở Việt Nam và Châu Á* (Mother Goddess Religion and Shamanistic Forms in Ethnic Groups in Vietnam and Asia), ed. Ngô-Đức-Thịnh, 221–234. Hanoi: Nhà xuất bản Khoa học xã hội.

Nguyễn-Thế-Anh. 1971. *Kinh tế và xã hội Việt Nam dưới các vua triều Nguyễn* (Vietnamese Economy and Society under the Nguyễn Rulers). Saigon: Lửa Thiêng.

Nguyễn-Thiệu-Lâu. 1951. "La réforme agraire de 1839 dans le Bình Định." *Bulletin de L'École française d'Extrême-Orient* 45:119–129.

Nguyễn Tùng, ed. 1999. *Mông Phu: Un village du delta du Fleuve Rouge* (Mông Phu: A Village of the Red River Delta). Paris: Harmattan.

Nguyễn-văn-Khánh. 1997. "Thêm một số tư liệu về VNQDD trên địa bàn Lâm-Thao với cuộc khởi nghĩa Yên Bái" (Additional Materials on the Vietnamese Nationalist Party in Lâm-Thao in Connection with the Yên Bái Uprising). In *Khởi nghĩa Yên Bái 2–1930: Một số vấn đề lịch sử* (The Yên Bái Uprising in February 1930: Some Historical Issues), eds. Sở văn hóa thông tin Yên Bái (Yên Bái Department of Culture and Information) and Viện Sử học Việt Nam (Vietnam Institute of History), 159–171. Yên Bái: Sở văn hóa thông tin Yên Bái.

Nguyễn-văn-Trung. 1963. *Chủ nghĩa thực dân Pháp ở Việt Nam: Thực chất và huyền thoại* (French Colonialism in Vietnam: Reality and Myths). Saigon: Nam Sơn.

Nguyễn-Xuân-Nguyên. 1942. "Enquêtes démographiques sur deux agglomerations annamites." *Bulletin de L'Institut Indochinois pour l'étude de l'homme* 5, no. 2:129–136.

*Nhân Dân*. 1954–1955, 1983–1988.

*Nhân Dân nguyệt san*. 1955–1957.

Olson, Mancur. 1965. *The Logic of Collective Action*. Cambridge, MA: Harvard University Press.

Paige, Jeffery. 1975. *Agrarian Revolution: Social Movements and Export Agriculture in the Underdeveloped World*. New York: Free Press.

———. 1983. "Social Theory and Peasant Revolution in Vietnam and Guatemala." *Theory and Society* 12:699–737.

Papin, Philippe, and Olivier Tessier, eds. 2002. *Làng ở vùng châu thổ sông Hồng: Vấn đề còn bỏ ngỏ:* The Village in Questions. Hanoi: Trung Tâm Khoa Học Xã Hội và Nhân Văn Quốc Gia, L'Ecole Française d'Extrême-Orient & Đại học quốc gia Hà Nội.

Phạm-Cường, and Nguyễn-văn-Bá. 1976. *Revolution in the Village: Nam Hồng (1945–1975)*. Hanoi: Foreign Languages Publishing House.

Phạm-Gia-Đức. 1986. *Lịch sử cuộc kháng chiến chống thực dân Pháp, 1945–1954* (The History of the Resistance to French Colonialism, 1945–1954). Hanoi: Quân đội nhân dân.

Phạm-Viết-Đào. 1996. *Mặt trái của cơ chế thị trường* (The Underside of the Market System). Hanoi: Nhà xuất bản Văn hóa thông tin.

Phạm-Xuân-Độ. 1939. *Phú-Thọ tỉnh địa chí* (Geography of Phú-Thọ Province). Hanoi: Nam Ký.

Phong-Châu, Executive District Committee of Communist Party, Vĩnh Phú Province. 1989. *Lịch sử đảng bộ huyện Phong-Châu.* Tập 1: *1939–1954* (The History of the Party Organization in Phong-Châu District. Vol. 1: 1939–1954). Việt-Trì: Ban Tuyên giáo Tỉnh ủy Vĩnh Phú.

*Phú-Thọ.* 1960–1968, 1997–2006

Phú-Thọ, Statistical Office. 2001. *Niên giám thống kê: Statistical Yearbook 2002.* Việt-Trì: Cục Thống kê.

———. 2004. *Niên giám thống kê: Statistical Yearbook 2003.* Việt-Trì: Cục Thống kê.

———. 2006. *Niên giám thống kê: Statistical Yearbook 2005.* Việt-Trì: Cục Thống kê.

Phúc-Khánh, and Đinh-Lục. 1986. *Cuộc kháng chiến chống thực dân Pháp xâm lược (9.1945–7.1954)* (The Resistance against French Invaders, 9/1945–7/1954). Hanoi: Sự thật.

Piétri, François. 1960. "L'affaire de Yen Bay." *La revue des deux mondes,* July 15: 278–288.

Popkin, Samuel. 1979. *The Rational Peasant: The Political Economy of Rural Society in Vietnam.* Berkeley: University of California Press.

Porter, Gareth, ed. 1981. *Vietnam: A History in Documents.* New York: New American.

Pouvourville, A. 1892. *Deux années de lutte (1890–1891).* Paris: Albert Savine.

———. 1923. *Chasseur de pirates.* Paris: Monde moderne.

Quốc-Anh. 1975. "Một vài ý kiến về mối quan hệ giữa các khuynh hướng chính trị tiểu tư sản với phong trào công nhân trong phong trào giải phóng dân tộc Việt Nam trước 1930" (A Few Ideas on the Relation between the Political Trends among the Petite Bourgeoisie and Workers' Movements in the pre-1930 Vietnamese National Independence Movement). *Nghiên cứu lịch sử* (Historical Research) 160:28–48.

Rambo, A. Terry. 1973. *A Comparison of Peasant Social Systems of Northern and Southern Vietnam: A Study of Ecological Adaptation, Social Succession, and Cultural Evolution.* Carbondale: Southern Illinois University Center for Vietnamese Studies.

Ravallion, Martin, and Dominique Van de Walle. 2008. "Does Rising Landlessness Signal Success or Failure for Vietnam's Agrarian Transition?" *Journal of Development Economics* 87:191–209.

Rouband, Louis. 1931. *Vietnam: La tragédie indochinoise.* Paris: Valois.

Sahlins, Marshall. 1981. *Historical Metaphors and Mythical Realities.* Ann Arbor: University of Michigan Press.

————. 1985. *Islands of History*. Chicago: University of Chicago Press.

Scott, James C. 1976. *The Moral Economy of the Peasant*. New Haven, CT: Yale University Press.

Scott, James George. 1885. *France and Tongking: A Narrative of the Campaign of 1884 and the Occupation of Further India*. London: Fisher Unwin.

Skocpol, Theda. 1979. *States and Social Revolutions*. Cambridge: Cambridge University Press.

Smith, Carol. 1984. "Local History in Global Context: Social and Economic Transitions in Western Guatemala." *Comparative Studies in Society and History* 26:193–228.

Sơn-Dương. 1942. *Sổ cải lương hương ước năm 1942 của làng Sơn-Dương* (Reformed Village Regulations in 1942 of Sơn-Dương Village).

Sơn-Dương. 1987. *Lịch sử xã Sơn-Dương: Sơ thảo* (A Preliminary History of Sơn-Dương Village). Published under the editorship of the [Communist] Party Executive Committee in Sơn-Dương Village. Việt-Trì: Sở Văn hóa Thông tin Vĩnh Phú.

Tạ-Long. 1976. "Đôi nét về các nghi lễ trong một năm ở Vĩnh Phú trước cách mạng tháng tám" (Certain Features of Annual Rituals in Vĩnh Phú before the August [1945] Revolution). *Tạp chí Dân tộc học* (Journal of Ethnology) 2 (1976): 74–84.

Tai, Hue-Tam Ho. 1983. *Millenarianism and Peasant Politics in Vietnam*. Cambridge, MA: Harvard University Press.

Taylor, Philip. 2007. *Cham Muslims of the Mekong Delta: Place and Mobility in the Cosmopolitan Periphery*. Singapore: National University of Singapore Press.

Tessier, Olivier. 2009. "Don *(giúp đỡ)* et réciprocité dans une société villageoise du Nord du Vietnam: Entre solidarité et dependence." *Moussons*.

Thụy-Sơn. 1942. *Sổ hương ước làng Thụy Sơn* (Village Regulations of Thụy Sơn).

*Tiền Phong*, 2005–2009.

Tô-Duy-Hợp, ed. 1997. *Ninh Hiệp: Truyền thống và phát triển* (Ninh Hiệp: Tradition and Development). Hanoi: Nhà xuất bản Chính trị quốc gia.

Toan-Ánh. 1969. *Miền Bắc khai nguyên*. Saigon: Đại Nam.

Trần-Đức-Lương. 1998. "Từ những việc xảy ra ở Thái Bình, Đảng, nhà nước và nhân dân ta rút được bài học qúy gía" (From the Events in Thái Bình: The Party, the State, and People Have Drawn a Valuable Lesson). *Sài Gòn Giải Phóng* 4 and 5 March: 5.

Trần-Huy-Liệu, Văn-Tạo, and Nguyễn-Khắc-Đạm. 1957. *Phong trào Văn thân khởi nghĩa* (The Aid-the-King Movement). Hanoi: Văn sử địa.

Trần-Trọng-Kim. 1964. *Việt Nam sử lược* (A Summary History of Vietnam). Saigon: Khai Trí.

Trần-Từ. 1984. *Cơ cấu tổ chức của làng Việt cổ truyền ở Bắc Bộ* (The Organizational Structure of Traditional Vietnamese Villages in North Vietnam). Hanoi: Nhà xuất bản khoa học xã hội.

Trần-văn-Thọ et al. 2000. *Kinh tế Việt Nam 1955–2000* (Vietnamese Economy 1955–2000). Hanoi: Nhà xuất bản Thống kê.

Trullinger, James Walker. 1980. *Village at War.* New York: Longman.

*Trung-Bắc-Tân-Văn.* 1930–1931.

*Trung tâm Lưu trữ quốc gia 1, Phú-Thọ* (TTLTQG1-PT), Files 133, 134, 472, 473, 480, 481, 482, 483, 484, 485, 534, 537, 1274, 1292, 1368, I234, I34.

Trương Bửu Lâm. 1967. *Patterns of Vietnamese Response to Foreign Intervention, 1858–1900.* New Haven, CT: Yale University Southeast Asia Studies.

*Tuổi Trẻ,* 2005–2009.

Verdery, Katherine. 1996. *What Was Socialism, and What Comes Next?* Princeton, NJ: Princeton University Press.

Vietnam. 1999. *Những văn bản pháp luật về dân chủ và quy định đảm bảo thực hiện* (Legal Documents on Democracy and Implementation Regulations). Hanoi: Nhà xuất bản Lao động.

Vietnam. 2005. *Văn bản pháp luật về nghi lễ, lễ hội, và trang phục của cơ quan nhà nước* (Legal Documents on Rituals, Festivals, and Clothing for State Agencies). Hanoi: Nhà xuất bản Chính trị quốc gia.

Vietnam and World Bank. 1999. *Attacking Poverty.* Hanoi: World Bank.

Vietnam Chamber of Commerce and Industry. 1996. *Vietnam Business Directory 1995–1996.* Hanoi: Vietnam Chamber of Commerce and Industry.

Vietnamese Communist Party. 2004. *Các văn bản hướng dẫn thi hành Điều lệ Đảng* (Documents Guiding the Implementation of Party Regulations). Hanoi: Nhà xuất bản Chính trị quốc gia.

*Vietnamnet.* 2004.

*Vĩnh-Phú.* 1968–1975.

Vĩnh-Phú Research Committee on Party History. 1971. *Bốn mươi năm hoạt động của đảng bộ Vĩnh Phú* (Forty Years of Activities of the Vĩnh-Phú Provincial Party Organization). Việt-Trì: Ban nghiên cứu lịch sử Đảng Vĩnh Phú.

Viollis, Andrée (pseudonym of A. F. C. d'Ardenne de Tizac). 1935. *Indochine: S.O.S.* Paris: Gallimard.

Vũ-Kim-Biên. 1999. *Văn hiến làng xã vùng đất tổ Hùng vương* (Village Culture in the Ancestral Land of the Hùng Kings). Hanoi: Trung tâm UNESCO thông tin tư liệu lịch sử và văn hoá Việt Nam & Sở văn hoá thông tin thể thao Phú-Thọ.

———. 2002. *Truyền thống giữ nước của nhân dân vùng đất tổ* (The National Defense Tradition of the People in the Ancestral Land). Việt-Trì: Hội Cựu chiến binh tỉnh Phú-Thọ.

Vũ-Quốc-Thúc. 1951. *L'économie communaliste du Vietnam.* Hanoi: Presses universitaires du Vietnam.

Vũ-văn-Tính. 1970a. "Những thay đổi về địa lý hành chính các tỉnh Bắc kỳ trong thời kỳ Pháp thuộc" (Administrative Geographical Changes of Tonkinese Provinces in the French Colonial Period), Part 1. *Nghiên cứu lịch sử* (Historical Research) 133:43–51.

———. 1970b. "Những thay đổi về địa lý hành chính các tỉnh Bắc kỳ trong thời kỳ Pháp thuộc" (Administrative Geographical Changes of Tonkinese Provinces in the French Colonial Period), Part 2. *Nghiên cứu lịch sử* (Historical Research) 134:53–63.

Wallerstein, Immanuel. 1979. *The Capitalist World-Economy.* Cambridge: Cambridge University Press.

Weller, Robert P. *Alternate Civilities: Democracy and Culture in China and Taiwan.* Boulder, CO: Westview.

White, Christine. 1981. "Agrarian Reform and National Liberation in the Vietnamese Revolution: 1920–1951." Ph.D. dissertation, Cornell University.

———.1983. "Peasant Mobilization and Anti-colonial Struggle in Vietnam: The Rent Reduction Campaign of 1953." *Journal of Peasant Studies* 10:187–213.

———.1988. "Alternative Approaches to the Socialist Transformation of Agriculture in Postwar Vietnam." In *Postwar Vietnam: Dilemmas in Socialist Development,* eds. David Marr and Christine White, 133–146. Ithaca, NY: Cornell University Southeast Asia Program.

Wolf, Eric. 1969. *Peasant Wars of the Twentieth Century.* New York: Harper and Row.

Wolf, Margery. 1972. *Women and the Family in Rural Taiwan.* Stanford, CA: Stanford University Press.

Wolpe, Harold. 1972. "Capitalism and Cheap Labour-Power in South Africa: From Segregation to Apartheid." *Economy and Society* 1:425–456.

Woodside, Alexander. 1976. *Community and Revolution in Modern Vietnam.* Boston: Houghton Mifflin.

World Bank and International Donors. 2003. *Poverty (Vietnam Development Report 2004).* Hanoi: World Bank.

Zinoman, Peter. 2001. *The Colonial Bastille: A History of Imprisonment in Vietnam, 1862–1940.* Berkeley: University of California Press.

# Index

Address, 60, 75, 79–80, 166, 170, 171, 175, 177, 244, 269

Adoption, 60–61, 201, 216

Affines, 61, 236, 243

Agriculture: calendar, 53, 158–159; division of labor in, 53; fertilizer, 158, 181, 190–191, 215–216, 219, 283; harvesting, 53; intensification of, 7, 158–159; irrigation fee, 10, 213, 215, 246, 249–250, 252, 254, 255; labor, hired, 215–216; plowing, 1, 53, 180, 188, 193–194, 215; taxes, 191, 213, 255; transplanting, 53; water control, 7, 10, 48, 64, 157–158, 176, 187, 190–191, 213, 215–217, 246, 249–250, 255, 293n1; weeding, 53. *See also* Animal husbandry; Commerce; Cooperatives; Crops; Economy, colonial; Economy, postcolonial; Household contract system; Household garden plots; Peasants; Rituals

Alcohol: illegal production, 46; monopoly by French colonial government, 46–47

Ân (Mrs. Ái), 92, 136, 141, 143, 149, 170, 176

Ancestor worship, 32, 38, 41, 61, 74–76, 78, 175, 201–202, 228–231, 238; and adoption, 60; expense coverage, 202, 229; and tombs, 208, 220, 228–231. *See also* Family; Kinship

Animal husbandry: chickens and ducks, 59, 182, 191, 282; fish, 216; oxen and buffalo, 1, 282, 193–194; pigs, 58, 69, 180, 182, 184, 191, 216, 282; as source of income, 164–165; swans, 184, 185; waste, use of, 158, 171, 181, 182

Annam (central Vietnam), 302n18; French administration of, 42, 46; political economy, 46, 85, 264–265, 267–268, 270, 304n9; resistance to French colonialism, 38, 87, 88, 142, 267; resistance to U.S. intervention, 267; social structure, 262–264, 269–271. *See also* Household contract system; Land reform

Anticolonial resistance (before 1925), 34–42, 48–50; French repression, 50

Anticolonialism: *See* Communist movement and party; Family; Guerilla warfare; Kinship; Tân-Việt party; Tradition; Vietminh; VNP

Areca nuts and betel leaves, 1, 162, 238, 239, 281

Associations: alumni, 235; bonsai, 307n4; ceremony assistance,

Credit: bank, 216, 220–222, 254,
305n10; cooperative, 161,
164, 166; to store customers,
220; sources of, 221. *See also*
Associations, credit
Crime, 137, 138, 178, 187
Crops: cash, 214–215; corn, 189,
191–192, 215; fruit, 53; peanut,
158, 189, 190; rice, 53–54; tea,
43; vegetable, 53; Wax-tree resin,
43; yield of rice, 157–158, 182,
184, 185, 189, 190, 192, 215,
304nl. *See also* Agriculture,
calendar
Cứu quốc (national salvation)
associations. *See* Vietminh, mass
mobilization

Đại-Việt party, 300n7
Democracy: as ideology, 82, 85, 88,
155; and nationalism, 18–19; in
post-colonial era, 251. *See also*
Communist movement and party,
ideology; Emerson, Rupert; VNP,
ideology
Diarchy, racial, 20, 52, 79, 80–82,
83–84, 95, 266, 271
Điện-Biên-Phủ, 154, 288
Discursive practices: and gender,
200; life-history narratives, 12;
in politics, French influence
on, 85, 98, 103, 123, 125; in
politics, influence of Vietnamese
tradition on, 84, 95–96, 98, 103,
124, 125; and power inequality,
32–33; and reality, 29, 100–101,
108–109, 116–117, 118–119, 146;
and sociocultural reproduction,
268–269; Vietminh, 123–125;
VNP, 83–86. *See also* Address;
French colonial system, discursive
practices and myths; Kinship,
terminology; Names
Đoan-Hùng, 41, 42, 128, 130, 132,
142, 296n14, 303n24
Đông Kinh Nghĩa Thục, 49, 91, 92,
287

Đồng-Xuân, 183–184, 304n8
Dục-Mỹ, 89
Dụng-Hiền, 44, 53–57, 72, 76–80, 109,
138, 163–165, 213, 287, 297n1,
297n3
Dương, Phạm Thành, 90, 106,
109–111, 291, 295n5
Durkheim, Emile, 13, 19–20, 261

Economy, colonial: agricultural
concessions to settlers,
43–44, 264, 296n14; capital
accumulation, 263–265; capital
investment, 43–44, 51, 296n14;
corvee labor, 43, 48, 127; 263;
dual structure, 48; government
monopolies, 46–47; government
revenues, 44–45, 47; inflation,
45; public work, 47–48; taxation,
43–47, 271; transportation
network, 42, 47–48. *See also*
Agriculture; Alcohol; Commerce;
Industry; Japan; Peasants
Economy, postcolonial: commerce,
188; corvée labor, 160; crisis,
185, 188, 273; employment,
non-agricultural, 217–218, 223;
integration with global economy,
273–274; land distribution, 194,
208, 213, 304n2; living standards
and consumer durables, 222,
258–259; price control, 182, 185,
188, 273; private enterprise, 188,
198–199, 207, 208, 217, 219–220,
234, 254, 305n5; regional
variation, 274–275; state role,
274–275; taxes, 213. *See also*
Agriculture; Commerce; Credit;
Handicrafts; Household contract
system; Household garden plots;
Industry; Labor exchange teams;
Land reform; Migration
Education: access to, under socialist
regime, 161, 203, 303n3; and class,
61, 63–64, 66–68; communal land
for, 56–57, 298n6; Confucian
examination system, 67, 72, 81;

# About the Author

**Hy V. Luong** is presently professor of anthropology at the University of Toronto. He has been conducting comparative research in both northern and southern Vietnam since 1987 and has published extensively on political economy, discourse, social organization, and migration in modern Vietnam. His recent books include the edited volumes *Postwar Vietnam: Dynamics of a Transforming Society* (2003) and *Migration, Urbanization, and Poverty in a Vietnamese Metropolis* (2009).